CORPORATE
AND INSTRUCTIONAL
VIDEO

CORPORATE AND INSTRUCTIONAL VIDEO

Second Edition

DIANE M. GAYESKI
Roy H. Park School of Communications,
Ithaca College
OmniCom Associates

Prentice Hall, Englewood Cliffs, New Jersey 07632

Library of Congress Cataloging-in-Publication Data
Gayeski, Diane M. (Diane Mary)
    Corporate and instructional video / Diane M. Gayeski.—2nd ed.
       p.   cm.
    Includes bibliographical references and index.
    ISBN 0-13-173253-6
    1. Video recording—Production and direction.   2. Television–
–Production and direction.   3. Industrial television.   4. Television
in education.   I. Title.
PN1992.94.G39   1991
070.1'95—dc20   90-44531
                                                         CIP

Editorial/production supervision
and interior design: *Carol L. Atkins*
Cover design: *Ben Santora*
Prepress buyer: *Ilene Levy*
Manufacturing buyer: *Edward O'Daugherty*

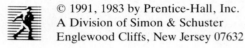 © 1991, 1983 by Prentice-Hall, Inc.
A Division of Simon & Schuster
Englewood Cliffs, New Jersey 07632

Printed in the United States of America
10 9 8 7 6 5 4 3 2 1

ISBN 0-13-173253-6

Prentice-Hall International (UK) Limited, *London*
Prentic-Hall of Australia Pty, Limited, *Sydney*
Prentice-Hall Canada Inc., *Toronto*
Prentice-Hall Hispanoamerica, S.A., *Mexico*
Prentice-Hall of India Private Limited, *New Delhi*
Prentice-Hall of Japan, Inc., *Tokyo*
Simon & Schuster Asia Pte. Ltd., *Singapore*
Editora Prentice-Hall do Brasil, Ltda., *Rio de Janeiro*

CONTENTS

PREFACE

Corporate and instructional video has gone from the basement to the penthouse. A decade ago, it was the province of a few "cameramen" and "A/V Coordinators" struggling to make a few good edits without glitches in a program that might be shown to a couple of people within the corporation. Today, it is a multi-billion dollar a year profession, involving thousands of men and women who produce programming that affects the bottom lines of thousands of organizations, with production values that many TV stations would envy.

Yes, the industry has matured; it's no longer acceptable to produce a program that "looks nice"; you've got to be able to use effective instructional strategies and prove that they worked. You've got to manage six-figure budgets and, in most situations, make a profit for your department or production house. You've got to keep up with fast-breaking technologies like digital video, computer animation, interactive videodisc, and satellite teleconferencing. *And,* you've got to sit in the boardroom and explain the role you have in accomplishing your organization's mission, in terms of profitability, employee training, morale, and public relations.

Quite a few books on the market today tell you how to produce a television program. This book tells you *why*—if you're a business, school, hospital, social-service organization, or any other group engaged in information or instruction—you might *want to.* Once you've decided you want to produce a program, it tells you how to *design* and *manage* a project from first request through distribution of the finished program.

This second edition builds on the core skills and concepts presented in the original book published in 1983. It covers the important aspects of dealing with clients, negotiating contracts, scheduling, budgeting, casting, scripting, organizing production and editing, evaluating, and disseminating programs. Numerous examples from the "real world"—both from my own work, and from outstanding professionals, give you concrete examples of models, forms, and scripts that you can use to build your own tools for individual projects as well as for managing an entire department or production house.

Special thanks go to the many colleagues and friends who contributed pictures, "war stories," computer print-outs, and scripts; my present and former clients who have given me myriad challenges and opportunities to build my expertise; my students who serve as a continual testing ground for my ideas and techniques; and my husband David, who encouraged me to do the book the first time around and to tackle it again and who has, with our son Evan, put up with staring at my back as I type on the computer.

Diane M. Gayeski, Ph.D.
Ithaca College
OmniCom Associates

1

THE CORPORATE VIDEO MARKETPLACE

The use of television in nonbroadcast settings—education, business, medicine, government and human-service organizations—has expanded rapidly during the last two decades. The decreasing cost and size of video equipment, coupled with its increasing reliability and ease of operation, have made the technology available to even the smallest organizations (not to mention individual consumers for home use). Nonbroadcast television goes by many names: corporate video, business TV, instructional television, small-format video, and the list goes on. In a way, it is a profession in search of an identity, since it has developed so rapidly and in so many forms. Its growth documents not only the ability of the medium to communicate successfully and efficiently, but also the exciting opportunities for careers in the field.

WHO'S USING VIDEO?

Who's using video? More aptly, we might ask: who's *not* using video? While television used to be the province of broadcast stations and a few large universities, today almost every type of organization is using the medium to communicate internally and/or externally.

The first large push into nonbroadcast video came from educational institutions who saw the medium as a way to extend their teaching staff. Universities such as Penn State in the 1950s used live closed-circuit distribution of lectures to compensate for the lack of large lecture halls (See Figures 1-1 and 1-2). Later, when videotape became available, professors were able to tape lectures for delayed or repeated viewing by classes or individual students. It was found, however, that the

Figure 1-1   An early use of instructional video was televising classes so that classes weren't limited to the capacity of a lecture hall. Here, an anatomy and physiology class is being broadcast around 1955 (*courtesy, Penn State University*).

Figure 1-2   An early control room at Penn State (*courtesy, Penn State University*).

"canned lectures" or "chalk talks" were not the best use of the medium, and soon more sophisticated production techniques prevailed.

In the early 1970s a number of government and private grants supported the production and distribution of television programs meant to replace classroom teaching. Such commercial ventures as "Sunrise Semester" did manage to capture small audiences who were motivated enough to watch these early-morning lectures, and a number of universities and community colleges followed this model. What we now know as public television was first envisioned to be educational TV or "ETV;" the concept was to find superior teachers and broadcast their lectures to a wide geographic area so that students might be exposed to the best instructors available. When carefully designed and produced, these broadcast lectures were effective: for instance, in the Washington County, MD, experiments funded by the Ford Foundation, students in the classes taught through the cable TV system showed remarkable gains in achievement (Saettler, 1968).

When the 3/4-inch U-Matic videotape recorders were introduced in the 1970s, for the first time videotape recording became inexpensive, reliable, and simple enough to appeal to schools, businesses, and social service agencies. As the equipment improved, its applications increased and became more sophisticated. Annual nonbroadcast video expenditures have now surpassed the $5 *billion* mark-up from a "mere" $1.5 billion in 1981 (Brush & Brush, 1986) and show no signs of decreasing, even in economic recessions. Corporate video is big business, and it got that way by proving its cost effectiveness, both to education (see Figure 1-3) and to business (see Figure 1-4).

Although business and industry are the heaviest users of nonbroadcast video, virtually every kind of organization uses and produces video: human-service agencies such as the Red Cross, medical institutions such as hospitals and clinics, government agencies like the Labor Department or the city of Baltimore, educational institutions, such as public schools, colleges, and universities, and religious groups, such as the Catholic Diocese of New York. These diverse organizations may buy "off-the-shelf" video for training, may produce programs in-house, and/or may hire production houses and freelancers to create custom programs for them. Even though video users are diverse, most of the major applications cross the boundaries of organizational types: 1) training/educational programming; 2) employee communications; 3) external public relations; 4) marketing/sales.

Training/Education

A major application of video within organizations is instruction—whether for students, employees, or customers. Although it is obvious how schools, colleges, and universities can use video for educational purposes, video's role in instruction for other kinds of institutions may be less clear—but certainly no less prevalent. Training in business and industry is a rapidly expanding field. According to a recent study sponsored by the Carnegie Foundation, corporations spend over $40 billion a year on employee education, not including trainee salaries. A Rand Report completed in 1986 reported that almost 40 percent of employees report having taken some training to improve existing skills while on the current job. Companies see training as an investment in greater productivity.

Why all this interest in training? First, organizations today typically are much larger than those of fifty years ago, and there has been a significant trend in the late 1980s toward consolidations and mergers. Traditionally, people could be taught "on the job," and skills learned were applicable for most, if not all, an employee's tenure within a company. Today, technology is rapidly changing the ways workers perform—from top managers down to the shipping clerks—and they need to learn new skills. Second, businesses worldwide are facing increased domestic and interna-

Figure 1-3 A modern class being taught at Syracuse University
using projected video as a teaching aid (*courtesy, General Electric*).

tional competition; employee productivity and morale is essential to stay in business, not to mention to make a profit.

Video has proven itself a viable answer to training needs. Its ability to inform, to communicate in a personal manner, to accurately simulate real-life situations, to motivate, and to record and transmit information accurately has been demonstrated repeatedly for diverse organizations. Because of the large number of employees hired or promoted each year and the specificity and complexity of their work, corporations must provide instructional programs to teach a range of skills. Although considerable instruction is still accomplished by stand-up training, video has become an even more popular way of training—in fact, it is the method most frequently used by corporations today (Lee, 1987). Not only can instructional video packages save the cost of hiring trainers and repeating lectures, but they can also

a

b

Figure 1-4 a, b Not all television consists of studios and taped shows. Here, AT&T uses this teleconference facility to enable personnel to conduct meetings via satellite with colleagues across the country (*courtesy, Lake Systems, Inc.*)

standardize training from person to person and plant to plant. Where it is impractical to assemble a whole class of trainees for a presentation, individuals may view prerecorded videotapes at their convenience. To accomplish this sort of mass training, organizations have established private *video networks* and have set up playback facilities in branch offices throughout their territories.

Video—with its capability to reproduce sound, motion, and color—is an effective and economical substitute for training on actual equipment. With its ability to zoom in close for a clear picture of a tiny object and to offer freeze-frame or slow-motion analysis, it can often surpass "hands-on" training. For these reasons, the Raymond Corporation in Greene, New York, uses video to train its dealers in selling and servicing new models of fork-lift trucks. The Cigna Corporation (an insurance conglomerate) teaches sales and management skills via video. Amway representatives learn about new products through videotapes. And if you work for McDonald's, chances are you'll learn to cook hamburgers and be told how to interact with customers by watching video (even corporate training *music videos*!) in the back room.

Big business isn't the only user of training programs, though. Naturally, educational institutions produce their own video programs for internal and external use—these days, most high schools and elementary schools like the Southern Cayuga school system in rural New York (Figure 1-5), have their own equipment (not to mention colleges and universities). These uses can range from simply taping a lecture for a professor who'll be going out of town to producing an elaborate series of documentaries to be shared with the public. For example, the State University of New York at Albany received a grant to produce a series of documentaries on Southern and Eastern European ethnic Americans which was subsequently distributed through a national clearinghouse. Hospitals, too, use video to train their own staffs as well as their patients. For instance, the Robert Packer Hospital in Sayre, PA, uses video to train student nurses as well as to inform patients about upcoming surgical procedures and outpatient care.

a

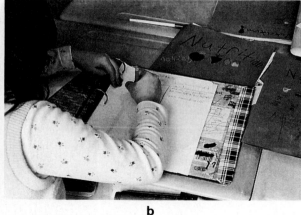

b

c

Figure 1-5   a, b, c, d   Elementary school students
learn to script, plan, execute, and evaluate their own
video productions (*courtesy, Cindy Sharshon,
Southern Cayuga School District*).

d

Many organizations are making use of new cable or satellite delivery technologies to provide live distance learning. Cable systems, microwave hookups, and ITFS (instructional television fixed service) have all been explored by a large number of school districts. Today there seems to be a resurgence of interest in this form of teaching, with a number of universities and school systems offering televised courses (Stern, 1987).

For instance, Ball State University broadcasts a number of its classes live to sites such as hospitals, high schools, and junior colleges throughout Indiana so that students in other areas can take part in and get credit for classes. IBM has a Satellite Education Network which broadcasts instructional and informational programming to their offices throughout the U.S., as does Eastman Kodak (Figure 1-6). The Hospital Satellite Network (HSN) is a nationwide provider of health-related programs for hospitals and nursing homes. And high school students in up-state New York can get college credit for advanced placement courses taught by a professor at Ithaca College over the local cable franchise.

Figure 1-6 The editing suite at KBTV, Kodak's Business TV Network. A team of production and management specialists plans and executes a variety of marketing and training programs each month (*courtesy, Holly Walkland, Eastman Kodak Company*).

Employee Communications

Although training has traditionally been the leading application for corporate video, recently employee information has been becoming a more popular use (Brush & Brush, 1988). As organizations get larger and their employee base becomes more highly educated, curious, and mobile, the need for organizational communication increases. It's no longer possible to assume that the President and CEO (Chief Executive Officer) can meet everyone in the organization—or even half of them. Many employees will never even have the opportunity to see the CEO in person. Nor can we assume that once employees are hired that they'll be content to sit back and ignore their company's mission statements, annual reports, or management plans. Organizations must compete for good employees and must actively keep them in the "information loop" in order to retain their motivation and loyalty (see, for example, Goldhaber, 1983).

Not only is there a need for "top-down" communication of policies, news, and so on, but there's a need for lateral communication—what are other individuals and departments doing—and who are they? Finally, upper management needs formal methods of knowing what the "troops" are thinking and doing.

Video is one answer to these needs. Of course, there are many media used for employee communication—meetings, bulletin boards, in-house newsletters, and the like. But increasingly, organizations are turning to video to communicate information of interest to their members. Most of these programs are one-shot efforts to

Figure 1-7 The studio at Federal Express; they use satellite-transmitted Business TV and state-of-the-art equipment to deliver company updates and training (*courtesy, Lake Systems, Inc.*).

deal with a specific news item or policy. For instance, when Marine Midland Bank introduced personal computers to each teller and customer service representative at their branches, a videotape was produced and sent around to acquaint employees with the new concept before the equipment arrived. Marine Midland also uses an orientation video to inform new hires of the Bank's many activities and sectors.

Many organizations are also involved in producing regularly scheduled news programs—some quarterly and some as often as every two weeks. Federal Express (see Figure 1-7) uses daily live satellite "feeds" to send news to employees worldwide. ConTel, a large electronics and communications firm, produces a quarterly video news program which updates employees on news from corporate headquarters as well as each of the branch offices. American Airlines also produces news programs which run continuously in public areas of their facilities, such as the waiting rooms in their training building where flight attendants and pilots often gather.

Because of video's ability to capture the personality of individuals, it is the next best thing to "being there." If you can't sit in your CEO's office and ask him how he thinks the company will fare next quarter, at least you can feel as though you were there if a reporter gets his response on video. Perhaps you've never been to your firm's Atlanta office, but you'd feel that you knew the faces behind those voices on the phone if the quarterly news magazine did a feature on your colleagues there. Good communication managers know how to get feedback from the field and collect questions and concerns which can be fed back to upper management, who can in turn address those issues in future video programs. So, employee communication programs are not only the conduit for information, but the "excuse" to do some field research and increase the flow of communication in all directions on the organizational chart—up to down, down to up, and side to side.

One additional use of video for employee communication is product launches—events ranging from sedate meetings to extravaganzas held in hotel ballrooms—which introduce a new product to the awaiting sales force. Often, these video programs are part of multi-media shows incorporating 36 or more slide projectors, indoor fireworks, and laser light shows (no exaggeration!) designed to "whip up" the team. The video portions may include interviews or montages—or in the case of a large pharmaceutical—contain scenes of the previous day's meetings and festivities. These programs, while they may be "informational," are not technically "instructional;" rather, they provide motivation for employees to sell a new product, as well as general knowledge of the corporation's plans and planners.

Video has proven to be tremendously helpful in times of organizational crisis. When the stock market crashed in October 1987, Merrill Lynch produced daily live satellite feeds featuring briefings by top management and phone-in questions from the field. Executives commented that the video department had proven its value to the company in an unprecedented way. SmithKline Beckman has aired a weekly "SKB TV News" program since 1979; this communication system was able to prepare employees fully for planned cutbacks and the closing of a Philadelphia plant, so that local media were surprised to find calm and informed employees rather than shocked and angry ones (Kleyman, 1988). You can't even put a dollar amount on the value of such an information tool in helping to create a more loyal and contented workforce.

Public Relations

All organizations depend on the good will of the public—they are potential customers, employees, stockholders, suppliers, and neighbors. With this in mind, many organizations are producing PR pieces on video (sometimes called video news releases or VNRs) which can overtly or subtly lead to goodwill. For example, when Steve Jobs unveiled his NeXT computer, a video news release was distributed via satellite so that TV stations could tape it, edit it, and use it in their news shows. According to the distributor of this VNR, 68 million viewers saw some or all of that program (Manoff, 1989). Many corporations publish a video "annual report" to be shown at the stockholders' meeting and given to those who can't be there in person. These programs can show vividly the activities and progress of a company. For example, in NCR Corporation's print annual report for 1987, a card was enclosed which, when sent to headquarters with $5, entitled the reader to a VHS copy of an interview with the company president on long-term corporate strategies.

Other PR programs are less directly tied to an organization's activities, but reap general benefits to the community. Georgia Power Company produces video and interactive video programs which acquaint executives looking for a new plant location with the Atlanta area. Although these programs don't overtly "pitch" Georgia Power Company, an increase in business in the area means the high probability of business for Georgia Power. Other organizations donate video programs to local charities, such as the United Way, to help them meet their fundraising goals.

Many not-for-profit organizations produce programs and/or spots to provide information to the public—and in so doing give themselves exposure. For example, Cornell University produced an award-winning series of public service announcements (PSAs) for broadcast on the subject of nutrition. Since Cornell is affiliated with the State Cooperative Extension, these spots drew attention to the university and their services.

As home VCRs become almost as popular as bathtubs and as cable TV reaches into more households, video becomes a more viable medium for general interest PR programs. Some corporations run programming on local cable access channels, and many will lend out programs to individuals in the community and to employees' families.

Marketing/Sales

Of course, we're all familiar with broadcast television ads. But increasingly, corporations are turning to nonbroadcast video to aid in sales as well. Since VHS tapes can cost only about $2 to duplicate, they are now being used along with or instead of company brochures. For instance, Shepard Niles, a manufacturer of industrial cranes, hoists, and monorails, uses several video programs as sales aids during meetings and trade shows to show unusual installations in large plants worldwide. These tapes are also mailed out to qualified prospects who indicate an interest in the company's products. Programs like this can not only vividly depict important facets of a product (such as the speed and quiet operation of a monorail), but can get a potential buyer's attention much faster than one more piece of paper.

Many companies are producing elaborate demonstrations of their products—for instance, many software companies now send out video demos. Microsoft Corporation ran ads on its new spreadsheet, *Excel*, and offered a videotape to anyone who would send in a coupon and $10. The tape turned out to be an elaborately produced and acted drama of how a small team within a company "snuck in" a powerful PC and *Excel* to turn out an exquisite report to their management—who, of course, after seeing that report, would buy them the hardware and software.

Video is also being used on the retail level. You may have seen video programs in hardware or department stores featuring products such as blenders. They provide information, light instruction on product use, and attract attention in an overcrowded environment. Interactive video is being used to let customers browse through inventory that might not be displayed fully in the store itself; such systems as the Levi's "Jeans Screen" let shoppers see what clothes look like on models—and some systems even let customers place orders through the use of a touchscreen. In other cases, video is being used as a subtle background, creating an appealing environment for shopping. For instance, Bloomingdale's, the large department store in New York City, has run store-wide themes featuring various exotic spots in the world. Video programs taking a documentary or travelogue approach shot by their crew play on monitors in various departments in the store, occasionally featuring products on sale in the store, such as designer clothing.

Data Collection/Retrieval

Although not programs *per se*, there are other uses made of videotape and videodisc within organizations. Video is often used as a feedback tool in education and training because of its immediate replay and reuse features. Trainees and students can be taped as they perform an activity—such as a tennis swing, a sales call, or a speech. Then, the tape is replayed for critique by the student and the coach or instructor. Many organizations also keep video archives—simple video recordings of a special event, such as the visit of a foreign dignitary or the opening of a new building. Data collection videotapes are used for research purposes. Cameras may be set up to record events in areas dangerous to humans or to accomplish long-term and unobtrusive observation of subjects. Finally, videotapes and videodiscs are used as visual databases—for instance, employees' photos may be stored on videodisc for access by security guards at building entrances. Many power plants have documentation of each area of their facilities on videodisc, and viewers can vicariously "tour" the plant by using a joystick to control the videodisc to move throughout rooms and hallways.

WHERE IS VIDEO PRODUCED?

So, who produces all of these programs, and where are they located? That's one of the biggest problems in corporate and instructional video—what to call the department whose responsibility it is to design and create video programming. But an even bigger issue is *whether* or not to produce video in house, posing the question, "in house or out of house?"

In-House Production

Many corporations prefer to establish their own video departments. There are many advantages to having an in-house unit:

- **Convenience.** Internal clients need merely to stroll into the video department for meetings or shoots. There may not be qualified independent production houses in the region.
- **Confidentiality.** Often companies produce programs with sensitive content, such as new product demonstrations or corporate planning. Keeping it in house reduces the possibilities of "leaks."
- **Familiarity.** An in-house department becomes familiar with the subject matter of an organization, whether that be insurance, medicine, or operating a nuclear power plant. That means that writers and producers can work more quickly and easily and also means that the video department already knows the politics and procedures of its own organization.
- **Cost.** By subsidizing an in-house department and keeping it a not-for-profit entity, programs *may* be produced more cheaply than by going to outside production houses who have to market themselves and turn a profit.

Video professionals are located in a variety of settings within organizations. Although they traditionally were part of training departments (under Human Resources or Personnel on the organizational chart), they have been migrating out to Marketing or Corporate Communications Departments (Brush & Brush, 1988). Now, media may be produced by a Corporate Communications Department, using the Training Department as an internal client. These production facilities range from a camcorder in a closet to an elaborate video center rivaling most broadcast TV stations. In fact, the average in-house video department has an annual budget of about $300,000—and a good number of these units have operating funds of over $1 million per year.

Not all in-house facilities work just for the company in which they're located, however. The video scene has gotten extremely complicated in terms of who works for whom and where the money and control resides. The following is an excerpt from a letter from a colleague who is the Director of Media Resources for a large state university campus. It gives you a good idea of the situation of many in-house video professionals today.

VIDEO MOVES UP AND OUT

Dear Diane,

Thank you for thinking of me as you update your 1983 book. It was my hope to have something for you but this has been an incredible year for this institution and particularly my department. Although we have been producing materials on a regular basis, many of these productions support the public service mission of the institution and not necessarily the instructional and research endeavors of our campus. The entire production function is dependent upon the income we can gather from any sources we can tap. On the one hand, this is quite exciting because we get involved in a variety of projects that can prove to be quite motivating. On the other hand it dilutes our purpose because we seem to be side stepping the need for this department to exist. As an example we are completing projects for area public school systems, the Chamber of Commerce, and the City.

. . . Another example of change is the fact that my unit will no longer report to the University Library but rather the Vice Chancellor for Faculty Relations and Academic Support. This moves our reporting structure much closer to the top and should translate into really exciting things for the department. I certainly hope so . . .

Anonymous Media Director, State University

Production Houses and Consultants

Independent production houses, consulting companies, and freelancers serve the needs of organizations who have no video facilities or whose facilities cannot accommodate excess work. This area of the marketplace has been growing rapidly during the past few years for two reasons: video *per se* has been growing, and the trend is for corporate video to be done at least partially *out of house.* Independent contractors offer several benefits:

- **Specific expertise.** Contractors may specialize in specific types of programs, such as interactive video, music videos, videowalls, humorous programs, and so on. While an in-house person may have limited exposure to these kinds of programs, an outside vendor can bring greater experience through work with a variety of organizations.
- **High-end equipment.** Production houses can specialize in keeping up with the latest technology and can market it to a variety of clients to amortize its cost. For instance, a $100,000 computer animation system might be used in a production house 30 hours a week for jobs for 15 clients, whereas an in-house unit may only need 30 hours of computer animation time per year and could not therefore justify its cost.
- **Flexibility.** An in-house staff of 3 (a typical size video department) may have nothing to do for three weeks and then have 5 programs to do the next 2 weeks. There are usually no "typical" days to provide a comfortable workload for a "typical" staff. Production houses and freelancers can be used to provide as much or as little service as necessary—without making long-term commitments to employees and in-house facilities.
- **Motivation.** Organizations often believe that competition improves performance both in terms of quality and cost. An in-house department with "captive" clients may not have the motivation to keep up with skills and technology and also may sometimes cost more *per se* than vendors.
- **Cost.** When an organization has many video programs of a similar kind to do each year, an in-house staff and facilities may justify themselves. But in current corporate climates of uncertainty, CEOs are cautious about adding staff and facilities. It may be more cost-effective to use a "pay as you go" approach and use outside vendors.

While video production houses were first clustered in large metropolitan areas, the need for video production by so many types of organizations has led to their establishment in other locations as well. Some of these firms specialize in one type of service—for instance, post-production editing, scriptwriting, or duplication. Facilities for such services can be specialized and expensive (see Figure 1-8). Others offer a range of services from needs analysis to production through evaluation.

Figure 1-8   Many of the programs used by corporations are produced at least partly by outside production houses. Here is an example of an elaborate editing suite at a post-production house. Note the areas for client observation, video editing, audio control, and the separate machine room for the videotape recorders (*courtesy, The Editing Company, Houston, TX*).

Production houses generally deal with a wide range of clients and topics. Most work on a contract basis with clients, being paid per hour, day, or program. Many video professionals work as free-lance writers, crew members, producers, or consultants on a daily or contract fee basis. Most work for a host of clients but have a few regular clients from whom they can count on work on a rather predictable basis. Although the term "freelancer" may conjure up images of the starving young person struggling to make it in the media business, independent producers and consultants are as a group the highest-paid workers in the nonbroadcast industry. Often these individuals started out working within a media department in an organization and became so skilled that they could draw their own clientele. Some production houses started out as in-house departments and were "spun-off" by their former corporate sponsors or were bought out by their employees.

THE GROWTH OF NONBROADCAST VIDEO

As we have seen, video has found its way into a great variety of organizations as an effective communicator, instructor, and motivator. From its modest beginnings in the recording of lectures, nonbroadcast TV has expanded through the 1970s and

1980s at a rate of 20% to 40% per year. Although the rush into electronic media may slow down, predictions are that more programs will be produced, more equipment sold, and more professionals hired.

Why this expansion of video? A number of social, technological, and economic factors account for the phenomenon.

- **Video is an effective communications tool.** Because of its ability to display sound, motion, and color, video can simulate "live" situations. It has proven again and again its power to teach and motivate.
- **Travel is becoming more expensive.** It used to be feasible to send sales representatives to many potential customers, trainees to seminars, or managers to branch offices. But the expense of travel and lodging has curtailed these activities. More and more (especially in two-career families), travel is a nuisance to employees rather than a glamorous benefit. Video, whether through teleconferencing, the use of a private network, or sending out tapes through the mail, can move *information* instead of *people*.
- **Organizations are becoming larger.** When face-to-face communication is not feasible, there is a need to communicate in a personal, yet standardized manner.
- **Video equipment is becoming cheaper, more reliable, and more portable.** Today's equipment is easily affordable in terms of both initial investment and maintenance. Its smaller size makes it easier to take into the field to get the shots that previously only film could accommodate. Most offices, schools, and even homes have VHS playback decks, so it can safely be assumed that anyone has relatively easy access to viewing facilities.
- **Video is cost-effective.** Because of the higher costs of travel, of hiring trainers or sales reps, and of training employees, together with the lower cost of video equipment, video has shown itself to be a time and money saver. Video tapes can take the place of "live" trainers—or at least make trainers more efficient. Often, too, trainees can learn faster and reduce the time away from the job.
- **People like video.** It seems obvious, but people will do what they enjoy doing. Most of us have grown up using television for entertainment and information, and this predisposition makes video an appealing form of training and motivation. While a person may toss out a memo or bury an instruction booklet, he or she will probably be intrigued by the prospect of a television program.
- **Video lets people learn at their own pace.** Videotapes and videodiscs allow the viewer to stop, replay a segment, slow down action, or speed through familiar material. Interactive video programs allow the viewer to "interact" with the material and, depending on personal needs or interests, to branch to various segments of a program.
- **Video programs never get tired or bored.** Imagine working in a personnel office and spending each day explaining your organization's benefit plan to new employees. Imagine demonstrating an office copier day in and day out. Imagine teaching six new patients each day how to clean their new contact lenses. Much of what people must communicate, whether as trainers, sales representatives, teachers, or physicians, is repetitive. Not only are endless repetitions of messages an inefficient use of a skilled person's time but the presentations become decreasingly interesting, thorough, and motivating. Video programs can repeat messages with as much clarity and enthusiasm the two-hundredth time as the first.

- **Video is immediate.** It can give a person an "instant replay" of a performance—then the tape can be erased and reused. Productions can be played back immediately—or information can be transmitted live.
- **We're learning how to use the medium.** Research and experimentation have developed effective methods of employing video. More and more people are being trained to use it, both as users (trainers, salespeople, etc.) and as producers. Video *per se* is not more effective than other media, but it is a powerful tool when the messages are designed correctly to use it. As more success stories are chalked up, more support and credibility are accorded it.

Besides the myriad of good reasons why organizations are using video, there are a few *bad* ones. Most of these center around the "bandwagon" or "magic" phenomena:

- **Keeping up with the Joneses.** Too many video facilities are installed because the President of Company X brags to the President of Company Y about their new television studio complex over a couple of drinks at a cocktail party. Of course, Company Y doesn't want to be seen as slipping backward, so the next thing you know, Company Y announces its new satellite TV network.
- **The "star" complex.** Some CEOs and managers are frustrated TV stars. They feel that they'll immediately be perceived as credible and friendly if they're put on "TV."
- **Video works magic.** Some organizations think that if they're having problems, all you have to do is throw money (video) at them. Some teachers think that using TV will improve their student ratings since kids "like" TV. Finally, some marketing departments feel that a good video will make up for an otherwise bad product.
- **Video looks like fun.** Many potential clients admit that they've always been fascinated with media and that the work looks like a lot of fun. These poor, misguided souls think that producing a program will be easy, exciting, and glamorous!

Fortunately, the sound approaches to the organizational uses of video have outnumbered the misguided ones, and the field has established itself in many organizations as an essential function rather than just a frill. The key to maintaining a strong video department is to make sure it has a direct impact on the organization's goals. Unlike broadcasting, where video exists for its own sake, the application of video in a company, school, or other institution is not its "product." The successful video manager knows how to tailor the medium to the needs and "culture" of the overall organization.

THE VIDEO DESIGNER/PRODUCER

The role of the organizational video designer/producer is a complex and fascinating one. Although many of the skills and duties resemble those in the broadcast realm, there are some significant differences. The broadcast industry focuses mainly on entertainment and news, whereas the nonbroadcast video profession concentrates on instructional and informational programming. Because video production is only a tiny part of what a company or school might do, video must be justified in terms of the organization's overall objectives. The industrial television producer, too, is usually a part of a very small unit—often a one-person shop.

Few people have been trained specifically for their jobs in corporate TV. Until quite recently, there were no academic departments or courses in this subject. Most people found their way into the field through training and experience in broadcasting, teaching, journalism, public relations, or sales. Most of them picked up the extra skills they needed through on-the-job experience, workshops, or part-time study. Today, however, as the field has grown, more and more young professionals are seeking explicit training to enter the field (see Figure 1-9).

Figure 1-9 Organizations investing in video need not only hardware, but skilled personnel to install and maintain it. Successful video is a team approach involving many varied specialities (*courtesy, Lake Systems, Inc.*).

HOW THE PIONEERS DID IT

It was 1966 and I was attending a conference for trainers. At the end of the day I was walking through the equipment display area when on a black-and-white monitor I saw a rumpled and disheveled guy with terrible posture. Then I saw that person straighten up, tuck in the shirt which had bloused over the belt, brush down the hair and—you guessed it, that was me seeing myself. Seeing myself and reacting to what I saw.

The first thought was about the miserable picture I was presenting of myself. Hard on the heels of that came the next thought. "If that equipment could make me do what I just did, what would happen if I used it in a supervisory training session where I wanted, and desperately needed, trainees to see themselves and how they acted and reacted in various interpersonal situations?"

So I convinced management to let me experiment with video in the training arena. My first intention was to use it purely as a "see yourself" device. To justify the expense, I was told to examine and experiment with the making of "training films."

The experiment with its use as a sell-yourself tool in the training room was an outstanding success. The making of the training film/video —an outstanding failure.

I was looking for some thing, some way, to increase the effectiveness of the training I was designing and presenting. I was looking for a better device than traditional role plays. For a long time I really didn't see "small format video" as anything but a tool to be used in the training room, especially after the first few attempts at producing a training package with this type of equipment.

I was now in our Headquarters Office (Federal Prison System) as Assistant Chief, Career Development. I used offices, conference rooms, empty spaces, and so on. But I did get some training and information programs produced. Rough and crude by film standards, but timely and topical. I could respond quickly, and I did concentrate on topics that management and line were interested in.

I signed up for some courses at a University—not a great idea, they were geared solely to teach students how to produce 30 minute news programs. Other courses again missed the target. Then I discovered an association made up of persons much like myself. The National Industrial Television Association (NITA) held conferences and training meetings with *experienced program producers* as leaders and instructors. I sometimes now joke that "experienced" meant that these people had done whatever they were talking about before I got around to trying it myself.

I could and did learn from these people. I also became a voracious reader of magazines and journals that featured articles from persons experienced in doing the types of productions that I envisioned for me.

Case studies, as training strategies, have been in use for a long time. The problem with them is that they can be very dry and boring unless very carefully written. My idea was to make the case study come alive by putting the principal characters into a realistic setting and videotaping them. I had an *investigative reporter* visit the prison and talk to the people concerned. While the learners listened to the Reporter, they gathered basic information that formerly had been delivered in print. Did it work? Oh my, did it work!

After a few hundred programs for my organization I retired. I now do only a few programs a year. Most of them are training materials. I have learned about video discs, about authoring languages, and about working with computer graphics, with the "all new" capabilities of the latest technoadvance.

If we pay attention to why we are doing interactive training, design programs to accomplish the stated objectives, and plan our learning strategies carefully, the decisions about form and format come easy. We must decide what we are going to do before we decide on how to package it. A trifling detail. As Michaelangelo said, "Trifles make perfection and perfection is no trifle."

Henry Bohne,
Video Consultant
Parker, Colorado

So, what do you need to know to be a corporate/instructional video professional? First, a general *liberal arts background* is helpful, since you will have to deal with a variety of familiar and unfamiliar topics and with a wide range of people. You won't be doing video programs on the topic of video programs! Of course, knowledge of *video production* is essential, and with it general competencies in other related media as well, such as graphic arts and audio. You need to know *how people learn*; some basic courses in teaching methods, educational psychology, and instructional design are invaluable. *Writing* is an essential skill, both for writing scripts, as well as for communicating with management and clients through proposals, memos, and reports. You must have good *interpersonal skills*. You don't produce programs for your own edification; whether you work for an in-house media center or a production house, you deal constantly with clients and content experts. During productions, you have to coach talent and keep your crew happy. You need to be a "people person" as well as a "button pusher." *Budgeting and financial management* cannot be escaped. You must keep productions within budget, forecast needs for individual programs as well as your entire department or production house, and provide cost-justification for your operation. *Organizational and management skills* are also helpful, both for working within your own video unit and for understanding the business environment of your total organization.

Most of all, perhaps, you've got to be a *good learner*. Most writers and producers are constantly translating unfamiliar and technical content into interesting video programs. You need to be willing and able to learn new information rapidly and to find sources for the information you need. You never know whether your next production will be on heat-treating gears, the legal aspects of firing employees, doing open-heart surgery, or selling luxury sports cars. Finally, you have to have that magic ingredient, *creativity*, to pull all this together.

Most people who work with corporate and instructional video "wear many hats" and possess to some degree all the skills and knowledge just listed. For example, see the job descriptions in Figure 1-10. You may find a job in which you would just write scripts, or run camera, or manage the production unit; these more specific jobs are available in organizations that have relatively large video staffs. The more specialized your capabilities and interests, however, the more difficult it is to find a suitable job—and one with an upward career path.

Generally, organizational media professionals hold a bachelor's degree, although some technical personnel hold only an associate's degree, and many managers have a master's degree in communications, instructional design, or business. In higher education and research organizations, it's not uncommon for a Ph.D. or Ed.D. to be required.

What's it like to work in corporate TV? Most people in the field will tell you there is never a dull moment. Because most departments have small staffs, people take on a variety of roles and generally see a project through from inception to production and evaluation. Unlike broadcast stations and networks which are generally unionized, corporate video departments allow and expect their staff members to do a variety of tasks. For instance, in broadcasting, a director may not touch a camera and a news anchor may not even touch a videotape. Many people leave broadcasting because they get bored in such rigid jobs and find more outlets for their creativity in nonbroadcast settings where they can try more things.

Field production is becoming increasingly common, so travel to on-location shooting sites is common. The instructional video producer is constantly working with new clients and different programs; there is no set format of the sort that characterizes commercial news shows or situation comedies. Along with the varied topics come an array of clients and content experts. Figure 1-11 illustrates the following scenario.

JOB DESCRIPTION GUIDELINES

MANAGER
   Responsible for planning, organizing, coordinating, budgeting, staffing,
   and overall administration of an audiovisual department.
   Develops, recommends, and coordinates policies, plans, and programs for
   application of existing and new audiovisual technology on a corporate-
   wide basis.
- Approves or recommends annual operational and/or capital budgets.
- Approves or recommends staff and salary changes, and expense accounts.

SUPERVISOR
   Supervises a media department or section.
- Works with users in planning maximum utilization of audiovisual media.
- Advises users on most effective uses of media, including content and
  organization of a given program.
- Coordinates scheduling of audiovisual productions.
  Directs all company media programs either directly or indirectly through
  delegation to a qualified staff member.
- Recommends annual operational and/or capital budgets.
- Develops department or section objectives.
- Recommends staff and salary changes.

PRODUCER/MEDIA DIRECTOR (PROGRAM SPECIALIST)
- Evaluates and interprets user needs.
- Analyzes the user audience and determines the program objectives.
  Writes a proposed treatment.
- Establishes budget.
  Assigns writer and/or writes.
- Responsible for the program being completed on time, within budget and
  to the user's satisfaction.
- Coordinates all aspects of assigned videotape productions. This includes
  developing information from content specialists; working with assigned
  writer, graphic designer, studio crew, and participants in the production.
- Evaluates program results.

DIRECTOR (VIDEO COORDINATOR)
   Directs the actual production, including making decisions on placement of
   sets, props, lighting, staging, audio timing, technical direction of
   cameras, and editing.
- Directs the activities performed by the assigned teleproduction crew,
  either on location or in the studio.
- Selects and directs the talent for the video productions.

WRITER
   Evaluates and interprets user needs.
   Takes suggested program ideas on an assignment basis and develops
   visualized scripts for television or any other medium.
- Researches source materials and interviews subject material experts
  including participating script outlines for approval.
  Writes the actual shooting script for the production.
- Evaluates program results.

Figure 1-10 Job descriptions for various corporate media
personnel (*courtesy, Mark Weiss, Georgia Power Co.*).

A CAMEL IN MY BEDROOM—AND OTHER JOYS OF VIDEO

Who says life in corporate video has to be boring? The in-house
media production department at Bloomingdale's traveled halfway
around the world to exotic India to shoot one of their spring promotions.
Trekking through the varied terrain of this picturesque land we encountered all the usual production mayhem . . . and the unusual.

Thousands of cows and camels roamed everywhere . . .

"Stop tape, there's a cow in the shot." Even as we traveled on the bus from location to location, we were delayed by the intense traffic caused by—camel crossing?

Well, if you can't beat them, join them. Hoisting the gear between the humps, we finally had a new means of transportation. Determination, patience, and creative thinking kept this production right on schedule. After three weeks of shooting this rich cultural heritage, somehow we got accustomed to this inscrutable nation. The camels and cows became our allies. Actually, one morning room service brought breakfast to my room and left it on a table near the window. I went to the bathroom and upon my return a camel had poked his head through the shutters and helped himself to the sweet rolls and orange juice—but the funny thing is—it didn't bother me. I knew then it was time to take the next flight home.

Steven Kasten, Producer
Georgia Power Media Services

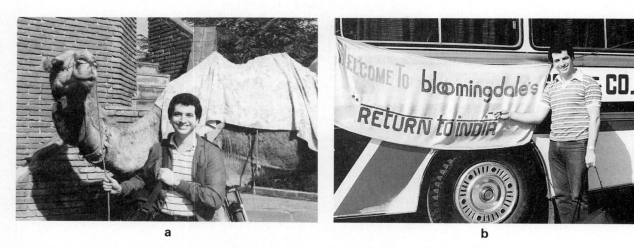

a   b

Figure 1-11   a, b   One thing corporate video is not, is boring (*courtesy, Steve Kasten*).

While some organizational video departments have facilities that would rival the networks, most have more modest equipment. However, many corporate programs use the facilities of the same production houses that produce the network sitcoms and programs like Sesame Street. However, budgets for nonbroadcast productions are usually considerably less than those for commercial programs. Because there is no advertising money coming in, programs must be cost justified by their benefits to the parent organization—through increased sales, more efficient training, and the like.

Careers in the nonbroadcast video field may be a bit more staid than those in broadcasting—which is a plus and a minus. While few people achieve stardom in corporate video, few are fired because they don't fit a new "image" or "format" or because this month's ratings were too low. Jobs tend to be more stable, because performance is related to meeting objectives rather than striking the public's fancy. Salaries are also quite competitive; most video managers make about $40,000; writers, producers, and directors around $25,000; and entry-level production personnel start out in the low—to mid-20s (in 1990 dollars). One major industry study, the *Hope Reports Corporate Media Salaries*, found that the average salary in 1988 for corporate media personnel was $31,653, having risen 13% over the previous three years. As is true for most jobs, salaries are higher on the East and West Coasts and are also higher in big business than in nonprofits or educational institutions.

Increasingly, video professionals are being called upon to provide more than traditional TV programming: they are involved in interactive videodiscs, teleconferencing, computer graphics, and even telephone and computer networks. It is those talented and motivated individuals who see their role beyond the video camera who eventually become the Vice Presidents of Corporate Communications—or the next successful entrepreneurs in a new communication technology.

BIBLIOGRAPHY

BERGER, W. (1989, April). "When the walls come tumblin' Down: Crisis video," *Corporate Video Decisions,* pp. 40–45.

BRUSH, J. M. AND D. P. BRUSH (1986). *Private Television Communications: The New Directions (The Fourth Brush Report).* Cold Spring, NY: HI Press of Cold Spring, Inc.

BRUSH, J. M. AND D. P. BRUSH (1988). *Private Television Communications: The Fourth Brush Report, Update '88.* Cold Spring, NY: HI Press, Inc.

BUNYAN, J. A. (1987). *Why Video Works: New Applications for Management.* White Plains, NY: Knowledge Industry Publications.

GOLDHABER, G. M. (1983). *Organizational Communication,* 3rd edition. Dubuque, Iowa: Wm. C. Brown Company Publishers.

Hope Reports Corporate Media Salaries (1988). Rochester, NY: Hope Reports, Inc.

KLEYMAN, P. (1988, November/December). "Employee Television," *Corporate Television,* pp. 21-25.

LEE, C. (1988). "Where the training dollars go," *Training, 24* (10), pp. 51–65.

MANOFF, M. (1989, March/April). "VNR's Carry the Message to the Public," *Corporate Television,* p. 31.

MUNROE, M. (1986). *Inside Corporate AV.* Torrance, CA: Montage Publishing.

SAETTLER, P. (1968). *A History of Instructional Technology.* New York: McGraw-Hill.

STERN, C. M. (1987). "Teaching the distance learner using new technology," *Journal of Educational Technology Systems, 15* (6), 407–418.

STOKES, J. T. (1988). *The Business of Nonbroadcast Television.* White Plains, NY: Knowledge Industry Publications.

2

WORKING WITH CLIENTS AND CONTENT EXPERTS

Whether you work for a production house, for a company's media department, or as an independent consultant, you deal with clients and content experts almost every day. Your competent interaction with them is a key to your success in organizational video. Video is often thought to be a technical profession, emphasizing equipment and engineering. However, corporate television producers are constantly working with people—solving their problems through media communication and learning their business, their jargon, and their needs. If it weren't for clients, there would be no shows to produce!

The role of a video producer within a business, school, hospital, or other nonbroadcast organization is often nebulous and misunderstood. Video, you see, is not what the organizations as a whole is about. Sometimes the video group is seen as an expensive "frill." Sometimes video seems like too much fun, and outsiders find it difficult to take the media professional's work seriously. Still others view television as confusingly technical—something to avoid lest they embarrass themselves. Finally, some people see video as a rival and threat to their jobs.

Yet these same people are potential clients for programs, and while it may not be fully possible to communicate all of the medium's nuances to them, your video operation cannot survive without clients and cannot grow without *more* clients. And good interpersonal relationships with clients are paramount—especially these days when your ability to produce a technically competent video program is assumed. Most clients come back to a production facility not because they necessarily have the latest equipment or even produce the flashiest or most clever programs— they come back because they like the *experience*.

Writers, producers, or media managers often cast themselves narrowly into roles, when it might be more helpful for them to think of themselves more broadly

Figure 2-1   Pre-production planning and a good rapport between
the producer and client are necessary for effective productions
(*courtesy, David Peltz*).

as *communication consultants*. This expanded definition brings to light the tasks
and skills video professional *beyond* just working with equipment.

The roles of a communication consultant are:

- **Teaching others about media.** Often clients will know very little about media
  in general and video in particular. In working with them, the communication
  consultant teaches them the terminology and technical facts they'll need to
  know in order to participate in the production. Moreover, clients will turn to
  you to learn about emerging technologies, such as teleconferencing, interactive videodisc, and new ones yet to be invented.

- **Maintaining good public relations for the video operation.** The consultant lets
  people know what the video production unit is doing and how media programs have been used successfully, and he or she encourages potential clients to use the facilities.

- **Analyzing communication problems.** Informational and training needs
  within the organization must be identified and possible solutions suggested.
  Sometimes the solutions will involve video, but not always.

- **Designing and producing video programs.** This, the most obvious role of the
  video communications specialist, includes the research, scriptwriting, shooting, and editing aspects of the job.

- **Designing and maintaining equipment and facilities.** The communication consultant is generally called upon to specify new production and playback
  hardware and to design and keep functional whole systems of equipment.

- **Administration of facilities, staff, and budget.** Whether for a single production or for a production center working on many projects, a communication
  consultant generally must handle the paperwork of contracts, budgets, hiring, correspondence, and scheduling.

- **Evaluation of programs.** Commercially available software on existing programs often need to be evaluated for effectiveness, and new programs must
  be field tested.

- **Professional development.** The media professional must keep up with the
  constant change in technology and techniques. This can be accomplished by
  reading books and magazines, attending seminars and conferences, and
  participating in professional organizations.

Obviously there's a lot more to being a successful video professional than knowing how to operate equipment (see Figure 2-2). Too often media personnel are seen as technicians or clericals rather than professionals. Because television is available to us so readily, at the flick of a switch, it's difficult for the lay person to comprehend the complexities of production. By emphasizing the broad range of skills and duties inherent in the "communication consultant" role, we can give a more professional character to the job.

What does it mean to be a "professional?"

- **Having specific education in your field.** Not everybody who can focus a camera is a video professional. Your specific technical and conceptual training sets you apart from the amateur.
- **Being called upon to diagnose and "treat" problems—not just dispense services.** Just as you can't walk into a physician and demand a prescription for penicillin, clients shouldn't expect you merely to crank out a program without first finding out what their needs are and prescribing an appropriate solution.
- **Having professional standards of operation and ethics.** Even though the corporate video field is rather young, there are professional associations for video producers, trainers, and communication specialists which provide continuing education, survey the field to establish job descriptions and appropriate salary ranges, and recommend codes of conduct.

```
                          ACCOUNTABILITIES
                         Revised: 06/14/88


ACCOUNTABILITY                              WEIGHT: 25%
NUMBER 01


     Serve as project manager on AV, print and video projects.

                     PERFORMANCE STANDARDS

(A) Work with a creative team representing the various departments.
(B) Create and maintain a production schedule, a cost/expense
    budget and a time budget based on input from team members.
(C) Provide all team members with input regarding deadlines and
    other important facts to assist them in fulfilling their
    responsibilities.
(D) Ensure that company resources are managed in a cost-effective
    way.
(E) Complete programs within negotiated and/or established time
    frames.  The sum of all completions will be considered as the
    total of all commitment codes except those delayed by Media
    Services. (90% Excellent, 85% Commendable, 80% Fully
    Acceptable)
(F) Complete programs within negotiated and/or agreed upon budgets.
(G) Maintain positive relations with team members throughout the
    project.
(H) Ensure that all required contracts, appendixes, expense
    accounts and invoices are completed and processed correctly.
```

Figure 2-2 Job accountabilities of corporate communication representatives at Georgia Power Company. Note that it's not enough just to know how to use equipment and "be creative" (*courtesy, Mark Weiss, Georgia Power Company*).

(I) Conclude the project by effecting a smooth transition from media programs to av responsibility.
(J) Ensure program is completed in standard format and placed in the library.
(K) Maintain a standard production file that thoroughly documents the project.

Accountability   **WEIGHT:** 25%
Number 02

Create media programs and materials for marketing, training and information purposes.

PERFORMANCE STANDARDS

(a) Create programs and materials which fully meet client's needs and expectations by meeting or exceeding the project's stated goals & objectives.
(b) Create programs and materials which meet professional evaluation criteria established by media services.
(c) Establish solid learning goals for programs.
(d) Use effective instructional techniques throughout each program.

Accountability   **WEIGHT:** 20%
Number 03

Provide input to the media programs supervisor to help shape departmental policy and to assist the section in functioning effectively.

TIME BUDGET: After the initial meeting with the client and before the treatment and/or scripting stages begin, the CCR is to provide the Supervisor of Media Programs with an estimate for the number of hours that the CCR believes will be required of their time to create the treatment and script. This estimate <u>could be</u> based upon previous project tracking reports of past projects which were similar and/or any other information that the CCR might have. Upon the approval of the final draft of the script, the CCR will develop the TIME BUDGET which is an estimate as to the number of hours that will be required of their time to complete the project. The approved script should provide the necessary information so that an accurate determination of the scope of the project and the number of hours that it should take all parties to perform their tasks can be projected. The TIME BUDGET will be developed by using the project tracking task codes and sheets.

ACTUAL/BUDGET ANALYSIS: At the conclusion of the project, the CCR will provide an accounting of the expenses incurred and how they compare to the budgeted expenses in the form of the ACTUAL/BUDGET ANALYSIS (A/B ANALYSIS). Because invoices can trail the completion of a project, for commitment code purposes, the project will be considered to be complete after delivery to the client. However, the CCR will be held accountable to submit the A/B ANALYSIS within a reasonable

Figure 2-2 Continued

time period (no more than one week after the receipt of the final invoice). It is important that projects be completed within the agreed upon budgets. Expenses that cause a production to run over budget must be communicated to the client for approval (preferably documented).

The TIME BUDGET will be compared with the actual hours compiled from project tracking reports. Time deviations within a variance level of (+) or (-) an agreed upon percentage for all tasks associated with the CCR will be considered acceptable. Deviations greater than the variance without reasonable explanations will be considered unsatisfactory. Therefore, greater emphasis will be placed on the weekly project tracking records that are submitted as well as the monthly reports. Though this system will be implemented in the near future, results derived will not be factored into the CCR's review in November 1989.

RATIONALE:

Consider the utilization of the above budgets as if we were a commercial production house. If a project is completed within or under the approved budget (**without compromising on quality**), the production house would have realized a profit. If the project came in over budget, either the client would have to pay more (and possibly eliminate repeat business) or the production house would need to absorb these expenses (decreasing the profit on the production and thus losing money). If more time is budgeted than actually required, future scheduling is affected which could mean turning down projects (loss of potential revenue). If too little time is scheduled, other projects could be adversely impacted.

PERFORMANCE STANDARDS

(a) Participate in section planning sessions to increase the team's effectiveness.
(b) Participate in section problem-solving sessions and serve on problem solving teams as required.
(c) Increase team building relationships within the Company.
(d) Ensure that all required administrative duties (staff notes, monthly goals, invoices, freelance contracts, project tracking reports, production filing reports and expense account statements are performed accurately and on time.

Accountability   **WEIGHT:** 10%
Number 04

Stay abreast of emerging technologies and business trends related to both the corporate television and utility industries.

PERFORMANCE STANDARDS

(a) Read professional journals.
(b) Attend professional meetings and approved seminars.
(c) Apply expanded and or new techniques and processes whenever appropriate.

Figure 2-2 Continued

METHODS FOR DETERMINING MEASURABLE GOALS
(Third Draft: 06/14/88)

BUDGETS:

During the preproduction stage of each project, the CCR will develop a **TIME BUDGET** and possibly, a **COST/EXPENSE BUDGET** if it is determined that the proposed project **could** incur expenses over <u>$1,000 for a slide/tape or multi-image program</u> and <u>$2,000</u> <u>for a video program</u>.

COST/EXPENSE BUDGET: A COST/EXPENSE ESTIMATE should be made early in the preproduction process, preferably <u>after</u> the treatment has been created and <u>before</u> scripting has begun. The COST/EXPENSE ESTIMATE will be an approximate <u>estimate</u> as to what the program could cost to produce based upon the treatment. This would include all expenses that could be invoiced to the project (talent, freelance, equipment, etc.) A review of this estimate is important so that the client can determine early in the process if there are adequate funds available to produce the proposed treatment. The C/E ESTIMATE or BUDGET might also be determined by a dollar amount provided by the client. Upon receiving preliminary approval of the ESTIMATE, the CCR can begin to fully research the subject and work towards developing the script. The final COST/EXPENSE BUDGET is to be developed and submitted to the client after the client approves the final draft of the script and before production begins. The script should provide the necessary information so that an accurate determination of the costs can be projected. The CCR will also share this information with the Media Programs Supervisor. No expenses for a production should made without the prior consent of the client.

THE PROJECT FILE:

Each CCR will be required to develop and maintain a project file that will contain the following: the final script (including music tracks used), invoices, budgets, communications, a copy of the production filing form, program set up instructions, etc. The purpose of the file is to provide a history of the production for future reference or revisions. The creation and maintenance of these files is imperative. Failure to maintain organized files could result in an unsatisfactory performance appraisal.

FEEDBACK:

At the conclusion of each production, the Media Programs' supervisor will conduct a performance/project review with the client requesting feedback on the client's satisfaction with the project as well as the CCR's performance. Points for evaluation could be the quality of the production, whether it met the stated goals and objectives and the turnaround time. The CCR could also be evaluated on their creativity, communication during the project, responsiveness, attitude, etc. (<u>NOTE: This feedback instrument will need to be developed</u>.) The CCR will also have the opportunity to evaluate the production to notate (or respond to conflicts, concerns, etc.). Both evaluations will be placed in the CCR's folder for use as a guide for the year end performance appraisal. The CCR's client feedback reviews for their projects during the year will be averaged together and count as 20% of the review.

Figure 2-2 Continued

WHEN AND WHEN NOT TO PRODUCE A PROGRAM

Whether working with an in-house facility or a production company, video producers find most of their assignments coming through direct requests from clients. Perhaps a manager will suggest a program to alleviate some training problem, or an executive may propose a motivational program to kick off a sales meeting, or a teacher might request a short documentary program for a class. Before jumping into the studio, however, you should address a number of questions.

It is difficult for a media producer to turn down an idea for a program. First, producing programs is what he or she is being paid to do. Second, we usually assume that a client has analyzed the needs and understands what a video program can do to meet those needs. Third, the client expects that the media producer is there to be told what to do.

Such assumptions threaten the whole life of media production units. First, unless you're working at a broadcast station, you're *not* being paid to "make videos." You're being paid to solve an organization's problems and in doing so create programs. Doing unwarranted or unneeded shows only makes you look foolish and wasteful and ties up time that could have been put to better use. Second, clients usually don't know much about video, and they may be so close to their problem that they can't judge how best to tackle it. Sometimes people who think they want a video program haven't thought out important considerations such as time, commitments, budget, and ability to distribute and play back the tapes or discs—not to mention the questions of appropriate use of the medium. We've all seen too many videotaped slide shows or "talking heads" programs to need to argue the latter point. Often, clients think that any problem can be solved by "throwing video at it."

Finally, a video production center is not like a typing pool where someone's scribblings are automatically transformed into some more polished form. Clients often regard a media production center as a general service unit, where jobs are turned in and accomplished without question. This attitude makes it difficult for the video producer to question the ill-advised requests that may come in.

Unfortunately, the producer who is *too* cooperative and unquestioning often winds up with very unhappy clients who don't like the final product. They won't understand *why* they don't like it—and they'll probably blame you. To avoid this, proposed videotape productions should undergo a screening process. This front-end analysis may be a formal one with written worksheets and documentation, or it may merely be a set of questions the producer asks when first talking with clients.

The first question to ask is: *What is the nature of the problem?* When employees' performance is unsatisfactory, for example, management often assumes that there is a training problem. However, lack of skills or information is not the only cause of poor on-the-job performance. There are four basic areas in which a person may be lacking: *information, skills, motivation, and personal inclination.* Not all these can be remedied by video, and even if you could solve the problem through video, you would use very different strategies for each.

The first step in analyzing a communication problem is to help the client state the problem in terms of *performance discrepancies*: what are people *not* doing that you want them to do (or conversely what *are* they doing that you *don't* want them to do). By breaking down the need into identifiable behaviors, you can begin to look at the reasons for the poor performance.

Let's look at a sample dialogue between a potential client (C) and a video producer (VP):

C: *I'd like a 10-minute video on our new office copier to show our sales reps so they understand it better.*

VP: *OK. What exactly are your objectives for the program?*

C: *I'd like the sales reps to know the features and benefits of the XY-500 so they increase their sales of it.*

VP: *So, the problem is that your reps aren't selling enough XY-500s?*

C: *Right. It's a great machine, but they're going nowhere with it. They need more training, I guess, to be able to do a really good sales job.*

Now, you need to determine if it's *really* a training problem, as assumed by your client. Is it that people don't *know* how to do something, or that they don't *want* to. Mager and Pipe (1984) suggest asking yourself the following question: Could they do it if their lives depended on it?

VP: *Have they been trained on the XY-500?*

C: *Oh yeah—when we first introduced it, we put them all through a one-day hands-on training session. But that was 6 months ago. And they have tons of literature on it—if they ever bother to read it.*

VP: *If they* really *had to, could the reps demonstrate all the features and benefits of the copier?*

C: *Well, probably. Maybe not all the features, but I guess if we really pushed them, they could do it. After all, they could brush up on it if they referred to the manuals they all have.*

VP: *So, maybe it's not a training problem after all. Do you think it's a problem of general sales skills?*

C: *No, most of them are super at sales. They're doing a great job with our other copiers, it's just this 500 that they're ignoring.*

So, you see, the producer has determined that perhaps it's not really a training problem. The reps could do a good demonstration if they really had to—they've already been trained once and have at least mediocre print materials for reference. Their sales skills can't be faulted, either. Wonder why they're not selling more of the 500s?

VP: *Well, it doesn't exactly sound like a typical training problem. You know, if we produce yet one more training session on the 500, it seems like we might not really address your problem—and increase sales. Is there some reason that they're not demonstrating the 500—or not doing a good job with it?*

C: *The 500 is a new animal for them. It has twice the power—and twice the price as our other models. It's a hard sell. To show it off well, you've got to put on an elaborate demo—you've got to show how it collates, reduces, and automatically staples—things like that. And it's also about twice the size of our other models, so it's harder for them to lug around.*

Aha! It now seems that the reps don't lack information about the new copier—it's just harder to sell. Some of these factors are beyond your control to change. But, you may be able to suggest another approach.

VP: *Well, it seems like the demo itself is tough to do. Maybe that's why they're putting more emphasis on the other machines that are easier to sell.*

C: *Sure, they know the other ones better—they've been around for 8 years now. And the smaller copiers are easier to sell. Since they're under $1000, you generally only have to sell one or two people in an office. The 500 goes for about $2000, so you need to convince more people—and show it to more people which is always tough.*

VP: *What about a demo on video? Almost every office has a video player these days, or you could provide a small integrated player and monitor to your reps to take with them. It would be smaller to carry than the 500 and could show more elaborate jobs. We could compress the time so that what might take 20 minutes to do as a live demo could be done in say 5 or 8 minutes on video. Then your reps could also leave the tape for their managers and purchasing agents to see at their own convenience.*

C: *Sounds interesting. . . .*

Of course, this scenario will have a happy ending for the client and the video producer. A marketing demo is just what the doctor ordered. But not all situations are so clear. Other organizational situations can't be solved easily—or at all—by video or by any other medium. Perhaps the sales reps aren't motivated to sell the model 500. Are the commissions worth the extra effort, or is it easier and more profitable to sell 5 model 100s? Does peer pressure *not* to work so hard keep ambitious sales people from outshining their colleagues? Is the newer technology just beyond the sales rep's understanding? Do customers react negatively when the product is presented? Or is it just a bad product?

This simple example suggests how many different factors may contribute to an organizational problem. Unfortunately, many managers find it easier to label the problem as a lack of training—thus shifting the problem to the producer. All the videotapes in the world, however, will not solve problems rooted deeply in management policy, personality conflicts, or personnel unqualified for their jobs. In these cases, the only thing a video program will do is to put some of the blame in a new place—the video department.

Once you have determined the general nature of the problem, the second question to ask is: *Can a videotape solve the problem?* If the problem is one of information or training, chances are that video can meet the need. If motivation is lacking, certain types of programs can enhance it—at least for a while. However, video alone cannot replace hands-on practice or overcome more deeply seated management or personality problems.

Finally, you should ask: *Is video the best medium?* Does the content lend itself to visualization? Can the same effect be accomplished by a less expensive medium? Are there appropriate playback facilities for viewing a videotaped program? Some topics are not suitable for the television medium but could be treated well by a workbook, a series of graphics, a slide show, or hands-on practice.

Video is good for showing live, moving events and for introducing people and places. It is not good for presenting a series of facts—that's usually done better in print, and print is easier for the audience to refer to later. Video also has limited utility in teaching hands-on skills. For instance, if you're teaching student nurses to administer injections, a video might show the procedure, but hands-on practice with real patients or at least simulated injection sites (like using an orange to practice with) is still necessary to get the "feel" of it.

The video producer can't assume that the client has thought out all these questions in advance. Working every day with television, it's easy to forget that concepts you take as second nature are not necessarily common knowledge. Beware of clients with ulterior motives. Sometimes a teacher or trainer will want to produce a videotape because it's "fashionable" to use media or because all his or her colleagues are producing video programs. Watch out for people who think that using and producing media is an easy way out of preparing lectures. Unless a client has specific objectives that can be successfully addressed by video, the producer will face an unending series of program ideas, script changes, and last-minute production modifications—because you can never meet nonexistent needs!

Interpersonal skills are extremely crucial in the early phases, when ideas are being developed with a client. A video designer must be a good interviewer and a good listener. A sense of trust must be developed. Often clients will come in with problems that are difficult to talk about. Perhaps a teacher is having a great deal of difficulty in getting across some specific concepts class after class. It takes a good deal of courage to admit this to someone else and seek help. A media designer with a know-it-all or condescending attitude will quickly find a shortage of customers.

In interviewing a client, you will have to be quick and efficient in gaining insights about the proposed videotape and its audience. You'll also have to be able to "read between the lines" to figure out if there are any hidden, deeper problems.

Clients often show their lack of knowledge about media. They may suggest, for instance, that it would be a fantastic idea to tape a three-day conference with one camera from the back of the room, so that those who couldn't attend will be able to watch the whole thing at another time. Or they'll assume that you edit by physically cutting the videotape. Diplomacy is the key in these situations. Of course, you can't let someone continue on with misunderstandings or ill-conceived ideas. But to laugh, to react with a sarcastic comment, or to officiously lecture the client is certainly unprofessional. If the client understood everything about video, who would need *you*?

HOW NOT TO DESIGN A PROGRAM

A number of years ago I was called by a manager from the headquarters office and told that I would be receiving about 4 hours of video tape and I should make that into a program about 40 minutes long. Honest—that was the request/order!

So, I asked what this was about. The answer: The video material had been recorded at a conference a week earlier and consisted of video from one unmanned camera set in the back and center of the room with available light and one microphone. What was the purpose of the program? The person on the phone didn't know; he had been told to contact me and tell me to get ready for the tapes, to do—something.

ME: "OK, are you prepared to do some narration, some additional visualization, some (did I dare say the word) scripting?"

About two more days passed, and then I got a message cancelling all plans for a video program. It seems (are you ready for this) when they looked at the tapes as requested, they found that the video heads had clogged after the first 10 minutes. All they had was 230 minutes of head-clog recording with audio. So—forget it.

Henry Bohne
Video Consultant
Parker, CO

Most people are anxious to learn about video production, once they overcome an initial hesitancy to ask "stupid" questions. Most clients also really want a good solution to their needs. Even if you decide that a video program is *not* in order, or that you can't assist them in a particular project, be sure to offer alternative solutions. Don't just say, "Twelve hours of a talking head is a terrible, boring idea. We wouldn't do a job like that!" Suggest another approach. Perhaps a written summary of the conference with copies of handouts would work. Or perhaps you could tape the conference, and later edit it down, using narration to summarize some points. Another idea would be to conduct short videotaped interviews with the presenters. Remember that you're a *communication consultant*. Perhaps you can identify a whole other topic or approach that *would* make a good video program. In any case, whether or not you decide to continue the development of an initial idea, leave the client with a positive feeling after talking with you.

The key to having good client relationships is having a *service-oriented attitude*. Producers aren't (or shouldn't be) prima donnas—they are there to serve customers and solve problems. As we saw in the last chapter, many in-house video departments are being increasingly challenged by outside facilities. For instance, many clients choose outside production houses when their own company may have a video department in the same building. Why? It usually isn't price or fancier equipment, as many in-house producers would complain. It's because outside contractors are *anxious* for the business and don't assume that clients *have* to choose them. Sometimes in-house producers get bored or "burned-out" with the job and the company's subject matter. Often they feel that they could do better work if they only had better equipment. While these are understandable feelings, clients don't want to feel that they're putting you out to do their programs. They'll take the trouble (and often pay the higher bill) to go somewhere where they're treated well. *Clients don't come back only because they liked the program—they come back because they like the experience.*

INSTRUCTIONAL DESIGN

After you've got a client, an idea for a program, and some assurance that the client's objectives can be met through a video program, where do you start? In order to assure that you proceed logically in attacking the problem, you should follow a systematic procedure for program development. Particular applications of general systems theory have been developed for instructional and informational use—they are called *instructional design models* or *instructional systems design*. A system is a flowchart, or map if you will, of steps to be taken in developing a program. There are probably as many systems as there are instructional designers, but all of them have some basic concepts in common. A system tells you where you're going, and how you can tell when you've got there. Don't let the word *instructional* throw you off either; these systematic procedures are useful for developing informational (marketing or update) programs as well as for traditional training applications. Look at Figure 2-3, now.

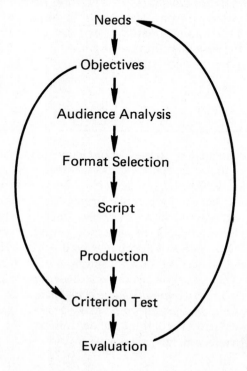

Figure 2-3 A general Instructional Design System.

The first step in systems design is to pin down the *needs*. What's the organizational problem? What could be improved? What information needs to be communicated? Usually this first step defines a problem, then suggests a general solution or broad goal.

The second phase involves specifying those general goals into *behavioral objectives*. What should the viewer be able to or motivated *to do* after watching the program? Behavioral objectives, as the term implies, identify desired outcomes or behaviors to be exhibited by the audience. Behavioral objectives are written in terms of the *audience's* desired behavior:

- specific
- measurable
- observable

An example of a behavioral objective is: "The trainee will list, in order, the six steps in preparing the deep-fryer for operation."

Notice that the objective covers one specific concept and describes an *overt behavior*. Stay away from objectives that try to describe feelings or inner motivations—these are difficult, if not impossible, to measure. Instead of "The viewer will gain an appreciation of the advantages of solar heating," write "The viewer will compare and contrast, in writing, the use of solar power and the use of petroleum-based fuels," or "The viewer will list verbally six advantages of solar heating." Be sure that you will be able to judge concretely and objectively whether or not a viewer can meet each objectives after viewing the material.

There are three types of objectives:

- cognitive
- affective
- psychomotor

Cognitive objectives are those involving concepts or definitions—"book learning." The objectives discussed above on solar heating are examples of cognitive objectives. Affective objectives deal with feelings or motivation. Although harder to measure, you *can* measure change in attitude through change in behavior. An example is "At least 60% of the viewers of the tape will donate at least $50 to the United Way drive." Another example is "When faced with the opportunity to divulge confidential client information, the employee will refuse to do so." Finally, psychomotor objectives deal with "hands-on" skills—things which require the development of a "knack." As mentioned previously, there's only so much a video can do to improve psychomotor skills—watching 200 hours of NFL football on TV doesn't make millions of Americans outstanding quarterbacks! A psychomotor objective might read something like "The trainee will load the 35mm film into a developing tank in complete darkness, completely covering the spool and without any film surfaces touching each other, within a maximum of 3 minutes."

Why go through such pains to specify each objective? First, it's the best way to narrow down the content and help your client decide upon the scope of the program. Second, it provides a means by which you can evaluate the finished product. Notice that in Figure 2–3 an arrow leads from "objectives" to "criterion test." This indicates that while you are developing your objectives, you should also be thinking about how you will test whether your objectives or criteria have been met. Remember, it's important not only to test your "students" but to *test the video program* to see if it works.

After you have narrowed the content and listed the specific objectives, you must *analyze the audience*. Why are they going to be watching the program? Who are they? How old are they? What kinds of jobs do they have? What are their motivations? What kinds of backgrounds do they have? Where are they from? The style and treatment of the video program should be tailored to the needs, interests, and culture of the intended audience. Something about the program (like the vocabulary or style of dress of the narrator) may be acceptable to your clients (generally management) but may not "wash well" with your audience.

The third step in systems design is the *selection of a format* through which to deliver the information. We assume here that you've done some preliminary investigation to discern whether video would be a viable medium. But what sort of program should be produced? Is it meant for individual or group viewing? How will the content be presented? How long should it be? The answers to these questions form the basis for the *treatment*, which is a narrative description of the way the program will look when completed. The treatment explains the style and format of the program, as if a summary were being made by a viewer while watching it.

After a treatment and format have been selected, the next stage is *writing the script*. Sometimes designers start with outlines and work up to fully developed scripts, letting the client check the work as it progresses. Some types of programs lend themselves to detailed scripts, with each word and shot planned before production. Other formats, such as the documentary, may not permit the designer to be so specific until the actual production takes place. For instance, if you were producing a program that included random interviews of people at a rally, you would not know what these people would say or how many interviews you'd actually use until the taping was completed. Even in this production style, however, the designer can block out segments of a script and sketch out suggested content, shots, and timing.

Once a script has been approved, the *production* occurs. "Production" may be a misleading label, because this phase includes not only the actual shooting, but also the pre-production planning, rehearsals, set construction, travel, and editing necessary to realize the script fully. If the previous steps in the instructional design system have been followed, the production phase should run smoothly. It is because the actual videotaping is so costly, whether a program is being produced in-house or through a production house, that the planning phases are so crucial. Changes are easy and cheap to make on paper, but considerably more troublesome on videotape.

Many producers end their involvement with a program with the end of the credits. However, a crucial phase in instructional development is yet to follow: *evaluation*. How do you know the program meets its objectives? How can you justify the cost of making it? This is where we look back to the behavioral objectives and criterion tests developed in the design stages. The criterion test is created right from the objectives, and it measures the learning or motivational outcomes of the program. If the program is instructional or technical in nature, the test can take the form of a written examination or a hands-on demonstration of mastery of a skill. If the program is informational—let's say something like a general company orientation, a news program, or a "pitch" for contributing to a charity, a test might be a simple questionnaire asking for the viewers' opinion. It may even consist of an informal interview to see what the viewers got from the program. Even more important, you should follow up to see what behavioral changes are made back on the job. Has the tape reduced production errors? Increased donations? Resulted in managers writing better appraisals?

The results of the testing should be summarized into an overall evaluation of the project. If certain spots seem weak or need correction, they can be redone. Even though it is complicated to make changes this late in a production, it is better to spend the time and money and have a product that meets its objectives. The information gained through this feedback will be useful in developing other programs as well as in justifying the work of the video department to the overall organization.

THE PARTICIPATORY DESIGN MODEL

As you've just seen, instructional design models follow the basic steps detailed in Figure 2–3. There are literally hundreds of variations on this general model—some may be more specific in discussing front-end analysis, such as analyzing the needs for a program or specifying the exact step-by-step procedures needed to complete a task which you'll be teaching. Others include more detail in the selection of media or in production.

My first major production contract was for a series of programs on ethnicity in America to be used in high schools and colleges. Because it was funded by a federal grant, we were required to have an advisory council consisting of scholars, ethnic community representatives, and potential users of the tapes. When I tried to apply the existing instructional design models I had studied, I found one thing missing: how to get "the" content. The models just assume that the content comes from "somewhere" and is unquestionably correct. That works if you're teaching $1 + 1 = 2$, but not when you're trying to teach something as nebulous and open to many interpretations as ethnic studies. There were *many* "correct" opinions and facts.

So, I developed a new model which deals with this difficulty; it grew into my doctoral dissertation. It has also grown along with my professional practice; it's not only government grant situations and "fuzzy" content like ethnic studies that produce these dilemmas. In working with corporate clients, we have found that:

- Different content experts have different ideas about what's needed and what's correct.
- They may not realize that their views aren't shared by everybody in the organization until you try to pin them down to a script.
- Unless you involve a number of content experts and deal with these diversities of opinion, your program will not be well-received in the field.

Using this Participatory Design Model is especially crucial in designing interactive video programs. Here, you'll be expecting your viewers (or more accurately, your *participants)* to respond in a conversational manner. How can they do this if they don't understand your vocabulary or if you haven't taken into account how something is done in *their* office?

Involvement in the program design process breeds commitment to using the program, both on the part of the client and the ultimate user, because they quite correctly feel identified with the program's success. People will spread the word about the program, and their colleagues will await its debut. You've gotten people in different areas of the company to "buy into" the program. Often, in fact, just having the client or expert working with representatives from the audience may itself foster good communication. When, for instance, a client representing management interacts with employees from the production line in pursuit of a common goal, understanding may be strengthened between the two groups. In summary, wide participation in program development equals program success. With that as an introduction, here's an explanation of how to use the Participatory Design Model (Figure 2-4).

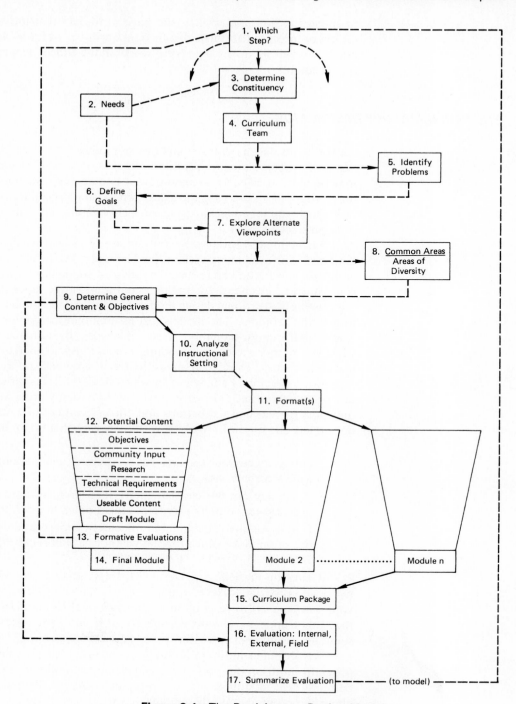

Figure 2-4   The Participatory Design Model

Step 1. Identify which processes have *already* occurred, and which have been skipped, in order to determine where to start in the design model. In the "ivory tower," things always start with a needs analysis, but in the "real world" you may find that some decisions and deliberations have already taken place.

Step 2. Analyze the overall need for the program.

Step 3. Determine your *constituency*: for whom and/or about whom are you producing the program? Your constituency is everybody who has ordered the program (your client) and everyone who will use the program (such as teachers, trainers, students, employees).

Step 4. Form a program-development team of content experts, media producers, and constituency representatives. For instance, you may have on your team an engineer who developed a new product, a scriptwriter, a video producer/editor, the client who is the product sales manager, a trainer who will use the tape within a classroom environment, an experienced sales rep who has worked with similar products, and a brand-new sales rep who has never been trained on such products.

Step 5. Identify existing needs and problems as seen by all members of the program development team.

Step 6. Define goals that address the identified problems.

Step 7. Explore all viewpoints represented with regard to achieving the goals and designing the program.

Step 8. Identify common areas of agreement and areas of diverse opinion within the team.

Step 9. Taking into account previous input, determine specific objectives for the program.

Step 10. Analyze the setting in which the program will be used. For instance, will people watch the program in a formal classroom, on their own time in the company library, as they socialize in the lobby or cafeteria, or in their own homes?

Step 11. Determine the program's format or format(s). Which media will be used, and which strategies for each media will be employed?

Step 12. Pool ideas for potential content. You'll probably find that there will be more than is wise to cover in one program. Screen these ideas by:
  • assessing how they address the objectives
  • seeking the constituency's reactions or additional suggestions
  • researching content for accuracy and duplication of other sources
  • determining whether the technical requirements of the medium will permit ideas to be implemented. Now you can produce a draft module or program segment (script or rough-cut). This step is repeated for each of several programs in a series or for several segments within a program.

Step 13. Have the entire program development team evaluate each module as it develops, through the stages of outlining, scripting, and production.

Step 14. Produce final modules or programs, using the feedback gained in formative evaluation.

Step 15. Put together the entire program package, which may include several programs or supplementary materials, such as workbooks or "live" training sequences.

Step 16. Have the program evaluated:
  • internally by the program development team
  • externally by other content and media professionals
  • in the field by users.

Step 17. Summarize the evaluations from these sources and feed them back to the program development team for possible revisions.

LEARNING ABOUT UNFAMILIAR SUBJECTS

Corporate video producers deal with a wide array of program topics; even those within an in-house production center may find themselves working on projects about technical skills, company policy, safety training, or management development. Producers within colleges and universities, as well as those working in medical applications, must often work with extremely abstract and esoteric concepts as well. How can you produce a program on a topic you don't understand? I've scripted programs on the theory of AC motors, on how to program computer-controlled lathes, and on patient information on experimental eye surgery—all without my having taken a course in physics or biology past 9th grade. While video writers and producers usually work very closely with a content expert or client, it is still necessary to develop some understanding of the subject matter in order to design the message effectively.

It is important to estimate how much time and money you will need to spend to become familiar enough with the content to produce a credible program. This item is often neglected in production schedules and budgets. There are three major factors to consider: (1) your knowledge of the subject, (2) the amount of help provided by the client, and (3) the format of the proposed program.

Obviously, if you are already familiar with the content, or if it is relatively easy to pick up, you will require less time to design and script a program. If the client can provide you with a content expert to write a draft script, or if there are other materials already available on the subject, your job will likewise be easier. Often, brochures or pamphlets on a topic are helpful in explaining material in a concise manner. For instance, if you're doing a general marketing piece for a client, their sales brochures or annual report will be useful.

Finally, the extent to which a program is scripted is an important variable. Of course, you really need to know very little to shoot a simple speech, report, or interview. A demonstration given by a skilled person is also easy to design (but may be *very* difficult to shoot unless the person is also good on camera). In these cases you need only provide appropriate backgrounds or locations and adequate camera coverage. An interview program may depend only upon a written outline of questions. However, if your talent or narrator is *not* a subject expert, if your program consists of dramatized scenes, or if you need to script fully and visualize the show for efficient production and client approvals, the demands upon your knowledge of the content are heavy. (See Figure 2-5.)

CONTENT EXPERTS: KEEP THEM AROUND

It was my first job after graduation. I was relatively unfamiliar with the product (highly technical computer-controlled machining centers)

We needed to show specific internal movements of the machine we produced. When setting up for the shot, we discovered a metal cover obstructed the moving assembly. I simply (naively) removed the cover, set up the shot and started the machine. We immediately discovered, however, why that cover had been placed there. A torrential shower of machine oil sprayed camera, crew, and cast within 15 feet of the machine.

LESSON: One should make a point of not being abandoned by one's content expert after the scripting stage.

Marty Brandt, independent producer

Figure 2-5 Producers and designers need to learn about many different subjects—some quite technical (*courtesy, Monarch/Cortland*).

In order to write good instructional programs, you must be a good student and a good teacher. You must be willing and able to learn about subjects that perhaps don't interest you. Often, existing sources on the topic are unsatisfactory—or nonexistent. In fact, probably the largest number of programs are produced about *new* products (which may not be documented or even fully developed before you need the script done). After mastering the content, you must be able to decide how best to communicate the instruction to the intended audience. While unfamiliar topics are certainly a challenge to work with, sometimes a certain "distance" is an advantage. Very commonly, subject experts or instructors are *so* familiar with or immersed in a topic that they find it difficult to explain concepts to a novice. The video designer and writer can help bridge that gap by taking the knowledge of the client and putting it into terms more easily grasped by the student.

As you've seen in the Participatory Design Model, subjects are usually best tackled by a *program-development team* consisting of subject-matter experts (sometimes called SMEs), media professionals, and representatives of the targeted audience. Not only is it important to cover the content accurately, but it is also crucial to consider the backgrounds, needs, and cultures of the potential viewers. Often programs fail because they do not relate to the values and social and work milieu of the audience. If the scriptwriter neglects to consult people representative of the intended audience, the language, dress, manners, or settings used in a program can quickly offend or amuse a viewer. The credibility and acceptance of a videotape can be ruined at the outset by the use of unfamiliar languages, the stereotyping of minority groups, or the use of wording with unintended double meanings.

For instance, if you were doing a program for distribution to your company's Middle Eastern branches or for guards in a federal prison (and you hadn't spent time in one), you should learn about their jargon, their work environment, and their attire.

AVOIDING MISUNDERSTANDINGS

Producing a video program is often a long and detailed process, in which many unexpected situations can arise. By its very nature, instructional and corporate video is a mixture of art and business, and often this combination leads to sticky situations. Often the "creative type" producer dislikes thinking about the legal and financial dimensions of video. More producers fail, however, because of their lack of business acumen than their shortage of media skills.

The one overall principle in dealing with clients is to *put everything clearly in writing*. Written records serve to clarify arrangements and to recall discussions that can easily be forgotten along the way. Make sure that you retain copies of all your correspondence and send copies to appropriate people who are involved in the production process. Written records serve several purposes:

- They remind people what was said.
- They can summarize discussions and put your understandings out on the table so that if the client had a different impression, he or she can clarify a position.
- They serve as a means for someone else to follow the project, in case the original client or producer can't follow the project through to its completion. Think of this: what would happen if someone else suddenly had to take over your role as producer of a program? Or, what would happen if your client suddenly left the company and someone else had to step in? A written "paper trail" is a good way for others to find out what has been done and agreed to in a video project. Figure 2-6 is an example of a good written needs analysis.

There are a few key questions to remember in entering an agreement with a client:

- What is the responsibility of each person or organization?
- What is the description of a satisfactory finished product?
- What are the financial considerations?
- When will the financial transactions take place?
- What are the "deliverables"?
- What happens if one party does not fulfill the stated responsibilities?
- Who has the authority to change the agreement and under what circumstances?
- Are there time deadlines—and if so, what are the penalties for not making a deadline?
- Who owns the rights to the final production, the script, and the by-products of the program (the set, slides, graphics, "raw" unedited tapes, and so on)?
- Who has the final approval or "sign-off?"
- Who has the legal responsibility for the accuracy of the content of the program?

These questions can be addressed in a formal contract (which is usually the case when two separate companies enter an agreement) or by a more informal letter of understanding (important even for the in-house producer). See Figure 2-7, which is a sample short contract. It is best to be extremely specific in the early stages of a

Division Transmission & Distribution Safety Presentation
Media Needs Analysis
Revised: September 08, 1988 Page 1

Contact Date: September 08, 1988
Requester: Todd Hartz
Department: Division Transmission & Distribution
Telephone Extension: 526-2425
Project Title: Division Transmission & Distribution Safety Presentation
Account Number/RC: 9900-588-190 / RC 9290 AC 0403
Project Manager: TODD HARTZ

GOALS & OBJECTIVES:

Define the program's final goal statement and objectives.

EDUCATE ALL NEW AND NON-OPERATING EMPLOYEES TO OBSERVE AND REPORT HAZARDOUS CONDITIONS ON THE COMPANY'S FACILITIES AND ELECTRIC SYSTEM. THE PURPOSE IS TO ELIMINATE PUBLIC INJURY ON THE SYSTEM.

Provide a brief statement of the Behavioral Goals (if more than one, rank the top three) that are to be reinforced, changed etc.

1. INCREASED EMPOYEE AWARENESS & OBSERVATION OF THE ELECTRIC SYSTEM.
2. INCREASED EMPLOYEE INVOLVEMENT IN HAZARD ELIMINATION.

Is the objective of the program to change viewer attitudes or just communicate new information?

BOTH

What type of behavior, specific skill, knowledge or attitude should be developed?

ALL EMPLOYEES NEED ENOUGH KNOWLEDGE TO RECOGNIZE POTENTIAL HAZARDS ON THE SYSTEM AND DEVELOP A POSITIVE ATTITUDE TOWARDS DILIGENT OBSERVATION AND REPORTING OF SAME. SEE ATTACHED LIST OF TARGETED EQUIPMENT CONDITIONS TO BE COVERED.

Division Transmission & Distribution Safety Presentation
Media Needs Analysis
Revised: September 08, 1988 Page 2

GOALS & OBJECTIVES (CONTINUED):

What should the viewer do or know as a result of the new skill, knowledge attitude or information that they received?
RECOGNIZE CERTAIN EQUIPMENT CONDITIONS THAT MAY POSE A PUBLIC HAZARD. KNOW THE PROPER PROCEDURE FOR REPORTING SAME TO OBTAIN REPAIR.

Figure 2-6 A needs analysis should be conducted before you even begin planning a video program (*courtesy, Mark Weiss, Georgia Power Company*).

Are there any constraints? Possible problems? Preconceived problems?

NO CONSTRAINTS. POSSIBLE EMPLOYEE APATHY.

How will the production and implementation of this program benefit Georgia Power?

REDUCE INJURY/PROPERTY DAMAGE CLAIMS & LITIGATIONS.

DEADLINES:

When is the program scheduled to be implemented?

JANUARY 1989

How much lead time to delivery?

2 MONTHS

PROGRAM APPROVALS:

Identify the individual or group that will approve the program for release.

MR. JACK LAWRENCE, V.P. OF POWER DELIVERY

Division Transmission & Distribution Safety Presentation
Media Needs Analysis
Revised: September 08, 1988 Page 3

PROGRAM CONTENT:

What is the projected length of the program?

20 MINUTES

Based upon the audience, what is the appropriate tone and style for the program?

INFORMAL — GOOD SAMARITAN ATTITUDE

Who will be the content expert? *TODD HARTZ, X2425, DIV. T&D*

List the specific subjects that need to be included (products, processes, persons, facilities).

SEE ATTACHED LIST

Rank the subjects in their order of importance (use % for weight of importance where the total equals 100%)

1. 20%   2. 5%   3. 5%   4. 10%

5. 10%   6. 20%   7. 30%

Figure 2-6 Continued

Are there any required shooting locations? *YES*

Are there any required on-camera persons (executives, content experts, spokespersons, actors, etc.)?

POSSIBLY — REQUEST ADVICE

Is there any existing visual material that can be used (video footage, film or slides)?

POSSIBLY — SLIDES FROM CLAIMS DEPT. FILES, METHODS & TRAINING DEPT. PROGRAMS

Division Transmission & Distribution Safety Presentation
Media Needs Analysis
Revised: September 08, 1988   Page 4

THE AUDIENCE & PROGRAM EVALUATION:

Who will the audience be? *ALL NEW EMPLOYEES IN ALL DEPARTMENTS, AND ALL EXISTING EMPLOYEES IN NON-LINE DEPT. CATEGORIES WHO HAVE FIELD EXPOSURE.*
Demographics:

Type of job: *METER READERS, COLLECTORS, MARKETING REPS.*

General educational background: *HIGH SCHOOL THRU COLLEGE*

Other factors

How many potential viewers will this program be made available to?
1000 — 1500

Is there specific information regarding the program's effectiveness that needs to be measured?

UNKNOWN

What would be the logistics of conducting the evaluation?

How much access to the audience is there for research and evaluation? Would it be appropriate to meet with representative members of the potential audience?

POSSIBLY

Figure 2-6   Continued

Are there any potential negative attitudes toward the subject?

Division Transmission & Distribution Safety Presentation
Media Needs Analysis
Revised: September 08, 1988   Page 5

PROGRAM UTILIZATION:

How much work and/or planning has already been done?

CONTENT HAS BEEN PLANNED.

How will the program be used?

VCR EXHIBIT DURING ROUTINE SAFETY PROGRAMS.

Will this program tie into a larger campaign?

Will the audience have access to print or other materials which also deal with the same subject? Will these pieces complement each other?

NO

If your request is for either a multi-image or slide/tape program, can you forsee the need for it to be transferred to videotape in the future?

N/A

How many copies will be needed in each format?

20 COPIES OF 3/4" VIDEO TAPE

Who will show the program? Will technical assistance be required?

SAFETY ENGINEERS & DEPARTMENT HEADS

Is equipment available at the location to show the program?

YES

Figure 2-6 Continued

OmniCom Associates

communication analysis, design & production

Proposal for the Design and Production of a Videotape on Widget Safety for Worldwide Utilities, Inc.

June 15, 1989

OmniCom Associates is pleased to propose the design and production of a videotape on widget identification, operation, installation, and related safety concepts. This proposal is based on a meeting with Suzy Supervisor on June 6, 1989.

OmniCom will design and produce a videotape approximately 30 minutes in length, following this outline:

- ° I. Introduction

- ° II. Overview of widgets - shot in widget lab in Geneva

- ° III. How to turn on widgets

- ° IV. Installing remote widgets in a customer's home

The videotape will feature actual demonstrations by WORLDWIDE UTILITIES, INC. employees, a voice-over narration, and several "video quiz points" to check trainee's comprehension of major topics.

OmniCom will, with the input of Suzy Supervisor and WORLDWIDE UTILITIES, INC. content experts during up to two days of pre-planning meetings, develop an outline script and treatment which will guide the on-camera interviews and demonstrations. Once this outline is developed, videotaping will begin. OmniCom will provide up to four days of video shooting on-site in the field and in WORLDWIDE UTILITIES, INC. offices within a 100-mile radius of Ithaca. All shooting will be based entirely on the approved outline script. WORLDWIDE UTILITIES, INC. will identify ap-

Figure 2-7 A sample proposal/contract. Note that it's important to define both what you'll do and what you except the client will do (*courtesy, OmniCom Associates*).

propriate content experts to be interviewed and videotaped for demonstrations, will assist OmniCom in coordinating production schedules, and will obtain all clearances and approvals to shoot in their facilities and in the field. WORLDWIDE UTILITIES, INC. will authorize one or more content experts who will be present for all videotaping of demonstrations to ensure accuracy of content and adherence to safety procedures and who will approve each segment as it is being shot. WORLDWIDE UTILITIES, INC. will also be responsible for the technical accuracy and completeness of the videotape, and will review the raw footage before it is edited to choose appropriate scenes for inclusion. Once all the shooting is completed, OmniCom and WORLDWIDE UTILITIES, INC. will write a voice-over script, and OmniCom will have it professionally narrated. All production will be done by fully qualified and experienced personnel using professional 3/4" U-Matic standard equipment.

Once the shooting and narration is completed, OmniCom will complete post-production of the program, including editing and inclusion of any titles or graphics specified in the outline script. All editing will be done using professional 3/4" U-Matic equipment. OmniCom will provide one 3/4" master suitable for duplication, and one VHS copy for immediate use. We can also coordinate duplication of copies. OmniCom will also provide one master copy of a short videotape guide suitable for duplication.

Schedule

OmniCom plans to conduct pre-production meetings and shooting in the period of July 10 - August 3, with post-production taking place in late August. We anticipate completion of the videotape and print guide by mid-September, given timely approvals by WORLDWIDE UTILITIES, INC..

Cost and Payment Schedule

due upon written acceptance of proposal............................$xxxxx.

upon approval of outline and treatment.............................$xxxxx.

upon completion of up to 4 shooting days...........................$xxxxx.

upon presentation of final tape & guide.............................$xxxxx.

TOTAL...$xxxxxx.

_____   _____
for OmniCom   for WORLDWIDE UTILITIES, INC.

_____   _____
date   date

Figure 2-7 Continued

client/producer relationship—even if the written agreement seems redundant to your discussions. It's surprising how much gets forgotten in the weeks or months of production—and how easy it is for misunderstandings to occur. Written agreements are also useful in drafting future contracts, in reporting activities to supervisors, in documenting your efforts, and in helping others to gain a quick understanding of the arrangements just in case someone is brought in as a replacement. Unfortunately, it's not uncommon to work with several contacts within a client organization as people shift projects and jobs.

Once an original agreement has been drawn up, don't think that you're off the hook: continue to document the progress of the production through memos, letters, or reports. Follow up phone calls with memos reiterating what transpired. It's also a good idea to remind people of upcoming deadlines and plans. Even if your client's involvement isn't necessary during certain stages of the production and you are tooling along with no problems, it's a nice idea to inform them about your progress.

It's smart to build certain checkpoints into the production process, during which the client can review the project, so that changes can be made before ideas are committed to videotape. Once a lot of time, creativity, and money have been invested, it's very difficult to make modifications, and usually both the customer and the producer leave feeling frustrated and not liking the final program. When the client has reviewed a portion of the project, you may have him or her sign off that it's approved; this can avoid your going over budget to reshoot, rewrite, or re-edit something later on. Cost estimates and quotes are important documents, too (see Figure 2-8).

Some producers approach project management and billing in stages; for instance, at OmniCom Associates, we generally use a three-stage plan: First, a needs analysis and treatment is contracted for and delivered. The writer is paid a specified fee for it. If the client likes the idea and *both* the client and producer decide they'd like to proceed with the project, a contract for a script and an estimated production budget are drawn up based on the treatment. Once the script is approved and delivered, the client is billed and a specific budget for the production is generated. Payment for the production and editing can occur at certain milestones (that is, after each major "shoot") or maybe in one lump sum upon delivery of the final edited program. This plan allows both the customer and the producer to assess the situation cautiously, without committing themselves to a large undertaking too soon.

Clients always want to know, "How much does a video program cost?" Before an adequate needs analysis and script have been completed, the cost is very difficult to estimate, and many a producer ends up in bankruptcy because of a bid that was too low—or because of too many bids that were so high that they were not accepted. Of course, this three-stage approach also lets the client "off the hook" easily, and it may set the producer up for more competition or fewer productions, since the client can back off after the needs assessment or the script are done. However, especially for the first-time client, it's usually easier to justify three small contracts than one large one.

Written messages shouldn't be reserved for contracts or complaints. Video professionals find that the old-fashioned thank-you note goes a long way in smoothing their way professionally. Once a project is done, it's good business to write a wrap-up letter to your client, citing particular people who were instrumental in assisting the project. These letters usually get passed on to a supervisor, who will be glad to know how nicely the project went when considering the *next* job.

```
                           VIDEO/AV COMMUNICATIONS
                         MEDIA PRODUCTION COST ESTIMATE


        CLIENT: _____   JOB NO. _____

        DIVISION/DEPARTMENT: _____

        LOCATION: _____   PROGRAM: _____

                                                              COST ESTIMATE

        PREPRODUCTION:
           (Includes such things as research, scripting,
           scouting, and all preparations for production.)

        PRODUCTION:
           (Includes such things as materials, equipment
           and crew, and travel.)

        POSTPRODUCTION:
           (Includes such things as editing, mixing, narration,
           ending up with a finished product.)

        DISTRIBUTION:
           (Includes duplication and shipping of completed
           program.)

        TOTAL ESTIMATED COSTS:                            _____


        PROVISIONS:
        1.  This is an estimate based on the job as of this date and is subject
            to revision.

        2.  After approval signature below, Video/AV Communications will process
            all individual invoices up to the total amount estimated above, plus
            or minus 10%, and forward directly to accounts payable.

        3.  Any cost variance above plus 10% will require the submission of a
            revised estimate to you, the client, for approval.


        REMARKS: _____

        _____

        _____

        _____

        _____

        _____


        REQUISITION AUTHORIZATION: _____
                                          (please print or type)

        SIGNATURE: _____   DATE: _____
```

Figure 2-8 Cost estimate forms are needed for clients to approve programs and see if they fit their budgets. Even within companies, each department must be responsible for maintaining its own budget, and each usually makes an internal transfer of money into the video production unit for their work (*courtesy, Union Carbide Company*).

BIBLIOGRAPHY

GAGNE, R. M. and L. J. BRIGGS (1979). *Principles of Instructional Design,* 2nd ed. New York: Holt, Rinehart, and Winston.

GAYESKI, D. (1981). "When the audience becomes the producer: a model for participatory media design." *Educational Technology 21*(6), 11–14.

MAGER. R. AND P. PIPE (1984). *Analyzing Performance Problems* (2nd ed.). Belmont, CA: D.S. Lake Publishers.

3

TRANSLATING IDEAS INTO VIDEO

You've got a client and an idea—now how do you communicate that message through television? Translating ideas into video is perhaps the most creative aspect of corporate video, and it takes a good deal of experience and talent. However, there is a palette of techniques that have been proven useful for certain types of messages, and the good video designer should be able to select and blend them with precision and artistry. Principles gained through research in perception, communications, psychology, and education are worth keeping in mind, too, when evaluating possible approaches. Scriptwriting is much more than putting correct information into correct columns on a page; it is, in fact, *message design,* and the creation of a blueprint for content approval, production, and budgeting.

TECHNIQUES THAT WORK

No magic formula will ever be discovered for designing effective informational video programs. Each topic, audience, and organization suggests different approaches, and in a given situation there may be several strategies that could be effective. Through research, however, a number of principles have been identified that can help the video producer decide how people learn and what they'll pay attention to. There are also a number of "standard" program formats that have been used successfully. Each format has its advantages and disadvantages, and you usually have to trade off the "ideal" for the "possible" in terms of time and budget.

In the earlier days of corporate and instructional video (way back in the early 80s!) many programs tried slavishly to copy broadcast TV show formats. While these basic formats (like news, panel discussions, or talk shows) can be effective, and can sometimes be used humorously in a satire script, most of the broadcast cliches have no place in nonbroadcast applications. Some producers try to adapt the trite "talk show" format with a host and one or more guests. While it may be effective to have someone interview a content expert or several business managers, the emphasis should not be on the "host." It's not the host's show—nor is the host the star like a Phil Donohue or an Oprah Winfrey. Even worse is the voice-over narration that introduces "your host for the program, Jane Doe," when Jane is merely an actress paid to read off a teleprompter for the afternoon. A big buildup introducing a narrator who has no particular expertise or name recognition always leaves the audience wondering who this supposed "expert" is and why he or she should be believed.

This "star" complex persists in the selection of narrators or actors and their attire. Everyone seems to have stepped out of a dress-for-success book. What mechanic is going to believe a perfectly groomed 25 year old in a three piece suit talking stiffly about tracing fuel-economy problems in cars? Talent can be distractingly good-looking and too formally dressed, so that the message fades out behind the glitter. Your audience is much more likely to believe and "relate to" people who look and act like credible and achievable role models. That's why it's often a good idea to use "real people" from within an organization to appear in video programs. Although they may be harder to direct and will certainly stumble through more "takes" than will professional actors, they will have the credibility to make the program "work."

The same thing is true in regard to special effects and expensive equipment. While technical production values can certainly add to a program, too many experiments with special effects will produce what looks like a demo tape for the switcher or digital effects generator manufacturer. Programs can look *too* expensive, too; your audience may wonder why you spent so much time and money on the program instead of on raises for them!

Imitation of broadcast programming is not without its merit, however. It's true that today's viewers are sophisticated and expect all television to look like network productions. Many of the techniques used by broadcasters are grounded in good principles of teaching and motivation. In fact, commercials are some of the best instructional television. By striving for broadcast quality, video professionals have become less sloppy and less likely to use the excuse that it's "only an industrial tape." Using familiar formats can be a nice way to introduce new viewers to the medium as an informational tool—but make sure that those viewers don't just sit back passively and see the program as entertainment.

Here are some general principles to keep in mind when designing informational or motivational programs:

- Get the viewer's attention first. Show them why they should pay attention to your program.
- People will pay attention to something a little bit different from what they expect; too similar or too different have the same effect—boredom.
- People will be motivated to learn something that seems to have a direct and immediate influence on their lives—relate your message to individual's needs and interests.
- Let the viewers know what a program's objectives are—and what's expected of them. These "advance organizers" help to create a mental model of the content.
- People will imitate a role model with whom they can identify.
- Provide introductions and conclusions. "Tell 'em what you're going to say, tell 'em, and tell 'em what you just told 'em."
- Use video and audio to reinforce one another; never present two unrelated or clashing pieces of information in the two channels.

- Make the viewers feel involved in the program; have them select answers or predict what will happen next—even if they're only answering "in their heads."

Increasing involvement = increased retention.

- Provide a structure to the program. Just as writing has the structure of chapters, paragraphs, underlined words, and diagrams, use transitions and visual emphasis to organize the video program.
- Tell as much of the story as possible through the visual channel.
- Show the viewers objects and processes from the same angle as they will view them in real life.
- Change the visual and aural pace within the program to relieve monotony. Intercut various interviews, different moods of music, or have the narration pause for visual montages, for example.
- Use special effects (audio or video) only when they add to the information.
- Show common mistakes as well as correct procedures—people need to learn what's a nonexample as well as what's a valid example of a concept.
- Make sure that the program is authentic and accurate from the audience's point of view. Little inconsistencies or awkwardnesses in an actor's presentation can lead viewers to doubt the value of the entire program.
- Zero in on the essential information through close-ups and/or simplified sketches or diagrams. Try to reduce complex visuals to the simplest, clearest form.
- Start from something the viewers are familiar with; don't overwhelm them with complexities too soon.
- Display unfamiliar words on the screen as they are spoken so that viewers can see and hear them.

PROGRAM FORMATS: FROM LECTURE THROUGH MUSIC VIDEO

A number of standard program formats are familiar to all of us through broadcast television. Certain topics lend themselves naturally to a specific treatment, but many can be approached in a variety of ways. The selection of a program format (or formats) is a first step in formulating a treatment (the narrative explanation of how the show will look). Some formats inherently hold more variety and interest than others, but these usually also require more time, money, and skill. Let's look at some formats, from the simple (and limited) to the more complex.

Lecture

If people know *anything* about video, they know that a "talking head" lecture is *boring*. But you still may get requests to tape a "class" that someone is teaching so that it can be recorded for posterity. Often, when a company buys a new piece of equipment, such as a phone system, the vendor will put on one or several "live" training sessions. But how will the training be handled once the trainer leaves? This is where the request for videotaping comes about.

Simply putting a camera at the back of a classroom and letting the tape roll will almost certainly result in a less-than-scintillating production. A static shot of a small talking head is very difficult to pay attention to. It may be difficult to hear what class members are saying. It also may be difficult or impossible to see what the trainer is writing on a board or displaying on an overhead or slide projector. So, should you refuse the request altogether? A better approach would be to take the contents of the class and redesign and reshoot it for video. You'll find that you can almost always reduce the time by tighter scripting and eliminating pauses for things like questions or writing on the board. But, you don't always have the luxury to redo the training.

If you *must* tape a lecture, here are a few pointers:

- See if you can get a copy of the slides, handouts, or overheads used. You can reproduce these on a computer graphics system and edit them in later so that the visuals are more readible.
- Make sure that you can pick up adequate audio from both the instructor and the class. You might, for instance, suspend a mike from the ceiling over the class, and put a wireless mike on the trainer.
- If the instructor demonstrates a procedure on some equipment, see if you can reshoot those demos at another time so that you can get close-ups.
- Put a "table of contents" and graphic "chapter markers" on sections of the tape so that viewers can later find the section they want to see.
- Sit down with your client and review the footage to see if anything can be edited out. You may write some brief transitions or summaries to be read later by a narrator which can help you to compress the time.
- If there's going to be a lot of interaction with the students, try to do a two-camera shoot and have one camera focus in on the students, and the other shoot the instructor. Get close-ups of faces—video loses a lot of detail in long shots and just a screenful of blurry colors is boring.
- See if you can include a workbook with the video which summarizes sections and/or reproduces visuals and handouts.

Interview

In the interview format, one or a few people are interviewed by a "host," either in the studio or in the field. This format is especially suitable when the focus is on an interviewee who is an expert, or a "personality."

The interview is one of the easiest formats to produce. Generally, the script consists of a brief opening and closing and a series of questions. The setting usually is a studio or a prearranged field location where lighting and production equipment can be set up beforehand and can remain stationary. Interviews ordinarily require little or no editing, minimal travel, and little production expertise. The interviewer needs little advance preparation or rehearsal, and the interviewee can respond naturally to questions, rather than being preoccupied with production requirements.

The interview, however, can become boring. Unless the subject or personalities hold some fascination for the audience, it's easy to tire of the same static shots of "talking heads." The format can be enlivened by taking the interview out of the studio and into the subject's home or workplace. You can also have the host and interviewee *move*—have them walk around a plant, through a park, or into an office building. Although it's difficult for the camera to follow them for too long, these roving shots can be used for transitions—characters can, for instance, walk into the interviewee's office and sit down for the rest of the program.

Several interviews can be combined into one program, with an introduction, transitions, and wrap-up by the host. Graphics, slides, or video clips can be inserted to illustrate the topic; these can be edited in after the interview so as not to constrain the speakers to a particular ordering of topics. Various clips of different interviewees can be intercut, so that they seem to be responding to or elaborating on each others' comments. This helps introduce visual and auditory variety (see Figure 3-1 for an example).

Open in black, with audio of soup kitchen. Video of food being spooned onto dishes, line of children and adults filling their plates.

MOST OF US HAVE ASKED OURSELVES, "WHAT DO I FEEL LIKE EATING TODAY?"

IT'S NOT OFTEN THAT WE THINK ABOUT THOSE WHO ASK, "WILL I EAT TODAY?"

Bring in basket graphic, title, "HELPING THE HUNGRY".

Video of St. Rita's kitchen.
Mary Haines VO: "For some of these people, it's the only hot meal they have all week."

MARY CATHERINE HAINES IS HELPING THE HUNGRY IN DUNDALK.

EVERY MONDAY, YOU'LL FIND MARY AND HER PARENTS IN THE KITCHEN OF SAINT RITA'S CATHOLIC CHURCH --- COOKING ENOUGH FOOD TO FEED AN AVERAGE OF 125 PEOPLE. WITH THE HELP OF LOCAL VOLUNTEERS, THEY HAVE BEEN PREPARING THE MONDAY SUPPER SINCE 1981.

Mary 35:09   "It's very important socially...
                    away from their environment.
Mary 36:11   For many of the elderly...budget the
                    whole month."

Wipe to Pam Addison inside, talking to client.

Pam 05:20   "Do your children get free lunch?"
                   ACROSS TOWN, AT THE STRAWBRIDGE OUTREACH CENTER IN BOLTON HILL, MORE OF MARYLAND'S HUNGRY ARE FINDING HELP.
                   PAM ADDISON IS DIRECTOR OF THE BREAD OF LIFE PROGRAM AT THE CENTER. SHE AND A GROUP OF VOLUNTEERS PROVIDE BAGS OF DONATED FOOD AND HOUSEHOLD ITEMS FOR THOSE IN THE NEIGHBORHOOD.

Pam   "Most are families....."

Video of packing bags, taking information.

Pam on camera interview   "What we try to include...
                    can't afford to buy food...
                    of that nature."

Fransciscan Center Kitchen
Women with turkeys.

                   MANY SOUP KITCHENS AND FOOD PANTRIES RELY ON HELP FROM VOLUNTEERS. HERE AT THE FRANCISCAN CENTER, VOLUNTEERS PREPARE AND SERVE A HOT LUNCH TO HUNDREDS OF PEOPLE ON A DAILY BASIS.
                   THE CENTER ALSO PROVIDES EMERGENCY FOOD ASSISTANCE TO ANYONE IN NEED.
                   SISTER CAROL RYBICKI (RYE - BIC - EE) IS ASSISTANT DIRECTOR AND PUBLIC RELATIONS REPRESENTATIVE FOR THE CENTER.

talkup 17:51
packing bags video   "Sometimes it's...no cooking facilities.
                     is a real challenge."
18:50
20:20

Exterior

                   SAINT AMBROSE COMMUNITY CENTER IN WEST BALTIMORE, OFFERS HELP IN A VARIETY OF WAYS TO THE HUNGRY AND THE HOMELESS.
                   IT'S THROUGH THE GENEROSITY OF PRIVATE DONORS THAT THE CENTER CAN OPERATE, ACCORDING TO ITS DIRECTOR, SISTER CHARMAIN.

Sr. Charmain on camera
                   "The people who do...consistent...
                   people we once helped.
                   It's not my project, it's the parish's
                   project...community....project.
                   If I...know them so well."
                   DURING THANKSGIVING WEEK, THE CENTER WAS ABLE TO GIVE OUT OVER ONE-HUNDRED FIFTY TURKEYS TO LOCAL FAMILIES.

                   IN ADDITION TO PRIVATE DONATIONS, MANY CENTERS LIKE THE ONES WE'VE JUST SEEN, PURCHASE FOOD FROM THE MARYLAND FOOD BANK.
                   MARKETING MANAGER BUY-ARD WILLIAMS EXPLAINS HOW THE FOOD BANK WORKS.

interview 05:39   "The Food Bank is...."

freeze frames of people from tape
                   YOUR DONATION OF FOOD WILL HELP PEOPLE LIKE THOSE YOU'VE SEEN HERE. WON'T YOU PLEASE JOIN THE ONGOING CAMPAIGN AGAINST HUNGER?

Figure 3-1 An example of an interview program tied together by an on-camera narrator (*courtesy, Mary Orlando-Llewellyn, Westinghouse Corp.*).

Panel Discussion

This format combines the lecture and the interview. A panel of guests is moderated by a host, and each presents a short talk and then discusses the topic in response to questions. This is a good format when opinions vary on a topic or when a number of experts must contribute in order to explore a subject fully.

The panel discussion takes the burden away from any one individual, but arrangements must be made to keep the group on the subject and to maintain a balanced approach—especially when the subject is a controversial one. It requires a host who's a good *facilitator* and leader of the discussion. It's a good idea to set a time limit on individual presentations and responses to questions and to have a definite idea beforehand of what each person is going to contribute to the discussion. For example, the interviewees should probably be given a list of the questions beforehand so that they can prepare some thoughtful responses. You might also want to have the guests meet each other prior to taping so that they don't interact awkwardly.

From the production standpoint, the panel discussion is an easy and inexpensive format, since little is changed from the typical round-table or living-room set. Panel discussions are useful in representing many sides or aspects of an issue as well as a variety of constituencies (academicians, business people, government officials, and so on). For instance, Texas Instruments has sponsored a series of teleconferences on artificial intelligence. They included round-table discussions by leading experts in the field who talked about current issues and responded to questions called in live by viewers of the teleconference.

Demonstration

When a subject expert is good on camera (and willing), a demonstration is an excellent way to teach "how-to" quickly and effectively. This format is more time-efficient than a voice-over since very little scripting is needed—*if* the talent knows what he or she is supposed to say and do. However, not too many content experts can, as we say, "walk and chew gum at the same time." It's difficult to do something and to talk about it smoothly. But, a person recognized as a credible authority is much more effective than an obviously coached actor. Furthermore, a demonstrator with whom the audience can identify, that they can enjoy and believe in will help motivation and retention of information.

If you decide to use an expert as a demonstrator, first have that person run through the demo without the camera. You can watch the demo, make suggestions, and decide how to shoot it. Then, have the person do the demonstration in small segments. Move the camera between segments to add to the visual variety and to enable smooth editing. The person can redo each small segment as many times as necessary without having to start at the top each time.

Another technique is to give your on-camera expert someone to talk to. It can be very disconcerting to have to give a demo to an unblinking camera lens—it's much easier to have a real person to talk to. For instance, in a series of videotapes on the operation of Carrier Corporation's new factory shop-tracking system, we had an actual supervisor familiar with the new system teach it to a colleague. He demonstrated how to call up screens on the system and enter data, and sometimes he looked at his student, and sometimes at the camera (as if it were another student). The on-camera student asked questions which made the production more interesting and also gave the expert a little "break" from constant lecturing.

If a professional actor must be hired, he or she must first learn to perform the demonstration with ease. Be sure to have a content expert with you while taping to ensure that the demonstration is being done accurately—you may miss small details that make a big difference later on. If there's a lot of technical dialogue to memorize, you can shoot some of the demonstration close-up and have the talent actually read the script off a teleprompter or a script just out of camera range. For instance, we shot a demonstration of programming a computer-operated lathe, and we had the talent deliver some lines on camera, and at other times he showed just his fingers entering numbers on a keypad while he was actually holding the script in his other hand and reading it.

You can also combine professional and "in-house" talent in a demo. Have the professional act as a "host" to introduce the program, make transitions, and deliver summaries. This person can then interact with the real expert who can talk less and demonstrate more. Figure 3-2 illustrates these techniques.

Voice-Over

In a voice-over program, a narrator who seldom (or never) appears on camera provides the audio track while complementary video shots reinforce what is being said. This is a common format for instructional or training programs, since it is an easy way to show procedures or places.

This format places a greater burden on the scriptwriter than do the previous ones, for unlike an interview or demonstration, it requires a complete script like the one in Figure 3-3 beforehand for each word and shot. The complete scripting is useful in highly technical areas, though, since everything can be checked over first by a content expert to see that it is accurate. Sometimes, an organization's legal department needs to review an exact script word for word before it is produced.

The information should flow in a logical and well-conceived manner; this is not always the case with interviews, which often get off the track. Visualization is important in this format, since you can't rely on shots of talking heads; every piece of narration must have a corresponding shot.

The voice-over requires a lot of pre-production planning and fairly extensive shooting. However, since everything is planned ahead of time, there is little wasted footage. Depending upon the topic, a variety of locations may be used, and careful editing will be necessary to keep transitions logical. Although the narrator may be on camera briefly, most of the narration can be read directly from a script, saving a lot of memorization and smoothing over any lack of on-camera acting technique. The narrator need not actually be able to demonstrate a task, and the on-camera demonstrator need not be able to speak well.

There's a trick to combining the efficiency in scripting of an on-camera demonstration by an expert and the professional delivery of a narrator: Videotape an expert doing a demonstration and talking about each step as it is done— but don't show his or her face. Transcribe the audio and edit what the expert said, using a word-processor. You'll probably find that you can eliminate a lot of wordiness and come up with smoother explanations. Have the expert check your edited script. Then, have a professional narrator read the edited script, and edit the expert's video demo with the narrator's audio track. We used this technique for a safety program for a major utility, and we found that we were able to edit the expert's demo down to about one fourth of the original time—and to have a much more lively and professional-sounding voice for the audience to listen to.

The voice-over is also a way to combine the credibility of an on-camera expert with the ease of having the expert read a script rather than memorize it and deliver it while smiling into that camera lens. For example, we produced a marketing program for a materials handling company using the company president as the narrator. He appeared in the beginning and the conclusion, and for transitions throughout the program—but each appearance was only about 15 seconds long. So, he only had to memorize and deliver two or three sentences at a time, and then he could read the voice-over for the rest.

SEGMENT 1	AUDIO
1) Fade up on CU of nameplate on office door. Slow zoom out to full shot of door	Customer's voice: And just how long have you been without one? Salesman's voice (timidly and questioningly): Well, ah, if you could tell me...I mean I haven't had a chance..... Customer's voice (impatiently): Well, I just don't know how you can operate without it.
2) Cut to side angle of door (full shot) Door opens and salesman walks out. Door shuts	Customer:..And please don't come back until you have it.
	②
~~3. Door closes abruptly behind~~ 2) cont Slow zoom in to salesman	Voiceover of salesman's thoughts (use a touch of echo): It! Everywhere I go lately I can't get anywhere because I don't have it. Did I lose it? Did I ever have it? Where in the world can I find it?

Figure 3-2   A Twilight Zone takeoff makes an on-camera demonstration a bit more entertaining (*courtesy, Avid Communications*).

SEGMENT 2

3) SLOW dissolve To LIMBO SET w/SERLING FULL ShoT	(Music up...Twilight Zone theme). (Music under) Figure (Rod Serling-type voice): Dave McBob, successful salesman with sales gone awry, is about to enter a new dimension....a dimension where sales success is measured in volts and amps and even in ohms. (Slow fade out of music during dialogue).
3) CONT: DAVE McBOB WALKS INTO SCENE IN BACKGROUND. CAMERA PICKS HIM UP AND PANS PAST SERLING. He stops	Dave McBob is about to enter.... (pause as action unfolds)
A GIANT MULTIMETER Lights up IN FRONT of HIM. He FREEZES IN FEAR While TITLE IS ClIPPED IN	the multimeter zone. (Music up full) (Music under)
DAVE BACKS up IN FEAR AND CAM FOLLOWS BACK TO SERLING. (DAVE CONTINUES BACKING up out of shot)	Now, journey with Dave into this new dimension of customer satisfaction. For, today, he will take an unusual detour in time and space.

Figure 3-2 Continued

4) CUT TO 2nd ANGLE of SERLING WITH BIG MULTIMETER IN BACKGROUND. BOX WIPE of DAVE REELING DOWN CENTER OF HALLWAY IS IN METER FACE.	Today, his travels will take him to the Reliance Electric training facility. And, here, in the multimeter zone, he will learn how to use _it_. (Music up full and out).
	/ = PAUSE
SEGMENT 3 5) DISSOLVE TO NARRATOR'S POV LOOKING OUT ON CLASS AS DAVE STUMBLES INTO BACK OF CLASS AND SITS DOWN 6) CUT TO MS of NARR. 7) CUT TO SHOT of DAVE LOOKING BEWILDERED 8) CUT TO FS FROM BACK of LAB SLOW ZOOM IN, STOP AT M.S. OF NARR. 9) CUT TO SIDE ANGLE of NARR. TALKING OUT AT CLASS. (TRY TO INCLUDE A FEW STUDENTS)	NARRATOR: Dave, glad you could make it . We've been expecting you./ We were just about to get started. -/At Reliance Electric (hold up multimeter) we have borrowed a technician's tool to use as a sales tool: the multimeter. We've done this because sometimes we're asked why an electrical device doesn't work right or it doesn't work at all. Frankly, though, we're salespeople, not technicians. But, because we're salespeople, we want to help our customers any way we can. And that's what we are going to do today: learn how to use the multimeter to help us help our customers. First, we'll show you

Figure 3-2 Continued

64) CONT. NARR. MAKES APPROPRIATE GESTURES	Make sure you don't touch any electrical conductor, including the enclosure, frame, or any other electrical component in the device, with any part of your body. And, of course, be careful not to reach across other live electrical components.
65) CUT TO SIDE ANGLE (F.S.) OF DEMO TABLE. NARR. SHOWS CORRECT PROCEDURES BY GESTURE	To take a measurement like this, you should extend the probes straight out from your body and touch them to the terminals. If you want to switch the probes, withdraw your arms from the test area and then exchange the probes. You should never cross your arms to reposition the probes.
NARR. PICKS UP ALLIGATOR CLIP 66) CUT TO C.U. of NARR PUTTING CLIP ON TERMINAL IN DRIVE	Whenever possible, use an alligator clip on one probe. Extend your hand into the test area and clip the probe on the terminal and place your free hand in your pocket.
67) CUT TO ANGLE SHOT WITH METER IN FOREGROUND. NARR. TOUCHING PROBE TO DRIVE IN BACKGROUND	So let's go ahead and measure the voltage between these two terminals. We see the needle move the scale and stop.

Figure 3-2 Continued

MONTAGE:
PERSON CAULKING WINDOWS
STEAK DINNER
FISH IN BAY
WOMAN READING PAPER
MAN AT DESK (FLOURESCENT)

PAINTERS AT WORK
BG & E EMPLOYEES (E.I. TEST
SHOP RBC WAREHOUSE CAPACITORS
AND TRANSFORMERS)

MCU NARRATOR, Z.O. TO
ESTABLISH NARR.
PCB GRAVEYARD

QUICK MONTAGE OF BG & E
CAPACITORS, TRANSFORMERS,
SWITCHERS, PCB DRUM

(MUSIC UPBEAT)

(MUSIC UNDER AS V.O. BEGINS)

V.O.

Familiar sights and experiences...

socially...professionally.

As natural as these scenes may

appear, there is something quite

common about them.

(JARRING TONE)

NARRATOR:

Concern over possible occupation-

al health and environmental

hazards continues. By now, most

of you recognize the source of

this concern: (NARRATOR GESTURES

TOWARD TRANSFORMER)...

Polychlorinated Biphenyls or PCBs.

(MUSIC MOTIVATES CUTS)

UP TITLE/SFX
PCBS: IT'S UP TO YOU

V.O.

Countless studies have been

performed, and many cases

Figure 3-3 A narrator who is occasionally on camera guides us through this program on toxic substances (*courtesy, Meta Ann Donohoe, Baltimore Gas & Electric Co.*).

MCU NARR.
RBC PCB GRAVEYARD

FOOTAGE OF OLDER PCB
NEW MINERAL OIL CAPACITOR

FIELD FOOTAGE

PCB APPLICATIONS

examined, regarding the toxic effects of PCBs. Although some hypotheses remain inconclusive, there are certain facts about the substance of which we are certain.

NARRATOR ON CAMERA

As of 1977, the production of PCBs has ceased. There is a reason why PCBs are no longer manufactured, and why, by the end of 1987, the Baltimore Gas and Electric Company will have phased out most of its PCB equipment.

Polychlorinated Biphenyls--upon examination--are quite complex. Used primarily as a nonflammable insulating fluid--or a dielectric--PCBs' chemical stability, low flammability, high heat capacity and low electrical conductivity, resulted in nation-wide usage. Many industries, including utilities, used PCBs from 1929 through the end of 1977.

Figure 3-3 Continued

CHYRON ROLL TRADE NAMES OVER PCB VIDEO.

Referred to as ASKAREL, PYRANOL, INERTEEN, CLORINOL...and a myriad of other trade names, their glorification period was relatively short-lived. Suspected health and environmental risks in the 70's raised national awareness.

NARR. ON CAMERA
RBC PCB GRAVEYARD

NARRATOR ON CAMERA
Since that time, the Federal Government, in the form of the Environmental Protection Agency has controlled the use, handling and disposal of PCBs. Why? Let's take a closer look.

PAGE TURN (TRANSITIONAL WIPE)

GRAPHIC: SINGLE MOLECULE (2 BENZENE, 2 CHLORINE)

CHYRON 209 COMBINATIONS
MOLECULAR COMBINATIONS
LIQUID PCB SUBSTANCE
WAXY SUBSTANCE

V.O.
PCBS exist as a family of compounds; there are two-hundred and nine possible chemical combinations, ranging from a watery-type liquid

Figure 3-3 Continued

	to a waxy substance.
TRANSITIONAL WIPES RIVER WITH FACTORY CHYRON: SLOW BIODEGRATION RATE	PCBs are pervasive. That is, they decompose slowly in our environment. Over a 50 year period, evidence of this chemical's slow biodegradation rate has
TRANSITIONAL WIPE MONTAGE OF NEWSPAPERS, CAULKING MATERIAL	become alarmingly evident. In the utility industry, PCBs are most commonly found in capacitors and transformers. But don't associate PCBs exclusively with electrical equipment.
FOOD SHOTS - GROCERY	Were you aware that low-level PCBs may exist in our food? (MUSIC CHANGE)
NATURE SHOT	The accumulation rate of PCBs in the environment is evidenced in
ESTABLISH FACTORY	the food chain through a process called Biomagnification. Simply,
GRAPHIC: FOOD CHAIN	fish in contaminated waters feed on phytoplankton and smaller life forms which have absorbed the PCB substance. Fish store this substance

Figure 3-3 Continued

GRAPHIC: FOOD CHAIN

primarily in the fatty cells of their bodies. These fish are consumed by larger fish. The process continues. Since PCBs do not easily break down, humans who ingest this fish stand the risk of introducing PCBs into their systems.

SLATE: CHYRON
PROGRESSIVE REVEAL

In addition to <u>ingestion</u>, PCBs can be introduced into the human body through <u>inhalation</u> and <u>absorption</u>. By-products of PCB combustion can be inhaled; or humans can come in direct physical contact with PCB thereby absorbing the chemical.

For the most part, physical contact with the substance results in relatively minor complications. But, like any other potentially harmful chemical, toxicity and damage is dependent upon exposure.

<u>NARRATOR ON CAMERA</u>

MCU NARRATOR: EXT.

(MUSIC CHANGE)

So, what was once considered a

Figure 3-3 Continued

MONTAGE: CU WARNING
SIGNS

C.U. LABELS
HIGHLIGHT AMOUNTS

positive attribute of PCBs--their chemical stability--is today regarded as a negative characteristic. PCBs hit home. Exercise responsibility when working near or with these chemicals. It's up to you.

Recognize these labels? They are one way of <u>informing</u> and <u>warning</u> you about PCB levels present within any given container. This labelling system is a result of the EPA's development of regulatory guidelines...designed for your safety. Zero to fifty parts per million designates a non-PCB item. Fifty to 500 parts per million means PCB contaminated and over five-hundred parts per million--a label that you should rarely see--indicates a high level of PCB concentration.

<u>NARRATOR ON CAMERA</u>

This all sounds comprehensive, but

Figure 3-3 Continued

	what exactly does parts-per-million mean? And how is it used as a unit of measurement?
GRAPHIC	Parts-per-million refers to the concentration of PCBs in any given mixture. A part-per-million is an extremely small amount; one part-per-million would be the same as one inch is to sixteen miles!
MCU NARRATOR-FT. SMALLWOOD	<u>NARRATOR ON CAMERA</u> Clearly, this substance demands special treatment in its handling and disposal. In response to the EPA regulations, BG and E has developed an active stance, instituting Corporate PCB Management Guidelines.
ROLL POLICY STATEMENT OVER MANUAL (AUTHORITY, PURPOSE APPLICABILITY...)	BG & E's Corporate PCB Management Guidelines outline our company's PCB policy, ultimately, however, <u>you</u> are responsible for policy implementation.

Figure 3-3 Continued

The voice-over puts the emphasis on the content rather than the personality. This fact, coupled with the format's intermediate ease of production and high visual interest, makes it a popular choice for informational and instructional programs. It is best used for relatively short, straightforward, objectively oriented topics, and it lends itself easily to be combined with other formats.

Dramatization

A dramatic treatment of a subject involves the acting out of scripted situations from which the viewer can derive information or general principles. This format is used primarily to provide a means for modeling behavior: the viewer sees how (or how *not*) to behave in certain cirumstances.

The dramatization is a captivating format, since it can involve a great deal of creativity in acting, writing, directing, shooting, and editing. It is an effective use of the medium, since video is so adept at recreating lifelike situations. The complexities of design and production, however, sometimes outweigh its advantages. The writer must be able to create realistic dialogue, evoking interest and emotion, without turning it into a soap opera (see Figure 3-4). Sets must be created, actors rehearesed and blocked, and camera shots practiced. Unless the program incorporates a narrator for explanations, the viewers may have difficulty in picking out the information they're supposed to acquire. And, if the scripting and acting aren't excellent, the whole thing looks awkward.

Generally, dramatizations are used to teach interpersonal skills or to present information in a "softer" form than a lecture. This is the best format for presenting role models to trainees or for stimulating the interest of otherwise unmotivated viewers. Also, some events simply can't be shot "as they happen." For example, we did a program for Marine Midland Bank on robbery and had to dramatize several kinds of hold-ups including a bank storming (Figure 3-5). We semi-scripted the program and used real tellers and managers as bank employees and also used two policemen who specialize in re-creating robbery scenes for classroom training simulations. While some of the robbery scenes were fully scripted and rehearsed, the actors (except for the robbers) were unprepared for the storming scene. We told them that we simply wanted general shots of a bank in operation—and before you know it, robbers with masks and sawed-off shotguns were screaming their way into the bank. We had two cameras tape the whole thing—and got very realistic reactions from the nonprofessional talent!

Other dramatic programs are shot in studios, such as the one done by Japanese TV illustrated in Figure 3-6.

News

This popular broadcast format has been adopted by many organizations to inform employees of current activities and policies. Like the documentary, it is more informational than instructional. Most corporate news programs mimic their broadcast counterparts by alternating studio-based segments with reports in the field. Many have one or two anchorpersons (who may *in fact* be network or station anchors or reporters) covering various stories. (There's usually no weather report—but many corporate news programs *do* feature reports about company or local sports activities!)

Once a format has been established, news programs are relatively easy to produce. The talent can read from scripts or teleprompters, and simple computer-generated graphics, slides, or stock footage can be inserted where appropriate. Depending upon the stories, travel may be quite extensive—and expensive. The purpose of many corporate news programs is to show employees what's happening in various branch offices or factories around the country or around the world. Some

General Telephone Company
V-4023 - Page 1
3/28/84 6/6/84

VIDEO	AUDIO

FADE IN
Ext. A small mom and pop coffee shop. We hear the voices of JOHN, a caucasian I&M man, and DARLEEN, a black cable maintenance girl. They are discussing 4-Tel. We've picked up their conversation in mid-sentence.

(MUSIC UP)

(MUSIC UNDER AND OUT)

DARLEEN (VO)

....I'll tell you what bugs me. On one hand they tell us how important people are....

JOHN (VO)
(picks up thought)
Right. And how they want you to do a good job....

Cut to Int. John and Darleen are seated at a table.

DARLEEN

Then they turn around and put in some machine to do the very thing you're good at!

JOHN

Me too....Yeah, and how about productivity and efficiency, they're always harping on that one. But from what I hear you've gotta go through about five steps just to shoot a short with 4-Tel. I can throw a tone/flicker across the line in a matter of seconds!

WAITRESS

A waitress arrives

What'll it be today?

JOHN

Just coffee for me Jan.

Figure 3-4 A dramatic treatment gets the audience's interest and sympathizes with their predicted attitudes to make this product introduction more effective (*courtesy, GTE California*).

General Telephone Company
V-4023 - Page 2
3/28/84   6/6/84

            VIDEO   AUDIO

                                                          DARLEEN

                                              Me too..It just doesn't make any sense!
CUT to Ext.
SUPER TITLE: (MUSIC UP)

4-Tel....A Sensible Change?

LOSE TITLE

A supervisor's truck pulls up
in front of the coffee shop.
TOM GONZALES, a first line sup.
gets out. He puts out his cones   (MUSIC UNDER AND OUT)
and heads for the front door.
                                                           JOHN
Cut to int.   John and Darleen   (With a cynical chuckle)

                                              Next week it'll be computerized repair

                                              people. Then they won't have to worry

                                              about us human beings at all......

Gonzales approaches the table   (STOPS MID-SENTENCE, REALIZING GONZALES
                                              HAS ARRIVED)

                                              Oh, hi Tom.....

                                                         GONZALES

                                              Hi, John....(TURNS TO DARLEEN).......

                                              Darleen.

                                                          DARLEEN

                                              Hi.

                                                         GONZALES

Gonzales takes a seat and turns   Bill can't make it tonight, so it looks
his coffee cup upright.
                                              like we're out a short stop.

                                                          DARLEEN

                                              He's probably still out trying to shoot

                                              that cross he had using 4-tel.

Figure 3-4 Continued

General Telephone Company
V-4023 - Page 3
3/28/84 6/6/84

<u>VIDEO</u>   <u>AUDIO</u>

<u>GONZALES</u>

Don't tell me. You two had your meetin
on it this morning.

<u>JOHN</u>
You got it....

Gonzales begins shaking his head
with a slight chuckle. Neither   <u>DARLEEN</u>
John or Darleen like this.
                                                           What....are we supposed to be overjoyed
CU Darleen
                                                           by some new computer that'll double

                                                           our work for no reason!?

                                                           <u>JOHN</u>
                                                           (To Darleen)
                                                           He thinks it's funny!

CU John   <u>GONZALES</u>
ON GONZALES
                                                           No....No I don't. Sorry. Look...I

                                                           can understand exactly how you guys

                                                           feel. It's just that it never ceases

                                                           to amaze me how we all seem to pass

                                                           judgement on new things without knowing

                                                           all the details!

                                                           <u>JOHN</u>

                                                           What do you mean?

                                                           <u>GONZALES</u>

Gonzales is controlled and   Ask yourself a serious question, John
convincing.
                                                           ....Do you <u>really think</u> the people who

                                                           made the decision to go with 4-Tel

                                                           would have spent the money to implement

Figure 3-4 Continued

General Telephone Company
V-4023 - Page 4
3/28/84

<u>VIDEO</u   <u>AUDIO</u>

                                                       <u>GONZALES</u> - cont'd
                                                       it companywide if it was a system that
                                                       <u>doubled</u> the amount of time it takes
                                                       people to do their jobs?!!
                                                       <u>JOHN</u>
                                                       Well....I....
Two shot   <u>GONZALES</u>
                                                       And Darleen....Did it ever occur to
                                                       you that since we're out here in the
                                                       field, in our own little operation,
                                                       we might only get to see a very small
                                                       part of the "big picture"....how 4-Tel
                                                       fits into the company's <u>overall</u> plans?
Darleen knows he's right, but   <u>DARLEEN</u>
she's being defensive   That's probably true. But I'm talking
                                                       about what 4-Tel means to <u>me</u>.
                                                       <u>GONZALES</u>
                                                       And you think it's going to mean more
                                                       work?
On Darleen--Now she's going to   <u>DARLEEN</u>
prove her point.   I'll put it this way. I can tell you
                                                       if there's a short on a line in about
                                                       ten seconds with a tone/flicker set.
                                                       From what I'm told, with 4-Tel, by
                                                       the time I dial it up, and go through
                                                       all the steps, it's gonna take a heck
                                                       of alot more than ten seconds!

Figure 3-4 Continued

Figure 3-5 Many productions are shot on location to enhance credibility, like this interactive training program for Marine Midland Bank (*courtesy, OmniCom Associates*).

Figure 3-6 A historical docu-drama being taped in a studio at NHK, the national broadcasting company in Japan.

investment is usually made in a set, and usually one or two steady anchorpersons are contracted in order to provide stability and credibility to a news series. Also, a rather "snazzy" animated logo is generally created to begin each program in the series, and certain stock computer graphic backgrounds can be developed for program segments. The editing involved may be extensive, but not usually complicated, since the stories are generally short and simple. See Figure 3-7 for an example of this format.

```
1.MAIN TITLE
WESTINGHOUSE LOGO TRANSFORMS INTO "ILSD TODAY"

                  MUSIC UP FULL

TITLE MOVES OFF SCREEN TO LEFT.


2.EACH STANDARD OF EXCELLENCE ENTERS SCREEN FROM RIGHT, MOVING OFF
SCREEN LEFT.
Pride - Desire - Teamwork - Attention to Detail - Follow Through

                                    NARRATOR: (VOICE-OVER)
                                    PRIDE...FOLLOW-THROUGH..
                                    DESIRE...TEAMWORK...
                                    ATTENTION TO DETAIL
3.GRAPHIC READS: STANDARDS OF EXCELLENCE

                                    ...FIVE STANDARDS OF
                                    EXCELLENCE.


4.GRAPHIC TRANSFORMS TO: TEAMWORK

                                    AND THE PIVOTAL
                                    STANDARD - TEAMWORK...


5.'TEAMWORK' TURNS TO REVEAL SINGAPORE FOOTAGE

                                    ...IS APTLY ILLUSTRATED
                                    IN A STORY ON THE
                                    SINGAPORE SERVICE CENTER
                                    COMING UP LATER IN THIS
                                    EDITION OF ILSD TODAY.


6.SINGAPORE FOOTAGE TURNS TO REVEAL LOGO
GRAPHIC: 50TH ANNIVERSARY LOGO

                                    ALSO COMING UP, THE
                                    50th ANNIVERSARY OF
                                    WESTINGHOUSE DEFENSE...


7.DISSOLVE TO STOCK PHOTOS OF HUNT VALLEY
2 PHOTOS

                                    ...INCLUDING SOME
                                    THOUGHTS ABOUT THE EARLY
                                    DAYS IN HUNT VALLEY FROM
                                    SOME PEOPLE WHO WERE
                                    THERE AT THE BEGINNING.
```

Figure 3-7 A corporate news program uses digital effects, graphics, and an anchor person, much like broadcast television (*courtesy, Mary Orlando-Llewellyn, Westinghouse Corp.*).

```
page 2

8.STANDING NEAR CAKE.
ZOOM OUT TO STAFF MEMBERS.
CONTINUE WITH CAFETERIA SHOTS.
                                        AND STRAIGHT AHEAD, OUR
                                        NEW GENERAL MANAGER GUS
                                        XINTAS, WAS ON HAND FOR
                                        THE CAKE CUTTING
                                        CELEBRATING OUR FIFTY
                                        YEARS IN MARYLAND...
                                        MEMBERS OF HIS STAFF
                                        SHARED THE HONORS.

                                        AS THE DRIVING FORCE
                                        BEHIND THE ILSD TEAM,
                                        MR. XINTAS BRINGS
                                        TWENTY YEARS OF
                                        EXPERIENCE WITH
                                        WESTINGHOUSE TO THE
                                        POSITION OF GENERAL
                                        MANAGER.

                                        OVER THE YEARS, HE'S
                                        HELD FINANCIAL AND
                                        EXECUTIVE MANAGEMENT
                                        POSITIONS...MOST
                                        RECENTLY AS BUSINESS
                                        OPERATIONS MANAGER FOR
                                        THE ENTIRE WESTINGHOUSE
                                        DEFENSE ELECTRONICS
                                        GROUP.

                                        WE'LL HAVE AN INTERVIEW
                                        WITH MR. XINTAS ON THE
                                        NEXT EDITION OF "ILSD
                                        TODAY".
```

Figure 3-7 Continued

The news format is appropriate for the organization that routinely (monthly, bi-monthly, or quarterly) desires to share short items of interest with its employees and investors. The format can be modified, too, to serve for individual topics, even when no regular news series is produced. Generally, these one-subject programs should use one or two reporters in the field, staying away from an institutional-looking studio set. These are more like the broadcast "special features" than the nightly news.

"Creative" formats

Whoever said that corporate and instructional video had to be boring? Many programs use sophisticated animation (see Figure 3-8). Some of the most creative and often funny programs are produced for nonbroadcast use. For example, a number of organizations have hired Jim Henson and his famous Muppets from Sesame Street to act as talent in their programs—aimed at adults, of course. The familiar and humorous Muppets can deliver messages that could be dull or even offensive if done by "real" people. Likewise, some of the biggest-selling videos have been produced by John Cleese of *Monty Python* fame. Their offbeat and slapstick humor can make a point memorable and bigger than life. Some of the programs they've

Figure 3-8 Many programs use animated characters to present information. They are appealing and are never dated (*courtesy, Children's Television International*).

produced are on topics like customer service or how *not* to conduct boring and lengthy meetings.

I once wrote an interactive video program to teach newly hired mechanical engineers how to see AC motors. I used a game show theme and called it "Rotor of Fortune" (see Figure 3-9).

MTV, anyone? Well, it's alive and well in corporate video, too. Music videos have become an acceptable format for many corporations who use this creative and current style to get viewers' attention and to communicate messages in a "fun" manner. For instance, a chain of private clubs produced a series of short "rap" videos where actors in the roles of various club personnel, like bartenders or wait staff, did raps humorously depicting what to do and what *not* to do to insure a happy customer. McDonalds did a music video for its teenage workers encouraging them to pay attention to their grooming; what could have sounded like a nagging mother telling you to brush your teeth was instead an upbeat and energetic "commercial" for a proper work image.

A combination of multi-image and video, videowalls, are also being used for high-impact presentations. These are sometimes displayed at trade shows (see Figure 3-10) or are set up in point-of-purchase areas to attract potential buyers.

Of course, these creative productions are among the most elaborate, expensive, and difficult to produce formats. Humor can work—sometimes. If your writing and actors are not superb, your program will fall on its face and probably even offend a segment of your audience. Clients often won't go for these offbeat approaches. And, the production elements of something like a music video are incredibly complex; you've got to be a songwriter, composer, choreographer, music engineer, stage director, videographer, sound mixer, and music video editor. But, as corporate video becomes more sophisticated, producers are being allowed more freedom to experiment with ways to communicate information. For example, read through the script in Figure 3-11.

Combining Formats

Most programs actually combine one or more formats. The intermixing of techniques is useful for two reasons: it allows you to fit the format to each concept, and it stimulates viewer attention, since the presentation mode is somewhat unex-

```
BASICS OF AC MOTORS   SCRIPT 3/5/86   OmniCom Associates (REVISED)
---------------
(computer)

Which would you like to do?
      1.  See this program for the first time
      2.  Continue previous work on this program
      3.  Review selected parts of the program
(if 1, begin program; if 2 or 3, present main menu)


---------------
(computer)

MAIN MENU

(this will be accessed after each section, or right at the
beginning for experienced users or trainees continuing the
program)

1.  Qualifying questions
2.  Basic motor operations
3.  Induction
4.  Motor performance
5.  What's in a motor?
6.  Frames & enclosures
7.  Mounting, frame sizes & service factor
8.  Motor temperature & insulation systems
9.  Final simulation

---------------
(QUALIFYINC QUESTIONS AND INTRO)
(video. game show setting with large "Wheel of Fortune" made up
as a Rotor and stater of a motor;  game show music up and under)
```

Figure 3-9 A game-show takeoff was the vehicle for an interactive video program on AC Motors; trainees became contestants and responded to questions via a computer-controlled videodisc (*courtesy, OmniCom Associates, Reliance Electric Co. and Avid Communications*).

MERV (voice over): When you saw us last, Joe Winding a motors distributor from Montrose, Colorado had just won an all expense paid trip to the birthplace of AC Motors London, England. Total cash and prizes $19,600. What's in store for our contestant today, lets find out, as we play another game of (crowd yells. ROTOR...OF.. FORTUNE). . And here's the host of the ROTOR OF FORTUNE... Johhhnny Barker.

HOST: Thanks Merv. Hello everyone and welcome to ROTOR OF FORTUNE. The game where you can make a fortune by showing your knowledge of AC Motors. Now join me in welcoming our hostess, here is the charming Heather White, oh Heather!? (crowd oohs and ah's) Time now for our contestant to be introduced. Merv why don't you introduce our guest.

MERV (voice over): Today's contestant is a sales engineer with Reliance Electric, a major manufacturer of electrical producing, and distributing equipment. Please welcome

(computer)
(generic title screen, requesting name and ID)

HOST: Welcome, glad you could join us. Well let's get on with the game, but first let's take a quick review of the rules. First you will enter the qualifying round. If you score well enough there, you will go right onto the Expert round. If you can score enough points in the Expert round you will win today's grand prize. Tell them what it is, Merv.

MERV (voice over): Well, Johnny today's grand prize is this beautiful 14 Karat miniature AC Motor. This prize is provided by Zuccis of Beverly Hills, total value $14,300. Good Luck!!

HOST: Sounds Great! If you don't score high enough in the expert round to win the grand prize, don't worry! There is still another way to win and here's how. You'll be presented with information on a variety of categories that are all concerned with today's main topic. Which Heather will help us select shortly. Questions will be asked by me or the game computer on each of these categories. If you accumulate enough points throughout these rounds you'll win. So if you are ready to play, Heather will help us select today's topic. Go ahead Merv why don't you tell us of today's possible topics.

MERV: Today's choices are Watts in a name, NEMA your poison, the Basics of AC Motors and Potluck (wheel is spun)...
and today's topic is the Basics of AC Motors (crowd cheers)

JOHNNY: OK, the "Basics of AC Motors" is today's topic, so let's get-to-it! Here we go with the qualifying round. Remember use your key board to answer the questions. Before we get into the subject of AC Motors, let's talk about the Basic principles that make them work -- magnetics. You are probably familiar with some of the general concepts of magnetism, so let's just try a few questions to see where you stand.

Figure 3-9 Continued

HOST V/O: What causes the magnetic field around a wire? (show picture of iron, wire, and magnetic field.)

1. the iron itself that the wire is wound on
2. the current flowing through the wire
3. rubbing the wire on the iron

(computer)
What causes the magnetic field around a wire?

1. the iron itself that the wire is wound on
2. the current flowing through the wire
3. rubbing the wire on the iron

(if 1)
(computer)
The iron itself is not magnetized until a current passes through it. Passing an electrical current through a wire around a piece of iron causes that iron to become a magnet with North and South poles.

(if 2)
(computer)
You're correct. Let's try another question.

(if 3)
(computer)
You're probably thinking of the way you might have made a magnet back in your grade school days - by rubbing a magnet on iron. But that's not how this iron is magnetized. It is magnetized by passing an electrical current through the wire around the iron this causes the iron to become a magnet with North and South poles.

(computer)
Magnets are surrounded by a magnetic field. This field is represented by "lines of flux". Do the lines of flux flow from:

1. North to South
2. South to North

(if 1)
(computer)
Right you are. Let's go on.

Figure 3-9 Continued

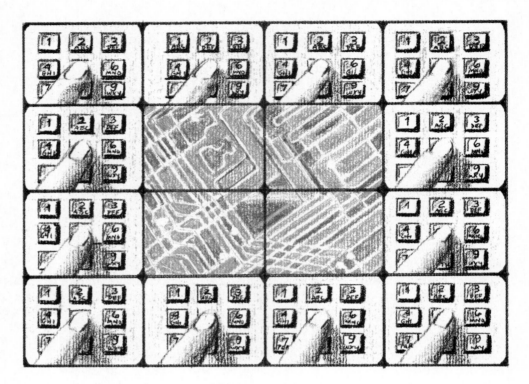

 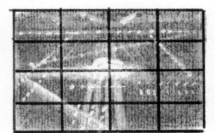

Figure 3-10 The storyboard for one section of a videowall display (*courtesy, M.J. Zink Productions*).

pected. Rapid changing of presentation modalities is used effectively in children's programming, such as *Sesame Street,* to deal with the short attention span of preschoolers. *Sesame Street* uses a range of production styles, from animation to live action to songs to dialogue with the Muppets; many segments are only 15 to 20 seconds long.

There are no rules about how to integrate different formats. The typical *magazine format* includes individual stories, ranging from one or two features to short "how to" segments. The interview/demonstration is a common combination, as is the voice-over/demonstration. It is important, however, to carry through an overall plan or theme within the program and not to hop and skip inconsistently among formats. You may wish to choose among two or three formats, using each several times throughout a program. If you're producing a series, you should keep the format and talent consistent throughout. The opening of a program can allude to the various segments to come, giving a glimpse at the way the various topics will be treated, so that the viewer is readied for the formats to follow.

FUDD:

Don't look at me. Last time I was

sick was the fall of thirty-two

-- when they elected that fellow

Roosevelt. And I think we can all

understand that.

ALL NOD IN AGREEMENT.

MELVIN:

Yes, but ... you see, it's actually

not for anyone here. You all look

great. Believe me, I don't think

I've ever seen you look healthier.

MEAGERLY: (NODS, TURNS TO OTHERS)

Is there any other new business?

MELVIN:

Well, actually, gentlemen, if I

can have just one more minute ...

well, ah ... you see, I was thinking

about the other employees.

BULK:

The ones on the floors below?

MEANLY:

Forget it, Melvin.

MELVIN:

Yes, but ... believe me, I can under-

Figure 3-11 A humorous script is difficult to write, but can be very
effective (*courtesy, ParTraining Corp.,* copyright 1980, 1985, 1989
from "Leadership and Teamwork" corporate training program).

stand your reluctance. But, well,
we have over seventy employees now,
and, gosh, it just seems to me that
we might want to consider having
some sort of health insurance for
them.

MEAGERLY:

Who's sick? We've never had this
problem before. Did you hire someone
who was sick, Melvin?

MELVIN:

No, no, it's nothing like that. It's
just that, well, sometimes people
get sick. They have, ah, operations!

BULK:

What kind of operations, Melvin?

MELVIN:

Well, gee, I don't know. Um, lots
of kinds. (SEARCHING) Sometimes
they have something removed.

MEANLY:

Ah, Melvin, maybe you don't understand
our policy here. When we hire a
person, we hire him whole -- and
we expect him to stay that way.

Figure 3-11 Continued

MEAGERLY, MEANLY, BULK,
AND FUDD LOOK STUNNED,
ABSOLUTELY HORRIFIED.
FINALLY, BULK, BREATHLESS,
LEANS FORWARD.

FUDD:

It's in the contract, Melvin.

MELVIN: (EXASPERATED, VERY EXCITED)

Yes, but, what if someone gets pregnant!

BULK:

Talk to him, Harold. He's your

nephew.

MEAGERLY: (AVUNCULARLY, BUT STERN)

Melvin, this is not a locker room.

MELVIN: (CONTRITE)

I'm sorry. I ... I got carried

away. But, maybe, maybe we could

just pay part of each employee's

health insurance. Not all of it,

just part.

FUDD:

How much, Melvin?

MELVIN:

Well, how about ... twenty percent?

ALL AT TABLE GASP AND GROAN.
BULK CLUTCHES CHEST AND
KEALS OVER BACKWARD IN
HIS CHAIR.

Figure 3-11 Continued

MEAGERLY: (RISING SLIGHTLY, LOOKING
                     OVER TABLE EDGE TOWARD
                     WHERE BULK WOULD BY LYING)

Hm, maybe we need some sort of health

insurance.

HOST   HOST:

There's no doubt about it -- Melvin

was dealing with some pretty tough

customers, and meeting some pretty

strong resistance. Oh, he was right;

his logic was flawless. However,

his listeners, like most people,

don't want to hear, "Yes, but."

And, sometimes, even the facts won't

make the problem go away.

So, how do you, as a leader looking

for committed decisions, deal with

resistance? How do you handle those

decision-makers who seem to have

a ready objection for every new

idea and a well-equipped arsenal

of reasons why not?

That's what this lesson is all about.

How to react to resistance in a

way that keeps a conversation alive.

And that's what you want to do.

You want to say, through your actions,

Figure 3-11 Continued

Here are some examples of *combination format* programs we've produced:

- training program for supervisors on how to write up performance appraisals consisted of:
  (1) short clips of interviews with supervisors talking about their feelings, experiences, and techniques for doing appraisals;
  (2) voice-over narration over shots of forms and character-generated graphics, giving basic instructions;
  (3) short dramatized sequences of sample employee situations which trainees would actually "write up" in their accompanying workbooks.
- program which introduced a new branch automation system for a major bank consisted of:
  (1) on- and off-camera narration by the Vice-President in charge of the new automation system explaining the benefits of the new system and describing its major components;
  (2) dramatized role-plays of how a new accounts officer would use the system to work with a customer;
  (3) short testimonials of actual employees who were using the system.
- series on ethnic studies used:
  (1) on-camera narration to introduce and explain major concepts;
  (2) documentary vignettes of ethnic events, such as ethnic festivals and families practicing ethnic traditions;
  (3) interviews with major ethnic studies scholars.

PROGRAM CONTROL, PRESENTER CONTROL, OR VIEWER CONTROL?

The video designer must also consider how a program will be viewed. How many people will be in the audience at any given time? Where will they see the program? Will individuals have control of when and how they see it? Will anyone else be around to answer questions or provide explanations? Will the program be viewed in an uninterrupted manner from start to finish, or will you anticipate that different people will see the program differently?

A stand-alone program is viewed under *program control*. That is, the audience is not meant to start or stop the program, replay segments, or alter the program's speed. This type of program is designed to be seen by more than one person at a time either in a single location or as distributed via broadcast, cable, satellite, and so on.

In the program-controlled program, you must be sure that the message is clear and concise enough that each recipient can fully understand it the first time through. This can be a difficult task if the audience is heterogeneous in abilities or backgrounds or if the material is supposed to be mastered in detail. Usually, these stand-alone programs are used for topics of a general informational or motivational nature. If you want to be *sure* that people have understood and remembered the content, you should probably provide them with additional means of practice or testing, such as giving them a workbook, job aid, or lab exercise.

An example of a tape to be viewed under *program control* is a mini-documentary we produced for the *World Game,* a live simulation based on concepts developed by the futurist Buckminster Fuller. This program was sent to television stations before the Game was to come to a given city to encourage the public to attend.

Presenter-controlled programs are meant to supplement face-to-face instruction or communication. The burden of complete communication does not rest on the tape or disc itself. Appropriate introductions, summaries, and the like can be given by the presenter and tailored to the specific audience. Often such programs use the video screen like an "electronic blackboard" to which an instructor can refer to show processes or equipment. Or, they might be used as sales tools by reps within a sales call to illustrate products in use. The program need not be as redundant as the stand-alone program, since the instructor can always repeat segments or present the same information in a slightly different way if clarification is needed. Since less of the entire presentation has to be prerecorded, many common sequences, such as relating the topic to the viewer's needs, can be eliminated and left to the live presenter. This technique actually makes the program more flexible for a wide variety of situations—*if* the speaker does his or her job well.

Some presenter-controlled programs have built-in pauses that instructors can use to time presentations to meet class schedules or to break for discussion. Teacher guides or student workbooks might be part of the package, integrating the video presentation with training exercises or problems. The program itself may ask questions; the teacher or trainer can stop the program for discussion of such questions or merely let the program play through and let the viewers answer the questions to themselves or via response devices like the ones pictured in Figure 3-12.

Figure 3-12   A speaker can obtain audience responses via keypad units tied into a computer which summarizes their inputs. It can also control a videotape or videodisc player and direct it to play an appropriate segment of video depending upon their responses (*courtesy, GenTech, Inc.*).

It's advantageous to produce an accompanying teacher's or user's guide with instructional programs. Often instructors don't have the opportunity or don't take the time to preview a program before showing it to a class. Occasionally, the presenter may not be very familiar with the subject matter. By providing a guide like the one in Figure 3-13 with a summary of the program, its objectives, perhaps the script, and some suggestions for its use, you will encourage presenters to use the program well and show it in its best light. Guides generally also include suggestions for further study, such as discussion questions, project assignments, problem sets, or bibliographies.

An example of a *presenter-controlled* program is one we produced for an electric and gas utility company on customer relations. The tape consisted of short dramatized clips of "difficult" customers. At the end of each sequence, a question appeared on the screen asking the viewers what they'd do in that situation. The group facilitator led the discussion and then continued the tape to show short interviews with other customer reps explaining their techniques for dealing with similar situations.

Viewer-controlled programs embody the assumption that the individual watching has control of the program's progression. The viewer may stop, rewind, fast-forward, slow down, or freeze the tape, or access another segment of the program through some sort of control device.

This style of presentation adapts well to the individual and is useful when the au-

BEFORE YOU USE THIS VIDEO PROGRAM.... Effective use of the program requires that you stop the videotape as instructed to think about or discuss how situations should be handled. The objective of this program is to present difficult situations in negotiating customer payment agreements, stimulate discussion about how similar situations might be handled and the feelings each might arouse, and finally, to hear reactions of and advice from actual customer service reps at NYSEG. Therefore:

1) Make sure you have **set up the program and equipment BEFORE** the class arrives; play the tape and set the volume level and picture controls. Then, cue up the tape to the beginning AFTER the color bars.

2) **Find the STOP control** on the video player so that you can get to it easily during the class. You might actually move the video player close to where you'll be sitting or standing so that you don't have to dash over to it during playback.

OUTLINE OF THE PROGRAM: After a brief introduction, the program presents several re-created scenarios of difficult customer situations. Following each scene is a question which remains on the screen for about 20 seconds. At the end of the question, stop the tape for discussion. After 5 seconds of black, a few responses from customer reps are presented, followed by another 5 seconds of black. If you wish, stop the tape again to discuss reactions to the reps' statements.

SCENARIOS:
    a) How do you open the conversation?
    b) How do you deal with a group of college students?
    c) What are some special considerations in dealing with the elderly?
    d) How can you deal with a mother and unruly children?
    e) What are some techniques for dealing with angry or abusive customers?
    f) How would you deal with an emotional or crying customer?
    g) Do you ever feel ripped off or angry with dishonest or "regular" customers?
    h) What are some especially difficult situations, such as dealing with someone whom you know?
    g) How do you wrap up the conversation, especially if the customer doesn't want to leave?

TIMING YOUR TRAINING SESSION: The entire program is about 32 minutes long; if your scheduled time is short, you may want to ask the group which situations they'd most like to discuss, and stop the tape to discuss ONLY those situations. You may or may not want to stop to discuss the reps' responses - depending on your time or the interests of your trainees.

Figure 3-13 A short guide for trainers helps them use a videotape more effectively. This one calls for the trainer to start and stop the video to show segments and lead a class discussion (*courtesy, New York State Electric and Gas Company*).

dience is not homogeneous or does not need to see the program at any one time. The physical environment must be conducive to viewer control: he or she must easily be able to reach and confidently manipulate the appropriate control functions and must be given the time and privacy to work through the program at his or her own speed.

Viewer-controlled programs may have accompanying workbooks, handouts, or lab exercises. Some programs are used as reference tools to which the viewers can refer as they go through some step-by-step process (see Figures 3-14 and 3-15). An important advantage of this program modality is that the student has the sense of being part of the program process, remains actively involved, and pays more attention. The crucial element here is informing the viewers of their ability (and giving them *permission and encouragement*) to control the program; otherwise, the presentation will in effect become program-controlled. Most people are used to sitting passively in front of a TV set and may also be afraid to "fiddle around" with a VCR lest they mess something up. We've actually produced short segments in the beginning of some viewer-controlled programs showing them how to start and stop the VCR and giving them some practice in doing so.

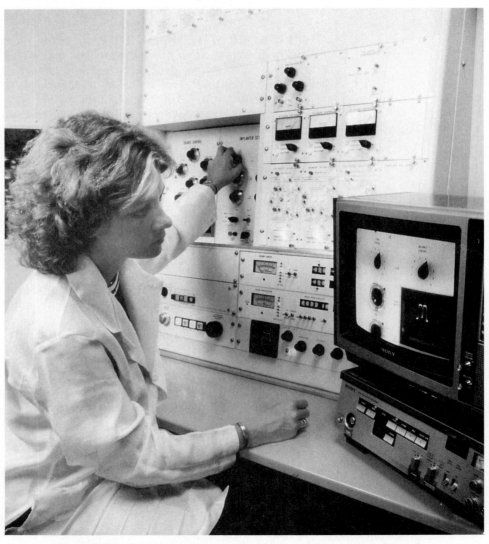

Figure 3-14   A trainee can control a desktop video unit to learn her job (*courtesy, Varian*).

<u>*Guidebook on Performance Appraisal*</u>

VIDEOTAPE SIMULATION

You should now view the next section of the videotape. You'll see short scenes of good and bad performance which are examples of things which our supervisors have reported in the field. *(Of course, the scenes are dramatized and do NOT reflect actual people or locations!)* Stop the videotape after each brief scene, and take notes on each as if you were the supervisor observing the scene. Of course a whole year's appraisal can't be written on one incident, but write down a few lines of what you might include in an appraisal if these situations were to represent a pattern in the employees' behaviors. **START THE VIDEOTAPE NOW.**

Chief line mechanic and line crew

Clerk

Gas fitter

Power plant laborer

Figure 3-15 A page from a trainee guidebook which accompanies a videotape on performance appraisal. Video doesn't have to be hooked up to a computer to be interactive. (*courtesy, New York State Electric and Gas Company*).

Here are some examples of *viewer-controlled* programs we've done:

- a stand-alone videodisc on sign language with an accompanying print guide which allows viewers to slow down the signing to observe it more carefully and practice interpretation.
- a videotape—workbook package on using a new computerized shop floor control system for first line supervisors which demonstrated a particular function, then told users to refer to their workbook for data and enter it, using the function just demonstrated, into a "live" on-line computer terminal located next to the VCR.

INTERACTIVE VIDEO

Viewer participation in a program is the key to interactive video, a technology that typically interfaces a microcomputer with a videodisc player. Interactivity, however, is a program *style* rather than a particular type of hardware. Interactive programs don't necessarily need to be driven by a separate microcomputer; some videodisc players have, in effect, a small microcomputer built in and can read data on the videodisc and control branching based on responses users make via a remote control. And conventional laser videodiscs are not the only way to get video into the system; interactive systems may use videotape or compact disc (CD) technology, like digital video interactive (DVI) (Figure 3-16) or even small amounts of video stored on a computer hard disc or WORM (write once-read many) magnetic disc.

Interactive video combines the advantages of computer-based instruction or

Figure 3-16 Digital Video Interactive allows video and computer displays to interactively respond to a user's needs and inputs. The video is digitized and compressed and can be stored on a computer hard disk or compact disk, eliminating the need for conventional videotape or videodisc (*courtesy, Intel Corporation*).

information and video programming: programs are tailored to the interests and needs of the viewer via the computer program and microprocessor control, and these branching programs have the sound, motion, and color inherent in video. Interactive programs are used for instruction as well as general information. For instance, we produced an interactive training program on how bank employees should behave to avoid fraud; the program shows a short clip of a customer doing something questionable, and the program asks "What would *you* do next?" Depending upon the viewer's response, the program branches and explains why their approach was correct or incorrect. An example of an information program is one we produced for the United Way. After a video "open" the program asks "What would you like to know about the United Way?" Through an "intelligent" analysis of the user's free-form response, the program displays the portion of the program which relates to their interests, covering the agency's methods of operations and the other community groups it supports. See Figure 3-17 for a flowchart of this program. Interactive video can also be used as a simulation device. For example, we produced a touch-screen videodisc simulator of a computerized lathe: trainees touched the device's controls on the screen to simulate actually using this huge, expensive (and potentially dangerous) device. Because of the way in which a designer can display and individually sequence information and assess a user's mastery of content or his or her need for information, interactive video is perhaps the most powerful communication tool available to us today.

Although interactive video has many advantages and has been around since the late 1970s, widespread adoption has been slow. Less than a quarter of all organizations are actually using it in training or marketing. Like any new technology, it is still in a development phase in which the skills needed to produce programs are not widespread, program creation is rather expensive, and the hardware lacks standardization. Unlike video, where there are perhaps two or three major playback standards, interactive video has no real standard. When you look at all the available models of touch-screen monitors, computers, videodisc players, and interface cards necessary to get the computer to "talk" to the disc player, there are tens of thousands of combinations of systems! It's simply not yet possible to walk into a big organization with an interactive program in your briefcase and hope to find a compatible hardware system to play it back on. However, just like "regular" video did in the early 1970s, interactive video will have its "shake down" period in which one or several standards will emerge, and more individuals will know how to design and produce for this technology.

Videodiscs are currently the most popular means for getting the video into an interactive video program. Videodiscs are similar to audio records, except that they contain 30 minutes of audio and video per side. That 30 minutes of "linear" video can also be considered 54,000 still frames: the video can be played at normal speed, slow or fast speeds, or one frame at a time (or any combination of these playback rates). Each frame is electronically numbered so that a videodisc player can find it precisely. The videodisc player reads the disc by means of a laser which bounces light off the surface: the disc is not actually touched by anything mechanical, therefore, there is no wear.

Levels of Interactive Videodisc

In order to sort out all of these thousands of standards into some more comprehensible categories, the interactive industry has developed some terminology called *"levels" of videodisc* programs. A *Level 1* program consists merely of a videodisc with no accompanying computer programming. The videodisc can be played and segments randomly accessed by using a remote control on the videodisc player. A *Level 2* program has some limited computer programming pressed right onto the

Tompkins County United Way
INTERACTIVE INFORMATION SYSTEM

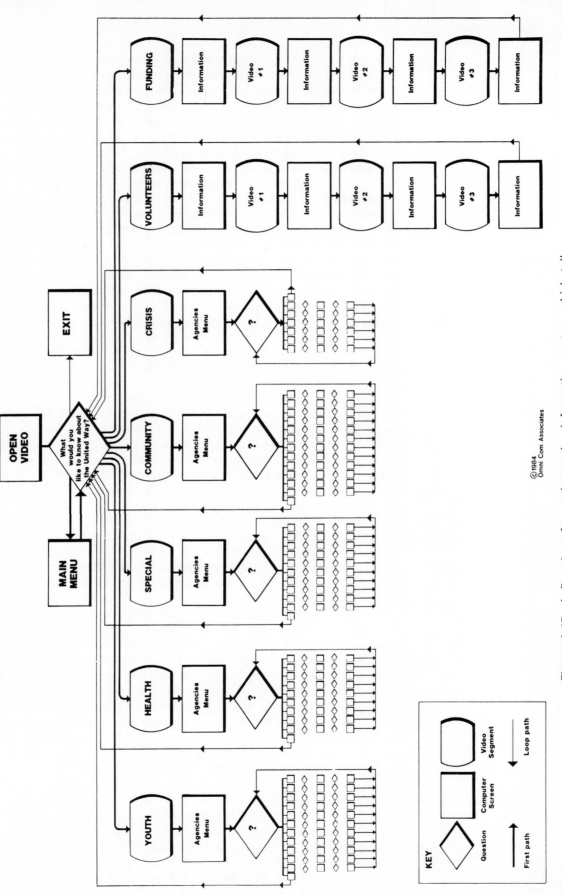

©1984
Omni Com Associates

Figure 3-17 A flowchart for an interactive information system which tells the public about services supported by the United Way (*courtesy, OmniCom Associates*).

disc. A special videodisc player with a small computer built in reads the computer programming; users then make responses to questions by pressing a button on a remote control, and the microprocessor in the disc player figures out where to branch. *Level 3* programs use both a computer and a videodisc player; the video and audio are contained on the videodisc, and the branching instructions and computer text and graphics are stored on a computer disc. This is the most complex and expensive level, but it also offers the most variations of questioning, branching, and record-keeping. Interactive systems can contain such peripherals as touch-screens, joysticks, or input devices for speech recognition, and may also be hooked up to various kinds of devices like CPR mannikins or driving simulators. Some systems like the one in Figure 3-18, use one monitor: computer text and graphics can be displayed alternately with video, or they can be combined—computer images can be superimposed over the video to provide for immediate updating of information without having to press a new videodisc. Other systems have two monitors—one for text and one for video.

Figure 3-18 A "Level Three" interactive videodisc program uses a computer, a videodisc player, and an interface card to display both computer and video information on one screen (*courtesy, Avid Communications*).

Advantages of Interactive Video

Interactive video programs are useful in holding viewers' attention, since the program follows each person's responses and won't proceed until a response is made. Testing can easily be done, since many systems record users' responses and then print out a summary for trainers. Besides its use in individualized presentations, interactive video can be used with small or large groups, with viewers discussing situations and responding based on consensus, or by giving each person his or her own small response device.

The advantages of interactive video are numerous:

- It allows for customized presentations, based on users' knowledge, learning style, mastery of content, or interest.
- It can be a high-level substitution for working with devices or situations which are dangerous or impossible to replicate in "real life."
- Programs can keep track of users' responses for later review by trainers or managers or follow-up of potential customers by sales representatives.
- It mandates active user participation in a program; therefore, retention of the material is usually higher than for linear presentations.
- Because each person only sees what he or she really needs to see, instruction can generally be done *about 30–50% faster than by conventional linear video or classroom instruction.*
- Testing is built into interactive instruction, so that no separate post tests are needed to see if the audience has understood the information—this can be important for safety or legal reasons.

How an Interactive Video Program Is Produced

Interactive programs are difficult to develop, since they contain not only a video program, but questions, branches, lesson flowcharting and authoring, and computer programming. A number of *authoring languages* and *authoring systems* are available that simplify the programming aspects for nonprogrammers; by using simple codes or simply picking items from a menu, an interactive developer can create the code that's necessary to display text and graphics, control the video player, and analyze users' responses.

Once a designer determines that interactive video is an appropriate medium for the message, he or she develops objectives. From there, a *flowchart* is developed which outlines the video and/or computer presentations, questions, menu choices, and branches. A flowchart uses standard symbols to represent video scenes, computer text, and decision points, and arrows connect the various elements to show the possible "flows" of a program.

The flowchart is then fleshed out into a complete script and storyboard like the NCR example in Figure 3-19. Then, two parallel production tracks occur: the video material is produced using normal video and/or film equipment; at the same time, the programmers create the code necessary to have the computer display its text and graphics and also to analyze user inputs and to branch based on them. The final video master has a time code put on it and is sent to a videodisc pressing plant (if you're doing a disc). Once the frame numbers for the in-points and out-points for each video scene are known, they can be inserted into the computer code. Once the videodisc comes back from pressing, the whole system is integrated and tested.

THINKING VISUALLY, WRITING FOR THE EAR

Most of us have a lot more practice writing letters, reports, and term papers than we do scripting video programs. Unfortunately, just about everything your high-school English teacher taught you about composition can be thrown out the window when you set out to write for television—except perhaps the grammar! The printed word leaves the reader free to skip around, reread sections, skim, or proceed slowly.

```
COURSE:  RETAIL ENVIRONMENTS: CONCEPTS          SEGMENT # A1 01 03
---------------------------------------------------------------------
DATE PRINTED:  12/19/86                          PAGE  1 OF 1
---------------------------------------------------------------------
SEGMENT DESCRIPTION:  TOUCH, FREEZE FRAME

VIDEODISC DELIVERY:   Motion — Graphic w/ Text

COMPUTER DELIVERY:  TEXT, TOUCH

EDITS:        INFO BOX:  2      HELP SEG:  2       LOCATE:  A1

COMMENTS:

=====================================================================
BELOW:  TEXT
---------------------------------------------------------------------
    EXERCISE 1 OF 5

    Touch all of the boxes that represent the
    "Primary" functions of retailing.

    Store          Buying          Displaying
    Security

    Money          Pricing         Product
    Control                        Testing

    Store          Product         Refund and
    Stocking       Repairing       Exchange

    Investing      Advertising     Selling of
                                   Goods &
                                   Services


    -----------------------------------------------------
    CORRECT. (Highlight all correct)

    No, the correct answers are highlighted above. (Highlight all
    correct)




=====================================================================
BRANCHING:
        SP - NEXT
```

Figure 3-19 An interactive video script has many sections to designate video footage, computer display, and proper branching for each possible response (*courtesy, NCR Corporation*).

Typographical cues such as chapter titles, headings, italics, and paragraphs give the reader hints on how to structure and interpret the information. Since most printed material is not designed to be read aloud, the writer need not be concerned with tricky word combinations or long phrasing, difficult to utter in a single breath.

Video, of course, is an entirely different medium, one that relies on images and spoken words. The most difficult thing for a novice scriptwriter to learn is how to turn verbal information into visual communication. The video producer must become *visually literate*—just as he or she is verbally literate. Visuals have a language of their own; most people within a culture are rather adept at "reading" the gross visual cues found in their environment. Red is a cue for attention or danger, a skull and crossbones means poison, a nod signifies approval. There are many cues, some quite subtle, that can be used within the frame of the television screen to enhance the communication of a message.

When first going through a sequence of information, you should constantly ask yourself, "How can I visualize this?" If you're showing a demonstration of some process, the subject of your shots is quite evident. But what composition is best, what angles? Abstract subjects present a much more difficult challenge. How can you visualize a company's new marketing strategy? A religious philosophy? A motivational message for a sales staff? Foreign diplomacy? While you decide what you will say, you must consider what you will show.

It's easy merely to present a "talking head." But before you take that route, try a few mental gymnastics to see if there's not a better way. Try to sketch a picture or graph of the concept. If you had to communicate with a foreign or a deaf person, how would you get this message across? What should people *do* if they follow your message? Is there a mental picture or a cartoon that captures the essence of the idea?

Generally, the narrative portion of a script is outlined first, but remember, make sure that each visual ties directly to the accompanying audio. There's nothing more distracting and confusing to the audience than trying to relate two divergent ideas presented simultaneously. Rather than starting with the words, try starting with the pictures. Sketch out a rough storyboard of the script—and then add only the words that are necessary.

Besides designing a visual message appropriate to the content, you must consider the shot composition. How will the colors reproduce on television? Is the detail too small to be seen clearly on the screen? How can the camera best cover the subject? The ways in which viewers respond to various television techniques can be summed up in a few general principles:

- Close-ups grab attention and signify that something is important.
- Long shots give a wide perspective and remove a viewer from direct involvement. There is less emphasis in this shot.
- A zoom-in zeroes attention on a particular aspect.
- A pan or truck across a scene gives the viewer the perspective of an array of related items and a sense of movement through a place.
- A long angle looking up at a person makes the person appear strong, powerful, and authoritarian.
- A high angle looking down on a person makes the person seem to be weaker or more fragile.
- Rapid editing of shots denotes life, vigor, and the perception that the viewer should look for an underlying theme.
- Slow dissolves and camera movements denote tranquility and emphasize the mood of each subject.
- Television is a medium of visual motion; avoid static shots whenever possible.

These techniques can be used to enhance the overall idea of theme of a program. We all know that pictures speak louder than words, so it's crucial to examine every shot to ensure that it is sending the correct message.

The audio portion of a program also takes a little creative thought. It's easy for the viewer to tire of the same voice rattling on and on throughout a program. Just as visuals need pacing, the aural channel of a program should provide variety and emphasis. Remember that you're writing for the *ear*, not the eye, so that you must remain conscious of what the words sound like. A conversational style is more appropriate than a formal tone; use short sentences and simple phrases so that the listener doesn't get bogged down following a thought through several subordinate clauses. Instead of:

"The widget is to be placed in the heat treater with the flanges facing up and at a 90 degree angle to the bridge. When the thermometer reaches 200 degrees for 10 minutes, the widget may be removed by the operator."

Write this:

Put the widgets in the heat treater like this: make sure the flanges face up and that it's at right angles to the bridge over here. The widgets have to be lined up just like this . . . not like this or this. Now watch the thermometer over here—when it gets to 200 for 10 minutes, you can take the widget out.

A friendly, personal tone is generally superior to a remote, third-person approach. Each viewer feels as though the television is addressing him or her individually, even if a program is being distributed to an audience of thousands. Narrators don't need to project their voices as if they were addressing a crowd or giving a stage performance; they should speak in a normal conversational tone—perhaps even more softly for greater attention.

Watch out for tricky word combinations that are difficult for your talent to enunciate. Long phrases can leave a narrator sounding out-of-breath. Often, good scripts will look disturbingly like third-grade readers—but when spoken aloud, they sound perfectly appropriate for an adult audience. It's much more difficult for a listener to process a flow of spoken words than to read and reread passages at one's own pace. Use the simplest, most precise terminology possible.

Don't be afraid to have a little silence! When the video channel is presenting something crucial, don't let the audio compete for attention. If a mood is being established, a visual montage with a musical background may convey the message far better than words. In fact, *some ambiguity* in a sequence may be desirable, because each person can interpret a message in his or her own way and take away a personal meaning. While this technique may not be appropriate for technical subjects, motivational or consciousness-raising programs can use it very successfully. Look at the advertising aimed at the general public, and see how visual montages and short, rather ambiguous phrases are used to make individuals use their imaginations to put themselves in the picture using the product. Coca-Cola's advertising campaigns, for example, have touted Coke as "The Real Thing" or promise that "Coke Is It!"

When a program relies heavily on the spoken word, hearing the same voice without a break may become monotonous. You may break up segments with musical themes. Another technique is to utilize two or three very different voices, alternating paragraphs or sequences. Various narrators may also take different parts or roles—for instance, one may play a trainee asking typical questions while another plays the expert mentor. Just as using a range of video shots increases attention and provides emphasis, variety in the audio track may increase a program's effectiveness.

Writing dialogue is especially tricky: this is perhaps the hardest thing for beginning scriptwriters to pull off. Be careful to not make the conversations sound stilted, like this:

JOE: *"Oh hello, Jane. I just came back from lunch. Gosh, what are you doing?"*

JANE: *"Oh hello, Joe. Did you have a nice lunch?*

JOE: *"Yes, thank you, I did."*

JANE: *"Well, Joe, I'm just looking through all these manuals to find out how to install my new printer. I just don't think I can figure it out."*

JOE: *"Well, Jane, did you know that we here at ABC Corporation have a new department called Corporate Computing that can help with just this kind of problem? Maybe you should try to call them."*

Rather saccharine, huh? Let's do a re-write.

JOE: *Hi, I'm back. Hey, what 'cha got there?*

JANE: *Ugh. Manuals.. Been trying to get this printer plugged in all morning. It's hopeless.*

JOE: *(Chuckles) Don't look at me!. Why don't you just call those guys in that new department downstairs—Corporate Computing I think they're called.*

The only thing harder to write than dialogue is a humorous script. While corporations have shunned anything but serious pin-striped programs for years, they're now loosening up and using funny and creative programs. But what's funny to you may not be funny to your client—or your audience. It takes a special knowledge of your audience to make something that's really funny. Some general "slap-stick" humor may be funny to almost anyone, but the "inside joke" can really be powerful. For instance, we produced an interactive video program using the theme of a bumbling, industrial spy who has been hired to find out about how our client was making so much money selling gears. (Of course, the program was for newly hired, young sales engineers on how to specify and sell gears.) The industrial spy's client was never seen, only heard on tapes or on the phone, and he had the distinct accent and charming turns of phrases of the audience's training manager. While the program was funny to almost anyone, the intended audience found this inside joke irresistible, and the humor broke the pace of the lengthy and technical content.

STAGES OF SCRIPTWRITING

Few writers can just sit down and rattle off a full script. In fact even if you *could*, in practice, you *shouldn't*; in almost every situation in corporate and instructional video, you're not writing the script for yourself, it's for a client. It's crucial to take scriptwriting and production slowly in stages, getting client feedback and approval at each benchmark.

The first step in scriptwriting is to develop a *treatment*. Look at Figure 3-20. This is a narrative of one paragraph to two pages or so in length that describes what the program will look and "feel" like. A treatment describes the general tone, length, scenario(s), characters, and an outline of the content. Once this program concept is approved, you can move into the detailed part of scriptwriting.

Many people confuse the word *script*; to them it means the "words to be spoken." In video, a script is much more; it's the entire blueprint for the production, including music, effects, camera angles and shots, and, of course, the spoken words. And that's what makes writing a script tricky.

Video scripts are usually written in a two-column format, the video on the left, and the audio on the right. Special effects, camera movements, and sound cues should also be included. A number of word-processors and specialized scriptwriting

AD CETERA Communications Incorporated

New Sponsoring Video - Trmt

COPY

Description: This new, 10 - 12 minute video program is designed to help Amway Distributors in North America sponsor new distributors. It will be brief and fast-paced, utilizing state-of-the-art video techniques and effects, computer graphics, original music, and the services of a "name" talent with mass audience appeal to heighten interest and lend credibility to the lives and motivations of real people as they share with the viewers their reasons for owning an Amway business.

We will see and hear the host at different locations within an ultra-modern airport; the setting itself, as well as what it symbolizes (options, choices, varying directions, excitement, a sense of adventure and progress), subtly underscores our theme of looking toward the future.

Selected distributors, meanwhile, will be videotaped on-location throughout North America, in settings that illustrate and reinforce the values and aspirations they've been able to realize as Amway people. They will be carefully chosen to demonstrate the diversity of individuals and interests found within Amway, as well as to illustrate Amway's compatibility with existing economic and social trends; their comments, woven together by the host, will convey our message: Amway is in tune with the times ... the trends are with us ... the future has already begun. And for those with vision -- and a willingness to work -- Amway offers an opportunity to turn their dreams for the future into reality.

AMW/8024 Treatment   9-06-88:Draft # 4   1/15

Figure 3-20 The scripting process starts out with a treatment, explaining the program's goals and intended "look" (*courtesy, Ron Brown, Amway Corporation*). Continued on next page.

software packages facilitate the layout of two-column scripts (see Figure 3-21). Sometimes writers use a teleplay format: a scene is described in a short paragraph form (sometimes written in italics) and the dialogue follows. Whatever style you use, special effects, camera movements, and sound cues should also be included. The video column is usually described in terms of shots, using standard abbreviations, like CU for close-up, MS for medium shot, LS for long shot, and so on.

To give the client an even better idea of what the final product will look like, many producers draw up a *storyboard*, which is a series of sketches of each shot with the accompanying audio written underneath (see Figure 3-22, pages 102–104). The storyboard specifies the visual composition of each shot and is helpful to clients unused to visualizing a program from a written description alone. Storyboards are also helpful in communicating the scriptwriter's ideas to the camera operator or director who will execute the script. The only problem with storyboards (aside from

AD CETERA Communications Incorporated

New Sponsoring Video - Trmt

Objective: As stated above, the ultimate objective of the program is to sponsor new Amway Distributors. It will accomplish this goal by meeting these immediate objectives:

1. Establish (both emotionally and intellectually) that current studies and demographic data enable us to identify -- and so to prepare for -- the sweeping social, economic and cultural changes that will shape all our lives well into the next century;

2. Establish that in two critical respects Amway is in position to ride the crest of the wave into the future, because,

   a) it is a mainstream business whose products and services correspond exactly to the consumer demands we know this changing world will create; and,

   b) it is an opportunity that enables people who own their own Amway business not merely to survive the coming upheavals in the workplace, but to thrive while doing so;

3. Establish that participation in Amway is the mark of one who is people-centered, visionary, willing to work hard, invigorated by challenge; and who looks forward to enjoying the rewards of financial success, recognition and personal fulfillment that result when those qualities are applied to the Amway opportunity.

To put it more succinctly, our objectives are to ensure that viewers seeing this program will

   * <u>feel</u> excited by the futuristic vision we present;
   * <u>believe</u> that Amway holds the key to their futures;
   * <u>want</u> to sign up as new Distributors.

AMW/8024 Treatment   9-06-88:Draft # <u>4</u>   2/15

Figure 3-20 Continued

the time and artistic skill needed) is *being able to follow one.* It's fine if you're producing a short, dramatized piece like a commercial and have the time and authority to arrange scenes and people the way you had envisioned. However, in many corporate and instructional pieces, you have to "wing it" in part on location and may not be able to reproduce exactly each shot as you had imagined it in your head.

So, in scripting you've got to be as detailed as is realistic. While you want your client to have a good idea of what you want the program to look and sound like (it's easy to make changes at this stage), you don't want to promise what you may not be able to deliver. On the other hand, don't wait to figure everything out in production when time is expensive and crews and talent get impatient. Decide now what elements of the script will be shot from what angles, and exactly how long each shot should be to cover your narration. You may not be able to go back and get that "one last shot" if you haven't planned carefully at this stage.

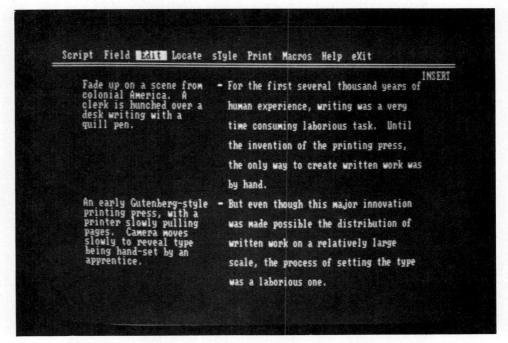

Figure 3-21 Scripting software like Scriptmaster makes it easy to write and revise scripts and print them in a standard two-column format (*courtesy, Comprehensive Video Corporation*).

THE FIVE BIGGEST SCRIPTING MISTAKES

Here's a quick rundown of mistakes to avoid in scripts:

- The "laundry list" syndrome: rattling off a list of facts, model numbers, names, places, and the like. Remember, viewers can only remember a limited number of things at once. "Chunk" information and give them an overall concept or frame of reference on which to hang the facts.

- The "who cares?" syndrome: beginning a program with details about a company or process before you've sold the viewers on why they'd be interested. For instance, don't start out a promotional script on a college about when it was founded, how many professors are on the faculty, and who is the president; start with something to entice the viewer to want to know more. Grab their heart-strings first.

- The "who are you?" syndrome: letting some unknown narrator expound on a subject or try to convince an audience when he or she lacks any real knowledge (or when his or her expertise has not been made clear). Instead, try to let "real people" explain who they are and then give the information; it is much more believable and motivational this way.

- The "so what do you want me to do?" syndrome: presenting all kinds of great information without a "call to action." Be sure to tell viewers specifically what you want them to do. If you're producing a great program on the Red Cross chapter in your city, tell them what you want them to do: donate blood, contact the Red Cross to be a volunteer, and so on.

- The "real people don't talk that way" syndrome: writing stilted conversations that sound unrealistic when spoken. Don't use whole sentences, let your actors hesitate or occasionally use less-than-perfect grammar, and use colloquialisms. Write in the active voice—avoid the passive voice at all costs!

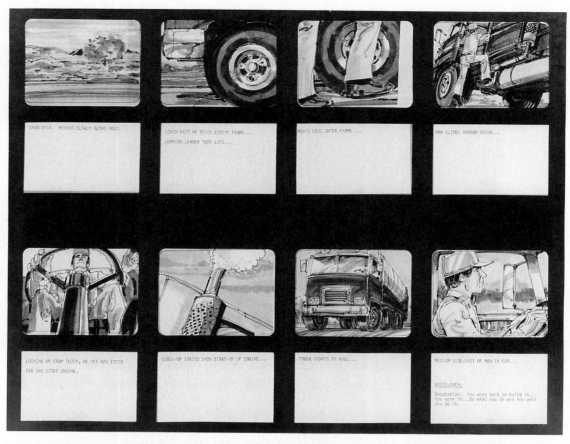

a

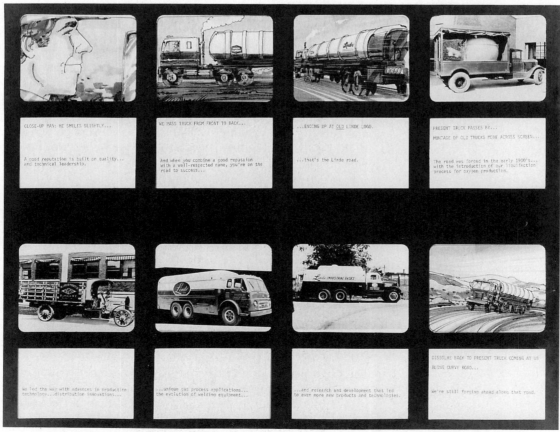

b

Figure 3-22 Sometimes a complete storyboard is drawn before a program is approved and shot. This designates each camera shot and its accompanying audio underneath (*courtesy, Union Carbide Company*).

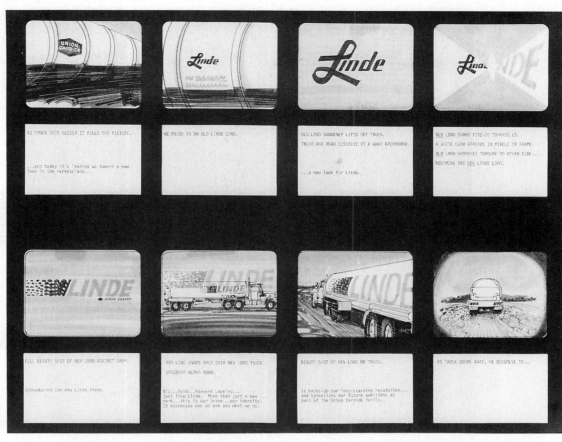

c

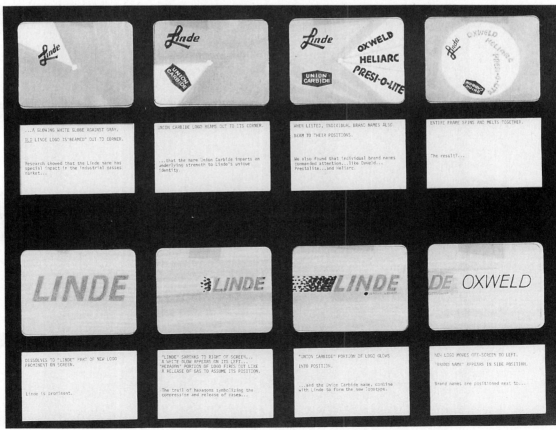

d

Figure 3-22 Continued

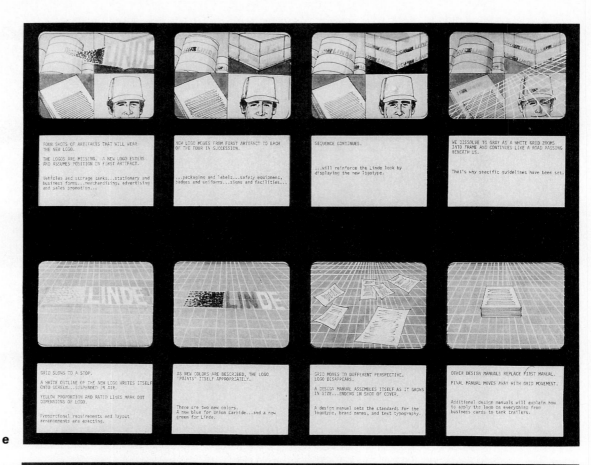

e

f

Figure 3-22 Continued

Figure 3-22 Continued

As video programs become more diverse and integrated with other technologies, their scripts will reflect this sophistication. The precise layout of the script is really immaterial as long as everyone involved can interpret it clearly and vividly. To minimize unpleasant surprises for both the client and the scriptwriter during the program's premier, you will need a well-planned, thorough, and understandable script.

BIBLIOGRAPHY

ARWADY, J. AND D. GAYESKI (1989). *Using Video: Interactive and Linear Designs*. Englewood Cliffs, NJ: Educational Technology Press.

FLEMING, M. AND W. H. LEVIE (1978). *Instructional Message Design*. Englewood Cliffs, NJ: Educational Technology Publications.

IUPPA, N.V. AND K. ANDERSON (1988). *Advanced Interactive Video Design*. White Plains, NY: Knowledge Industry Publications.

MATRAZZO, D. (1980). *The Corporate Scriptwriting Book*. Portland, OR: Media Concepts Press.

4

BUDGETING AND FUNDING

Organizational and instructional video is highly dependent upon the support it receives from management, from its audience, and from other interested agencies. That support is most concretely represented by the funding it receives. The successful producer is also a capable business manager, experienced in acquiring, forecasting, contracting, and justifying financial support. For most institutions, effective television programs are *cost*-effective programs; the expenditures incurred in creating the program must relate directly to an increase in profits or a decrease in spending. Therefore, the media professional must be able not only to handle the video budget but also to relate that set of figures to the overall organization's finances.

THE VIDEO DEPARTMENT BUDGET

There are a number of factors to consider when developing an overall budget for a video production center, whether it is a separate company or a department within an organization.

- Salaries. The total amount paid to all regular employees—including their fringe benefits such as contributions to Social Security, insurance, and so on. To calculate total salaries, add about 30% (or whatever your organization's rate happens to be) for fringe benefits onto the annual salary for each employee.
- Overhead. Rental or purchase of space, heat, light, utilities, any corporate overhead assessed, and so on.
- Capital equipment. The cost of major equipment to be purchased each year, including production gear and office equipment.
- Depreciation. The total price of each piece of major equipment, divided by the number of years of its estimated life span. This cost should be calculated

each year for tax purposes. For instance, if you buy a $25,000 video editor, you usually won't "write off" the total cost in one year, but rather would depreciate it over 3 to 5 years. Organizations vary in the method they use to depreciate various types of equipment, and the estimated life span can vary from one to seven years.

- Consumable production, maintenance, and office supplies. Videotape, stationery, repair materials, film and graphics stock, lamps, and the like.
- Travel. The total budget for travel to locations for shooting or research, or for travel for professional development for the staff to attend conferences and the like, as well as local mileage for routine business-related trips.
- Professional materials. Reference books, dues for professional associations, periodicals, and so on.
- Maintenance and repair. The estimated cost for parts and labor for all equipment for the year.
- Rentals. Telephone lines, business machines, computer lines, specialized production equipment you may rent rather than buy, and the like.
- Licensing fees. Charges to secure the rights to stock footage, pictures, recordings, or videotape or computer programs.
- Communications. Phone calls, computer terminal charges, postage, shipping, and similar items.
- Wages and fees. Including per-hour or per-day charges for talent, narrators, specialized crew members, consultants, and so on.
- Instructional materials. A budget to purchase such items as software as an alternative or supplement to producing your own video programs.

Each organization has a different approach to budgeting; budgets may be broken into very specific items or account numbers or may merely provide an overall lump sum within which to operate. Video managers are usually responsible for developing a proposed budget for the coming fiscal year. Rather than merely adding on a set percentage increase to the previous year's budget, it is more sound to start from ground zero and build a new budget based on proposed programming needs. This allows for flexibility to increase and decrease budget categories according to specific objectives for the next year, and it provides a more thorough justification to management for requests.

Various methods are used in financing in-house video departments: the *direct annual budget*, the *client charge-back* system, the *soft-money* approach, and, of course, combinations of the above approaches. In the annual budget approach, the organization allocates to the video department a yearly sum that is to cover all expenses in producing programs for any in-house clients. Client charge-back systems operate by charging clients for the total cost of producing their programs—including "their share" of salaries, overhead, and so on. Soft money refers to grants, donations, special contracts or other outside funding that cannot be counted upon from year to year. The combination system, of course, is a mixture of two or more of these approaches.

Each underwriting approach has inherent advantages and disadvantages. The direct annual budget provides a secure base of operation; each year the video manager knows exactly how much is available to spend and can plan accordingly. There is never a worry about finding clients to support personnel and overhead costs. However, this approach is not equitable to all departments in an organization, since the cost of the video operation is borne by all departments equally, but invariably some departments make use of its services much more than others do. It is difficult for the video manager to apportion the budget among potential clients;

conceivably one client could propose a series of programs on the first day of the fiscal year that would expend the entire annual budget! While this is certainly not a common occurrence, it does put the video center's "goodies" on a first-come, first-served basis. Departments funded in this manner also do not have to be as responsive or outgoing to clients, since no matter how many productions they do nor how excellent their work, they will get the same amount of funding for that year. Clients are also forced to use the in-house facility (unless an unusual need can be demonstrated).

In the charge-back system, the video department bills other departments for their services. Some bill as if they were an outside production house—each program requested pays not only for the direct expenses incurred, but for a share of the department salaries and operating expenses. Other departments may be allowed to charge clients only for direct expenses. They do not charge for salaries or overhead and cannot accrue profits. Charge-back systems are equitable to each department within the organizations, since clients pay as they go. The video manager is free to take on as many projects as feasible without the fear of running out of money. This approach encourages responsiveness to clients, allows for flexibility in undertaking projects within the fiscal year, and encourages video producers to seek more clients, since they can gain more staff and facilities this way. In fact, if there are too *few* clients, the video department can disappear! However, the charge-back system can discourage potential clients because they *do* have to pay for the services. Only those departments with a sufficient budget can gain the benefits of the medium. If in-house charges become too high, or if the quality is perceived to be lower than appropriate, clients may start looking for out-of-house production houses or freelance consultants.

The soft money approach is generally used by independent producers or nonprofit organizations who depend solely upon some sort of grant support to underwrite their existence. Usually, these video centers are quite small and vary in size and activity from year to year. Many agencies producing children's television, video art, or documentaries survive on a relatively continuous stream of government funding, private donations, and support from foundations. Producers with a specific subject area of expertise or with a definite concept of programming they wish to produce may systematically seek funding for their proposals. This approach leaves them free from seeking clients or working with topics they don't care for. Needless to say, this funding method is not for the weak-hearted, since the cash flow from year to year can never quite be predicted, except for the very largest and most successful non-profit groups.

The combination funding approach, used wisely, can combine the best aspects of each system. Many video departments receive an annual allocation to cover the fixed costs of salaries, overhead, and equipment. Clients are then charged just for the out-of-pocket expenses of consumables used on each production. For instance, the client pays for video tape, direct travel, set construction, any elaborate graphics or animation done out-of-house, and other items directly related to a specific project. Soft money is used by many nonprofit educational video centers to fund "extras," such as a large production on a topic of interest, or the hiring of some additional staff members.

Some video departments have become independent *profit centers*. The department operates as if it were an independent company and takes on clients from within and from outside the company. Within more and more corporations nowadays, the video department is, in fact, a separate profit-making entity. Although this approach is cost-effective from the organization's viewpoint, if video departments need to seek outside clients to keep themselves going, their responsiveness to in-house needs can suffer, too. In an era of cost consciousness and cutbacks, some organizations have virtually eliminated their video departments through *divestiture*.

The equipment is sometimes sold to the former employees of the video departments, and they become independent production houses; often their former employers become major clients.

For example, Avid Communications started out as part of the training department in Reliance Electric, a major manufacturer of industrial motors. In lean times for the company, the manager proposed that they become a profit center for the corporation. He did so in lieu of having his department cut or being forced to seek new employment. Before breaking into semi-independence, the company's senior slide producer was brought aboard Avid to complete the AV/Video house. They now do work for Reliance but have also successfully established themselves as a regional media production house.

BIDDING AND SPECS

Few moments in the professional life of a video producer can match the joy and anticipation of those in which you discover that there's finally going to be enough money in next year's budget to buy that new piece of equipment you've been longing for. Hot upon the heels of the good news, however, comes the realization of the paperwork required to consummate those purchases. For most organizations, it's not as easy as trotting down to the local video retailer with a blank check and picking out the shiny new toy that catches your fancy.

Most companies consider purchases over a certain amount (such as $500) to be *capital equipment*, specified and justified in an annual budget. So, if in September you decide that you'd like a new camera but the previous fall you didn't put it in the budget to go into effect during the current fiscal year, you're out of luck. Most organizations also require that major purchases be put out on bid. You describe what you want in a spec; your purchasing department sends copies of that, called a *request for quotation* or *RFQ* to qualified suppliers or vendors, and they in turn respond with sealed bids. At a specified time, the bids are opened, and the lowest one gets the contract. This method ensures that the company gets the most for its money and avoids "sweetheart deals" in which one supplier with the right "connections" gets all the business regardless of price.

This is all well and good, because you do want the most for your money. However, this procedure imposes several extra demands upon you. First, bidding is a slow process, usually taking four to six weeks. This means that it's risky to try to buy any major equipment near the end of the fiscal year. Why? In most organizations, whatever is left over in the budget at the end of a fiscal year *reverts* back to the organization: there's no such thing as saving from year to year. If the bidding process takes a little longer than expected and you wind up actually receiving the equipment in the *next* fiscal year, the money will come out of the next year's budget; the money earmarked for the new gear in last year's budget will have reverted to the general operating fund of the company. The moral: Buy early in the fiscal year.

The second complication of the bidding system is writing up *specs* or specifications for equipment. In order to assure that you don't pass up a certain brand or model that meets your needs at the lowest cost, most purchasing systems require that you draw up specs for the equipment. Instead of merely ordering a certain model, you list the particular characteristics of the equipment you need; a bidder can then supply a quote on any make or model meeting those specifications. Therefore, it's necessary to do a little research into the exact characteristics of the hardware you require, so that you can write a complete and accurate description of your needs. Besides performance standards, you'll need to consider size, weight, compatibility with existing equipment, and any other criteria you deem important. See Figure 4-1 for a sample spec sheet and Figure 4-2 for a purchase order. Many media

SPECIFICATIONS

■ COLOR VIDEO CAMERA KY-25U
Optical system: 2/3" F1.4 RGB prism system
Pickup device: 2/3" Interline-transfer CCD, 3-chip
Picture elements: 360,000 (effective),
  Total picture elements: 380,000
Encoder: NTSC (Wide-band R-Y/B-Y system)
Synchronizing system: Internal/External
Optical filter: Closed, 3200°K, 5600°K, 5600°K + 1/8 ND
Lens mount: 2/3" bayonet
Sensitivity: F5.6 at 2000 lux (186 fc)
Minimum illumination: 23 lux (2.2 fc) at F1.7 with +18 dB
  switch ON
S/N: 60 dB typical (Contour correction OFF, Gamma 1,
  Bandwidth 4.2 MHz, Matrix OFF)
Horizontal resolution: 700 TV lines (at center)
  530 TV lines (R/G/B)
Registration: 0.05 % (without lens distortion) in all areas
Contour correction: Horizontal: Dual-edged
  Vertical: 2H
Color bar generator: Provided (full-field)
Gain boost: +9 dB, +18 dB
Output signals: Video signal
  1. Composite video signal: 1.0 Vp-p, 75 Ω (BNC, 26P)
  2. Separate Y/C signal: Y: 1.0 Vp-p C: 0.286 Vp-p,
    75 Ω (7P, 26P)
  3. Component video signal: Y: 1.0 Vp-p
    R-Y/B-Y: 0.486 Vp-p, 75 Ω, (26P)
  4. R/G/B signal: R/G/B: 0.7 Vp-p, 75 Ω (26P)
    (2, 3 or 4 is selectively output from the same 26-pin
    connector.)
  Test signal: Composite/R/G/B selectable (BNC)
  Audio signal: −52/−20 dBm selectable (Stereo/
    Monaural applicable)
  Audio monitor signal: 8 Ω (From VTR)
Input signals: Return video signal: 1.0 Vp-p, 75 Ω
  Genlock signal: VBS: 1.0 Vp-p, 75 Ω
    BB: 0.43 Vp-p, 75 Ω
  Microphone signal: −52 dBm (Stereo/Monaural
    applicable)
Power requirement +12 V DC
Power consumption: 1.5A (with 1.5" viewfinder VF-P10U)
Ambient temperature: −5°C to +45°C (23°F to 113°F)
Dimensions: 113.5(W) x 277.5(H) x 276.5(D) mm
  (4-1/2" x 11" x 10-15/16") (with camera head, camera
  adaptor, carrying handle and shoulder pad)
Weight: 3.0 kg (6.6 lbs.) (with camera adaptor)

■ VIEWFINDER VF-P10U
CRT: 38 mm (1.4") diagonal
Resolution: 400 lines
Provided circuits: Top tally lamp (ON-OFF switchable)
  LOW-L (Low light)/BATT (battery) warning (Red)
  REC (tally)/ALARM (VTR) lamp (Green)
Power consumption: 12 V DC, 250 mA (provided from
  Color Video Camera)
Ambient temperature range: −20°C to 50°C
  (−4°F to +122°F)
Weight: 650 g (1.4 lbs)

■ VIEWFINDER VF-P400U
CRT: 94 mm (4") diagonal
Resolution: More than 500 lines
Tally lamps: Top: filament lamp (12 V)
  Screen side; LED
Power consumption: 12 V DC, 750 mA (provided from
  video camera)
Ambient temperature: −20°C to +50°C (−4°F to +122°F)
Weight: 1.8 kg (4.0 lbs)

■ 13X ZOOM LENS HZ-513U
Focal length: 10 mm — 130 mm
Zoom ratio: 13 to 1
Relative aperture: f/1.7; 10 mm — 110 mm
  f/2.1; 110 mm — 130 mm
Minimum object distance: 1 m (3.28 ft)
Macro distance: 90 mm (3-9/16")
Front thread diameter: 72 mm dia. P = 0.75 mm
Weight: 1.35 kg (3.0 lbs) without lens hood

■ 16X ZOOM LENS HZ-516BU
Focal length: 9.5 mm — 152 mm
Zoom ratio: 16 to 1
Relative aperture: f/1.8; 9.5 mm — 114 mm f/2.3;152 mm
Minimum object distance: 0.95 m (3.12 ft)
Macro distance: 70 mm (2-3/4")
Front thread diameter: 77 mm dia. P = 0.75 mm
Weight: 1.4 kg (3.1 lbs) without lens hood

■ 12X ZOOM LENS A12X9BERMU
Focal length: 9 mm — 108 mm
Zoom ratio: 12 to 1
Relative aperture: f/1.7; 9 mm — 99 mm f/1.9; 108 mm
Minimum object distance: 1 m (3.28 ft)
Macro distance: 70 mm (2-13/16")
Extender: X2, built-in
Front thread diameter: 72 mm dia. P = 0.75 mm
Weight: 1.3 kg (3.0 lbs) without lens hood

■ 15X ZOOM LENS J15X95BKRSIIU
Focal length: 9.5 mm — 143 mm
Zoom ratio: 15 to 1
Relative aperture: f/1.8 to f/2.1
Minimum object distance: 0.95 m (3.12 ft)
Macro distance: 10 mm (7/16")
Front thread diameter: 82 mm dia. P = 0.75 mm

■ 15X ZOOM LENS J15X95BIRSU
Focal length: 9.5 mm — 143 mm
Zoom ratio: 15 to 1
Relative aperture: f/1.8 to f/2.1
Minimum object distance: 0.95 m (3.12 ft)
Macro distance: 10 mm (7/16")
Extender: X2, built-in
Front thread diameter: 82 mm dia. P = 0.75 mm
Weight: 1.6 kg (3.5 lbs) without lens hood

■ BATTERY PACK DC-C11U
Type: Ni-Cd battery
Output: +12 V DC, 2.2 Ah
Weight: 1.0 kg (2.2 lbs)
Dimensions: 68(W) x 142(H) x 76.5(D) mm
  (2-3/4" x 5-5/8" x 3-1/16")

■ Ni-Cd Battery NB-G1U
Type: Ni-Cd
Output: +12 V DC, 2.2 Ah
Weight: 0.6 kg (1.3 lbs)
Dimensions: 79(W) x 43(H) x 103(D) mm
  (3-1/8" x 1-3/4" x 4-1/16")

■ REMOTE CONTROL UNIT RM-P200U
Output signals
Composite video signal: 1 Vp-p, 75 Ω x 2
R/G/B signals: 0.7 Vp-p, 75 Ω x 1 each (without SYNC)
Y/R-Y/B-Y signals: Y; 1 Vp-p, R-Y; 0,486 Vp-p,
  B-Y; 0,486 Vp-p, 75 Ω each
Y/C 358 signals: Y; 1 Vp-p, 75 Ω, C; 0,286 Vp-p, 75 Ω
  (burst level)
Intercom signal: Two-wire system, −10 dB, 600 Ω balanced
  (R/G/B, Y/R-Y/B-Y, YC 358 should be selected at camera
  head. The primarily output is R/G/B.)
Input signals
Genlock signal:
  Composite video signal 1 Vp-p, 75 Ω or high
  Black burst signal 0.43 Vp-p, 75 Ω or high
AUX signal: Composite video signal 1 Vp-p, 75 Ω or high
Intercom signal: Two-wire system, −10 dB, 600 Ω balanced
Tally signal: Make-contact or power (5 — 24 V DC or
  6 V AC) supply
Power supply: 120 V AC, 60 Hz
Ambient temperature: −10°C to +45°C (14°F to 113°F)
Power consumption: 11 W
  65 W (with camera and 4" viewfinder)
Weight: 5 kg (11.1 lbs)

■ AC POWER ADAPTOR CHARGER AA-P250U
Output:
  CAMERA mode — 12.5 V DC 3.5 A
  CHARGE mode — 12 to 17 V DC 2.2 A
Power source: 90 V — 130 V AC, 50/60 Hz
Power consumption: 60 W
Usable Battery Pack: JVC Battery Pack —
  Ni-Cd type, DC-C11, NB-G1 or DC-C50
Operational temperature:
  CAMERA mode; −20°C to 50°C (−4°F to 120°F)
  CHARGE mode; 10°C to 35°C (50°F to 95°F)
Weight: 1.7 kg (3.7 lbs)
Charging indicator: QUICK/TRICKLE
Charging time: DC-C11; approx.60 min. NB-G1; approx.
  60 min. DC-C50; 95 min. (after normal discharge)

■ AC POWER ADAPTOR AA-P200U
Output: 12 V DC, 3.5 A
Power source: 90 V AC — 130 V AC, 50/60 Hz
Power consumption: 54 W
Operational temperature: −20°C to 50°C
  (−4°F to 120°F)
Weight: 0.8 kg (1.8 lbs)

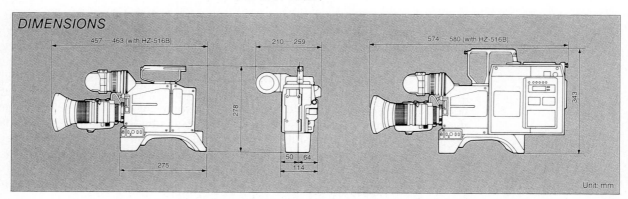

DIMENSIONS

Unit: mm

Design and specifications subject to change without notice.

Figure 4-1 Buying equipment starts out with research, reading, and deciding upon the exact specifications you desire (*courtesy, US JVC Corporation*).

producers find themselves "stuck" with second-rate equipment because they failed to write the specs in sufficient detail—they wind up with something that meets the incomplete description they wrote and happened to come in at the lowest cost.

Besides the usual criteria of price and characteristics, there are several additional factors to consider when purchasing equipment:

- What is the essential delivery date?
- What is the warranty for parts and labor, and how long does it last?
- Who is available to service the equipment if it needs repair—and how fast can someone get you back in service?
- What is the availability of replacement parts?
- How easy is it to maintain and repair?
- Are operating manuals and schematics included?
- What accessories, such as cables, covers, or batteries, are included?
- Who will install the equipment?
- If it is an equipment package or system, how *must it work together?*
- What will the penalty be if the vendor does not meet any of the conditions listed in the purchase offer?

A smart video manager will know how to write specs and contracts to get what is needed in a timely manner. One colleague responsible for the installation of a complex post-production suite contracted to a vendor for design, equipment, and installation. The specs included a date by which the system needed to be fully functional (he specified exactly what the system would need to do to be fully functional) *and* specified a penalty for each day overdue. As it turned out, that spec pushed the vendors to work hard on his system—but despite their motivation, they could not meet the deadline. My colleague wound up with a very functional edit suite—albeit a few weeks late—at quite a discount!

PRODUCTION BUDGETING

Probably the first substantive question any prospective client asks (or at least thinks about) is, "How much will it cost?" This is like asking, "How much does a house cost?" The cost of producing video varies greatly, not only with the quality, complexity, and length of a program, but also with its format, the location(s), the fee structure of the video department or company, and so on. Per-minute averages are sometimes useful for giving clients a ballpark idea of costs; a typical figure is $1500 to $2000 per finished minute for programs done out-of-house and $500 to $1000 for in-house projects *if* the department only charges for out-of-pocket costs. Of course, there's no such thing as the "average production." What are the major factors, then, that contribute to production costs?

- Program format. How much scripting, shooting, and travel does the format require?
- Technical quality. What kind of equipment will be used (such as consumer cameras versus broadcast-quality equipment).
- Client support. How much research, scripting, or personnel will the client provide, and what is the experience of those assigned to help?
- Program length. What is the estimated number of minutes of finished product?

ITHACA COLLEGE
Ithaca, New York 14850
PURCHASE ORDER

DATE:
To:

PURCHASE ORDER **028990**

THIS NUMBER MUST APPEAR ON ALL INVOICES, PACKAGES AND OTHER CORRESPONDENCE RELATIVE TO THIS ORDER.

IT IS THE POLICY OF ITHACA COLLEGE THAT DISCRIMINATION ON THE GROUNDS OF SEX, COLOR, RACE, RELIGION, NATIONAL ORIGIN, AGE, MARITAL STATUS OR HANDICAP, WILL NOT EXIST IN ANY AREA, ACTIVITY OR OPERATION OF THE COLLEGE.

DELIVER TO:

FREIGHT
☐ PRE-PAY AND ADD
☐ CARRIER TO BILL DIRECT
☐ PRE-PAY AND ALLOW
☐ CARRIER SPECIFIED

THE ARTICLES SPECIFIED FOR PURCHASE HEREIN ARE FOR USE OF ITHACA COLLEGE, TAX EXEMPT CERTIFICATE NO. EX-112761

PURCHASING COPY

BUDGET APPROVAL _____ DATE _____

ACCOUNTING APPROVAL _____ DATE 9/18

M 33579

REQUISITION NUMBER

USING DEPARTMENT

QUANTITY	CATALOG NO.	DESCRIPTION	UNIT PRICE	AMOUNT
200		EG Scotch VHS Tape		
2	TVS/54	Luxor AV/TV Carts		
4	VT3044	Hitachi VHS – 4 Head		
5	WM10-PRO	AZDEN 10 Wireless Microphones		
4	QKTH30	Quick Set Tripod		
		CONFIRMING ORDER – DO NOT DUPLICATE		

DATE IN	COND.	DEPT. ACCOUNT	SUB CODE ACCT CNTL.
		2-14020-3110	3363.50
		2-14020-8360	300.00

TOTAL

SPECIAL INSTRUCTIONS

BY:

PURCHASING DEPARTMENT (PURCHASERS NAME)

RECEIVED BY USING/REQUESTING DEPARTMENT DATE

SHIP NO.	DATE IN	ORDER COMPLETE		GOODS RECEIVED		
		YES	NO	ACCEPTABLE	DAMAGED	
1						
2						
3						

PAYMENT APPROVAL _____ DATE _____

REMARKS:

Figure 4-2 Once you decide on specs, a purchase order is written (courtesy, Ithaca College).

- Shooting ratio. How much tape will need to be shot in relation to what's likely to be used? How much editing will be necessary?
- Talent. Who are needed to be on camera or to narrate, for how long, and for what fees?
- Set and graphics. How much peripheral support is needed in terms of graphics, film, costumes, set, or props?
- Special effects. What kind of computer graphics, special effects (like split screens or digital wipes), or animation are necessary?
- Travel. How many sites will be covered, what is their location, and how expensive will it be to travel to (and perhaps stay over) at those locations? For foreign travel, are visas or other legal documents needed?
- Size of crew. Will you need to send only one camera person to shoot, or will you need a larger crew to light, direct, provide production assistance, or use more than one camera?
- Duplication. How many copies of the final program are needed and in what format?

It is useful for each video department to calculate its own estimates for productions, based upon the common types of programs requested and the local costs of operation. Commercial production houses use rate cards to itemize rental and service prices for potential customers; many in-house production units have similar documents. Typical rate cards list per-hour and per-day rentals for field production units, studio time, editing suites, and duplication services. Usually, they are broken down by the type of equipment used and the size of the crew supplied. (See Figures 4-3 and 4-4.)

Many facilities also offer other services, such as *standards conversions* in which video tapes are dubbed onto machines using a foreign video standard. The United States, Canada, and several other countries use the NTSC system; other systems used abroad include PAL, PAM-M, and SECAM. *Dubbing* or duplication from tape to tape, disc to tape, or film to tape, is another common option. Special effects, computer animation, or technical correction of tapes with electronic faults are also offered by some production houses.

If you will be using an outside production house, it pays to look into their policies. Look at Figure 4-5. Here are some things to consider:

- What are their charges for overtime for production facilities and crew, and what are considered "normal" business hours?
- What personnel (how many and their qualifications) are provided with the rental of equipment and facilities?
- Are you or members of your staff allowed to operate the production house's equipment?
- What are their *personnel fees* and mileage *charge* for travel to location shoots?
- Is there a minimum fee for short jobs (such as 1/2 day)?
- Who assumes liability for damage to software or hardware or for accidents?
- Is there is special discount for large projects or for not-for-profit organizations?
- Who pays for "down time" when their equipment breaks down?
- Who keeps the sets, graphics, and "raw" unedited tapes used in the program?
- Is there a deadline before which cancellations must be made?
- Exactly what equipment is included in the rental package (for instance, do you have to pay extra for an extra battery or extension cord)?

```
            VIDEO EFP/REMOTE PRODUCTION

                            STATE      ENDOWED    OUTSIDE
EQUIPMENT
    EFP Package             $350/day   $350/day   $500/day
        Betacam or SONY 350
        Camera, Lights, Monitor,
        Audio (any kit), Tripod,
        Dolly and/or Jib if desired

    Van                     20/day     20/day     30/day
        (plus .25/mile for shoot
        exceeding 50 miles round-trip)

    Camera/Tripod only
        Betacam or SONY 350  100/day   100/day    200/day
        Portable Beta deck for 350 100/day 100/day 200/day

    Lighting only (per kit)  25/day     25/day    35/day
        Soft lights, Cool-Lux Minis,
        Lowell D kits, Tota-kit

    Dolly only (tracks opt.)  50/day    50/day    75/day

    Jimmy Jib only            50/day    50/day    75/day

PERSONNEL
    Producer/Director         N/C       N/C       $30/hr.
    Video Engineer          $11/hr.*   11/hr.*    27/hr.
    Audio Operator          $20/hr.    20/hr.     25/hr.
    Videographer            $20/hr.    20/hr.     25/hr.
    Production Assistant (opt.) $20/hr. 20/hr.    25/hr.


    *Cornell clients charged 1/2 of Engineer costs, officially
        $22/hr.

One-half day minimum -- up to four hours at .5 times daily
rate.  EFP package rental requires full crew; camera or jib
rental requires videographer. Tape stock not included. Client
also charged for meals, travel and other unusual costs.

A PRODUCTION DAY IS 7 WORKING HOURS.  OVERTIME IS CHARGED
AFTER 7 HOURS. A FULL WEEK OF PRODUCTION IS BILLED AS 4 DAYS.
```

Figure 4-3 A rate card for EFP (Electronic Field Production) units at Cornell University. Note that they have different scales for State-supported units of the University, the endowed colleges, and outside clients (*courtesy, Cornell University ETV Center and Media Services*).

SIFFORD VIDEO SERVICES, INC.

PROPOSAL

VHS and BETA DUPLICATION
(Includes tape, slipcase and generic typed labels)

Length:	5 min.	10 min.	15 min.	30 min.	60 min.	90 min.	120 min.
Quantity		(Price per cassette)					
1-5	$11.50	$12.00	$13.00	$13.50	$14.50	$15.50	$16.50
6-100	9.65	9.90	10.15	11.20	12.75	14.00	15.25
101-200	7.80	8.00	8.20	9.25	10.60	12.55	14.40
201 +	Call For Quotation						

VHS and BETA DUPLICATION ONLY
(No Tape)

Quantity		(Price per cassette)					
1-5	$7.55	$ 8.00	$ 8.95	$ 9.30	$10.00	$10.50	$11.30
6-100	5.70	5.90	6.10	7.00	8.25	9.00	10.05
101-200	3.85	4.00	4.15	5.05	6.10	7.55	9.20
201 +	Call For Quotation						

EXTRA CHARGES

REEL CHANGES: (Combining copies from more than one master)

    One Reel Change   – No Charge

    Two or More Reel Changes   – See Selective Dubbing

SELECTIVE DUBBING: $3.00 per minute from start to finish of job plus standard duplication charges.

OPTIONS

VHS or BETA Black Plastic Slipcases	– $ .60 each
VHS/BETA Black 1/3 Pocket Vinyl Case	– .85 each
VHS/BETA Full Pocket Vinyl Case (Black or White)	– .90 each
VHS or BETA Shipper/Storage Case	– 2.50 each
Labels (Sifford stock, typed and applied)	– .30 per cassette
Typing of Customer Supplied Labels	– .05 per label
Application of Customer Supplied Labels	– .10 per cassette
Shrink Wrapping	– .10 per cassette
Mailers (Padded Envelopes or Cardboard)	– .60 each
Distribution: 1 to 100 locations	– 1.25 per location
101 plus locations	– 1.00 per location

TERMS AND CONDITIONS: C.O.D. – Credit may be established by contacting the Credit Department.

F.O.B. Nashville, TN

5/89

Figure 4-4 A rate card for tape duplication (*courtesy, Sifford Video Services, Inc.*).

EDIT SUITE I   *TERRY MOORE*

Base rate includes: CMX 3600 Editor, Ampex AVC-23N Effects Switcher with Extended Panel Memory, black and white graphics camera, Tascam M-250 20x8 audio mixer, character generator and one VTR any format................. $ 200/Hour**

2 VTR Edit any format........................... $ 250/Hour**
3 VTR Edit any format........................... $ 300/Hour**

Additional effects and up to 6 VTR's may be added at the rate listed on page 4.

1

EDIT SUITE II   *DAVID TANNER*

Base rate includes: Grass Valley 41 Editor, Ampex Vista-18 Switcher with Digi-loop and Effects Memory, black and white camera, Studiomaster 8x4 audio mixer, character generator and one VTR with time code any format.......... $ 110/Hour*

Additional effects and up to 5 VTR's may be added at the rates listed on page 4.

2

EDIT III

This complete Sony offline package featuring 5800/5850 editing with a RM450 controller is bookable in 1/2 day or full day blocks of time.

4 Hours (unsupervised)................................ $ 100
8 Hours (unsupervised)................................ $ 200

An Editor may be furnished at an additional rate.
(Minimum charge for Edit Suite III - $ 50)

3

ADDITIONAL EQUIPMENT

1" Machine.......................................	*$ 90/Hour***	*Teac 25-2 ATR (Edit Suite II) ....*	*$ 10/Hour**
Betacam Machine............................	*$ 55/Hour***	*Color Camera...................................*	*$ 50/Hour**
3/4" Machine..................................	*$ 35/Hour***	*Compact Disc Player.......................*	*$ 25/Hour**
ADO (Edit Suite I)...........................	*$175/Hour***	*Turntable...*	*$ 15/Hour**
NEC E-Flex....................................	*$110/Hour***	*Audio Cassette Playback.................*	*$ 15/Hour**
Quantafont Character Generator		*ADO Disc...*	*$ 10/Each*
Pre-Programming...........................	*$ 60/Hour**	*Edit I Switcher Memory Disc.............*	*$ 10/Each*
Tascam ATR-60 1/4" (Edit Suite I)		*Edit I or II EDL Disc........................*	*$ 10/Each*
with centertrack Time Code...........	*$ 25/Hour**		

*1 Hour Minimum
**1/2 Hour Minimum

4

Figure 4-5 Rate card for a post-production house; note the explicit charges for various additional services and the terms and conditions of work (*courtesy, The Editing Company*).

SPOT DUPLICATION

1" (:60 or less)
*Price includes tape stock, reel, box and label.**
1 - 10	$22/Each
11 - 25	$20/Each
26 - 50	$16/Each
51 +	Call for bid

Betacam, 3/4" or 1/2"
*Price includes tape stock, jacket or sleeve and label.**
1 - 10	$30/Each
11 - 25	$25/Each
26 - 50	$20/Each
51 +	Call for bid

PROGRAM DUPLICATION

1" to 1"	$180/Hour***
1" to Betacam	$145/Hour***
1" to 3/4" or 1/2"	$125/Hour***
Betacam to Betacam	$110/Hour***
Betacam to 1/2"	$ 80/Hour***
3/4" to 3/4"	$ 70/Hour***
3/4" to 1/2"	$ 60/Hour***
1/2" to 1/2"	$ 50/Hour***

Rates do not include tape stock.
Rates apply to format in either direction.
Multiple copies-call for bid.

* Add $5 for each additional spot on same dub.
*** 1/4 Hour Minimum

5

ADDITIONAL TAPE ROOM SERVICES

1" Machine	$ 90/Hour***
Betacam Machine	$ 55/Hour***
3/4" Machine	$ 35/Hour***
1/2" Machine	$ 25/Hour***
Time Base Correction	$ 90/Hour***
Blanking Correction	$125/Hour***

Window Dubs/Time Code on an audio or address track	Transfer Fee + $15
Interformat transfers	See Program Rates
Editech assembly	See Program Rates

*** 1/4 Hour Minimum

MISCELLANEOUS SERVICES
Conference/Screening Room
includes 3/4" and 1/2" viewing	$ 50/Hour*
With 1" viewing	$125/Hour*

TAPE STOCK

			Time Coded
1"	per minute	$3.00	4.50
	(3 minute minimum)		
Betacam	20 minute	25.00	40.00
	30 minute	30.00	50.00
3/4"	5 minute	15.00	25.00
	10 minute	20.00	30.00
	15 minute	22.50	37.50
	20 minute	25.00	45.00
	30 minute	30.00	50.00
	60 minute	40.00	70.00
VHS	All lengths	10.00	
Betamax	All lengths	10.00	
1/4"	Audio Tape	1.00	
	(Audio Tape per minute)		
1" Metal Reel		5.00	
1" Spot Reel		3.50	
1/4" Reel		3.50	

6

TERMS AND CONDITIONS

ACCEPTANCE-The use of The Editing Company (the Company) facilities and/or service shall signify that the Client accepts the following terms and conditions of doing business.

RATES-Rates charged shall be those of the Company in force at date of use of the Company's facilities and services. Rates shall be based on elapsed time of use and not on program running time. Rates for additional facilities and services not shown will be quoted upon request. Local, state and other government charges for sales, excise and like taxes shall, where applicable, be due and payable by the Client. All rates are subject to change without notice. Unless otherwise stated in writing, all post production expenses will be billed at cost to the Client. Standby charges will be at 100% of the facilities and labor scheduled.

LIABILITY-The Company shall not be liable for any injury to person or property of the Client, its agents or other personnel, occurring in or about the facilities owned or leased by the Company. Should an equipment failure occur during a session, the Company will be responsible only for expenses specifically related to services we are supplying. The Company shall not be liable for any Client loss whatever due to delays, equipment failure, or problems in storage caused either directly or indirectly by acts of God, natural elements, power failures, strikes, flooding, fire, war, failure of transportation, failure of other to deliver, or inability to obtain. The Company shall not be liable for any lost profits or other damages caused by the loss,

damage or destruction of any materials belonging to the Client or to any other person unless caused by the negligence of the Company, in which event, the liability of the Company shall be limited to the replacement of a similar quality of material which is lost, damaged or destroyed, except for such replacement, the Company shall have no further liability regarding the loss, damage or destruction of such materials. The Company shall not be liable to the Client nor to any other person for any act of omission of any person selected by the Company to perform services or furnish materials for the Client.

PAYMENT-All work is done on a C.O.D. basis unless prior credit arrangements have been made. Client agrees to pay the Company for all services performed and invoiced to Client within thirty (30) days after services are performed. An interest charge of 1 1/2% per month will be charged on any unpaid balance after the due date. Any claims for adjustment in connection with an invoice must be presented to the Company in writing within fifteen (15) days from the date of the invoice in question. Client hereby waives any claim for adjustment in billing which is not presented in a timely manner according to the provisions of the paragraph. No processing, transferring, dubbing, editing, or other work which is to be billed to a third party will be performed by the Company without prior written authorization from said third party. No Client's master will be processed, transferred, dubbed, edited or other work performed by the Company on behalf of a third party without the written authorization from the Client. All rates for facilities, services, and quantities not covered or described herein are available upon request.

Continued

CANCELLATIONS-Cancellations within 24 hours of scheduled production will be charged at 100% of rates for total scheduled facilities and actual expenses incurred.

MINIMUMS-All personnel and facilities are charged from time in to time out and will be charged with specific minimums and by the minute thereafter unless otherwise specified or negotiated.

LABOR/OVERTIME-Straight time labor is that which occurs between 9:00 am and 6:00 pm, Monday through Friday, not exceeding 8 hours total duration. All other labor utilizing the daytime staff will be charged at applicable overtime rates. Overtime rates of $35 per person will be charged for each hour before 9:00 am and after 6:00 pm. All work performed by the daytime staff on weekends or holidays will be billed at applicable labor overtime rates in addition to the facility charge incurred.

MEAL PERIOD-A period of at least 1/2 hour must be allowed for meals after every 5 hours of work. Any session booked across the 11:00 am to 2:00 pm period will require a 30 minute meal break. Cost of lunch for the session will be included on Client's invoice.

OWNERSHIP OF ELEMENTS-Client warrants that it has the legal right to possession and use of all elements delivered to us and agrees to hold us harmless from all liability arising therefrom and further agrees to defend us at Client's expense, from any action or proceedings arising from such liability.

SHIPPING-All materials shipped to and from the Company shall be shipped at Client's expense and risk.

TAPE STORAGE-The Company offers tape, art and computer medium storage as a convenience to our Client at the Client's risk. In no event shall the Company be held responsible for more than the replacement of the supplies only.

LIENS-Client agrees that those properties delivered to the Company are accepted on the express condition that the Company will, at the time of delivery, acquire a lien on said property to secure payment of any amounts due the Company by Client.

INDEMNITIES-The Client will indemnify and hold the Company harmless for all suits, claims, demands and other liabilities and expenses (including attorney's fees), arising out of any goods or services performed and/or delivered by the Company.

NOTES

Figure 4-5 Continued

Rates can vary by as much as 500% from one production house to the next. The amount and technical sophistication of both the equipment and the personnel have a major effect on the price, but there are other factors as well. Geographic location plays a large role; the large East and West coast cities predictably have the highest rates, with the Midwest and South or small towns often being substantially less. Production houses have rapidly sprung up even in rural areas; these companies are successfully competing for clients from larger cities who are willing to travel to save production dollars. It's a good idea to collect rate cards to compare prices before you make a decision to use any specific production house.

Budgets can perhaps best be calculated using a four-part equation:

pre-production + production + post production + duplication = project total.

Once you have established in-house rates and have acquired figures for any out-of-house services required, the next task is to estimate the number of hours and the materials needed to accomplish the production. The process of costing out a program can vary greatly from situation to situation. Sometimes a client gives you a specific budget range within which to script and produce a program; other times you may be given a full script and asked to cost out its production. In perhaps the most common situation, you are given a very rough idea of the limit of the client's finances, and you rewrite or pare down the production costs until the client is satisfied with both the concept and the price.

The major categories of any production are:

- design/production personnel
- equipment rental
- travel
- talent
- materials
- raw tape stock
- licensing/production of music, graphics, and so on.

These categories should be broken down to reflect as much detail as can be provided for each program. For instance, the personnel category could be broken down to include scriptwriter, crew members, a producer/director, an engineer, and clerical staff. Each line should reflect the estimated number of hours or days or items, the cost per unit, and the total cost. See Figure 4-6 for a good example of an in-house budget.

Most budget developers add 10 to 15 percent to each conservative estimate for unexpected overruns. The larger and longer the production, the more chances for error and bad luck. The weather may be uncooperative, causing delays in shooting. Equipment can break down, segments may need to be reshot, and prices may increase between budgeting time and production time. While it's unwise to pad the budget excessively, it is always better to come in under budget than to exceed it. Of course, all the calculations mentioned so far will merely cover the costs of a production; if your department is a profit center, or if you work for a production house, you'll need to help the company make a profit, too. Remember, you need somehow to cover the costs of new equipment, overhead, staff training, and *then* make a profit for the owners or stockholders.

Writing up the budget is just the first stage, though. Budget management is an ongoing process throughout the project. The producer must keep tabs on the expenditures under each category to ensure that they stay within the allotment. This accounting should be done on a regular basis whenever payments are made, keep-

```
GEORGIA POWER COMPANY - TRAINING & MEDIA SERVICES      PRODUCTION BUDGET

PROD. # 860156     'WHEN THE LIGHTS GO OUT'                      01/12/87

CLIENT: CONSUMER AFFAIRS                  CONTACT: LYNN MILLER / 526-2334
------------------------------------------------------------------------

ABOVE-THE-LINE:
PRE-PRO/SCOUT   : T. BOISSEAU          (FLAT) -      100.00       100.00
SCRIPTWRITER    : S. SHOER             (FLAT) -    1,500.00     1,500.00
TALENT #1       : G. HOLLYFIELD        2 DAYS X      381.70       763.40
TALENT #2       : TBA                  (FLAT) -      150.00       150.00
CONTINGENCY     : CONTINGENCY          (FLAT) -    1,175.00     1,175.00
COURIER         : FLASH                1 TRIP  X        8.00         8.00
                                                              ------------
                      ABOVE-THE-LINE SUBTOTAL - $             3,696.40
PRODUCTION:
LIGHTS          : BOISSEAU/PSA         2 DAYS  X      476.00       952.00
EXPENDABLES     : MISC. ITEMS          2 DAYS  X       68.00       136.00
LIGHT DIRECTOR  : T. BOISSEAU          2 DAYS  X      200.00       400.00 *
CAMERA OPR. #1  : J. GODWIN            3 DAYS  X      225.00       675.00 *
MAKEUP          : D. CHURCHMAN         2 DAYS  X      200.00       400.00 *
GRIP TRUCK      : T. BOISSEAU          2 DAYS  X      135.00       270.00
COURIER         : FLASH                4 TRIPS X        8.00        32.00
3/4 in. TAPE    : MINI CASS.          10 EACH  X       21.85       218.50
AUDIO TAPE      : VO NARRATION         1 EACH  X        9.95         9.95
STOCK FOOTAGE   : STORM FOOTAGE        (FLAT)  -      650.00       650.00
PROPS           : PROPS                (FLAT)  -       50.00        50.00
        (* PERSONNEL - $     1,475.00)                        ------------
                      PRODUCTION SUBTOTAL - $                 3,793.45
POST PRODUCTION:
3/4 DUBS        : PROGRAM DUBS         5 EACH  X       17.55        87.75
MISC.           : 30:00 CASS.          3 EACH  X       17.55        52.65
                                                              ------------
(B-T-L SUB. = $  3,933.85)    POST PRODUCTION SUBTOTAL - $        140.40
                                                              ============
                      TOTAL BUDGET =              $           7,630.25


 BUDGET SUMMARY FOR PROD. # 860156



    ABOVE-THE-LINE SUBTOTAL -                    $   3,696.40



    PRODUCTION SUBTOTAL -             $   3,793.45



    POST PRODUCTION SUBTOTAL -        $    140.40
                                                 ------------
    BELOW-THE-LINE SUBTOTAL -                    $   3,933.85
                                                 ------------
    TOTAL BUDGET =                               $   7,630.25
                                                 ============
```

Figure 4-6 A typical budget for an internally-produced program (*courtesy, Georgia Power Company*).

ing an accurate balance and forecasting future expenditures. If certain categories seem to be running over the estimates, prompt action should be taken. You may be able to pare down future expenses, transfer money between budget categories, or perhaps even negotiate for an increase in the budget from your client. Crucial to this process is staying on top of the actual balance from day to day and not letting the paperwork build up and costs get out of hand. Most budget overruns happen when a large number of small expenses suddenly and unexpectedly mount up at the end of a project.

Accounting should be done on ledger paper or on a computer spreadsheet, with separate sections for each budget category. (See Figure 4-7). The item description, the person or company paid, the amount, the date, and the method of payment (cash, purchase order, charge, or whatever) should be recorded. Don't wait for your organization's budget printout to see where you stand; they're often four to six weeks behind. Save all receipts; this is especially important when crew members purchase items in an emergency, using their own money, and need to be reimbursed later. Receipts and accurate records are, of course, also mandatory for tax purposes.

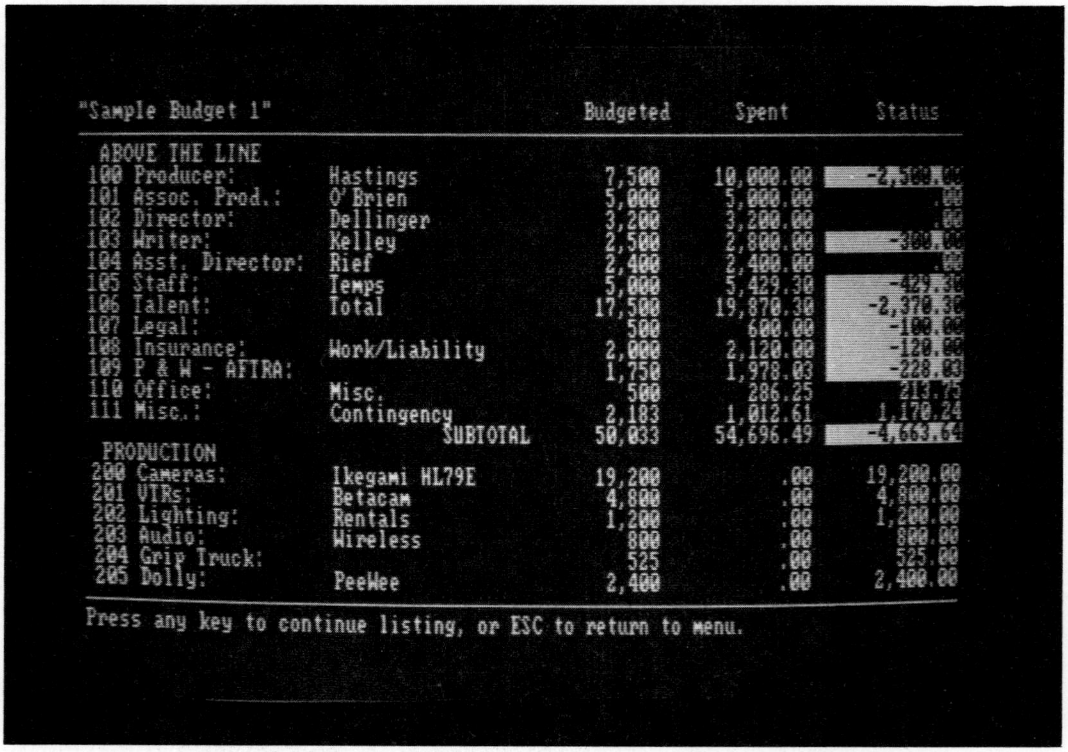

"Sample Budget 1"		Budgeted	Spent	Status
ABOVE THE LINE				
100 Producer:	Hastings	7,500	10,000.00	-2,500.00
101 Assoc. Prod.:	O'Brien	5,000	5,000.00	.00
102 Director:	Dellinger	3,200	3,200.00	.00
103 Writer:	Kelley	2,500	2,800.00	-300.00
104 Asst. Director:	Rief	2,400	2,400.00	.00
105 Staff:	Temps	5,000	5,429.30	-429.30
106 Talent:	Total	17,500	19,870.30	-2,370.30
107 Legal:		500	600.00	-100.00
108 Insurance:	Work/Liability	2,000	2,120.00	-120.00
109 P & W - AFTRA:		1,750	1,978.03	-228.03
110 Office:	Misc.	500	286.25	213.75
111 Misc.:	Contingency	2,183	1,012.61	1,170.24
	SUBTOTAL	50,033	54,696.49	-4,663.64
PRODUCTION				
200 Cameras:	Ikegami HL79E	19,200	.00	19,200.00
201 VTRs:	Betacam	4,800	.00	4,800.00
202 Lighting:	Rentals	1,200	.00	1,200.00
203 Audio:	Wireless	800	.00	800.00
204 Grip Truck:		525	.00	525.00
205 Dolly:	PeeWee	2,400	.00	2,400.00

Press any key to continue listing, or ESC to return to menu.

Figure 4-7 Budgeting software, like Budget Master, assists you in developing and maintaining production expenses (*courtesy, Comprehensive Video Corporation*).

Interactive video programs add even more complexity to the budgeting process (Figure 4-8). In addition to video production, you need to account for programming, videodisc pressing, and often specialized design and hardware resources. Don't forget to budget in money for duplication and distribution, also.

Let's try an example of budgeting: You are contracted to produce a program featuring a new method of teaching wildlife education to elementary school students. You need to tape an approximately one-hour lesson in each of three schools:

```
MARKETING SERVICES   -   INTERNAL QUOTES   (Confidential)
NIT Production Support

Project:_____          Project #_____


                        Planned      Unit      Item
ITEM                    Weeks        Cost      Totals
--------------------    -------    -------    --------
DIRECT LABOR - NIT
   Project Admin.                     .00       .00
   Script/Storyboard/Plan             .00       .00
   Video Producer                     .00       .00
   Graphic Producer                   .00       .00
   Software Producer                  .00       .00
   _____              .00       .00
                        -------               --------
Sub-Total Dir. Labor    .00 weeks              .00
   (100% Burden)                               .00
                                             --------
TOTAL DIRECT LABOR                                        .00

                        QTY   PER UNIT   TOTALS
INDIRECT EXPENSES
   SME's (42.50/52.50)                         .00
   Equip. Rental                               .00
   Facilities Rental                           .00
   Set/Prop Rental                             .00
   Talent/Announcer                            .00
   Music                                       .00
   Supplies:                                   .00
      BETACAM Tapes                            .00
      One Inch Master Tapes                    .00
      Diskettes/duplicated                     .00
      Slide Film/Processing                    .00
      misc.                                    .00
   Checkdiscs                                  .00
   Videodisc Mastering                         .00
   Replicates/Duplication                      .00
   Art/Text Editing                            .00
   Printing                                    .00
   Package Assembly                            .00
   Mail (Shipping)                             .00
   Photography                                 .00
   Travel (Air/Miles)                          .00
      Lodging/day                              .00
      Meals/day                                .00
      Car Rental/Taxi/etc.                     .00
   _____                       .00
   _____                       .00
   _____                       .00
                                             --------
TOTAL INDIRECT EXPENSES                                   .00
                                                      ==========
TOTAL PROJECT QUOTE                                       .00
```

Figure 4-8 The budget for an interactive video program adds things like software producers and videodisc mastering to the cost (*courtesy, Darlene Spence, NCR Corporation*).

one is within your town and about ten minutes from your door; one is two hours away; and one is five hours away. All the lessons are done in the morning. After each lesson, you are to tape some interviews and testimonials with teachers and students. You will be the producer, but you need to rent out portable production equipment and hire two crew members. What are the budgeting factors to consider here?

First of all, remember travel. Although you might not be taping, you are tying up the equipment and the crew. Check with your rental agency and see what their rates are for travel time.

Second, remember that equipment cannot be set up instantly. Generally, it takes about an hour to unload, set up equipment and lights, get audio levels, and begin taping.

Therefore, for the five-hour distance, you'll need to leave the day before. For the two-hour distance, you may be able to leave early in the morning—if your crew is willing to get up early. Don't forget that it takes time to pick up and load the equipment and crew, too.

Finally, remember that it will probably take at least two hours to tape the lesson and the testimonials.

Therefore, you can see than an hour of "shooting" is really more like a half-day (for local shoots) to a day and a half (for out-of-town shoots) and you need to budget accordingly. You'll have to pay the crew's hotel and meal charges for the overnight and pay at least car expenses and lunches for even the local shoots. Work out with any crew you'll hire exactly what they charge for travel time.

FINDING ADDITIONAL RESOURCES

All too often, a video producer finds that funds are insufficient to produce a program of the quality desired. This is unfortunately a common situation among independent producers, not-for-profit organizations, and educational institutions. But it occurs as well in business and industry. When this happens, you might think of turning to outside or nontraditional funding sources: grants, contracts, bartering, sponsorship, and selling programs.

Grants. These are funds provided to an individual or organization (almost exclusively to not-for-profit agencies) for a specific type of work that is seen as beneficial to the public. Grants come from two major sources—the government and private foundations. It takes quite a bit of legwork to find a funding source appropriate to a particular concept for a program, but it's well worth the effort. There are literally millions of dollars available each year for the production of video programs; the only trick is finding an agency and convincing them that you have a worthwhile idea.

The first step in getting your idea funded is finding out who has the money and what they're interested in supporting. The *Catalog of Federal Domestic Assistance* lists funding programs sponsored by government agencies; of course, you will find many that are unsuitable for your needs, but quite a few do support public information or educational goals that could be accomplished through video. The catalog is available from the Government Printing Office in Washington, D.C. Other sources may also list government grants: the *Federal Register, Commerce Business Daily, The Chronicle of Higher Education*, and the newsletters or magazines of many professional associations will keep you informed about programs and the deadlines for submission of proposals.

Government-sponsored endowments, such as the National Endowment for the Arts (NEA) and the National Endowment for the Humanities (NEH) also commonly support media productions. Each of these agencies has a number of funding programs aimed at different goals with different guidelines. The National Endowment for the Humanities also funds state humanities agencies, which in turn fund programs related to humanities issues within the state (Figure 4-9). The grants offered by state agencies are smaller, but they are a bit easier to obtain and have simpler proposal formats.

Private foundations are another source of funding, although they are a bit trickier to find. The Foundation Center in New York City is a clearinghouse for information about private foundations. Often large companies, such as Exxon, or individual family businesses, such as Rockefeller, Newhouse, or Annenberg, set up large trusts of money to be donated towards the support of some particular stated goals.

In order to get funding, you need to write a proposal. Some agencies have specific programs with set criteria for what will be funded, who is eligible, what the funding limit is, and how the proposal should be written. The agencies send out a *request for proposals* (RFP) detailing their guidelines and the submission deadline. You can get on an agency's mailing list, or watch the periodicals in which programs are announced, and write each agency for a copy of its RFP.

Other organizations merely announce their objectives and accept unsolicited proposals at any time. Often you can start with a brief letter of inquiry to see if they're interested in your general idea before writing up a full-blown proposal. This practice is more typical of private foundations than government agencies.

When looking over an agency's programs, don't look only for something specifically dealing with "media" or "video" or "television:" These are merely a means to an end. Programs that support art, public information and debate, or education often will fund video programs that can help accomplish their goals. For instance, the Department of Education or the Department of Energy might have specific branches that fund the dissemination of information or curriculum materials, which could include video. Your organization may have a file of funding sources, which might be appropriate targets. It's always a good idea to see if anyone else in your organization has had experience in getting similar proposals funded. Most organizations, in fact, require that you develop proposals with their office of contracts and grants or the director of development, since they are the professionals in money-raising and need to coordinate a formal sign-off committing your organization's resources to a project.

Proposal writing is an art and a science: in a few pages you have to establish a strong argument in favor of an agency's funding your program idea. Although formats vary, every proposal seeks to answer the basic questions:

- What is the need for the program?
- What is your specific program idea, and how does it effectively address the stated needs?
- What are your (your organization's) qualifications to do this?
- How will you go about doing it?
- How can you do it better than other competing applicants?
- How much money are you requesting, and how do you intend to spend it?
- Are any other organizations (including your own organization) donating money or in-kind services towards the project?

Usually, RFPs set down specific requirements for the proposal format, the number of copies to be submitted, and guidelines for how the proposals will be evaluated. Most of them have tight deadlines, and many proposals have their finishing touches written in the taxi on the way to hand deliver to the agency! Time

NEH APPLICATION COVER SHEET

OMB No. 3136-0086
Expires 2/29/89

1. Individual applicant or project director
a. Name and mailing address

Name _____
(last)   (first)   (initial)

Address _____

_____

_____
(city)   (state)   (zip code)

b. Form of address: ⬚

c. Social
Security # _____ Date of birth _____
(mo day yr)

d. Telephone number
Office: _____/_____ Home: _____/_____
(area code)   (area code)

e. Major field of applicant
or project director _____ ⬚
(code)

f. Citizenship ☐ U.S.
☐ Other _____
(specify)

2. Type of applicant
a. ☐ by an individual   **b.** ☒ through an org./institute
If a, indicate an institutional affiliation, if applicable, on line 11a.
If b, complete block 11 below and indicate here:
c. Type
d. Status

3. Type of application
a. ☐ new   **c.** ☐ renewal
b. ☐ revision and resubmission   **d.** ☐ supplement
If either **c** or **d**, indicate previous grant number:
_____

4. Program to which application is being made ⬚
  Humanities Projects in Media
Endowment Initiatives: _____
(code)

5. Requested grant period
From: _____   To: _____
(month year)   (month/year)

6. Project funding
a. Outright funds $ _____
b. Federal match $ _____
c. Total from NEH $ _____
d. Cost sharing $ _____
e. Total project costs $ _____

7. Field of project ⬚   **8. Descriptive title of project**

9. Description of project (do not exceed space provided)

10. Will this proposal be submitted to another government agency or private entity for funding?
(if yes, indicate where and when):

11. Institutional data
  a. Institution or organization:

(name)

(city)   (state)
  b. Name of authorizing official:

(last)   (first)   (initial)

(title)

(signature)   (date)

c. Name and mailing address of the institutional grant administrator

(last)   (first)   (initial)

_____

(city)   (state)   (zip code)

Telephone: _____/_____ Form of address ⬚
(area code)

12. Federal debt status
I certify that I am not delinquent on repayment of any federal debt.

This institution certifies that it is not delinquent on repayment of any federal debt.

_____
(signature, person named in Block 1)

_____
(signature, authorizing official named in Block 11b)

Note: Federal law provides criminal penalties of up to $10,000 or imprisonment of up to five years, or both, for knowingly providing false information to an agency of the U.S. government. 18 U.S.C. Section 1001.

Please check appropriate boxes:
☐ Adult   ☐ Radio   ☐ Planning   ☐ Production
☐ Children   ☐ Television   ☐ Scripting

For NEH use only
Date received
Application #
Initials

Figure 4-9 Grants for educational and public-service programming can be obtained by writing proposals to agencies; note all the detail and work that goes into a grant application (*courtesy, National Endowment for the Humanities*).

Continuing Information Sheet

The following information must be provided on the first page of the proposal. Do not exceed one side of one page. Please write at the top of the page: COVER SHEET CONTINUATION (in capital letters, underlined). NOTE: This is an important part of the application and should be prepared carefully and thoughtfully.

(a) Give a brief history and description of the organization or entity proposing this project.

(b) Identify the specific humanities theme(s) and areas on which the project will be based.

(c) Define the specific program format and length.

(d) List the principal professional staff and key consultants who will be working on this project. Underline their names, and identify them by occupation or institutional affiliation. Tell what role or title each will have in the project.

Budget (see page 36) NOTE: Applicants proposing production projects may use the standard industry form in place of the NEH budget form. However, those doing so must complete the NEH Summary Budget page (Section B, page 4).

Table of Contents

Application Narrative

The project narrative provides a substantive description of the concepts informing a project and the format for conveying them. THE APPLICATION NARRATIVES FOR ALL CATEGORIES OF SUPPORT (PLANNING, SCRIPTING, AND PRODUCTION) SHOULD PROVIDE A DISCUSSION OF THE FOLLOWING ITEMS:

- A description of the request and of future requests anticipated from the Endowment for the same project. Example: "This is a request for planning funds leading to the development of a project about....We anticipate that subsequent proposals will be made to the Endowment for scripting and production support." Example: "This is a request for funds leading to the completion of a dramatic script for a thirty-minute pilot television program. The eventual series will contain thirteen thirty-minute programs, and it is anticipated that a subsequent proposal will be made to NEH for a pilot production and full series funding. It is anticipated that the total cost for the series will be...."

- A concise explanation of the subject matter, its significance to a broad national audience, and the concepts and themes to be explored. The presentation should be analytical, rather than descriptive, and should clearly articulate the project's theoretical framework. This section should also discuss how the project will advance public understanding and appreciation of the humanities.

Figure 4-9 Continued

- A brief description of the history of the project. Indicate the source of the ideas, the research conducted, the collaboration of scholars from disciplines in the humanities, and any previous financial support the project has received.

- A rationale for the proposed format. Justify the medium and the proposed documentary or dramatic format and style in terms of its feasibility, its appropriateness to the topic, its consonance with the project's intellectual and artistic vision, and its ability to fulfill the program's educational goals.

- When appropriate (for example, in proposals for anthropological studies, community studies, etc., whether in a documentary or a dramatic format), the applicant should discuss the history and nature of the relationship between the filmmakers and the community or subject that is the focus of the program. The applicant should be able to provide reasonable assurance that the producers will have access to the people being studied and that the nature of the relationship between the filmmakers and the subjects will not be one of exploitation.

- A clear description of the qualifications and roles of key personnel including an identification of the scholars whose expertise is appropriate for the project and an indication that the professional experience of the production personnel is commensurate to the needs of the project. (Resumes for each and their written commitment to the project should be included in the proposal's appendix; see page 34.)

- A clear, detailed, and comprehensive plan of work for the grant period that gives evidence of continuous collaboration between scholars and production personnel.

- When appropriate, a concise bibliography and/or filmography of relevant items.

IN ADDITION, APPLICATIONS FOR <u>SCRIPTING GRANTS</u> SHOULD PROVIDE THE FOLLOWING:

- If applicable, an explanation of accomplishments made under previous NEH grants to this project.

- An identification of possible scriptwriters(s) with professional experience commensurate with the needs of the project.

- A treatment that illustrates what will be in the script, together with a detailed narrative account of the content and format of the proposed program.

IN ADDITION, APPLICATIONS FOR <u>PRODUCTION GRANTS</u> SHOULD PROVIDE THE FOLLOWING:

- If applicable, an explanation of accomplishments made under previous NEH grants to this project.

Figure 4-9 Continued

- A completed script if the request is for a drama or if it is for a documentary, either a script or a detailed treatment. If the latter, the treatment must include a detailed explication of the themes and issues to be explored, the narration and/or voice over, the visual elements that will be used (including archival footage, photographic stills and location shots), the interviews that would be conducted, and the questions to be asked.

IN ADDITION, PROPOSALS FOR <u>CHILDREN AND YOUTH</u> SHOULD PROVIDE THE FOLLOWING:

- A description of the age group that the program is intended to reach and a rationale that links the subject matter with the age level, the format, and the length of the program.

- An indication of the active collaboration of at least one individual--a child development specialist, child psychologist, children's writer, producer, librarian, or teacher--who can verify that the content and format of the project are appropriate to the age group to which the program is directed. (A resume and written commitment should be included in the proposal's appendix; see below.)

5. <u>Appendices</u>

    (a) <u>Resumes</u>

        <u>A resume should include</u> information on the person's education (including places and dates of degrees and any graduate or advanced professional education). Producers, directors, and other media professionals should list their credits and previous humanities work. <u>No resume should exceed two pages.</u>

        <u>All resumes must be attached in the appendix to the application and be received by the deadline.</u>

        If the resume of a key member of the project's staff cannot be obtained in time for the mailing of the application, applicants may include in its place a one-page summary statement of the person's knowledge, experience, and role in the project. This document, certified by the project director's signature, will serve as the resume for the project participant. <u>Please note, however, that it is most beneficial for applicants to provide the resume of each member on the project's staff and that this substitution should be submitted only in extraordinary circumstances.</u>

    (b) <u>Documentation of Commitment of Participants</u>

        On or attached to each resume, please supply a signed and dated letter of commitment from all key personnel, including consultants, indicating that they have agreed to participate in the project for

Figure 4-9 Continued

the time specified in the proposal, if funded. Such statements are often useful places for participants to indicate their understanding of the project and the degree of collaboration to which they are committed. (Such documentation is unnecessary for clerical staff.)

(c) <u>Treatments and Scripts</u> (for scripting or production applications).

(d) <u>Supporting Materials</u> (visual or audio samples).

A sample of the production work of the key production personnel on the project <u>must be submitted with applications for all categories of support</u>. If possible, provide a work that illustrates an approach similar to that proposed. Please note that the Endowment will not use its copies of previously supported films, tapes, or audiocassettes for this purpose.

(1) The sample must be accompanied by a letter clearly explaining the roles of the project personnel in the production of the sample and the positions they will hold in the proposed film. The applicant may also want to explain how the sample is related to the proposed work.

(2) Samples must be either on 16mm film, 3/4" or 1/2" videocassette, or audiocassette. Films should be loaded on standard projection reels, heads out, in cases.

(3) Films on 35mm and 1", 2", or some foreign videotapes cannot be projected or played for the panel. Please check with the program staff if there are any questions about the program's ability to show the sample film or tape.

(4) It is crucial that applicants preview tapes before submitting them to ensure that there are no technical problems (faulty dubbing, over modulation, cross-talk, etc.) that might interfere with the panel's review of the work.

(5) Producers submitting proposals for post-production or works in progress must send samples of that work.

(6) A pilot program should be submitted if the request is for additional programs in a series.

(7) All sample works will be returned after the panel review. The Endowment cannot be responsible for any loss or damage.

All samples must be clearly labeled to indicate:

(1) the name of the project for which it is submitted as supporting material;

(2) the title of the production with a brief description; and

(3) the complete mailing address to which it should be returned.

Figure 4-9 Continued

must also be left for circulating your proposal to the appropriate officers of your organization for their approval; most proposals won't even be accepted by agencies without the signature of your chief executive officer, since the request for a grant implies a significant commitment of resources and administration on the part of the organization as a whole.

RFPs or foundation brochures will always include the name of a person to contact if there are questions. It's advisable to chat with this person to see if your ideas coincide with the agency's and to ascertain better what your chances are of actually being funded. Only a very small number of grant proposals actually get funded, since the competition is generally stiff. If you are not funded, however, federal agencies are required to give you reasons why you were turned down. Seeking grants is always a gamble; there's a lot of energy expended in the proposal writing and a relatively small chance of success. However, many organizations survive quite nicely on grants from various sources, so it *can* be done.

Contracts.   These are more specific than grants. An agency that has a *specific* idea for a product will issue an RFP or an *RFQ* (Request for Quotation) for a contract job. For instance, rather than merely supporting general consumer information materials such as a grant would, a contract would call for the production of twelve 30-second broadcast television spots on food shopping. With contract proposals, you don't have to spend time presenting a needs analysis—the agency has already done this. They know what they want; you just tell them how you will do it and how much it will cost. Contracts certainly don't give you the flexibility to propose your own ideas, but they do make specific exactly what they're interested in funding. If that happens to coincide with *your* interests and expertise, then they're a viable financial alternative.

Contracts and grants can come from government agencies or foundations, or you might try private businesses if your program concept is related to their activities. For instance, if you were interested in teaching children about computer technology, you might approach major computer manufacturers to see if they had any programs that supported this type of objective. Combinations of funding sources can also be sought for large programs, each contributing to a portion of the expenses. In fact, many agencies require that you obtain *matching funding* from other sources. Some agencies will match dollar-for-dollar the amount you can obtain from donations or other grants.

Bartering.   "Swapping" or bartering is a technique that more video producers should employ. Rather than focusing on *money*, the focus is on the *service* needed. For instance, an organization might need several reels of film transferred to videotape but may have no film chain. By calling around to other local video producers, they may be able to trade several hours of use on someone's film chain in return for the use of some of the equipment or personnel. Such cooperative efforts can save the purchase cost of equipment that would seldom be used, and it not only promotes facilities sharing but also idea sharing among professionals.

Another intangible trade-off is experience. What seems like work to you may be an opportunity for a student seeking experience in video. Many colleges, universities, trade schools, and even high schools have internship or cooperative education programs, placing students in jobs for varying lengths of time. These students are generally well trained and highly motivated and can extend a staff at no cost to the participating organization. If a school hasn't called you, call them. Try departments of communication, radio-TV, educational technology, or engineering.

If you need actors or narrators, you might also try drama departments, community playhouses, or dinner theaters. Often aspiring actors welcome the opportunity to work with video. You may be able to trade the production of a short resume tape in return for a free actor or narrator. Musicians and composers are sometimes willing to donate their services in return for a copy of the final production with their names in the credits.

Sponsorship. This is another viable financial support method—especially for independent producers and not-for-profit organizations like public TV stations. In this system, a producer finds a company or companies who may be interested in sponsoring a program. Why would they wish to do this? First, the program may support their product or services; for instance, a program on nutrition might enhance viewers' understanding and use of dairy products, or a program on office automation might feature a particular brand of computers. Second, companies can use donations to a nonprofit group as a tax deduction. Their sponsorship of a successful program providing benefits to the public is good for their image in the community. Sponsorship can imply an outright cash donation or an in-kind contribution of supplies, locations, services, or personnel.

Selling your product to other organizations may be another way to recoup costs. Programs produced for in-house training may be useful to other similar organizations. You can try to market programs to other institutions directly or through a professional association or commercial distributor. Rental or sale of training materials is becoming an increasingly popular means of supporting in-house productions. General information or entertainment programs may also be sold to cable, broadcast, or pay-TV stations and networks.

Many associations or cooperatives for independent producers are being established primarily for the purpose of marketing programs. As distribution channels to the public multiply, the idea of "narrowcasting" special-interest programs is becoming more viable, and the need for well-done informational programming is increasing.

VIDEO AND THE ECONOMY

There's no question that the video budget of an organization is tied to that organization's financial situation. However, the *way* a company responds to its media department when it's having financial headaches depends greatly on the savvy of the video manager. You'd think that when costs must be shaved, the video department would be one of the first things to go; this is the nightmare of many a producer when a company's profits start to slide. After all, video is not the company's product, and the company *could* get by without it. But *should* it?

If the organization's leaders see video as a "frill" or an "extra," its stability is highly dependent on the overall economy and the whims of management. However, if training and communication have been shown to be cost effective, then those programs should flourish—even more so in the face of financial adversity! The key is in linking the benefits of video directly to the bottom line. For instance, well-trained employees are more productive, make fewer mistakes, and have better safety records. Employees kept informed of the company's news and policies may feel a stronger commitment to the organization and may be more motivated to work harder.

Video can also be shown to hold down costs. How much money is being saved in travel by shipping video programs rather than people? Can video be used to "stretch" a teaching staff so fewer people can teach more students? Can teleconferencing widen the circle of employees able to participate in decisions, since they don't have to travel to meetings? Do the flexible hours of video viewing encourage more students to enroll in educational programs or courses?

The response of management to the video department is one that must be

DATE: October 31, 1988

  RE: <u>MEDIA PROGRAMS' THIRD QUARTER 1988 REPORT</u>

FROM: Mark Weiss

  TO: Don Kiblinger

I have compiled the following statistics from the attached
Media Programs' project reports for the third quarter of
1988.

From July 1 through September 30, 1988, Media Programs
received 29 requests for services and completed 38 projects.
An analysis of the commitment codes reveal that:

```
63% (24) projects were completed on or ahead of schedule (#1)
 5% (02) projects were delayed by client changes (#2)
 8% (03) projects were delayed by higher priorities (#3)
 5% (02) projectS were delayed by the client (#4)
 0% (00) projects were delayed by Media Services (#5)
19% (07) projects were cancelled by the client or Media
         Services (#6)
```

During the second quarter of 1988 (April 1 through June 30)
Media Programs received 45 requests for services and
completed 45 projects. An analysis of the commitment codes
from that quarter reveal that:

```
65% (29) projects were completed on or ahead of schedule (#1)
11% (05) projects were delayed by client changes (#2)
09% (04) projects were delayed by higher priorities (#3)
02% (01) project was delayed by the client (#4)
00% (00) projects were delayed by Media Services (#5)
13% (06) projects were cancelled by the client or Media
         Services (#6)
```

A review of the first three quarters of 1988 (January 1
through September 30) reveals that Media Programs received
126 requests for services and completed 117 projects. An
analysis of the commitment codes from the first three
quarters of 1988 reveals that:

```
62% (73) projects were completed on or ahead of schedule (#1)
 9% (10) projects were delayed by client changes (#2)
10% (12) projects were delayed by higher priorities (#3)
 4% (05) projects were delayed by the client (#4)
 1% (01) project was delayed by Media Services (#5)
14% (16) projects were cancelled by the client or Media
         Services (#6)
```

Figure 4-10 The smart video manager keeps accurate track of the
"big picture" in the department and can clearly articulate their
productivity (*courtesy, Mark Weiss, Georgia Power Company*).

The table below summarizes the number of new requests and completed projects for each period.

PERIOD	NEW REQUESTS	COMPLETED
========	==============	===========
07/01-9/30/88	29	38
07/01-9/30/87	40	26
04/01-06/30/88	45	45
04/01-06/30/87	25	36
01/01-03/31/88	52	34
01/01-03/31/87	29	30
01/01-09/30/88	126	117
01/01-09/30/87	94	92

Note:
Monthly blanket numbers have not been included as new projects or completions in the totals.

The table below summarizes the numbers and percentages of new requests received between July 1 and September 30, 1988, and compares the results for the same period in 1987.

	07/01-09/30/88		07/01-09/30/87	
Video	17	59%	19	50%
Slide/Tape, Multi-image	10	34%	14	37%
Print	2	7%	5	13%

A detailed report for the previous quarters of 1988 and 1987 is included under the heading "Media Programs: Projects Received (3rd Quarter 1988)" in with the other printed reports.

MARKETING PROJECTS:

The table below compares the number of Marketing related requests for assistance received by Media Programs and the number of projects completed by the section in the first three quarters of 1988 and 1987. Percentages of those numbers to the total number of requests received and projects completed for each period has also been provided:

PERIOD	NEW REQUESTS	% OF TOTAL	COMPLETED PROJECTS	% OF TOTAL
========	======	======	==========	======
07/01-09/30/88	10	34%	4	11%
04/01-06/30/88	21	47%	8	17%
01/01-03/31/88	17	33%	11	32%
01/01-09/30/88	48	38%	23	20%
01/01-09/30/87	20	21%	9	10%

This report continues to show both the progress and success that Media Programs, the Audio Visual and Graphics sections have accomplished by increasing communication, cooperation and planning between the sections when working on joint projects.

The Media Programs section is appreciative of the professionalism and the efforts that the other sections expend to make the system work.

Figure 4-10 Continued

cultivated. Don't expect to pull off dazzling statistics overnight when you've just been faced with bad news. Tabulate data on the costs and benefits of video regularly, and be sure to keep management up-to-date on your activities. Show that you understand the "bottom line;" be sure to explain your need for expensive new equipment. Look at Figure 4-10, and study the way in which video activity is documented. It's easy for new gear to look like overpriced playthings when their use is not justified.

When asking for a budget increase, be sure to tie it into the results you desire from the extra support. Document the services requested that had to be denied because of lack of facilities or personnel. Show management an example of a production done using the equipment you *want* to buy, and compare it to what you're able to do now.

All of this is not to say that in-house video departments have no worries. In the late 1980s "merger mania" led many companies to abolish or combine the media departments of what was formerly two companies. Many facilities were completely closed; those who fared better merely had staff cutbacks. Many organizations are convinced of the merits of video, but not of doing it *in house*. Companies need to examine if they really need to maintain the overhead of personnel (with benefits and ever-increasing salaries) and equipment when they can conveniently go to the rising number of independent production houses.

Few video departments or production houses close because their programs weren't good enough—it's more often because their financial management wasn't good enough. Be willing to be as careful and creative in your finances as you are in your producing. Be willing to experiment, document, balance budgets, persuade, and seek alternative methods of support—and then enjoy the fruits of your labor.

BIBLIOGRAPHY

BRANDT, R. (1987). *Videodisc Training: A Cost Analysis.* Arlington, VA: Future Systems, Inc.

SCHMIDT, W. (1980). *Media Center Management.* New York: Hastings House.

VAN DEUSEN, R.E. (1984). *Practical AV/Video Budgeting.* White Plains, NY: Knowledge Industry Publications.

5
PRE-PRODUCTION PLANNING

A lot happens between the scripting and the shooting of a production. This crucial set of countless activities and details is generally called *pre-production planning*, and it just may be the key to a producer's success—not to mention his or her sanity.

The efficient use of facilities and personnel necessitates a good deal of production management, so that during the expensive production stage no time is wasted. Talent and crew must be selected, locations scouted out and secured, schedules drawn up (and followed!)—and the list goes on. How much time this all takes varies, of course, but most professionals plan to spend about 60 percent of the working time of a program on preproduction planning.

SCHEDULING

"How long will it take?" That's the next question after "How much will it cost?" Sometimes you won't have much choice in scheduling a production; a client's firm deadline may mean that you have two options: turn down the job or live with the schedule. Many in-house departments take a third approach—take on the job, but sub-contract it to an out-of-house company. In any case, coming up with an accurate schedule is right up there on a list of important skills with coming up with an accurate budget. Examine the critical path in Figure 5-1. Scheduling can be approached in two ways: starting at a given date and working up to a comfortable deadline, or starting with the deadline and working backwards. Using the latter approach, you may often find that you should have started a month ago!

Scheduling is a matter of figuring out two things: how fast can *you* do what's needed and how fast can *others* do what you need them to do. You can probably figure out that the latter is a much harder job. In most of my work, I've found that

Critical Path Production

DATE _____ PROGRAM NO._____

PROJECT NAME_____

COMPLETION DATE: (Target) _____

Job Description	Scheduled Starting Date	Scheduled Completion Date	Actual Completion Date
PREPRODUCTION			
Determine Objectives			
Determine Audience			
Script Meeting/Approval			
First Draft			
Script Meeting/Approval			
Second Draft			
Script Meeting/Approval			
Third Draft			
Arrange Graphics			
Story Board			
PRODUCTION			
Arrange Remotes			
Remote Shoot			
Remote Shoot			
Remote Shoot			
Studio Shoot			
POST PRODUCTION			
Edit			
Approval/Viewing (Work Print)			
Re-edit			
Duplication			
Distribution			

AV0003 Printed in U.S.A.

35000 Curtis Boulevard/Eastlake Ohio 44094-4825/216-266-7551

Figure 5-1 Pre-production planning worksheet (*courtesy, Avid Communications*).

clients don't have a good idea of the amount of time they'll need to spend in order to give you what you need to get the production done to meet their deadline—most delays are because the client gets tied up doing other things or because others within the client's organization want to get involved, too. You'd be surprised how slowly the wheels of major corporations can turn—especially when you're waiting for needed approvals on scripts or locations. A friend of mine in the computer media business prides himself on being able to complete a job before his major client organizations can even complete the paper work to give him a purchase order!

If the program is a complex one, the schedule may reflect an intricate series of interdependent and concurrent activities (see Figure 5-2). Sometimes the timetable takes the form of a list of processes and the days by which each is to be accomplished. Calendars for each project can be useful in laying out dates and locations.

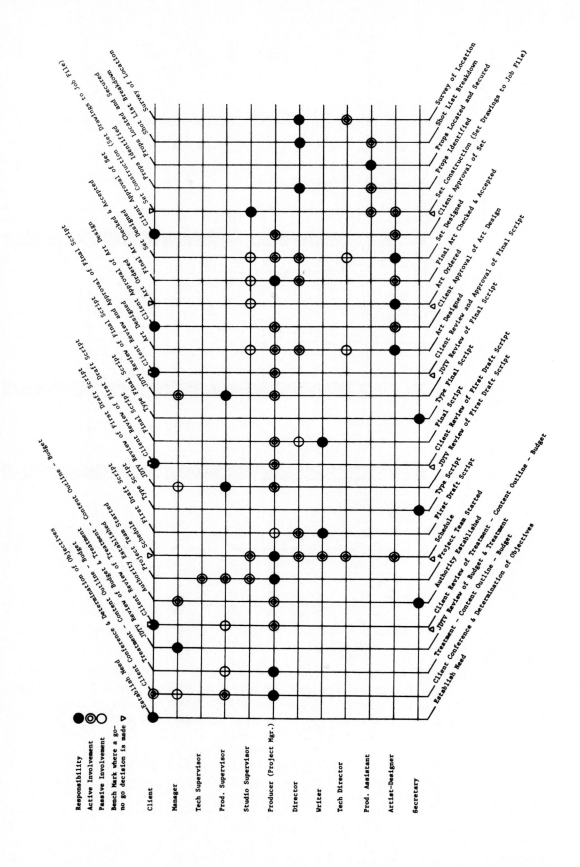

Responsibility ●
Active Involvement ◉
Passive Involvement ◯
Bench Mark where a go-
no go decision is made ▽

Client
Manager
Tech Supervisor
Prod. Supervisor
Studio Supervisor
Producer (Project Mgr.)
Director
Writer
Tech Director
Prod. Assistant
Artist-Designer
Secretary

Survey of Location
Shot List Breakdown
Props Located and Secured
Props Identified (Set Drawings to Job File)
Set Construction of Set
Client Approval of Set
Set Designed
Final Art Checked & Accepted
Final Art Checked & Approval of Art Design
Art Ordered
Client Approval of Final Script
Art Designed
Art Review and Approval of Final Script
Client Review of Final Script
JDTV Review of Final Script
Type Final Script
Final Script
Client Review of First Draft Script
JDTV Review of First Draft Script
Type Script
First Draft Script
Schedule
Project Team Started
Authority Established
Client Review of Treatment - Content Outline - Budget
JDTV Review of Budget & Treatment
Treatment - Content Outline - Budget
Client Conference & Determination of Objectives
Establish Need

136

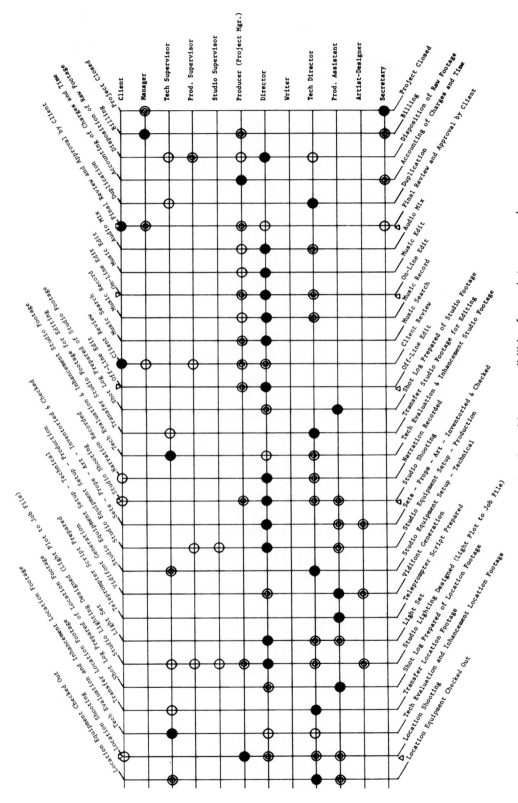

Figure 5-2 A production timeline with responsibilities for each team member (*courtesy, John Deere Television*).

More complicated techniques, such as the PERT chart (for Program Evaluation and Review Technique) designed by the military, are useful in visualizing complex schedules. Today, a number of clever software packages can help you make better decisions about scheduling; they can produce PERT and GANTT charts and show you trouble areas if you get behind in one phase of the project. Other programs let you schedule facilities and staff, and help you in assigning personnel to particular projects. When you've got 13 programs and 6 staff to coordinate over a couple of months, it's important to know when any given project can get into the studio, when it can have access to the editing equipment, or when you will have any 3 people available on the same day to go on an out-of-town shoot.

Before attempting to fix taping dates, rework your script into a *shooting script* which separates out all the shots done in the same location. In this way you can see how much is to be shot in each place and how many locations are necessary. Take a look at the planning documents in Figure 5-3. In producing a schedule, the producer should keep in mind some basic questions:

- How many days will it take to accomplish each specific task?
- How much travel is necessary, and how do travel days figure into the picture?
- What tasks can be done concurrently?
- What events have fixed availability dates—such as special events that must be shot or approvals that must be granted by a company officer who will be in town only during a certain time span?
- What allowances should be made for "rain dates," re-scheduling, or re-shooting?
- How do other productions or personnel commitments impact on the schedule?
- What approval points must be built in, and what happens if one element does not receive approval?
- Is there a date that the client needs the program, such as for a specific presentation or for airing over a satellite teleconference on a specific day?

A good way to lay out a schedule is to write each production step down on an index card or post-it note and then estimate the number of days it will take to accomplish each step. Start laying out the cards in a horizontal fashion. Position those tasks that must be accomplished first to the *left* of each step Those steps that can be worked on simultaneously can be positioned above or below, making vertical columns for concurrent activities. Star those items that, if delayed, will cause hold-ups in accomplishing other jobs. For example, if a script has not been approved, you can't record the narration. You can now transfer this time plot to a calendar or time line.

Remember, this is your best estimate of the production schedule. One of our clients gave us *his* version of how to come up with a target completion date for a project:

Take your best estimate of the time it will take to complete the project. Add one. Then increment it by the next level of time. For example, if you think the project will take 4 weeks, add one to get 5 weeks, and then increment the measure of time from weeks to months. So, your project will really take 5 months. A two-day job will take 3 weeks; a five-hour edit session will be done in six days. Sounds depressing doesn't it?

This "formula" may be a bit extreme, but it does put into perspective that, unfortunately, few project are done "on time." Great, you think—I'll have longer to do my projects, then. Yes, but it'll be longer until you get paid!

We usually plan to have at least one extra shoot on complex productions "just in case." Clients never mind if things have gone so well that a shoot can be cancelled. However, adding a shoot is not so easy—and it can be embarrassing if the fault was yours. I also tell my students to expect that one shoot will be completely "blown." Especially in an academic environment with well-worn equipment and novice crews, it's probable that something will go wrong. When that one shoot turns out to be totally worthless, my students just say to themselves, "Well, that was it, just as I had expected." They and their clients aren't so horrified that the entire production from then on has a cloud over it. You might also tell amateur talent that you want to do a complete "rehearsal"; in your mind, you hope that it will in fact be the final shoot, but the talent is more relaxed thinking that it's only practice. If it turns out OK, your talent and clients are incredibly pleased . . . again much better than having to "re-shoot." **The rule: always add one.**

How long does a shoot take? That's a good question. Novice producers (and almost all clients) grossly underestimate this. If you're going to shoot a 5-minute interview in somebody's office, how long will it take? **My rule of thumb: nothing takes under half a day**. Remember, you've got to spend some time talking to the client and talent, arranging audio and lighting levels, doing some rehearsal, and looking at what you've done. If your shoot is on location (as most of them are these days), you've got to find the building (leave some time to get lost or tied up in traffic), park, unload, scout the building, unpack, shoot, wait until the lights have cooled off to re-pack, and so on. See what I mean?

Once a schedule of events has been fixed, you should prepare a more detailed list of all the individual tasks necessary to the administration of the production. For instance, when talent is used, how will the performers be selected? Who will find out what actors or narrators are available, and how will they be screened? When should letters confirming the various production dates and places be sent? When should supplies be ordered and checked? Although these picky details seem insignificant, many a taping has had to be called off at the last moment because someone didn't remind the talent when to show up or because the crew suddenly ran out of videotape stock.

Just like budgeting, scheduling is about 75 percent a maintenance function. That is, the job's not through when the dates are laid out. If a given event can't occur on schedule, it may knock the whole remainder of the schedule out of kilter. Then the whole process of reserving equipment, facilities, and personnel time must begin again. When working with outside rental facilities or in a busy in-house production center where there's a heavy demand for equipment and where many simultaneous projects are being produced, readjusting schedules may turn into a nightmare. For this reason, producers usually reserve more time than they estimate will be necessary to ensure equipment availability in case of delays. Remember, however, that most production houses and freelancers require a 24—to 48-hour notice of cancellation, or else normal fees will be charged whether or not the services are actually used.

The key to staying within a schedule is twofold. One, *experience* is needed in estimating the time necessary to accomplish the various phases of production; if you don't have the experience, ask someone who does. You need to know how fast your particular crew can do a job. For instance, I know that a certain kind of production usually takes 1 hour of editing for each finished minute of program. I also know that it usually takes 3 hours to set up, record, and strike equipment for a finished 10-minute piece of narration (and more if we're using nonprofessional talent or un-

```
SCENE/SHOT  PROPS REQUIRED
----------  ------------------------------------------------------
0002/0002   SWEATER, GLASSES
0003/0001   TEA POT, TEA BAGS, A RADIO, COOKING UTENSILS
0003/0002   RADIO
0003/0003   RADIO
0003/0004   RADIO, FLASHLIGHT
0003/0005   FLASHLIGHT
0003/0006   FLASHLIGHT
0005/0004   CLIPBOARD, HARDHAT
0006/0001   TELEPHONE, TABLE, CUP OF TEA, SAUCER, SPOON, CONDIMENTS
0007/0002   FLASHLIGHT, TRANSISTOR RADIO, BATTERIES
0007/0003   CANNED FOOD
0007/0004   BLANKETS, SWEATERS
0008/0001   GPC RESIDENTIAL CUSTOMER HANDBOOK, (SEE 0006/0001)
0010/0002   FLASHLIGHT
0010/0003   PHONE BOOK, FLASHLIGHT
0011/0001   SWEATER, SOCKS
0012/0001   CURTAINS, WINDEX
0013/0001   TELEVISION, TOASTER, MR. COFFEE, REFRIGERATOR
0014/0001   KITCHEN SINK
0016/0001   REFRIGERATOR
0017/0001   MATCHES, CANDLES, CANDLE HOLDERS
0018/0001   CAN OPENER, CAN OF TUNA FISH, LOAF OF BREAD
0023/0001   FIREPLACE, KNITTING NEEDLES, AFGHAN, CAT, LOGS
0025/0001   FIREPLACE, KNITTING NEEDLES, AFGHAN, CAT
0026/0001   TELEVISION, TOASTER, REFRIGERATOR
```

```
SCENE/SHOT  PROPS REQUIRED
----------  --------------------------------
PROP SOURCE: ANN RUSSELL
-----------  --------------------------------
0003/0001   COOKING UTENSILS
0003/0001   TEA POT
0007/0003   CANNED FOOD
0007/0004   BLANKETS
0007/0004   SWEATERS
0010/0003   PHONE BOOK
0017/0001   CANDLES & CANDLE HOLDERS
0018/0001   CAN OF TUNA FISH/LOAF OF BREAD

PROP SOURCE: GLADYS HOLLYFIELD
-----------  --------------------------------
0002/0002   GLASSES
0002/0002   SWEATER
0011/0001   SOCKS
0023/0001   KNITTING NEEDLES

PROP SOURCE: H. HARRINGTON
-----------  --------------------------------
0023/0001   FIREPLACE

PROP SOURCE: LYNN MILLER
-----------  --------------------------------
0003/0001   RADIO
0003/0001   TEA BAGS
0003/0004   FLASHLIGHT
0008/0001   GPC RESIDENTIAL CUST. HANDBOOK
0013/0001   TOASTER
0023/0001   AFGHAN

PROP SOURCE: MARK WEISS
-----------  --------------------------------
0018/0001   CAN OPENER (HAND)

PROP SOURCE: MEDIA SERVICES
-----------  --------------------------------
0007/0002   BATTERIES
0012/0001   WINDEX

PROP SOURCE: TELECOMMUNICATIONS
-----------  --------------------------------
0006/0001   TELEPHONE
```

Figure 5-3 Pre-production planning includes prop lists, audio requirements, graphics, and locations; database management software can help keep track of the details and print out production reports (*courtesy, Mark Weiss, Georgia Power Company*).

SCENE/SHOT: 0001/0001
DESCRIPTION: SHOTS OF STORM: GREY SKIES, RAIN, LIGHTNING, ETC.
AUDIO SOURCES: BGS/WEATHER SFX/MUSIC #1-IN

SCENE/SHOT: 0002/0001
DESCRIPTION: DISSOLVE TO W.S. OF MARTHA'S HOUSE
AUDIO SOURCES: BGS/WEATHER SFX/MUSIC #1

SCENE/SHOT: 0002/0002
DESCRIPTION: ZOOM IN TO MCU OF DOOR AS IT OPENS & MARTHA LOOKS OUT
AUDIO SOURCES: BGS/WEATHER SFX/MUSIC #1-OUT

SCENE/SHOT: 0003/0001
DESCRIPTION: DISSOLVE TO MS MARTHA IN HER KITCHEN MAKING TEA
AUDIO SOURCES: BGS/MUSIC FROM RADIO #2-IN,OUT

SCENE/SHOT: 0003/0002
DESCRIPTION: CU OF RADIO, MARTHA MOVES TO MAKE IT LOUDER
AUDIO SOURCES: BGS/VO FORECAST-IN

SCENE/SHOT: 0003/0003
DESCRIPTION: MCU MARTHA LISTENING TO THE RADIO
AUDIO SOURCES: BGS/VO FORECAST

SCENE/SHOT: 0003/0004
DESCRIPTION: WS MARTHA TURNS OFF RADIO, LOOKS FOR FLASHLIGHT & TESTS
AUDIO SOURCES: BGS/VO FORECAST-OUT
NOTES 1: MARTHA TESTS FLASHLIGHT BY SHINING IT INTO THE CAMERA

SCENE/SHOT: 0003/0005
DESCRIPTION: CHYRON: WHEN THE LIGHTS GO OUT IN GEORGIA.......
AUDIO SOURCES: BGS
NOTES 1: MARTHA TESTS FLASHLIGHT BY SHINING IT INTO THE CAMERA

SCENE/SHOT: 0003/0006
DESCRIPTION: CHYRON: (SAME 0003/0005)....GEORGIA POWER IS THERE
AUDIO SOURCES: BGS/SYNC
NOTES 1: MARTHA TESTS FLASHLIGHT BY SHINING IT INTO THE CAMERA

SCENE/SHOT: 0007/0000   TYPE: GRP
SCENE NAME: STORM PREPARATION (GRAPHIC)
DESCRIPTION: GRAPHIC WITH WINDOW FOR B-ROLL INSERTS
AUDIO SOURCES:
NOTES 1:
NOTES 2:

SCENE/SHOT: 0008/0002   TYPE: GRP
SCENE NAME: RES. CUST. HANDBOOK PAGE (GRAPHIC)
DESCRIPTION: CHYRON: GEORGIA POWER'S STORM PLANNING TIPS
AUDIO SOURCES: VO-NARRATOR
NOTES 1: SEE SCRIPT FOR POINTS, CLAP OF THUNDER AT END OF SCENE
NOTES 2:

SCENE/SHOT: 0010/0003   TYPE: KEY
SCENE NAME: POWER OUT (GRAPHIC)
DESCRIPTION: CHYRON: REPORT OUTAGE TO GEORGIA POWER
AUDIO SOURCES:
NOTES 1: GRAPHIC IN: "....FIRST, REPORT THE DAMAGE TO GA. POWER...."
NOTES 2: GRAPHIC OUT: GRAPHIC OUT WITH CUT AT END OF SCENE

SCENE/SHOT: 0011/0001   TYPE: KEY
SCENE NAME: SWEATER & SOCKS (GRAPHIC)
DESCRIPTION: CHYRON: DRESS WARMLY
AUDIO SOURCES:
NOTES 1: GRAPHIC IN: "LIKE MARTHA......"
NOTES 2: GRAPHIC OUT: "...SENSITIVE TO THE COLD."

SCENE/SHOT: 0012/0001   TYPE: KEY
SCENE NAME: CLOSING CURTAINS (GRAPHIC)
DESCRIPTION: CHYRON: CLOSE CURTAINS TO KEEP HEAT IN
AUDIO SOURCES:
NOTES 1: GRAPHIC IN: "...CLOSE YOUR CURTAINS...."
NOTES 2:

SCENE/SHOT: 0012/0001   TYPE: KEY
SCENE NAME: CLOSING CURTAINS (GRAPHIC)
DESCRIPTION: CHYRON: OPEN CURTAINS WHEN SUNNY TO LET WARMTH IN
AUDIO SOURCES:
NOTES 1:
NOTES 2: GRAPHIC OUT: GRAPHIC OUT WITH CUT AT END OF SCENE

Figure 5-3 Continued

```
1/12/87                WHEN THE LIGHTS GO OUT: MARTHA'S HOUSE              Page    1


   LOCATION:   MARTHA'S HOUSE - BEDROOM
   ---------   ------------------------------------------------

      SCENE/SHOT: 0007/0002       TYPE: INT
      SCENE NAME: STORM PREPARATION-FLASHLIGHT & RADIO
      DESCRIPTION: MS MARTHA PLACING FLASHLIGHT & RADIO IN DRAWER
      AUDIO SOURCES: BGS/VO-MARTHA
      PROPS REQUIRED: FLASHLIGHT, TRANSISTOR RADIO, BATTERIES
      NOTES 1:
      NOTES 2:


      SCENE/SHOT: 0007/0004       TYPE: INT
      SCENE NAME: STORM PREPARATION-BLANKETS & SWEATERS
      DESCRIPTION: TILT DOWN BLANKETS ON SHELF TO SWEATERS HANGING
      AUDIO SOURCES: BGS/VO-MARTHA
      PROPS REQUIRED: BLANKETS, SWEATERS
      NOTES 1:
      NOTES 2:


      SCENE/SHOT: 0011/0001       TYPE: INT
      SCENE NAME: SWEATER & SOCKS
      DESCRIPTION: MS MARTHA PUTTING ON AN EXTRA SWEATER & SOCKS
      AUDIO SOURCES: BGS/SFX-WIND/VO-NARRATOR
      PROPS REQUIRED: SWEATER, SOCKS
      NOTES 1:
      NOTES 2:


   LOCATION:   MARTHA'S HOUSE - BREAKFAST AREA
   ---------   ------------------------------------------------

      SCENE/SHOT: 0006/0001       TYPE: INT
      SCENE NAME: MARTHA'S PHONE CALL
      DESCRIPTION: WS MARTHA ANSWERS TELEPHONE, SITS DOWN AT TABLE TO TALK
      AUDIO SOURCES: BGS/PHONE SFX/SYNC
      PROPS REQUIRED: TELEPHONE, TABLE,CUP OF TEA, SAUCER, SPOON, CONDIMENTS
      NOTES 1:
      NOTES 2:


   LOCATION:   MARTHA'S HOUSE - DEN
   ---------   ------------------------------------------------
```

```
1/09/87                WHEN THE LIGHTS GO OUT: SORT/LOCATION               Page    1


   LOCATION: GPC STOCK FOOTAGE LIBRARY
   --------- ------------------------------------------------
      SCENE/SHOT: 0001/0001   TYPE: EXT
      SCENE NAME: OMINOUS WEATHER
      DESCRIPTION: SHOTS OF STORM: GREY SKIES, RAIN, LIGHTNING, ETC.
      AUDIO SOURCES: BGS/WEATHER SFX/MUSIC #1-IN

      SCENE/SHOT: 0004/0001   TYPE: EXT
      SCENE NAME: BRANCH TRIMMING
      DESCRIPTION: SHOTS OF TREES & BRANCHES BEING TRIMMED
      TALENT: GPC LINECREW
      AUDIO SOURCES: BGS/VO-NARRATOR/MUSIC #2-IN
      NOTES 1: GPC LINECREW TRIMMING  TREES AND BRANCHES

      SCENE/SHOT: 0005/0003   TYPE: INT
      SCENE NAME: STORM CENTER
      DESCRIPTION: MONTAGE OF STORM CENTER ACTIVITY
      AUDIO SOURCES: BGS/VO-NARRATOR/MUSIC #2-UP

      SCENE/SHOT: 0005/0004   TYPE: EXT
      SCENE NAME: STORM CENTER
      DESCRIPTION: LINE CREW REVIEWING DAMAGE AND TAKING NOTES
      AUDIO SOURCES: BGS/VO-NARRATOR/MUSIC #2-OUT
      PROPS REQUIRED: CLIPBOARD, HARDHAT

      SCENE/SHOT: 0007/0001   TYPE: EXT
      SCENE NAME: STORM PREPARATION-HOUSE INSULATION
      DESCRIPTION: INSULATION, CAULKING & WEATHERSTRIPPING ACTIVITY
      AUDIO SOURCES: BGS/VO-MARTHA

      SCENE/SHOT: 0009/0001   TYPE: EXT
      SCENE NAME: OMINOUS WEATHER
      DESCRIPTION: LIGHTNING AND DARKENED SKY
      AUDIO SOURCES: SFX-THUNDER
      NOTES 1: ANOTHER CLAP OF THUNDER AND THEN CUT TO LIGHTNING OUTSIDE

      SCENE/SHOT: 0019/0001   TYPE: EXT
      SCENE NAME: DOWNED POWERLINE
      DESCRIPTION: SHOT OF A POWERLINE IN THE STREET
      AUDIO SOURCES: BGS/VO-NARRATOR/MUSIC #3
```

Figure 5-3 Continued

Figure 5-4 Project directors and talent conferring on the planning of a televised educational series (*courtesy, Children's Television Workshop*).

usual settings). Second, *keeping on top of details* is necessary to ensure that little problems don't cause major delays. In this regard, a production assistant or administrative aide can make a production run much more smoothly by making the phone calls and taking care of the correspondence necessary to reserve and confirm facilities, personnel, travel arrangements, supplies, and contacts.

TALENT AND CREWS

Another responsibility of the video producer is the coordination of personnel, both in front of and behind the camera. In some productions there is no choice about the personnel; the talent is an identified subject-matter expert or executive, and the crew may consist of the entire in-house staff. However, when working with freelance personnel, the screening and selection process may be a large part of the pre-production schedule.

Choosing on-camera narrators and actors is a key element in production design. Too many programs fail because a narrator stumbles through a script or because amateur actors play their roles stiffly and unconvincingly. A big question for organizational video producers is whether or not to use in-house talent.

In-house talent has two big advantages: *credibility* and *price,* and the first factor may just be *the* most important consideration in selecting on-camera people. Nothing turns off an audience faster than obviously coached "pretty faces" reciting memorized lines. Why should anyone believe *them*? Often, they're a sure-fire loser in programs aimed at line workers or employees in "hands-on" kinds of jobs, since they represent "management" or those people who obviously never get their hands dirty in the actual work. An in-house employee with experience who appeals to the audience, and with whom they can identify, is a better choice. For example, I've produced a number of programs for Marine Midland Bank, and we chose to use actual tellers because only they could count money convincingly with the speed and style of a true professional. Marriot Hotels redid an interactive video program on customer relations because the original one using actors looked too "phony." Some companies, like Fisher Scientific, (see Figure 5-5) have used managers as actors,

(a)   (b)

Figure 5-5 In-house talent can add credibility—and sometimes humor—to productions. Here the Chairman of the Board and a division President of Fisher Scientific Company dress up as historical figures for their parts (*courtesy, Fisher Scientific Company*).

even in humorous roles. Also, of course, you can usually get company staff released for a television appearance at no cost.

What about the *disadvantages* of using in-house talent? Again there are two factors: *lack of experience* and *negative recognition*. Most nonprofessionals are awkward at first on camera and may be overly self-conscious. In fact, you may find it difficult to find a willing subject. You may have to spend a great deal of time teaching the amateur about television production and answering endless questions. Often it's difficult to find a subject expert who looks and sounds good on camera and who can be fluent in explaining concepts or adept at memorization. We once had to do more than 30 "takes" of a young engineer explaining, in his own two sentences, what he did every day. Negative recognition occurs when the audience is so wrapped up in watching a familiar person on the screen that the message is lost. This is most frequent in situations calling for the acting out of roles in dramatizations; the viewer may pay so much attention to comparing that role to the person's actual personality that little else is learned. If the person on the screen happens to be an unpopular co-worker, the message may be ignored. If a staff member plays the "bad guy" in a program, it could unconsciously affect the way co-workers would view him or her in the future. Finally, many organizations want to avoid spotlighting a particular employee in case he or she leaves the company.

Freelance talent has the advantage of experience and anonymity—but you pay the price. The cost, however, may be well worth it in terms of the "polish" of the final program and the hours of retakes saved. Many production houses have lists of available actors, as do talent agencies, and local chapters of AFTRA (American Federation of Television and Radio Artists) or SAG (Screen Actors Guild). You might also try colleges and local theater groups for alternatives. You will want to audition prospective talent and probably have your client in on the final selection.

THE "PRISON PLAYERS"

During the mid 70s I was doing lots of drama in my training programs, using actors and actresses from the Baltimore and Washington stage and theater companies. We asked them to play many different types of roles portraying employees and inmates. They became known as the "prison players."

We shot these scenes in a small studio, with sets that didn't do more than approximate the interiors of cells, offices, dayrooms, and so on. Our first set of jail bars was a small piece about 3 feet wide and 5 feet high made of wooden dowels. We did dress the inmates in clothing such as that found in our prisons, and employees wore uniforms or business clothing.

It was not unusual to get calls from field people that had seen the latest training program asking about one or another of the talent. These field people were convinced that they had supervised that individual as an inmate some time in the recent past.

To my knowledge, none of our "prison players" had ever done time, but they could act as though they had. Employees would remark that, "They know exactly how inmates talk and act, they must have done time. I still think I supervised . . . here about four or five years back."

Henry Bohne
Video consultant·
Parker, CO

For voice-only narrations, the range opens up. Since the person need not appear on the screen, he or she can read the script. The criteria here are voice quality and diction—and the ability to read easily without stumbling. Besides the sources listed above, you can look to local radio stations. There are also audio production houses that have numbers of narrators available—most of whom can send you an audio demo tape, and some of whom can offer auditions over the phone.

When working with professional talent, you may find that many are members of AFTRA or SAG. Members of these unions have minimum fees or *scale* which may be quite high, as well as stipulations about calculating fees and setting working conditions.

Selection of crew members is another facet of production administration. Although you might think that for an in-house production, your crew is already picked out for you, increasingly this is not the case: many large video departments have only producer/directors on staff, and they use freelancers as camera operators, audio engineers, editors, and so on. If you are choosing from an in-house crew, assignments are generally rotated among personnel, and people with special skills (and sometimes even special interests) are put on appropriate productions. For instance, someone specializing in lighting may be called upon for location shoots for which you know in advance the lighting will be complicated. Often, outside consultants will be brought in to help with program design, interview questions, interactive video computer programming, or evaluation.

Unions also represent many technical personnel. The International Association of Theatrical and Stage Employees (IATSE), the National Association of Broadcast Employees and Technicians (NABET), and the International Brotherhood of Electrical Workers (IBEW) are unions representing camera operators, engineers, and stage hands at various television stations and production houses. Where union contracts are in place, minimum wages as well as specified overtime and working policies must be considered. Nonunion personnel may also be forbidden to touch certain equipment—so beware of bringing in your own help to unionized production houses. Another union, DGA (Director's Guild of America), covers program directors, production assistants, and floor managers. Their contracts spell out wages and travel policies, as well as their ability to exercise creative control of a production.

Although freelance help is usually abundant, beware of "throwing together" a crew at the last minute. A show cannot progress smoothly until everyone understands its purpose, gets acquainted with co-workers, and knows his or her role and equipment. Every television professional has a slightly different way of approaching a task and uses a slightly different technical language. If you're forced into the situation of assembling a crew from scratch, have a thorough pre-production meeting with all members present, and if possible, schedule a "rehearsal" or easy shoot for the first time. A successful taping session, even involving a limited number of people on a one-camera shoot, is the result of cohesive teamwork. Try to keep the same crew for an entire production—and try to have the person who'll edit the program be in on all or most of the shoots.

SECURING RIGHTS

If you intend to use material (either video or audio) copyrighted by another organization, you need to secure permission for its use. This includes background music, photographs, and clips from other film or video programs. Almost all records, magazine photos, and media programs *are* copyrighted—even if they *aren't* marked as such. Under the new copyright law, all materials that are recorded by print, audio, video, and so on, are *automatically* copyrighted by the producer. Virtually everything is copyrighted—except for government publications and some materials specifically funded by the government for general distribution. **Even if your production is for nonbroadcast, noncommercial, nonprofit use, you still may not violate the copyright laws.** So, who will find out if you sneak in a clip of a Hawaiian beach you taped off the air at home? The answer is probably nobody—but it's stealing nonetheless. And if someone *does* find out, you'll be in court (along with your company), and you'd better look for another profession. **Even "old" material is probably copyrighted**; let's say you want to use a section of Bach's Brandenburg Concerto that you found on an album downtown. You know Bach's been dead for awhile now, and you remember that copyright was only good for something like 100 years. Yes, but the *performance* is copyrighted; look on the album, and you'll see that it's been copyrighted by the company noted on the record label.

In requesting permission to use copyrighted work, you must first find out who holds the copyright. This can be a tangle, because in many cases a number of people own the copyright to different parts of the work (the script, the production itself, and the like). Start by contacting the person or company whose name is listed as the copyright holder (usually at the end of the credits of video or in small print on print materials or records). Then, you must provide the holder of the rights answers to some basic questions:

- What *exactly* do you want to use? (Identify each segment and its length. Tell whether it will be edited, and so on).
- How do you intend to use it?

- What portion (approximately) of your final production will the requested material comprise?
- What is the nature and purpose of the completed program?
- Where and how will the program be distributed?
- Is the program being done on a commercial or nonprofit basis?
- Do you want *exclusive* rights (which would preclude other similar uses of the material by other organizations) or *nonexclusive* rights?
- Do you want rights just for the U.S., several specific countries, or do you need worldwide rights?
- What credit (if any) do you plan to give the holder in the program?

Your inquiry should be addressed to the permissions or legal department of the company. Often you will find that they are exceedingly slow in responding; it may take some persistence to get through to the right person. Once you get an answer, you'll be told if you may use the requested material, what the restrictions might by on its use, and what fees will be charged.

There are, of course, alternatives to using copyrighted materials. You can use materials in the *public domain*—those with no copyright or with expired copyrights. Various branches of the government have uncopyrighted stock footage or photographs on a wide variety of topics—check with the Government Printing Office in Washington, D.C. You can have music or art composed and executed specifically for your production. Or you can secure audio or video segments from commercial libraries handling production music or slides.

Background music is perhaps the most common "ready-made" program element sought by video producers. Although there may be a familiar tune that fits the mood of the show, avoid using popular music. Audiences tend to get so involved in "singing along" with the music that the content is lost. A number of production music libraries exist to provide this type of musical bed for organizational video programs. Generally, albums, tapes, or CDs consist of several brief cuts of tunes with similar orchestrations and moods. Although they can sound terribly boring alone, they blend in well with video and are easy to edit to desired lengths. Refer to Figure 5-6 for a sample catalog and licensing agreement.

Production music libraries operate in any or all of three ways:

- You buy the records, CDs, or tapes outright along with permanent nonexclusive rights to their contents.
- You buy the records and pay a *per needle-drop licensing fee* for each use. Each time you "drop the needle" to play a new segment or to repeat a segment, you must pay a fee—even within the same program.
- You buy the music and pay an *annual licensing fee*, entitling you to unlimited in-house use for a year.

Most of these fees are on a sliding scale, calculated by identifying the type of production, the purpose of the production, its distribution, and the nature of the producing organization. For non-broadcast use, a few minutes of a few cuts of music usually run $100 to $200. Audio is playing an increasingly important role in video (Figure 5-7).

Just like stock music, there are companies that license stock stills and video animation which are very useful, especially for introductions, titles, or credits. They operate in much the same way as licensing music.

If a company hires someone specifically to compose and/or execute music or artwork for a program, the company owns the rights. Full-time staff of an in-house

OMNIMUSIC

52 MAIN STREET   PORT WASHINGTON, N.Y. 11050   (516) 883-0121

Licensee: Invoice to:

Date: License #:   Terms:

For and in consideration of:

the undersigned, as owner or agent for owner of all rights in and to the musical compositions listed
below does hereby grant to the licensee listed above (hereinafter referred to as "licensee") the
irrevocable right to mechanically reproduce and synchronize those compositions as background music
in the production listed below in accordance with the following terms:

1. This license is valid for this production only; alteration of the production may
   require an additional license.
2. The licensee is permitted to duplicate up to 10,000 copies of this production.
3. When productions are licensed for broadcast use, the licensee shall notify stations
   or networks to give performance credit to the publishers.
4. The territory covered by this agreement is the world.
5. The musical compositions may not be duplicated or offered for sale or lease except
   as an integral part of this production.
6. All rights not herein granted are reserved by the undersigned.

Production Title:

Rights Granted:

Compositions:

a

Authorized Signature

Figure 5-6   Sample music licensing contract and catalog listing for
production mustic (*courtesy, OmniMusic*).

production center generally can claim no rights to the work they do there as part of
their jobs. A production house generally has no rights to a program they've done as
work for hire. If you're hiring freelance artists or musicians, it's best to state in their
contracts the fact that you will retain rights to use their work. You should describe
the nature of the intended use and indicate if you even foresee that you'll use it
again at another time.

When you use pictures or recordings that plainly identify individuals, you
must get a *model release* from them (see Figure 5-8). A release form grants an
individual's permission to use his or her likeness or voice for a production. This
procedure is not necessary for crowd shots or for instances when people are not
plainly identified. Other exceptions include photos or tapes of *bona fide* news
events or public figures. Get model releases even from people who work within
your own company—just to be sure. Minors (children under 21) need the signatures
of a parent or legal guardian. So beware if you're going to shoot in a school or day
care center—get those model releases to the teachers and home to parents well
before you plan to shoot—and *don't* get a child in the shot if you don't have a
release.

TITLE	CD#	LP#	TITLE	CD#	LP#
COUNTRY & WESTERN: MEDIUM TEMPO (cont.)			**DRAMATIC (cont.)**		
			Secret Agent	24	154
Hot Saturday Night	20	109	Stake Out	11	151
One of Those Days	20	109	Starship	5	140
Sagebrush	20	123	The Chase	11	151
The Dulcimer	19	109	Twilight	24	127
The Open Road	28	158	Undercover Cop	11	151
			Undercurrent	24	127
COUNTRY & WESTERN: SLOW TEMPO			Urban Jungle	7	143
			ETHNIC		
Bayou Blues	28	158	Aegean Rendezvous	16	138
Meadowlark	20	123	Antigua	16	138
My Breakin' Heart	20	123	Cafe Espana	16	138
River City	20	123	Confrontation	16	138
			Follies Fantasy	16	138
			Fun in the Sun	16	138
DIXIELAND			Havana Express	16	138
			Luck o' the Irish	16	138
Dixie Blue	16	130	San Juan	16	138
Jazzin' out Back	16	130	Tangiers	16	138
Ramblin' Down South	16	130	The Great Wall	16	138
The Joint Is Jumpin'	17	149	Tribal Rhythm	16	138
Uncle Joe's Cafe	16	130	Trouble in the Casbah	16	138
DRAMATIC			**FANFARE OPENINGS**		
Adrenaline	24	127	Championship	14	124
Claws	24	127	Decade of Challenge	23	114
Climax	24	127	Newsmaker	15	148
Covert Operations	24	127	Opening Day	29	159
Discovery	1	145			
Emotion Cues	24	127			
Escape	24	154	**FANFARES: BRASS**		
Footsteps	24	154			
High Voltage	23	113	Building Fanfare #1	15	148
Ice Caves	25	155	Building Fanfare #2	15	148
Ice Man	1	145	Dramatic Fanfare	15	148
Insanity	24	154	Heralding Fanfare	15	148
Intrigue	14	120	Independence	4	139
Night Magic	19	102			
Nowhere to Run	24	127			
Prowler	24	127			
Race Against Time	5	136			

b

Figure 5-6 Continued

CHOOSING LOCATIONS

Selecting taping locations is yet another crucial step in pre-production planning. The proper setting for your talent, the subject matter, *and* the technicalities of the medium is not always easy to come by. Travel budgets, too, are greatly affected by your decisions, and they can be a big portion of the overall production cost.

The primary question is *studio or field*? Studios have one major advantage—*control*; field work has one major advantage—*realism*. Obviously, certain productions lend themselves naturally to one mode or the other; many others use a combination of the two settings. The studio offers built-in lights, soundproofing, cameras, VCRs, and so on, *including* the crew and back-up equipment. But studio sets often look staged and stiff, and often they just cannot recreate the necessary shots. Field production is exciting—and tiring and challenging. Everything must be transported and set up in locations not acoustically, architecturally, or electrically designed for media production. Travel is expensive, tiring, and time consuming. But the richness of the settings usually overrides any inconveniences encountered.

Figure 5-7 Music is an important part of most productions; most production centers license music libraries on compact discs (*courtesy, Avid Communications*).

So important is remote production that many organizations who are heavy media producers have no studio. Instead, they have elegant portable recording equipment and editing suites, and perhaps they may have a small room or *insert stage* used for recording simple narrations. Since so many organizational video programs deal with large immovable equipment (like assembly lines or surgical theaters) or with distant places and events, field production has become increasingly important.

If remote production is selected, the next questions are "Where?" and "When?" Some of the characteristics of good locations are:

- Sufficient room to set up equipment and lights and to obtain a comfortable distance between the camera and the talent
- Ample electrical service for lights
- Pleasing backgrounds with enough detail to provide depth and interest, but not "busy" or "messy" enough to be distracting
- A quiet atmosphere without a lot of noise from people, machinery, traffic, or wind
- Potential for even lighting without glare from windows or large shiny objects
- Freedom from congestion, away from areas where you will disturb or be disturbed by others
- Easy access for loading and unloading equipment

in Cayuga, Schuyler and Tompkins

Healthy Heart Program
Tompkins County Office
401 Harris B. Dates Drive
Ithaca, New York 14850-1386
(607) 273-7272

RELEASE

I give the Cayuga-Tompkins Healthy Heart Program the absolute right and permission to record me by any electronic or photographic audio and/or video means.

I understand that the Cayuga-Tompkins Healthy Heart Program will use the recorded material only for the purposes of promoting the Healthy Heart Program and/or educating an audience about heart disease.

I also release and discharge Cayuga-Tompkins Healthy Heart Program from any and all causes of action and claims on account of or in any way growing out of any known or unknown personal injury, death and property damage resulting or to result from any injuries that might be caused while or because Cayuga-Tompkins Healthy Heart Program is recording me. I also hereby waive any right that I may have to inspect the finished product(s) or their use(s).

Notwithstanding the above, Cayuga-Tompkins Healthy Heart Program appreciates your participation in this activity and believes that it will be mutually productive.

Recorded Subject: _____

Address: _____

Date:_____

If child under 18, please have the following completed:

Parent or Guardian_____

Address_____

Date:_____

A New York State Healthy Heart Program

Figure 5-8   Sample talent release (*courtesy, Tompkins-Cayuga Healthy Heart Program*).

When scouting out potential locations, be sure to inquire about how to obtain the necessary permissions to tape in each place. You just can't march onto private property and start taping! Even in some public parks in Washington, D.C., you need to have a "tripod permit" to take professional photos, film, or video using a tripod. Proper authorities should be contacted in writing; when shooting in certain public areas, permission is required from the local police. Remember that taping can infringe on the privacy of others. It's important to let people know just what to expect when a TV crew will descend upon them, how long the set-up, taping, and strike should take, what objects may have to be moved, and what ordinary activities might be disrupted.

WHO SAYS VIDEO IS GLAMOROUS?

Our crew was scheduled to shoot a promotional documentary on a method of teaching foreign languages. The schedule had been set to tape the last meeting of a desired class at the community college campus where they met. Wanting to show the college off in its best light and have the most spacious and attractive classroom possible, we made special arrangements to tape in a new classroom in the Student Union. We scouted the place out, and it seemed perfect—that is, until the evening when we arrived to do the shooting. It seems that the student government was staging a "battle of the bands" to raise money, and you guessed it, the music and dancing were taking place right across the hall from our meeting place. Since it was after hours, no other space was available to us, and this was the last chance to get this group of students. The first problem was in getting through the admissions gate without paying for the concert; fortunately, one of the student leaders was impressed with our video gear, and every time we came in the door with yet another armload of cases, he'd tell the guard, "TV, TV, they're OK!"

Of course, once we got into the classroom, we could barely hear ourselves think. Undaunted, we decided to soundproof the room. We found an old rolling blackboard and set it up as a baffle outside the door. We then raided the men's and women's rest rooms for all the toilet paper and towels we could find, wadded it up, and taped up these sound-absorbing clumps to the walls with gaffers tape, put an extra layer of soundproofing around the edges, and began to tape. Our mikes didn't pick up a note of the music outside.

Unfortunately, our audio problems were not totally cured. The Student Union also housed an AM carrier-current radio station piped to the campus through the electrical wiring. In the middle of our foreign language program, we got a second track of foreign language—the Spanish program being broadcast by the radio station picked up through our VCR right from the power line!

DMG

Even if you have permission from the "top" of an organization, be sure that *everyone* in a location knows you're coming and what you'll be doing. We shot some general scenes of a client's assembly area for a training video we were doing, and we almost were the cause of a strike. A union worker some 500 feet away complained to his steward that the videographer was distracting him, and that he could not produce as many products as he could ordinarily have—and thus, he might be denied a bonus he otherwise might be able to obtain for outstanding production. Of course, we really *weren't* distracting him, but the union was about to enter negotiations and was sensitive about what we might be taping and *why*. Don't forget, to the uninformed, you may look like "spies."

OUT OF BOUNDS

We were shooting a training video deep in the lower regions of the Federal Medical Center for Prisoners on a quiet Sunday morning. The program had roles for inmates and employees. We were using employees as the actors for all roles.

One scene called for the employee-actor dressed as an inmate to enter the medical area from an outside corridor and walk to the registration desk. The action would be viewed from behind the desk and start with the corridor door opening. All the crew, the other actors, and myself were inside the suite.

Actor outside. Crew ready. Roll tape. "Action,"—and nothing. No door opening and entry as rehearsed.

A louder "Action." Still no response from outside.

I rushed over, opened the door to call "Action," and saw our employee-actor being marched away in the firm grip of a Correctional Officer who was saying, "I don't know you; you're out of bounds; and Lieutenant will decide what to do with you."

I hurried to the pair and began to discuss the situation with the Correctional Officer. His answer, "I don't know you either, but I remember something about a TV crew, but this inmate's out of bounds, and I'm taking him to the office."

The employee-actor was new, so the Correctional Officer didn't recognize him. Also, the actor had no ID on him and couldn't quickly prove who he was. The Correctional Officer hadn't been properly informed about our taping and decided (correctly) that he had an out of bounds prisoner and had taken appropriate action.

Henry Bohne
Video consultant
Parker, CO

If you're going to be shooting indoors, you've got to be sure there's adequate electricity to carry the load of lighting and recording gear. Even though most contemporary cameras can make surprisingly good pictures in low light, most indoor shots need supplemental lighting to look good—especially when those shots are taken down several generations while editing and copying. Lighting is by far the biggest drain on power; the camera and deck take relatively little and can be run on battery anyway (this also eliminates a few more power cords of the spaghetti). Not only will you need to find enough outlets (or plan to bring your own power boxes and lots of extension cord), you'll need to see if the amperage is sufficient. A good formula to remember is

$$\text{watts} / \text{volts} = \text{amps}$$

Calculate the number of watts you require (this is listed on each piece of equipment and on each light bulb). Volts in the United States can be estimated to be 110 (or 100 just to keep it really simple). The formula will then give you the amps you require.

Most homes and offices are wired with 15-amp circuits; that is, each group of outlets connected to a given fuse or circuit breaker is supplied with 15 amps. If you try to draw more than that, you'll trip the breaker. If you plug three 500-watt lights, 10 watts worth of video equipment, and 75 watts of room lights into one circuit, what will happen? Plug the numbers into the formula and see for yourself. It's a lot less embarrassing to blow fuses "on paper" than to cause a local power outage in an office building. Be sure to find out how many outlets are on the circuit you plan to use, and find out what's plugged into each one. The building maintenance department is a good source. If, for instance, a copier in the office next to the one in which you're taping is suddenly used in the middle of your shoot, you may trip the fuse—and cause an hour of fumbling around to find the building supervisor and the fuse box in the basement.

When setting up dates for taping, be sure to inquire what else will be happening at that site on that day. Even the simplest taping does disrupt the normal routine, and you should make sure that the situation will be conducive to allowing the crew some extra consideration and cooperation. For instance, if you're shooting in an office, you might have to ask people to stop using a printer for a while to cut down on the background noise; you don't want this to happen in the middle of a pressing deadline for their work.

For economy's sake, it's good to look for one location that can serve as a background for many shots. If there's enough visual variety in the immediate area, you can save a lot of needless travel. For instance, one conference room can be set up cleverly to look like at least three different offices by changing the chairs, plants, pictures on the wall, and camera angles. This is where the shooting script comes into use; it's important to remember each shot and plan its location, so you don't wind up having to travel a few thousand miles to get that "one last shot."

Once locations are chosen, the next questions are "How to get there?" and "What to take?" The further from home base you travel, the more difficult the process. Even though field equipment is "portable," it's not always too happy being bounced in and out of cars and airliners. It seems that the further you travel, the more numerous the problems.

There are two approaches to outfitting a traveling crew with the necessary equipment: carrying your own or renting it on location. When using your own equipment, you have the advantage of being familiar with its idiosyncrasies—and of saving rental fees. However, additional expenses may be incurred in transporting equipment. While the practice of renting equipment certainly saves a lot of wear and tear on both the crew and the in-house gear, it can be a risky proposition unless you deal with a known and reliable rental agency. Then, too, there's the problem of hooking up with that new equipment in a strange city—and of shots done with different cameras and VCRs possibly not matching well in the final edit. Sometimes producers and talent will fly to a city and have a local crew handle the equipment and the shooting—at least they're familiar with the equipment. However, unless you've worked with them before, this can lead to delays or problems. Generally, if you're going to rent something, make it something bulky and standardized—like lights; avoid renting gear central to the production, like the camera and VCR.

A full complement of production hardware and software (camera, VCR, lights, mikes, tripods, monitor, tapes, test and repair equipment, cables, and so on) weighs in at quite a few hundred pounds. This, in addition to a small crew's luggage, exceeds the limit of baggage normally allotted by airlines. Advance arrangements should be made with the carrier to reserve space for the equipment; sometimes, special fees are also charged for the transportation of the gear, and these should be ascertained and included in the transportation budget. You might also check on your equipment insurance to see if it's covered if it's out of your corporate headquarters.

If you're traveling across national borders, you will probably need papers, sometimes called *carnes*, which document the equipment you're bringing in—and out—of the country and for what purpose. Border guards must be sure that you're not bringing equipment across a border to sell it without paying duty. The forms and paperwork are long and cumbersome. You need to list *every* piece of equipment and where it's packed—down to the last cable—so plan ahead.

Estimate the cubic dimensions of the gear packed for travel. Local travel may permit odds and ends to be transported loosely; airline travel, however, requires that everything be packed in secure shock-resistant boxes (which are sometimes as expensive as the gear packed inside). Often this bulk will not fit in a compact car—especially when a few people also must ride along! When using rental cars away from home, be sure to reserve a large enough car—preferably a minivan or full-size station wagon—at least two weeks in advance. Trends among rental agencies are to carry only smaller cars, and outlets in small towns or airports often have a narrow selection.

Needless to say, you must also reserve hotel rooms, get directions, and plan transportation schedules. When traveling with a full complement of expensive production equipment, it's a good policy to check out hotels' facilities for securing large valuables. Some hotels have special rooms in which such gear can be safely stored; others may have their security department double-lock your rooms when you're not there. It's definitely unwise to leave equipment packed overnight in cars.

PLANNING GRAPHICS

Most programs make use of graphics, at least for titles and credits. Once these are scripted, the producer must decide how they will be executed and by whom. Still visuals, whether sketches, diagrams, text, or charts, can be created in a variety of ways, but increasingly they are computer generated.

Let's first examine some traditional methods. Artists can create *graphic cards*, using traditional poster-board materials. A variety of lettering aids are available to expedite this process, including rub-on or stick-on letters, lettering templates, or typesetting devices that produce strips of lettering. Slides can be produced from these graphics to be run through a slide chain onto videotape or the graphics can be shot directly on camera. Be sure that all graphics are in a 3-to-4 aspect ratio (the shape of the TV screen) and allow a wide margin around the essential area of information. Since not every TV monitor scans exactly the same way, you must be sure that no important information is lost around the edges. Examine Figure 5-9.

Most text shown on video is created by a *character generator*, a computer-like device which can display a variety of fonts, sizes, and colors, which then can feed its signal directly into a video production or editing system. Some personal computers, like PC-type MS-DOS machines and Apple Macintoshes, can be adapted to output standard video and can work as character generators. Other simple character generators (starting at around $2,000) can store limited numbers of graphics "pages" in memory, so that they can be called up instantly during a production. Most can also *roll* or *crawl* the text (move it vertically, like credits, or horizontally, like the weather report on electronic store signs). More expensive character generators have more storage capacity and virtually unlimited colors and types of text.

Most video systems also have more advanced computer graphics and animation capability (see Figures 5-10 and 5-11). Starting from inexpensive consumer computers, like the Commodore Amiga system for about $2,000, and ranging to elaborate mainframe computers for complex animation costing millions of dollars, video graphics is a rapidly expanding part of the business. Artists can sketch in

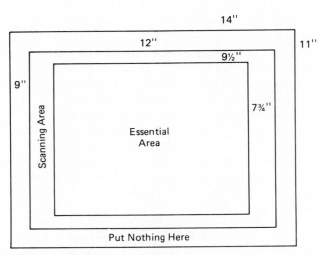

Figure 5-9   TV graphic specifications. On a 14 by 11 inch card, keep essential information within 9.5 by 7.75 inches.

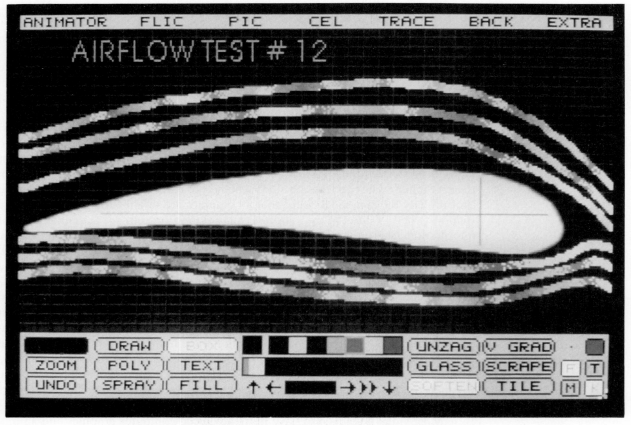

Figure 5-10   PC-based software for creating computer animation (*courtesy, Autodesk, Inc.*).

Figure 5-11 High-end computer graphics systems like this Paintbox provide high-resolution output (*courtesy, Quantel*).

graphics, or "snap" a still-frame from video, or scan in a print-based image. Then, using a paint system, the graphic can be manipulated, colorized, and even automatically turned into 3-D and animated. Animation software, even for PCs, can let you specify the path for objects to take, the kind of surface they have (metallic or flat), and place "lights" within the frame—and then automatically animate the scene.

The enormous range in price for computer graphics and animation has to do with several variables: (1) the resolution of the image (does it look like "real" video or is it stair-steppy?); (2) the complexity of the animation; (3) the rapidity of generation; can it do the animation in "real time," or does the computer slowly construct each frame and record it frame-by-frame on a VCR (which could take several full days to do a minute or so); and (4) the artistic talent behind all those buttons.

Computer graphics are not just used for pretty pictures and snazzy effects; they can make good instructional sense. If you're trying to teach about something that can't be seen by the naked eye (like the structure of a molecule or how the inside of a motor works), computer graphics can make the point clearly. Real scenes can be "touched up" to remove extraneous objects or to highlight salient points. Furthermore, as the field progresses rapidly, prices are dropping steadily and computer graphics and animation will soon be a part of every video production system.

PRE-PRODUCTION PLANNING FOR NEW TECHNOLOGIES

The advent of new technologies, such as interactive video systems and teleconferencing, has introduced additional steps into the pre-production planning of many programs. The production of interactive video adds another whole dimension of production, scheduling, budgeting, and support staff. Concurrent with the video, the computer program that "drives" the branching and provides computer-generated text and graphics must also be developed. The crew may include not only camera operators and engineers, but computer programmers and simulator designers as well. The duration and complexity of this process, of course, vary with the sophistication of the program and the viewer response/simulation device.

Most videodiscs are simulated in tape form to check for correct programming and branching before they are mastered and replicated. Since the exact frame numbers on the disc are not known until pressing and because frame numbers may be necessary for programming, often an intermediate "check disc" is produced to provide that information.

Teleconferencing brings with it the complexity of having to do things perfectly—and strictly on time. You must arrange for the satellite time, and also check out your up-link equipment and all the down-link sites. You may also be in charge of setting up meeting sites around the globe!

As video becomes more integrated with the products of other print and electronic systems, the video manager/producer increasingly is required to oversee the design, production, and distribution of these other products. As I noted earlier, you're not just the video specialist, but the "communications consultant."

BIBLIOGRAPHY

BLANK, B. AND M. GARCIA (1986). *Professional Video Graphic Design*. White Plains, NY: Knowledge Industry Publications.

KENNEDY, T. (1986). *Directing the Video Program*. White Plains, NY: Knowledge Industry Publications.

McQUILLAN, L. (1986) *Computers in Video Production*. White Plains, NY: Knowledge Industry Publications.

WERSHING, S. AND P. SINGER (1988). *Computer Graphics and Animation for Corporate Video*. White Plains, NY: Knowledge Industry Publications.

6

SELECTING EQUIPMENT

Another job of the video producer is that of selecting the appropriate equipment—either through purchase or rental—to carry out productions. With the wide array of hardware available today and the innovation that constantly brings new products to the marketplace, this task is not an easy one. The key is compatibility; ensuring that the individual pieces of equipment work together and that the technical quality of the hardware is appropriate to each given program. Selecting equipment is not just picking out the best individual piece of hardware; rather it's designing a system of interrelated parts, all of which work together efficiently and easily.

VIDEOTAPE AND VIDEODISC FORMATS

The major variable to consider when selecting video hardware is the *video format*. This term refers to the physical size and configuration of the videotape or disc used as well as the way the signal is recorded and played back. Don't confuse this with *program format*, which is the style in which a show is scripted.

A source of great consternation is the seemingly endless introduction of new (and incompatible) formats of video recorders and players. While each new format offers advantages over existing models, it seems as though equipment becomes obsolete almost as soon as it is purchased. However, some general principles should be kept in mind when selecting the format to buy or rent.

The first step is to consider *separately* the kind of equipment you will use for *production* and the format you will use for *distribution*. There are very different criteria for each purpose, and it may be difficult to find one format suitable for both. Most video departments, in fact, use one format for production (a high-quality but expensive one), and one format for distribution (usually consumer-level

159

VHS or industrial quality 3/4 inch). Let's look at the major current video formats—from the highest quality (and most expensive) to their simpler and less expensive cousins.

Digital (D2)

The D2 format was introduced in the late 1980s and promises to be the look of things to come. Using metal tape, these high-quality and large machines cost (in 1990) about $100,000 and were available only as studio machines, rather than including smaller portable units. However, their video and audio reproduction are outstanding: the 100th generation copy looks as good as the original. Signal correction circuits can even make up for drop-outs on the tape. At this writing, D2 is still an exotic format—but digital technologies will most likely be the norm in the decade to come.

Figure 6-1   Digital VTR (*courtesy, Panasonic*).

One-inch Type C

A common (but expensive) format for production and post-production is one-inch Type-C. Although portable 1-inch machines are available, they are bulky and have virtually been replaced by some newer high-quality formats such as Betacam or M-II. One-inch offers high resolution and the ability to freeze-frame or slow-motion tape in post-production; since it loses relatively little quality as copies are made, it is a good format for editing complex special effects which require a number of generations of tape. One-inch editing machines cost about $50,000. This format is the most vulnerable to the invasion of D2.

3/4-inch U-Matic

If anything approaches being an "industry standard" format, this is it. The U-Matic cassette was the first format sufficiently cheap, reliable, and easy to use to gain widespread popularity outside of broadcast applications, while retaining high enough quality to meet broadcast standards. There are over a half-million of these VCRs in the United States today. All 3/4-inch machines are compatible: 3/4-inch cassettes can be played back on any 3/4-inch video tape recorder or player, regardless of the manufacturer. Although the quality does not equal that of the 1-inch type, Betacam, or M-II formats, the machines are cheaper and are useful for both production and playback. A number of manufacturers make field recording decks that are relatively small and are battery operated. They take smaller 3/4-inch "mini-cassettes" which can record up to 20 minutes. Studio U-Matic VCRs use tapes of up to 60 minutes.

A newer version of 3/4 inch, called *U-Matic SP* has been developed by the Sony Corporation; these 3/4-inch machines offer superior resolution and hold up better in copying than does standard 3/4 inch. Regular 3/4-inch U-Matic tapes can be played back on an SP deck, and vice versa, but tapes recorded on SP tape must be edited on an SP machine to avoid edit glitches. Standard U-Matic editing machines cost about $8,000 and 3/4-inch U-Matic SP editing machines are about 50% more.

Betacam

Perhaps the most popular format for high-quality field recording is Betacam. It allows you to "dock" a small field recorder to a camera, making a one-piece camcorder. Don't confuse this with the obsolete Betamax consumer format. Although it uses small 1/2-inch tape, its recording and playback performance are about equal to 1 inch, and the portability is excellent. You can record for 30 minutes in the field, and the studio edit decks can take tapes of up to 94 minutes.

Betacam also comes in a version using metal tape, called Betacam SP. Editing decks cost about $20,000 for regular Betacam and about $30,000 for the SP variety.

M-II

The VHS version of Betacam is M-II. It uses 1/2-inch VHS format metal tapes and also delivers quality approximating 1 inch. The field recorders are dockable to portable cameras and can record 20 minutes. The studio editing machines can use tapes of up to 90 minutes in length. It is about neck-and-neck to Betacam in performance but is slightly less common. The studio editing decks cost about the same as regular Betacam, about $20,000.

S-VHS

S-VHS is a high-quality version of regular VHS—you might think of it as "professional" VHS. It uses a different way of encoding its signal than do the regular consumer VHS machines, and it can record up to 400 lines of resolution—higher than the 260 of regular U-Matic, and actually very close to Betacam and M-II. However, its signals do not hold up as well as its larger counterparts in dubbing and editing. To take advantage of S-VHSs high quality, you must have a "total" S-VHS system, including the recorder, camera, editing system, and even the monitors. You need special S-VHS tapes, and you cannot play back S-VHS tapes on a regular VHS machine. However, you *can* play back regular VHS tapes on an S-VHS system, and you can override the S-VHS mode and make regular VHS-compatible tapes on an S-VHS system.

This format is extremely small and portable, making an ideal low-cost field format. You can record up to 2 hours on one field tape and up to 3 hours on a studio recorder. Editing decks cost about $5,000. Many schools, small production houses, and in-house production departments that want lightweight and inexpensive gear have adopted this format.

Figure 6-2   New York Phone company uses M-II equipment (*courtesy, Panasonic*).

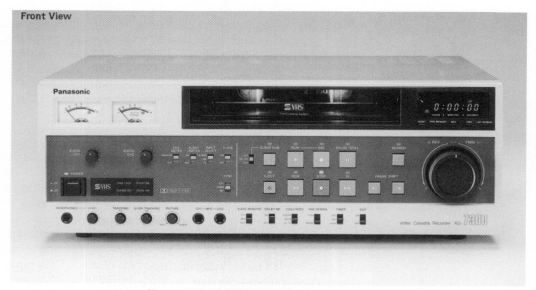

Figure 6-3   S-VHS recorder (*courtesy, Panasonic*)

8mm High Definition

A newcomer in the field, 8mm high definition or hi-8 offers extremely small size and weight with high quality, rivaling S-VHS with about 400 lines of resolution. It uses metal tape and can record up to 2 hours in the field or studio. This format can also record up to 12 channels of conventional audio and one channel of high-fidelity audio.

These units are just being released in 1990, and even so, the cost of an edit-capable studio deck is under $2,500. HD machines will play back regular 8mm tapes, but HD tapes cannot be played back on a regular 8mm system.

VHS

In an effort to further reduce the size and cost of video, manufacturers in the late 1970s developed a number of half-inch cassette formats. They were originally designed for the home market, but soon more professional versions of the machines were developed for the industrial market. VHS is undoubtedly the most common format, both for consumer and corporate playback use, and for "quick-and-dirty" documentation. *Betamax* is also a 1/2-inch cassette format, but is now obsolete.

While each of these formats is at the low end of the cost scale, they are more suitable for playback than production, since the quality degrades very quickly through tape generations. For instance, while an original VHS tape may look quite good, a copy of a copy of that master tape will have very blurry color and will lack detail. Popular consumer camcorders are useful for data collection and for use as a feedback device within training sessions. You can buy a consumer VHS recorder for several hundred dollars almost anywhere, but an industrial version capable of editing will cost about $2500.

8mm

This format is actually Sony's answer to their failed Betamax format and a challenger to VHS. The tapes and camcorders are a bit smaller than VHS and they offer up to 12 channels of audio and up to 2 hours of field recording. The picture quality is about the same as VHS, making it unsuitable for professional recording. Time will tell whether it will gain the acceptance as a playback format needed to become a real challenge to the penetration of VHS.

Laser Optical Videodiscs

After some confusion of standards in the early 1980s the videodisc world has somewhat settled on two major standards. Today, most laser disc players will play back both *CLV* and *CAV* discs. CLV (constant linear velocity) discs can play back up to one hour of motion video on a 12-inch disc side, but it is not as easy to access randomly given frames or sequences as is required in interactive video. This format was basically developed for consumer use in watching movies. CAV (constant angular velocity) discs can hold up to 30 minutes of moving video per 12-inch side, which also equals 54,000 still frames. This format makes it possible to access quickly any frame on the disc. There are also smaller 8-inch discs which can be used in more portable machines—these are capable of displaying up to 14 minutes of motion video.

Laser videodiscs are generally applied only in interactive video applications, where it's necessary to access quickly and accurately any frame or segment of a video program. Laser discs must be pressed from master tapes, and this process is done only at a handful of pressing plants throughout the world. Low quality, fast "check discs" can be gotten for a few hundred dollars, but high-quality pressed discs generally take about a week to turn around and cost about $1200 per side to make the original disc and about $25 per copy after that (until you get into pressing thousands, at which time the price per copy drops significantly). So, laser discs are slower and more expensive to have made, and the players cost from $1,000 to $3,000, depending on the features you want.

Because there is no physical contact made with the videodisc during playback, laser discs don't suffer from progressive "dropout" as do tapes, which also makes them ideal for continuously running programs such as you'd find in public kiosks.

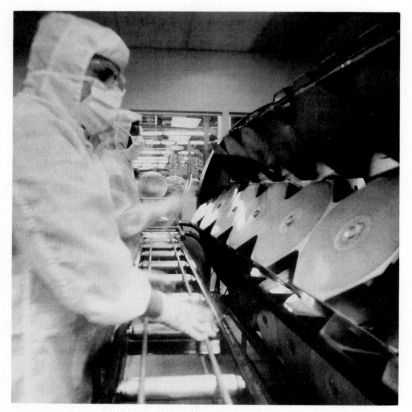

Figure 6-4 Conventional videodisc mastering and replication is a specialized process (*courtesy, Pioneer*).

DRAW Discs

Many people would like the advantages of videodisc without the delay and possible breaches of security involved in sending out a tape to be pressed. DRAW (direct read after write) disc formats have been developed by such companies as Panasonic and TEAC. The blank discs are expensive and are not re-usable—that is you can record on them only once. They are ideal for systems in which you need to record video still frames or short segments in an ongoing fashion and then call them up for instant replay. Such an application might be in a building security system, where you'd want to store each employee's picture on a videodisc to be called up under software control. These formats are not interchangeable with each other or with laser optical videodiscs. Some DRAW discs are being used in high-end editing systems to make off-line "rough cuts" of movies or elaborate productions. Because of the speed of random-access of segments, editing can go faster and be more accurate.

Insert fig

SELECTING A VIDEO FORMAT

Generally the more expensive the hardware, the better the quality. But how good is good enough? A lot depends upon what you're going to do with the tape.

Let's look first at selecting a production format. It's important to estimate

Figure 6-5 A desktop optical videodisc recorder (*courtesy, Panasonic*).

how many copies or *generations* of an original recording will be made. The tape on which the material was originally recorded is called *first generation;* a copy of it is *second generation;* a copy of a second generation tape is *third generation* and so on. As you lose a generation, you also lose quality—just like making a photocopy of a photocopy. When you edit, you always lose a generation, since in electronic editing, you copy parts of your original tape onto your new *edited master* tape. So, tapes that get distributed are copies of the edited master tape, and are at least third generation.

You may easily lose more generations in editing; for instance, if you want to do complex special effects, you may have to make a number of copies of a scene as you gradually build up more picture enhancements or special effects. So, you may be looking at certain parts of your program being fourth or fifth generation by the time your audience uses them.

Another question to consider is the nature of the visual material. Is detail important? Are color (hue) and saturation crucial? These technical elements get degraded in the duplicates. Yet another factor is ease of operation. Smaller formats are more easily transported, while some formats, such as consumer-level 1/2-inch, are quickly learned by nonskilled personnel.

What is your format for distribution? If you're using 1/2 inch to distribute copies of the program, copies made from lower-quality masters will look worse than copies made from higher-quality masters. For instance, a third-generation copy of a program shot and edited on 1-inch tape and dubbed to 3/4 inch will look much better than a third-generation dub of a 3/4-inch master. A third-generation 3/4-inch tape may be acceptable, but a VHS third-generation tape (even if the original and the edited master were on 3/4 inch) may not be suitable for your purposes.

Finally—the bottom line—what's your budget? Although a clean, crisp dub may please you and your engineers, chances are that your audience will not be so critical. They're used to looking at poor dubs of home movies on misadjusted TV sets in their living rooms, and usually if the content's really good, nobody notices the resolution. Is a slightly better image worth $10,000? The answer *may* be yes, if you need to see accurate color or detail (say, in a program teaching surgery), but for the vast majority of programs, it may not be worth the cost.

Distribution formats are chosen by different criteria. Although certainly the equipment's technical quality and expense are important here, there are new factors to consider. Characteristics such as ease of operation by the viewer, small size and weight for mailing and storage, and cost of raw tape stock are important. Whom do you wish to see the program? What format or formats are they likely to be able to play back?

These criteria lead many organizations to record and edit on expensive formats, such as one-inch or Betacam, and distribute copies on 3/4 inch or VHS. Federal Express, for example, uses a number of formats, as you can see in Figure 6-6. Although equipment may change from year to year, and even from month to month, a wisely chosen video format should serve your organization well for years to come. Beware of fads and isolated formats only used by one manufacturer. And remember, you can always dub from one format to another.

Most manufacturers make both studio and field VCRs. Studio models are larger and are meant to be operated on regular electric current; field models are meant to be carried over the shoulder or within a hand-held camera and run off batteries. VCR editing machines have special circuitry that allows them to make clean edits between segments and to be controlled by a remote edit interfacing unit. Often portable VCRs accommodate only shorter lengths of tape in order to keep the size down.

When choosing a given model of tape recorder within a selected format, look for specifications as to its *resolution* or picture sharpness and its *signal to noise ratio (S/N)*. Then find the features that are important to your application. Also check on a machine's ability to be serviced easily within your shop, or locally.

Selecting Interactive Video Formats

If you think selecting a video recording format is difficult, it doesn't even come close to deciding upon an interactive video format. Although laser optical discs

Figure 6-6   Federal Express Company's master control room contains a variety of tape formats (*courtesy, Lake Systems, Inc.*).

are a standard format, most interactive systems involve some sort of computer control to access information on the disc. That's where there's currently *no* standard!

In selecting interactive video formats, you must consider:

- the model of videodisc (or compact disc) player
- the way in which the computer "talks" to the videodisc player (either through simple "dumb" cables or through interface cards)
- the method of user input (touchscreen, mouse, keyboard, and the like)
- the number of screens used, and whether the computer text and graphics are to be superimposed on the video

Hardware is determined by its intended location (a trade-show kiosk like the one in Figure 6-7 for example) and by the kind of features needed in a given program.

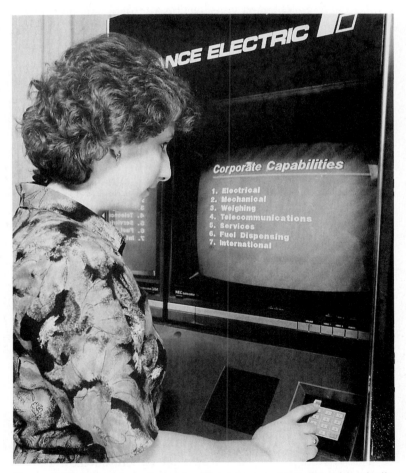

Figure 6-7   This interactive video kiosk uses a videodisc with a built-in keypad for accessing segments (*courtesy, Avid Communications*).

As you can see, there are many choices, leading to there being many *thousands* of *incompatible* interactive video systems on the market. Needless to say, this is a great source of frustration, and it has been holding back on the ability of producers to market generic courseware.

There is not even a standard protocol within manufacturers indicating how to "talk" to a videodisc player to control it. For example, different Pioneer videodisc players use different computer commands to search for a given frame and pause on it! So, if you've written software for a given system—even if the computer, interface card, and touchscreen are identical—but the videodisc models are different, the program won't run. Of course, you can develop programs which contain different versions of the control codes, but this requires time, patience, and constant updating as new models are released.

Currently, a major trade industry, the IVIA (Interactive Video Industry Association) is trying to get manufacturers to pull together and decide on a standard—much as manufacturers did in the early 1970s when they developed the EIAJ standard for the old 1/2-inch open-reel machines. Time will tell . . .

CAMERAS

The next big selection after a videotape format is that of the camera. An obvious first question back in the 1970s was "black-and-white or color?" But today monochrome cameras are used only for surveillance purposes or kid's toys; even inexpensive consumer camcorders reproduce color.

The most outstanding feature separating cameras is the pick-up mechanism: one tube, three tubes, one chip, or three chips. The tubes are the sensitive devices which detect the light signals passed through the lens, and in general, the bigger and more numerous the tubes, the better the picture. Inexpensive cameras have one tube which produces all the colors; the result is a somewhat "muddier" picture, especially in low light, or when dropped down several generations. Better cameras have three tubes, one for each of the primary colors of red, green, and blue. Three-tube cameras offer richer colors and higher *resolution* or sharpness of image. A more recent introduction is a "chip" or CCD camera (like those in Figures 6-8 and 6-9) which uses a light sensor on a circuit chip instead of a tube. These chips are tiny and lightweight, and are less sensitive to burn-in or jarring than tubes, and they last longer.

These days, most cameras come with power zoom lenses, automatic f-stop (which automatically sets the lens for the appropriate amount of light), and automatic white-balance (which automatically sets up the camera to reproduce accurate colors). Almost all professional cameras include the following:

- **Internal sync.** If a single camera is being used for recording, as in portable field work, the camera must supply its own synchronizing pulses or control track to keep the video stable

- **External sync.** When two or more cameras of other video sources (such as a character generator) are used together, they must be tied into a common sync source. This enables them to be switched among each other or mixed together without any disruptions or "glitches" in the picture. An external sync option on a camera enables it to operate from your "studio sync" being fed to it, and the option will allow it to be used in a production system.

- **Low light level gain.** Most cameras have an extra boost of sensitivity for low light levels, expressed in db or decibels. Although this boost also increases the noise in the picture (making it look a bit snowy), it is useful where adequate light is not available.

- **AC-DC power.** Some cameras designed solely for the studio use standard alternating current. Other cameras are designed to work from batteries in the field—either their own battery pack, a battery belt, or the VCRs battery.

3·CCD COLOR VIDEO CAMERA KY-17U

⑲ Phase adjustment control (PHASE) (SC, H)
⑳ Mic output level select switch (AUDIO LEVEL)
㉑ VTR triggering mode select switch (VTR)
㉒ Operation mode select switch (MODE)
   (VTR, Y/C 358, RM)
㉓ Power select switch (POWER)
㉔ Intercom level (INTERCOM LEVEL)
㉕ Y/C 358 output connector
㉖ Intercom jack (INTERCOM)
㉗ Genlock signal input connector (GENLOCK IN)
㉘ Test output connector (TEST OUTPUT)
㉙ Mic input (XLR-3) (MIC INPUT)
㉚ Exclusive microphone mounting shoe
㉛ Exclusive microphone input socket
㉜ Mic mode select switch (STEREO/MONO)
㉝ VF AUX video select switch (RET)
㉞ Gear for chest rest (KA-111)
㉟ Battery Guide
㊱ Earphone jack (EARPHONE)
㊲ DC 12V IN connector
㊳ Camera cable connector (RM/VTR)

Figure 6-8 Features of a typical CCD camera used in business and education (*courtesy, US JVC Corporation*).

❶ Viewfinder (VF-P10)
❷ Tally ON/OFF (TALLY)
❸ Contrast control (CONT)
❹ Brightness control (BRIGHT)
❺ Carrying handle (KA-231)
❻ 13 to 1 zoom lens (HZ-713)
❼ Shutter speed select button and indicator lamp (SHUTTER)
❽ Filter turret (3200K, 5600K, 5600K + 1/4ND, CLOSED)
❾ Operation switch (OPERATE) (CAMERA/ VTR)
❿ Sensitivity select switch (HI-SENS) (0, +9 dB, +18 dB)
⓫ "ZEBRA PATTERN" ON/OFF switch
⓬ Display select button (DISP SELECT)
⓭ Camera/color bar select switch (MODE) (CAMERA, BARS, NEGA)
⓮ White balance mode switch (W. BAL) (AUTO 1, AUTO 2, PRESET)
⓯ Shoulder pad (KA-220)
⓰ Top tally
⓱ Auto setup button (AUTO SETUP)
⓲ Video recorder start switch (VTR)

Figure 6-8   Continued

Figure 6-9 CCD camera which can be interfaced with a conventional portable or studio VCR (*courtesy, Panasonic*).

- Most DC cameras have an AC converter box, which allows them to be plugged into conventional electrical outlets.
- **Viewfinders.** All production cameras have electronic viewfinders (small TV monitors to show what you're shooting). The configuration of these viewfinders differs. When the camera is meant to be hand-held, it rests on the operator's shoulder and the viewfinder sits out to the left of the camera to bump up into the operator's eye with a rubber eyepiece. When a camera is meant to be used on a tripod, you may choose to purchase a large viewfinder that sits on top of the camera so that the operator can see the picture from arm's length directly behind the camera. Most monitors can also display a tape that is being played back on a VCR hooked up to the camera, so that the operator can check what has been recorded.
- **Remote controls.** When working in a studio configuration, optional zoom and focus controls can be attached to tripod arms so that the operator doesn't have to hunch over to reach the lens itself. For studio work, cameras should also be able to have their color balance and video levels controlled from a remote room, where an engineer can easily set up all the cameras at once and "match" them. Cameras designed for portable use have remote control buttons which can be triggered by the operator's thumb to start and stop the VCR. Little lights in the viewfinder indicate whether the VCR is in the "record" or "pause" mode, and many flash when the tape is almost at its end, or when the battery is almost dead.

Choosing cameras is not an easy task, since there are so many on the market. Resolution and ease of set-up are important for all applications. Size, weight, balance, and power consumption are criteria to be considered for portable cameras. If you're trying to set up a single camera/VCR hand-held unit, like the one shown in Figure 6-10, check to see which VCRs a particular camera can "dock" with. Check out the *signal to noise ratio* usually expressed as S/N; this is a ratio of the desired picture to the unwanted background "noise" at a given light level. The higher the ratio, the better the picture. *Resolution* usually is measured in lines at center—the number of lines that can be clearly distinguished in a picture in the center of the screen. The higher the resolution, the sharper the picture. Finally, consider the type of use and the kind of users in terms of the camera's ruggedness and ease of use.

Figure 6-10 Camera docked to a VCR allows for self-contained operation (*courtesy, Panasonic*).

STUDIOS

Often video producers are given the responsibility of selecting rental studios or designing a new studio for themselves. Although the technical specifics of studio design are the province of engineers, producers do need some background in studio layout and hardware. Today, "studios" range from large network-style caverns full of computer-controlled lighting grids, sets, and cameras to little more than a semi-soundproofed storage area for gear where someone can do a simple "stand-up" narration. In fact, the trend today is *away* from studios, since most programs need shots gathered in the field rather than the antiquated "interview set" look of a studio program. But, even video departments that do mostly field work need an area in which they can record narration and do simple shots of products or graphics in a controlled area.

Figure 6-11   Studios have to be designed to accommodate a
variety of sets, camera angles, and lights (*courtesy, GTE CAlifornia*)

Cameras and VCR formats are the primary concern in studio design, as they are the major determinants of a facility's quality and cost. A number of other factors also enter into the design of a workable studio:

- *Size.* Most studios are at least 20 by 40; this allows room for the construction of several moderate-size sets and for camera movement. Remember, cameras can't be on top of the talent, especially if you need to get wide shots of two or more people. Some organizations just use small "insert stages" for recording graphics or narration; these may be as small as 15 by 20 and just house one camera.
- *Location.* The studio should be easily accessible to a loading dock for receiving props and sets. Elevators (the large freight variety) should be available if the studio is not on the ground floor. Narrow halls or sharp turns on the way to the studio must be avoided—again, for the easy movement of large objects. The studio must also be relatively isolated from noise and vibration.
- *Ceiling height.* Most studios have at least 16-foot ceilings to make room for handling lights and to allow for proper picture composition. Since the video aspect ratio is 3 by 4, a set 12-feet wide would require at least 9 feet of vertical space in the shot.
- *Lighting.* One of the advantages to studio production is flexibility in lighting. This calls for a healthy complement of spot and flood lights that can be moved, focused, and dimmed. Most large studios have large dimmer control boards which can have different scenes preprogrammed in so that at the flick of a switch, the lighting can be changed (perhaps to move from one set to another or to dim all the key lights).
- *Soundproofing.* Studios should be free of echoes and of noises from the outside, from other parts of the building, and from plumbing and ductwork. In fact, most studios are designed as isolated rooms within a room.

- *Air conditioning.* All those lights can make a studio uncomfortable for people and "unhealthy" for the equipment. An air conditioning system for a studio must not only be powerful but also must be quiet, so that vibrations or rushing air sounds don't get picked up on the mikes.
- *Backdrops.* Studios should have a built-in selection of wall surfaces. Generally, the walls themselves may have portions painted in various colors; commonly one of these is "chroma-key blue" used to facilitate the keying in of different scenes or graphics from other sources. Nonreflective black curtains are another staple. Many organizational studios have permanent sets with the company's logo and special props or equipment about which programs are often produced.
- *Special hook-ups.* Water and gas hook-ups are often available in studios for the production of cooking, arts, or scientific programs. Some studios also have compressed air and 220-volt electricity to run machines, like lathes, that the company manufactures or uses.

The typical studio adjoins the control room (see Figure 6-12), with a large window between the two allowing the director to see the action in the studio. VCRs, camera control units, and film chains are generally located in a separate master control room. This arrangement is not always followed, however, and is not necessarily the best for all situations. Often control rooms must be set apart so that no direct sight of the studio is possible; this seemingly negative situation may yield a positive result in that the director has no choice but to focus on the monitors. Smaller facilities often combine master control and studio control rooms, keeping the VCRs close to the audio and video controls so that fewer crew members are needed. It's not uncommon to have the camera setup, audio, video switching, VCR control, and directing done by the same person for simple productions. Other facilities may combine the edit suite with the control room; this makes a lot of sense

Figure 6-12   Federal Express studio control room (*courtesy, Lake Systems, Inc.*).

for departments with small crews, since the same switcher, audio console, and VCRs can be used for both studio productions and for editing.

Although many factors must be considered when designing or choosing a studio, probably the most attention gets focused on the control room. It's in these dimly lit areas, full of shiny gadgets with glowing lights and panels full of buttons just waiting to be pushed, that you can really sense the "glamor" of the business. However, some of the best-looking control rooms are nightmares to work in. Equipment should be clearly labeled, logically arranged, and above all, engineered to work together. Getting cameras, VCRs, and special-effects devices to work together is no mean feat; just a little discrepancy in camera cable lengths, timing, or signal levels can mean that sources won't dissolve between each other or make clean transitions.

When evaluating a studio's electronic capabilities, here are a few questions to ask:

- How many cameras do you need to use?
- Do you need teleprompters?
- How many audio channels will you need, and from what kind of sources (mikes, CDs, audiotapes, videotapes, and so on)?
- What kinds of special effects will the switcher be called upon to accomplish?
- Will you need a digital-effects unit to "squeeze" or "spin" video pictures?
- How many sets will you use?
- Do you plan to incorporate slides or motion picture film?
- Will you need to roll in previously recorded videotape to a production, and if so, in what format(s)?
- Do you need to chroma-key in video backgrounds or graphics?
- How many crew members do you need? How many crew members can you afford?
- What kinds of electronic titles and graphics/animation are needed?

SPECIAL EFFECTS DEVICES

Video seems especially adaptable to special effects, and a number of devices available will produce an amazing array of tricks. Although the list lengthens almost daily, a few of the most widely used are:

- VCRs or videodiscs capable of playing back video in slow or fast motion
- Time-base correctors, VCRs, or graphics units capable of "grabbing" and displaying a video still frame
- Digital video effects devices (DVEs) used to alter video pictures by shrinking or stretching them or moving them around the screen. A number of video images can be combined and manipulated on the screen, giving the effect of "moving snapshots" traveling around the frame, zooming in and out, and rotating in space (see Figure 6-13).
- Graphics generators or sophisticated character generators used to create electronic graphics (see Figure 6-14). Some of these are small personal computers modified with a special card which allow them to output a standard NTSC video signal. Others are dedicated electronic generators having a number of standard symbols and type fonts that can be called up. Some are used to animate still graphics by generating layers of colors, moving patterns, or sequences of "cells."

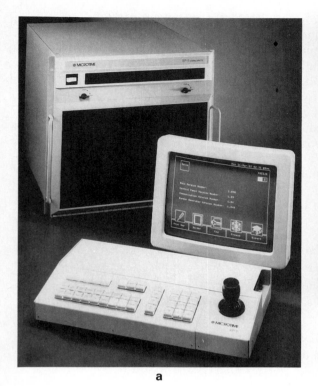

a

b

Figure 6-13   Digital effects devices enable the creation of effects like this 3-D rotating cube (*courtesy, Microtime*).

Figure 6-14   Lettering and titles can be done by specially-equipped personal computers, like this system (*courtesy, Comprehensive Video Corporation*).

Although special effects devices can be used to great advantage in visualizing or analyzing processes and in adding an exciting "professional" look to productions, they should not be used as a crutch. Fancy image manipulation never makes up for dull scripting or poor instructional design. Such devices are costly, too, and are time consuming to use. But properly selected and utilized, they can add to the impact of an instructional or motivational program.

POSTPRODUCTION FACILITIES

As field production has become the norm, the technology and facilities for postproduction have expanded. Hardware for editing, mixing, and enhancing audio and video is a necessary component of any complete video production center. Virtually all videotape editing is done electronically by dubbing the desired parts of one or several tapes onto an "edited master" tape. A special video tape recorder/editor is necessary so that those segments can be assembled smoothly, with no interruptions or "glitches" in the signal. It is usually accompanied by a host of other devices to make editing easier and to achieve special effects.

The design of editing areas is oriented today as much to human comfort as to electronic engineering. Whereas in earlier decades editing tended to be done in odd corners, the 1980s ushered in the era of the plush living-room suite, designed to ease the strain of long hours at the editing controls. Consoles are designed to put controls at exactly the right angle and distance for efficient access (see Figure 6-15). They're padded to make the inevitable leaning upon the desktop surface comfortable. Sometimes, noisy VCRs are kept in another room to provide a quieter atmosphere (and to keep them from the client's drinks and smoke). Couches and coffee tables (complete with catered food) are not uncommon; they keep the onlooking client a little more patient and happy as the production reaches its final stages.

Figure 6-15 Editing suites like this one at Federal Express have become one of the most important areas in a video unit (*courtesy, Lake Systems, Inc.*).

A more detailed description of editing systems and techniques follows in Chapter 8. Here are a few questions to ask when choosing editing facilities:

- Is the editing done by computer-generated edit list (on-line editing), or manually by setting up each edit (off-line)?
- What videotape formats are available to edit *from* and *to*?
- Can two or more VCRs be used as sources, combined through a switcher to do dissolves, wipes, and so on? (See Figure 6-16.)
- Is it possible to fade to or from black with a switcher while editing?
- Is an external camera available to add graphics or titles?
- Is there a film chain to add slides or film clips?
- Is a character generator included, and can it be keyed in over a video source?
- How accurate is the system in editing precisely on the frame you have chosen?
- Can the video signal be enhanced or reprocessed during editing to reduce picture degradation or to correct errors in the original footage? How about audio?

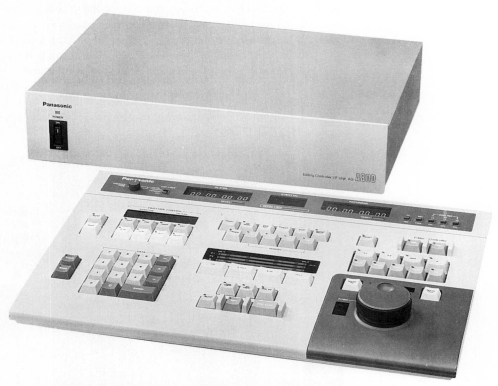

Figure 6-16 This compact editing controller also can control special switcher effects (*courtesy, Panasonic*).

Most post-production facilities make use of *time-base correctors* (TBCs). They're used basically for two purposes: (1) to correct minor flaws in the sync signal so that the tape is more stable, and (2) to synchronize a VCR to another VCR or studio signal so that it can be combined through a switcher with other sources. Because of minor fluctuations in tape speed, tape stretching, alignment, and so on, the signal on most small-format videotapes is imperfect. When you try to duplicate the tape (as you do when you edit), these problems are magnified. To rectify these errors, a time-base corrector is used between the master (playback) VCR and the slave (recorder/editor) VCR. Time-base correcting is usually necessary to bring small-format tapes up to broadcast quality. When two video sources are to be mixed through a switcher, a time-base corrector is used on each machine to synchronize them so that their outputs can be dissolved, superimposed, wiped, and so on, just like the outputs of two cameras in a studio.

MAINTAINING COMPATIBILITY

It's obvious that one of the most important considerations when selecting equipment is compatibility. There are really two issues here: what equipment *can* work together, and what equipment *makes sense* to work together. For example, you can't play back a VHS tape on a U-Matic machine. A camera without external sync drive can't be used as a synchronous source combined with other cameras in a studio. A VCR without editing functions and remote controls can't be used within an editing system. But some things that *will* work together shouldn't.

A primary example is combining very poor-quality equipment with very expensive high-quality gear. It makes no sense to use an old one-tube camera with an expensive 1-inch VTR. Although this is an extreme example, occasionally you do see producers with an odd marriage of hardware. For example, S-VHS tapes will play back on any VHS player, but you won't see the advantage of its extra resolution unless you also have an S-VHS playback deck *and* monitor. A sixteen track audio console may be nice, but is it needed for your simple training productions? Perhaps the money would be better spent on higher quality microphones or on better acoustics for the studio.

Compatibility also extends to questions of equipment maintenance. Unless good equipment is kept up, you'd probably be better off with something cheaper and simpler to maintain. An expensive camera with worn-out tubes certainly belies the original intent of its purchase. And if nobody knows how to align the tubes after the camera has been moved around a lot, the sharpness will be worse than that of a cheap one-tube camera that doesn't need alignment. Maintenance is one big reason to stick with a particular model or brand for all VCRs and cameras. Replacement parts can be more easily stocked, equipment can be substituted in a system, engineers become more familiar with the hardware, and operators have less trouble moving from one machine to another, making it less likely that misuse will occur.

When working in foreign countries, you also have to be aware of technical standards regarding the way that the visual information is generated and recorded. These standards have to do with how many frames per second and lines per frame make up the video picture and with how color information is encoded. Without getting too technical, there are three major standards: NTSC, PAL, and SECAM. The United States, Japan, Canada, Korea, and Mexico are among the users of NTSC: 30 frames per second, 525 lines per frame, using 60-cycle electricity. Most European and African countries use PAL, and France, French-settled African countries, and much of the Middle East use SECAM. All components of a video system: cameras, VCRs and monitors, must be of compatible standards. If you want to use, for instance, a PAL tape from England in your US production, you must first have a standards conversion done on the tape. This service is offered by a growing number of duplicating houses, but may cost as much as $100 per minute! Refer to Figure 6-17 for a more comprehensive list of foreign countries and their standards.

VCRs and monitors are now being manufactured that can play back two or more standards. As many corporations become multinational and programming is

DEVLIN
WORLD VIDEO STANDARDS

	COUNTRY	LINES/FIELDS	COLOR	VOLTAGE (V)	FREQUENCY (Hz)
A	AFGHANISTAN	625/50	PAL	220	50
	ALBANIA	625/50	SECAM	220	50
	ALGERIA	625/50	PAL	127-220	50
	ANDORRA	625/50		220	50
	ANGOLA	625/50	PAL	220	50
	ARGENTINA	625/50	PAL	220	50
	AUSTRALIA	625/50	PAL	240	50
	AUSTRIA	625/50	PAL	220	50
	AZORES	525/60	NTSC	120	60
B	BAHAMAS	525/60	NTSC	120	60
	BAHRAIN	625/50	PAL	220	50
	BANGLADESH	625/50	PAL	230	50
	BARBADOS	525/60	NTSC	120	60
	BELGIUM	625/50	PAL	220	50
	BERMUDA	525/60	NTSC	120	60
	BOLIVIA	525/60	NTSC	115-230	60
	BRAZIL	525/60	PAL M	220	60
	BULGARIA	625/50	SECAM	220	50
	BURUNDI	625/50		220	50
C	CAMEROON	625/50		127-220	50
	CANADA	525/60	NTSC	110-240	60
	CANARY IS.	625/50	PAL	127	50
	CENTRAL AFRICAN REP.	625/50		220	50
	CEYLON	625/50		230	50
	CHAD	625/50		220	50
	CHILE	525/60	NTSC	220	50
	CHINA (PEOPLES REP.)	625/50	PAL	220	50
	COLOMBIA	525/60	NTSC	110-220	60
	CONGO (PEOPLES REP.)	625/50	SECAM	220	50
	COSTA RICA	525/60	NTSC	110	60
	CUBA	525/60	NTSC	120	60
	CURACAO	525/60	NTSC	120	60
	CYPRUS	625/50	PAL	220	50
	CZECHOSLOVAKIA	625/50	SECAM	220	50
D	DAHOMEY	625/50		220	50
	DENMARK	625/50	PAL	220	50
	DOMINICAN REP.	525/60	NTSC	110	60
E	ECUADOR	525/60	NTSC	120	60
	EGYPT	625/50	SECAM	220	50
	EL SALVADOR	525/60	NTSC	110	60
	ETHIOPIA	625/50		127	50
F	FIJI	625/50		240	50
	FINLAND	625/50	PAL	220	50
	FRANCE	625/50	SECAM	115-230	50
G	GABON	625/50	SECAM	127-220	50
	GAMBIA	625/50		220	50
	GERMANY (DEM. REP.)	625/50	SECAM	220	50
	GERMANY (FED. REP.)	625/50	PAL	220	50
	GHANA	625/50		230	50
	GIBRALTAR	625/50		230	50
	GREAT BRITAIN	625/50	PAL	127-220	50

	COUNTRY	LINES/FIELDS	COLOR	VOLTAGE (V)	FREQUENCY (Hz)
	GREECE	625/50	SECAM	110-220	50
	GREENLAND	525/60		220	50
H	GUAM	525/60	NTSC	110	60
	GUATEMALA	525/60	NTSC	110-220	60
	GUINEA	625/50	SECAM	127-220	50
	GUYANA	625/50		127	50
	HAITI	625/50	SECAM	115-220	50
	HAWAII	525/60	NTSC	117	60
	HONDURAS	525/60	NTSC	110-220	60
	HONG KONG	625/50	PAL	220	50
	HUNGARY	625/50	SECAM	220	50
I	ICELAND	625/50	PAL	220	50
	INDIA	625/50		230	50
	INDONESIA	625/50	PAL	220	50
	IRAN	625/50	SECAM	220	50
	IRAQ	625/50	SECAM	220	50
	IRELAND	625/50	PAL	230	50
	ISRAEL	625/50	PAL	220	50
	ITALY	625/50	PAL	127-220	50
J	IVORY COAST	625/50	SECAM	220	50
	JAMAICA	525/60	NTSC	110	50, 60
	JAPAN	525/60	NTSC	100-200	50, 60
	JORDAN	625/50	PAL	220	50
K	KENYA	625/50	PAL	240	50
	KOREA (NORTH)	625/50			
	KOREA (SOUTH)	525/60	NTSC	100	60
L	KUWAIT	625/50	PAL	240	50
	LEBANON	625/50	SECAM	110-190	50
	LIBERIA	625/50	PAL	120	60
	LIBYA	625/50	SECAM	120	50
	LUXEMBOURG	625/50		120-208	50
M	MALAGASY REP.	625/50	SECAM	127-220	50
	MALAWI	625/50		220	50
	MALAYSIA	625/50	PAL	240	50
	MALI	625/50		125	50
	MALTA	625/50		240	50
	MARTINIQUE	625/50	SECAM	127	50
	MAURETANIA	625/50		220	50
	MAURITIUS	625/50	SECAM	220	50
	MEXICO	525/60	NTSC	127-220	50, 60
	MONACO	625/50	SECAM	120	50
N	MONGOLIA	625/50			
	MOROCCO	625/50	SECAM	115	50
	MOZAMBIQUE	625/50	PAL	220	50
	NETHERLANDS	625/50	PAL	220	50
	NETHERLANDS ANTILLES	525/60	NTSC	120-220	50, 60
	NEW CALEDONIA	625/50	SECAM	220	50
	NEW ZEALAND	625/50	PAL	230	60
	NICARAGUA	525/60	NTSC	117	60
	NIGER (REP.)	625/50		220	50

	COUNTRY	LINES/FIELDS	COLOR	VOLTAGE (V)	FREQUENCY (Hz)
	NIGERIA	625/50	PAL	220	50
	NORWAY	625/50	PAL	230	50
O	OMAN	625/50	PAL	220	50
P	PAKISTAN	625/50	PAL	220	50
	PANAMA	525/60	NTSC	110	60
	PARAGUAY	625/50	PAL	220	50
	PERU	525/60	NTSC	115-220	60
	PHILIPPINES	525/60	NTSC	115	60
	POLAND	625/50	SECAM	220	50
	PORTUGAL	625/50	PAL	110-220	50
	PUERTO RICO	525/60	NTSC	120	60
R	RHODESIA	625/50	PAL	220	50
	RUMANIA	625/50		220	50
	RWANDA	625/50		220	50
S	SAMOA	525/60	NTSC	120	60
	SAUDI ARABIA	625/50	SECAM	125-230	50, 60
	SENEGAL	625/50	SECAM	120	50
	SIERRA LEONE	625/50	PAL	230	50
	SINGAPORE	625/50	PAL	220	50
	SOMALIA (REP. OF)	625/50		220	50
	SOUTH AFRICA	625/50	PAL	220	50
	SPAIN	625/50	PAL	127-220	50
	SPANISH SAHARA	625/50	PAL		
	ST. KITTS	525/60	NTSC	220	60
	SUDAN	625/50	PAL	220	50
	SURINAM	625/50	PAL	115-127	50, 60
	SWAZILAND	625/50	PAL	220	50
	SWEDEN	625/50	PAL	220	50
	SWITZERLAND	625/50	PAL	220	50
	SYRIA	625/50	SECAM	115-220	50
T	TAHITI	625/50	SECAM		
	TAIWAN	525/60	NTSC	100	60
	TANZANIA	625/50		230	50
	THAILAND	625/50	PAL	220	50
	TOGOLESE REP.	625/50		127-220	50
	TRINIDAD & TOBAGO	525/60	NTSC	117	60
	TUNISIA	625/50	SECAM	117-220	50
	TURKEY	625/50	PAL	110-220	50
U	UGANDA	625/50	PAL	220	50
	UPPER VOLTA	625/50		220	50
	URUGUAY	625/50	PAL	220	50
	U.S.A.	525/60	NTSC	110	60
	U.S.S.R.	625/50	SECAM	220	50
V	VENEZUELA	525/60	NTSC	110-220	60
	VIETNAM	525/60	SECAM	120	50
	VIRGIN IS.	525/60	NTSC	115	60
Y	YEMEN	625/50	NTSC	220	60
	YUGOSLAVIA	625/50	PAL	220	50
Z	ZAIRE	625/50	SECAM		
	ZAMBIA	625/50		230	50

Figure 6-17 International video standards (courtesy, Devlin).

addressed to a worldwide audience, issues of video standards will be as common a consideration as tape format.

BIBLIOGRAPHY

BENSON, B., ED. (1986). *Television Engineering Handbook.* White Plains, NY: Knowledge Industry Publications.

HELLER, N. (1988). *Understanding Video Equipment.* White Plains, NY: Knowledge Industry Publications.

SCHWIER, R. (1987). *Interactive Video.* Englewood Cliffs, NJ: Educational Technology Publications.

UTZ, P. (1989, April). "A confederacy of formats—Part I," *AV/Video,* pp. 54–62.

UTZ, P. (1989, May). "A confederacy of formats—Part II," *AV/Video,* pp. 44–51.

UTZ, P. (1987). *Today's Video: Equipment, Setup, and Production.* Englewood Cliffs, NJ: Prentice-Hall.

7

PRODUCING THE PROGRAM: STUDIO AND FIELD

Now that you know how to justify, script, and plan productions and have gotten yourself outfitted with appropriate equipment, it's actually time to get your ideas from paper onto the monitor. Many people think of production as being an engineering process—and that's right. But it's far more a question of *human* engineering than *electronic* engineering. Exactly where your first video segments get shot and how smoothly productions go are the result of extensive, meticulous planning. The production phase of a project is almost universally the most expensive and exhausting. It demands the most efficient use of human and nonhuman resources.

STUDIO VS. FIELD PRODUCTION

Portable video equipment has made possible—if not always easy—*electronic field production,* sometimes called *EFP.* Field production brings the producer flexibility, which in turn requires decisions. Sometimes the decision is clear: certain shots can be captured only on location, or particular sets must be constructed in a studio. In many cases, organizations don't even have studios. However, often the material can be shot in a variety of ways. A person can be interviewed while walking through a plant, sitting in someone's office, or appearing on a studio set. A narrator can stand in a factory next to the equipment to which he is referring, or he and the equipment may be brought together in the studio.

Studio and field production each have their advantages. If an appropriate setting can be created in the studio, shooting there is usually easier and cheaper. However, if a studio setting will look phony, stiff, or contrived, field production is called for. The studio offers built-in control of lights and acoustics; equipment is already in place, so set-up and tear-down time is minimized (see Figure 7-2). You're

Figure 7-1 A New Jersey Bell crew on a shoot in the field; most corporate productions take place outside a studio (*courtesy, Panasonic*).

Figure 7-2 Studios allow for complete control of factors, such as lighting. This lighting board contains computer-controlled pre-sets for various lighting scenes (*courtesy, Nautilus productions*).

not disturbing other people and offices. Perhaps, most important, back-up equipment and additional personnel are there when you need them. The "outside world" eliminates the need for set construction and often puts the talent in a much more comfortable or credible situation. You can go to the talent so that they don't have to come to you. And field production can often be accomplished with fewer crew members.

Unless you have a remote van with several cameras and a switcher, every change of angle or shot in field shooting means a lot of work. You must stop tape, reposition the camera and sometimes the lights, start rolling again, and later edit all the segments together. This is sometimes called *film-style shooting*. In a studio, shot changes can be made with a simple push of the switcher button. Special effects, such as wipes or split screens, are simple to set up "live" in a studio but require lots of time and patience when constructed during post-production as they usually will be if your segments are shot in the field. Therefore, when the setting is not important, studio shooting is generally the best choice. Additionally, programs that are broadcast "live," such as teleconferences or telecourses, must generally be done in studios so that multiple cameras and video sources, such as electronic graphics, can be used.

Fortunately or unfortunately, the atmosphere usually *is* crucial in instructional or informational programs. Many times, there's a need to see equipment or demonstrations that simply *can't* be moved into a studio, like a surgical procedure or a demonstration of landing an airplane. The out-of-doors has all the light and background variety you could ask for—providing, of course, the weather's good. Location shots also assist the viewer in applying the information in the proper context.

To Summarize, Shoot in the *Studio* When:

- You feel the background is not important;
- You need a number of different angles or shots for a scene taking place in one setting;
- You have a crew large enough to handle all the equipment;
- You don't have time or money to travel;
- You need a complete program either "live" or in a very short turn-around time;
- You need special lighting or audio effects.

Shoot on *Location* When:

- Your subject matter calls for a specific setting;
- You have the time to pack up, travel, and set up equipment;
- There is a short supply of help for production;
- Time and money are available for post-production;
- A great deal of visual variety is needed;
- Natural surroundings are important for the talent's ease or the audience's understanding;
- The talent can't come to you.

SETTING UP THE STUDIO

If you've chosen to use a studio, you'll use a number of procedures to get ready for taping. It's important to minimize the studio time you use—especially when you're renting the facilities. Even if the studio is your own and the cost doesn't affect you, ill-planned productions generally result in fidgety crews and talent who have lost their spontaneity and enthusiasm.

The first step in studio production is *set design*; this can be as simple as finding a stool and a black velvet backdrop for a narrator set in "limbo" or as complex as drawing scale renderings of several complete scenes, including flats, furniture, and props. Rather specialized or complicated sets like news sets often are designed by professional theater or media set designers. A knowledge of perspective, how things appear on camera, and how colors will reproduce is necessary to create a set that will look right on the video screen. Often designs that look small and spare "in person" look luxurious and spacious when seen through the eye of the camera.

Generally, sets are drawn to scale on graph paper and also sketched to depict more clearly how they'll look in three dimensions and color. Next, the *lighting plan* is drawn, showing the types of instruments to be used and their positions in relation to each set. This plan is also drawn to scale; plastic templates can be purchased that have outlines of the various types of lights, as well as measurements that simplify the task of converting feet to inches on the plan.

The next step is *blocking the scenes* or establishing where on the set the talent will be at any given time. Following the script line by line, the movement, angle, and relative positions of all actors or narrators are described. Next *camera positions* are plotted to achieve the proper shots, given each person's position on the set. In order to do this accurately, you must know the zoom range of each camera lens; the angles of view at the widest shot and the tightest shot can be calculated so that you can see how far back a camera will need to be to get a cover shot or how close it must be to achieve a certain tight close-up. You also have to make sure that cameras will be out of each others' shots!

In order to facilitate directing the program, the director will *mark up* the script, as shown in Figure 7-3, noting which camera is being used for each shot and writing cues for upcoming events, such as rolling in film inserts or changing electronic graphics. Each director has his or her own style of "shorthand"—the important thing is to have the notes serve as effective prompts when following the script during production. There is often so much going on, and there are so many directions to give various crew members, that the task becomes nearly impossible without some sort of written aid. Some directors mark up a script with different colored pens to signify different actions: one color can represent stand-by reminders, another can represent the actual command that should be given to a crew member at a particular time. The important thing is to be complete without covering the script in unreadable scribble.

Once the shots and their respective cameras have been chosen, often *shot sheets* (Figure 7-4) are made up for each camera operator. These list in order the shots for that particular camera, assisting the operator in efficiently setting up the next appropriate camera composition while freeing the director from having to tell each cameraperson what his or her next shot will be. Shot sheets are simply written or typed notes to be taped to the back of the camera during production.

Communicating with the engineering staff is of the highest importance. The engineering department should receive copies of the set and lighting plan. Often they are the people responsible for setting up the lighting and perhaps even the scenery. **The rule: the engineers are your friends—be sure you treat them as such.** A complete checklist of all equipment needed should be submitted well before the taping date. Look over the example in Figure 7-5. This request should include:

- Number and format of recording VTRs—including back-ups
- Number and format of playback VTRs
- Cameras (how many and where they should be placed)
- Microphone number, type, and placement—including back-ups

Audiovisual Script Format

Georgia Power ▲

PROGRAM TITLE				
PROJECT INTERCONNECTIONS: "A NEW WAY OF LIVING"				

SCRIPT NUMBER	COPYWRITER	LENGTH	DATE	PAGE NO.
FINAL	STEVE KASTEN	15 MINUTES	9/87	1

VIDEO	AUDIO
Open title and graphic	——————————— *MUSIC UP* **ROSALYNN CARTER OFF—CAMERA NARRATION** ————— *music under*
Slide/B&W *alleyway*	They linger for days on end in dark alleyways,
Slide / B&W *Street scene*	on streets,
SLIDE / B+W *storefront*	near storefronts..........
SLIDE / B+W *CU feet Bathroom*	The word home can mean the restrooms of a bus depot,
SLIDE / B+W *Vacant lot*	a vacant lot,
SLIDE / B+W *broken down steps*	the steps to a desolate building,
SLIDE / B+W *Street Scene*	or the stark cold pavement....
SLIDE / B+W *dumpster*	They scrounge for morsals of food through refuse and garbage cans.....
SLIDE / B+W *Soup Kitchen*	Some, find their way to soup kitchens for a hot meal.
SLIDE/B+W *CU food*	Finding a few pennies, may mean the difference of eating or starving for a day.
SLIDE / B+W *shelter scene*	Many times they find themselves in overcrowded shelters which cannot handle their special needs......
SLIDE / B+W *Shelter scene*	Their regimen of personal hygiene is minimal, and they are completely deprived of any privacy.........
SLIDE / B+W *Person*	Their integrity and pride sink below the soil they walk on.......
SLIDE / B+W *Person*	They are....... the abandoned,
SLIDE / B+W *Person*	the mentally ill,
SLIDE / B+W *Person*	the homeless.

701111—3M—3-78—20

Figure 7-3 Before taping, the director marks up a script to denote actions like slide changes, camera moves, and audio (*courtesy, Steven Kasten, Georgia Power Company*).

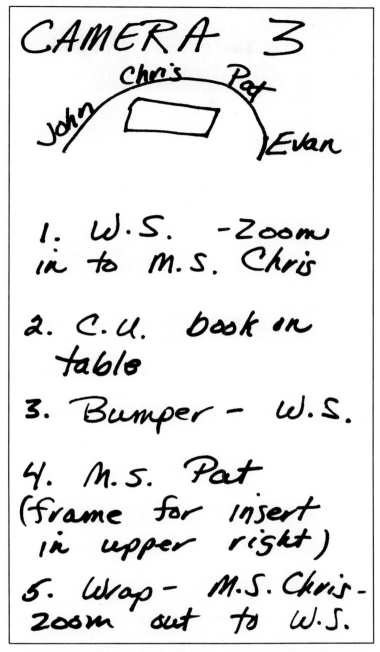

Figure 7-4 Many directors prepare shot sheets to be hung on cameras during productions to cue camera operators.

- Special effects desired, such as chroma-key or digital manipulation
- External video inputs such as film chain or computer graphics
- Audio sources, such as records, reel-to-reel tape, CDs, and cartridges
- Number and position of lighting instruments
- Number and placement of teleprompters
- Number of crew members and placement of headsets/intercoms
- Any video playback needed in the studio itself
- Approximate recording and rehearsal time

video AV communications (UNION CARBIDE)

ENGINEERING CHECKLIST

DATE: _____

TITLE:_____

PRODUCER: _____

CLIENT: _____

JOB #: _____

PRODUCTION

LOCATION: SETUP DATE:_____
                             SHOOT DATE: _____
                             FAX: _____

CAMERA(S):

MIKES: RF _____   LAV _____   OTHER_____

PROMPTER:

LIGHTING:

MAKEUP:

PROPS:

GRAPHICS:

COMMENTS:

Figure 7-5 To reserve and prepare studios, checklists like this are prepared (*courtesy, Union Carbide*).

If there is acting or narration involved, rehearsals and walk-throughs will be necessary. The first step is to have talent read through the lines aloud so that they get a sense of the content and so that the producer and client can suggest emphasis and check on pronunciation. Walk-throughs, where the actors read their lines as they assume the positions blocked, allow everyone to get a sense of space and motion. These first two stages are often done out of the studio to save rental or to make room for others doing actual taping. Finally, rehearsals are conducted on the actual set, using teleprompters, or after the actors have memorized their lines.

There's a delicate balance to be struck between "beating the script to death" and not providing enough rehearsal time. However, more productions suffer from under-preparation than from over-practice. Even actors who know their parts thoroughly may find it a bit disconcerting to perform in a studio amidst bright lights and moving cameras. The entire production crew also must have time to get used to working as a team and to "get the feel" of the program. Pretaping run-throughs not only give people practice but also give crew members a better idea of the style and purpose of the show. Every person involved, from the producer to the talent to the lowliest cable-puller, should understand what the show is about and feel that he or she is welcome to make suggestions. The increased motivation that comes from showing everyone on the crew this kind of professional respect pays off in a much more responsive team and often in a number of good ideas as well.

TAPING IN THE STUDIO

If the pre-production steps have been followed thoroughly, the actual studio taping should be quite uneventful. However, a few routine procedures, as well as some human management techniques, can help to make the process run smoothly. Two principles—efficiency and good communication—apply here particularly. Because so many people are involved and time is so valuable, the producer must be well organized and able to communicate directions to the crew clearly and accurately. He or she must also be able to keep the crew's motivation and morale high through what sometimes are long and tedious hours.

When taping starts early in the morning, nothing perks up a crew and sets a tone of cooperation like coming in with coffee and doughnuts. What sounds like a trivial gesture says a great deal about the producer's attitude toward co-workers and establishes an atmosphere of mutual respect and consideration. The few minutes taken in enjoying a snack are quickly made up in renewed energy and a spirit of teamwork. If this sounds like something out of a Boy Scout manual, rest assured the most experienced and respected producers will say the same thing. Directing a show usually calls for rather terse and authoritarian communication between the producer/director and the rest of the team—especially during the actual taping. It's good to take a few minutes out and let everyone know you're human and that you're considerate of their feelings, opinions, and needs.

It's usually a good idea to have a staggered crew call—that is, to ask different members of the production team to show up at different times, depending on their duties. Although the producer/director should always be there from the very beginning, usually engineers arrive early to unlock the facilities and fire up the equipment. The lighting, unless it's very simple, should have been set up in advance so that the cameras can be balanced for the required scene. If not, arrange the set and lights first thing. Cameras are then adjusted so that they reproduce as accurately and clearly as possible and so that the color, level, and contrast of each camera matches the others.

Mikes and other audio sources are set up and tested next so that relative levels can be set. Other video sources, such as character generators, film chains, and playback VTRs, are checked out. Finally, the video recording equipment is cleaned (if necessary), and a test recording is made to see that everything is working as expected.

Once the basic engineering aspects are taken care of, the crew can be called in. If the talent needs to get into makeup or costumes, they can also show up at this time and prepare for taping. The crew is given a brief overview of the anticipated schedule, and then each person "plays with" his or her own gear—camera, switcher, audio board, or whatever—to practice maneuvers needed during taping. This time is especially important if you're using freelancers (a popular option these days), since they don't work with your equipment every day.

Once the crew is on board, and everyone has checked out the equipment, the director can rehearse a few moves or scenes and make sure that everyone can hear the commands clearly. If there are shots involving no talent, such as graphics, equipment, and the like, they can be taken now to be used as "inserts" in editing or to cover any bad video or production mistakes later. Otherwise, these equipment shots can be saved until the end, after the talent has been released.

The talent should be spared from spending needless time under hot lights, pacing around nervously (and expensively!) while the crew takes care of technical matters. Not only does this tire out even the experienced actor or narrator, but it gives the novice enough time to get really nervous! Certainly, talent should be familiar with the studio and crew before taping, but this familiarity is usually gained during rehearsal. Impatient and tired people can't cover their moods well on a close-up medium like video.

When the studio and crew are at last ready to go, the talent can arrive on the scene and last-minute touch-ups can be made on lighting, camera positions, and mike levels. Always make a brief test recording before getting into the real program—just to make doubly sure that the equipment hasn't developed a problem.

Usually a few minutes of color bars and a test tone are recorded at the head of the tape to assist in adjusting playback equipment when the program is edited or seen by viewers. A *slate* or title graphic with the show name, tape date, producer, and so on, is also often included, as may be a *countdown leader* so that the program can later be cued up easily. Sometimes more than one VCR is used for recording: a second can be run as a back up, or the cameras can each have a VCR—called *isolation* or *iso*—recording their own outputs at all times. These tapes can be edited together later to select camera angles for the finished product in postproduction.

During the taping the director *calls the shots*, telling each camera operator what kind of shot to compose and the technical director (TD) which camera to put "on the air" (on tape) by means of the switcher. Sometimes the director also acts as the technical director and uses the switcher himself or herself—and may also control the audio levels. As the program progresses, the director communicates by means of headsets to the crew, giving them "standby" cues or warning of what's coming up, and then giving specific commands or directions. A floor director signals the talent by means of cue cards or hand signals—usually regarding how much time is left in a program, which camera to look into next, or when to move to a new position or change the topic. (See Figure 7-6.)

Sometimes studio productions are shot straight through, as if they were live. In other cases, they're shot in short segments, perhaps out of sequence, to be edited later. Obviously, the more that can be taped in one segment means that less editing will need to be done later on. Often, though, very complex special effects are needed that can't be done in real time, so small sections of a script are laid down on tape as if you were producing a program in the field.

When the program is completed, a few *cut-away* or *cut-in* shots may be recorded for later editing—either to add visual variety or to cover a bad shot or visual mistake. The same is true for audio—if you know that a certain line was "blown," you might be able to redo just that section. Before the talent changes clothes or anyone leaves, it's imperative to watch the entire tape from end to end—just to make sure there are no mistakes or "glitches" on the tape itself which make the audio or video break up.

Etiquette comes into play again after a taping; the producer should make sure that everyone is thanked and complimented for his or her work. If a crew has worked unusually hard, it's fun to give each of them some remembrance of the production—whether it's a piece of the set, a graphic, or a picture featuring the person taken during the taping. You can be sure that when it comes time for your

Figure 7-6 In the studio, a floor manager communicates the director's instructions via hand cues to the talent (*courtesy, Avid Communications*).

Figure 7-7 The control room is used to coordinate which video and audio goes onto tape, including inputs from cameras, mikes, video and audio tapes, and other special effects devices (*courtesy, GTE of California*).

next production, you'll have a willing crew and a great reputation to precede you. **The rule: always thank the crew.**

Of course, there's usually some work involved after the taping in striking the set, putting the equipment back into place, coiling cables, and cleaning the studio. Be sure you don't play *prima donna* and leave all the dirty work for the crew.

PREPARING TO SHOOT ON LOCATION

It seems that the further from home base a producer goes, the more things go wrong. Cables that have worked properly dozens of times suddenly turn up with broken connectors; mikes develop shorts; monitors turn everything strange colors; and VTRs suffer from unexpected spasms. Not only is this frustrating—since just the replacement part you need always seems to have been left back at the office— often the field shooting is a once-in-a-lifetime opportunity, or the trip to the site cost thousands of dollars. But since the vast majority of video production *is*, in fact, done in the field, there are ways to minimize problems.

The first important principle in planning field shoots is to *scout the location* (if possible). You should go to the site and note such factors as lighting, room size, noise, and electrical supply. Therefore, when you're planning the shoot, you should have a good idea of shots, camera positions, and the number and types of production gear required. Sometimes you just *can't* get to each production site, because of time and budget. Perhaps you can have your client scout out the location for you. For example, we taped a series of elementary school curriculum modules and couldn't get to see each classroom ahead of time. However, our client needed to be in those schools ahead of taping anyway, and she was able to sketch out each room in terms of size, window location, and outlets, and she also took Polaroid pictures of each place.

Extension cords, cables, and lights to be used will vary with the situation. Will the shooting be outdoors or indoors? During the day or night? Will the shots be taken mostly from a fixed location on a tripod, or will it be necessary to move quickly with a hand-held camera? How many minutes of tape do you expect to use from the shoot, and what do you anticipate the *shooting ratio* will be? The *shooting ratio* is the ratio of minutes shot to the minutes actually used. Typically it's about 6 to 1. That's not because of mistakes, but because you'll want to take advantage of being on location to get as much footage as you think you'd ever need—both for the current production and possibly for subsequent ones as well. For example, we produced a marketing video for a company that sells industrial tramrails. The video featured their customers' application of equipment throughout the US and Europe. Even though we only used about 2 minutes from each location in the initial program, while we were there, we shot about 20 to 40 minutes worth of footage, which was used in later productions. **The rule: plan on taking lots of tape**.

Because so much equipment may need to be packed up, and some of it can so easily be misplaced, having a specific place in an equipment case for each item is handy. Equipment cases can be custom fitted with foam padding to fit gear exactly; another helpful hint is to list all items, down to the smallest adaptor, that should be found in each case and tape the list to the inside of the lid. This provides a handy checkpoint when packing gear or trying to find a specific item on location.

Having a back-up for each easily breakable piece of equipment should be a goal of every field producer. In the rough handling and packing of cases and the unpredictable world outside the studio, many things are apt to happen. To have to cancel a shooting because of a broken cable or mike or because a battery wore out too quickly is a sure disaster. Besides replacement gear, repair manuals and a simple tool kit can also save the day. Even though most camera operators and producers aren't engineers, everyone can learn to solder a cable or clean the heads of a VCR. Carrying around the phone number of the company from which you bought or rented the equipment is also handy; often a call can help solve a simple problem or get replacement equipment to you. Finally, be sure to check out the equipment back in the office before it's packed up; a final "tweaking up" and examination here where troubles can be more easily repaired is worth the effort. Be sure you open and check all cases before you put them in your car. Once, we had rented some lights from a company we used frequently and just assumed that they had put the right instruments in the case. As luck would have it, we got onto the site (at night) and found the wrong gear; the lights would have made a nice spotlight in a football stadium but were totally unsuitable to softly illuminate our conference room. **The rule: always check your equipment before you go.**

VIDEO AT SEA

My media war story deals with my first experience "at sea." A contract field production job for the Coast Guard occurred shortly after my coming to the Maritime Institute of Technology and Graduate Studies. In two separate episodes of the same inbound trip, I thought that equipment and self were bound for a dunking! The first near miss occurred about 134 miles out into the Atlantic while trying to transfer from a pilot launch to the ship. It was winter and a nor'easter was blowing through. The problem of transferring 400 pounds of gear aboard was greatly hampered by the 12-foot swells.

I followed the gear (which went up by a one-inch heave line) using a 40-foot rope ladder on the side of the ship. I later found out that a spreader bar (or two) was missing, and because of this instability suddenly found myself with a VCR backpack looking out at the water instead of at the ship. The solution called from below was for the crew to flip the ladder around when the launch came up on the next swell. The swell came, the rope ladder was flipped (luckily with me still clinging), and I continued aboard. Later when I was transferring back to a tug, a wooden ladder was used to ease the problem. Unfortunately in their haste to insure safety, the crew brought the ladder higher on the tug than normal, which made the ladder more horizontal to the water. When I came across with the VCR backpack, the ladder began doing a sag routine with me caught between the ship and the tug looking down at the "quick water." I said a quick prayer and moved very rapidly to the safety of the tug.

From a more practical sense of production problems, I have shot around double corners of large machinery using two broken pieces of a Woolworth dressing mirror, shot XLSs of the deck of a ship while clinging to a three-inch mast 12 stories above the waterline, and done field repair of VCRs using only a borrowed soldering iron, a pen knife, and a paper clip. When anyone asks me how to prepare best for a field shoot, I usually begin by saying, "You can't!"

Lee Klima, Director of Media Resources
Maritime Institute of Technology and Graduate Studies

Items Normally Taken on a Shoot in the Field

- Camera and camera to VCR cable
- VCR
- Monitor and cables
- Mikes
- Lights and stands
- Tripod
- Shoulder brace for camera
- Videotape stock
- Mike mixer
- Extension cords for power and for audio/video cables
- Test tape
- Set-up charts for white balancing and registering camera
- Slate for graphic label to be recorded on each tape
- Model release forms
- Headphones to monitor audio
- Adapters for cables
- Colored gels for lights to match daylight
- Batteries for camera and VCR
- AC adapters for VCR and camera

Some other gear, a little less obvious, is equally as helpful:

- Gaffer or "duct" tape to secure cables, tape up pieces of scenery, wrap around cable connections, and so on.
- Clothespins for tacking lighting gels to the "barn doors" on lights, for adjusting hot barn doors, for holding cables in place, and a myriad of other creative applications
- A nightlight to check to see that outlets have power or to see which outlets are tied into a specific circuit breaker
- Pens and pencils to take notes, sign release forms, and label tapes
- A battery charger
- A tool kit for making minor repairs and cleaning
- A set of walkie-talkies to communicate to crew members at a distance (such as when one person goes down to a basement to check out the power supply or the producer goes into a crowd to check out possible locations)
- A "loading equipment" sign with your video logo to help prevent parking tickets. You'd be surprised at how cooperative people suddenly get when "TV" is involved!
- A company logo for the camera—especially when shooting in public—to answer the endless questions of "What TV station is this?"
- First-aid supplies for human breakdowns
- A credit card for emergency rentals or purchases
- Itineraries complete with addresses and phone numbers for each member of the crew *and* the colleagues back home
- A backpack or satchel for carrying extra tapes, model releases, and batteries when shooting hand-held equipment and moving among locations

- A cart or dolly to assist in loading and unloading equipment
- Copies of letters of permission to use facilities—just in case anyone questions what you're doing
- Plastic covers to act as raincoats for the equipment should a storm suddenly occur (garbage bags work well)
- C-clamps for fastening lights to supports, and the like
- Asbestos gloves for handling hot lights
- A set of adapters so that cable connecters can be modified to work several ways
- A dark cloth to cover up distracting objects
- Wind screens for the mikes
- A 35mm camera and film to capture production shots or stills for credits and/or souvenirs
- Extra tape for "that one last shot"

Hardly a field shooting goes by that producers don't wish they had brought along just one more gadget. While knowing what to take is crucial, it's also helpful to know where to draw the line. Portability and ease of set-up are also keys to field production. Bulk and weight can make traveling more expensive and less pleasant. Each producer and taping situation differs, calling for varying complements of hardware. For example, now that more producers are using Betacam and M-II equipment, the camera and VCR are one unit, so there are fewer concerns about cabling, and the like.

So, how does a producer decide what to take? First, by doing a careful analysis of the script. Second, by scouting out each location in person, if possible, or at least by getting a description of the setting on the phone or by a sketch. Last, by making lists and notes, and by sketching out possible equipment configurations. The more shoots you go on, the more adept you become at anticipating needs and packing wisely. Also, it never hurts to have someone else check over your lists and equipment as an extra measure of precaution.

SHOOTING ON LOCATION

Field production conjures up a variety of images: travel to distant and exotic places, taking the camera "where the action is," interviewing interesting people—and aching muscles, uncooperative weather, flight delays, and endless packing and unpacking. Some people love it, some people hate it—but most feel both ways—depending upon when you happen to ask the question! Because of the predominance of location shooting in contemporary organizational video, corporate video specialists at least have to get used to, if not actually love, travel.

Of course, the key to successful field production is careful planning. However, once you're out on location, you'll need to remember a number of specific techniques, since the production activities themselves differ significantly from studio production. Specifically, you must shoot with an eye towards editing. Since most field production takes place with one camera, typically you will be shooting many more shots than you will actually use. You'll probably shoot them out of order with respect to the script, and you'll have to try to imagine how the shots will look during post-production when special effects such as wipes, split screens, and superimposition of words and graphics may be added.

a

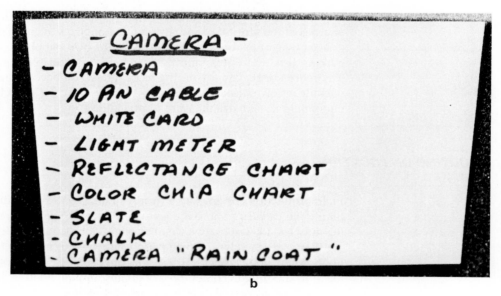

b

Figure 7-8 A good way to keep track of field equipment is to create equipment checklists for each case.

FORKLIFTS AND ME

Working in industrial video, the media person occasionally discovers that an adversary relationship has developed between human and machine. In my case, forklift trucks have proved to be a major humbling influence.

The first experience occurred days after starting my first work in the world of industry. I was dressed appropriate to my first assignment, which was to script a maintenance training tape. An emergency order arrived in the office to get footage of the dynamic testing procedures of a large machine that were about to take place in the factory. Allowing no time to change, the area had to be set up for a shoot. I was well remembered as the strange new person who, dressed in business suit and heels, was hanging off the top of a fully extended forklift clamping lights to the rafters of a twenty-foot-high ceiling in the testing bay. The shoot was successful, but anticlimactic.

New job, new start—this time as media manager for a machine-tool company. The inherent dignity of this position lasted only a matter of weeks. I was asked to get exterior shots of our newly expanded plant. With all the new landscaping, the shots had to be taken from a position above ground level. The obvious means of gaining elevation was a forklift. To record the variety of angles required, the most practical system was to cruise up and down the highway in front of the plant atop the extended forks. The highway travelers were amused, but this time my fellow employees were more subdued. I was accompanied on this assignment by the General Manager and International Vice President of the corporation. I'm not sure if I suffered less because of his esteemed company, or if we are both now seen as certifiable but harmless eccentrics.

Jerri Wells, Media Manager
Monarch Cortland

What to Do Once You Arrive on Location

Step 1. The first step upon arriving on location has nothing specifically to do with video—it is to find the proper authorities. Depending upon the situation, these can include the local police precinct, the person who arranged for your visit, the building supervisor, or the security guards. These people will need to be told that you're there, and *why* you're there, and they can arrange for you to get where you need to be or will tell you where you're not allowed to go. Nothing can spoil a shoot like getting arrested or spending a lot of time trying to avoid it. If you're shooting in public, cooperative police officers can often help keep crowds away or allow you to park in otherwise illegal zones—if you ask them first. Building security guards can often open locked emergency exits to facilitate your loading and unloading and will likewise assist you in finding convenient parking. Building supervisors can help you use freight elevators and tell you about the electrical system to help you find the necessary amps for your lighting and equipment. Be sure to ask about fire, heat, and smoke alarms, since sometimes the extra heat from lights can set them off.

Step 2. The next step is to find the easiest way to transport the equipment to its destination. Along with finding an appropriate parking spot, see if you can garner a cart or dolly—or perhaps even an extra hand—to help you unload your equipment. You may need to have someone watch your equipment while you carry portions of it to its destination. Ask your local contact to help you find the easiest path to the spot for your first shoot, and have the person tell people in the area that you have arrived and remind them what you'll be doing.

Step 3. Now it's actually time to set up the equipment. If you've scouted out your location, you should know exactly where you want to set up—if that was not possible, have someone watch the equipment while you take a brief tour. If you're indoors, you need to be sure of your power consumption and the available electrical supply. If you're outdoors and operating on battery power, you've got to be aware of how much battery time is available. Selection of camera position and shots is the next item on the agenda: remember to choose your angles in terms of achieving a pleasing (interesting but not busy) background and adequate and balanced lighting. Indoors, of course, you will generally supplement the illumination with portable spot and flood lights; outdoors, the sun determines the lighting. It may be necessary to move furniture around a room in order to make space for the hardware and achieve the desired background. First, set up the camera on its tripod and get a preliminary picture through your viewfinder and a separate monitor, if you have one. Have your talent or a stand-in get into position, and compose your shot.

Step 4. Keep talking to your clients and your hosts on location. It can be rather disconcerting for a manager to see her office being torn apart or for homeowners to see their living room suddenly redecorated. While the crew is arranging the equipment and furnishings, it can be very useful to have the talent and/or occupant of that space somewhere else. This is not the time for your client to be breathing down your neck nor for someone who will soon be interviewed to have a chance to become anxious. The first few moments of equipment set-up are usually pandemonium: the equipment may not be hooked up exactly right, the picture is usually not color balanced, and the lighting may not be turned on yet or may look quite unflattering. The video pros know that all this gets straightened out soon, but novices begin to doubt your expertise and their desire to participate after all. Therefore, it's wise to schedule a room for equipment *set up only* an hour or so before you want to begin taping and to find another place for its usual occupant to go. If possible, the producer or interviewer can take the person to another room and discuss the production—or perhaps take the person's mind *off* the production for now.

Step 5. Once the camera is in place and the location arranged, it's time to light. Of course, this is usually necessary indoors, and it's even sometimes a consideration outdoors. Although the sun is generally your lighting source outside, you can use reflectors or small battery-operated lights to help eliminate shadows. Lighting in the field is a real skill: once you step out of the studio, you lose the flexibility of high ceilings, plenty of lights, and dimmers. Indoors you have to worry not only about *how much* light is available but also *what kind* of light. Tungsten lamps have a *color temperature* of 3200 degrees Kelvin and emit a yellowish light. Fluorescent light is about 4800 degrees K and is bluish or purplish, and natural light outdoors ranges from 5000 to 7000 degrees K and is quite blue. Even though we don't notice these differences with our eyes, the video camera is sensitive to them.

Cameras must be *balanced* or set for different types of light so that they can reproduce color accurately. This is done by first setting the filter wheel behind the lens to its proper setting for the color temperature and then by white-balancing the camera by aiming it at a white card and pressing the white-balance button. So, what would happen if you were taping in a cafeteria with sunlight streaming through one side window, but you needed to balance that with artificial light from the opposite side? Both color tempera-

Far & Wide Kit

Sophisti-kit

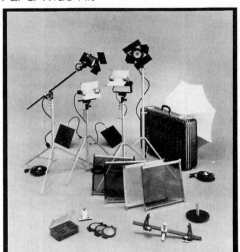

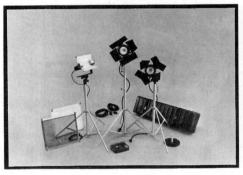

Intro-kit

All Pro Kit

Figure 7-9 Portable lighting packages are an important part of field gear (*courtesy, Lowel Light.*)

tures would have to be matched; either a bronze-colored gel could be attached smoothly to the window (very difficult, as you can imagine), or more commonly, blue gels could be used on the lights to convert them to daylight temperature. You would then set the camera for the specific color temperature achieved.

Lighting in the field is generally accomplished with two to three lights per subject: a *key light* on one side, slightly brighter than a more diffused *fill light* on the other. To provide definition between the subject and its background, a *back light* or *kicker* can be used. By checking recommended light levels for your camera with a light meter and experimenting with various setups, you can determine the best configuration for a particular situation. More light always means a sharper picture and brighter colors. However, in many cases, it's virtually impossible to light your scene. If you need a long shot of a factory floor, you generally don't have the time or number of lights to illuminate the whole place. Contemporary cameras are much better at reproduction in low light levels; you can set the *gain* control to give you more "oomph" in the picture. Most cameras have at least a 12db gain, which can in many cases eliminate the need for lights.

AN ENLIGHTENING EXPERIENCE

We were interviewing the Mayor of Baltimore alongside the inner harbor on a rather threatening day. Everything had been prepared hours in advance, including the placement of a small battery-operated light near the Mayor's mark to fill in some of the shadows anticipated by the sun's position. The interview began and everyone was in deep concentration on his task—the interviewer (me) and Mayor on each other, the cameraman on his viewfinder, the engineer on the audio and video meters, and the guards on the slowly gathering crowd.

Unfortunately, in the middle of the segment, a gust of wind appeared out of nowhere, toppling the spindly light and stand onto the Mayor's foot. Luckily, no one was injured; the guest was able to regain his composure, the crew their dignity, and the light its barn-doors, and the interview proceeded. Needless to say, this experience points out rather graphically the necessity for public relations skills as well as for safety precautions. And whenever I see the Mayor (now Governor) on TV, I look to see if he's still limping!

DMG

Step 6. After the lights and camera are in place, set up the audio. String the mike and have a crew member test out the levels. Now, neaten up the area. If extension cords or cables are used, it's a good idea to secure the connections with gaffer's tape and tie a loose knot in the cable right near the jointure. In case of a slight tug on the cable during production, the knot provides strain relief and the tape keeps the connection tight. All cables and wires should be straightened out, bundled together, and kept against walls away from traffic as much as possible. Lights and cameras can come plummeting down if someone catches a shoe in a cable, so safety precautions should always be a foremost concern.

Step 7. Now make a test recording—this can be done with a stand-in for your actual talent. Check out video and audio levels, and make sure that mikes and lights are out of your shots, even when the lens is zoomed out to its widest shot. Play back the video and make sure it looks and sounds right. Do you hear an air conditioner rumble in the background? Is there a reflection spoiling the shot? You may also wish to fast-forward and rewind each blank tape you plan to use to make sure it's running smoothly and to adjust its tension and wrap.

Rolling Tape

Now, you can finally bring in the talent and fine-tune the lighting, camera angles, and mike levels. To start each tape, record about a minute of color bars, and then a *slate*: this is a simple graphic displaying the subject, production name, and the date. Many producers also record the names of the principal crew members and what equipment was used. Blackboards or laminated boards are useful for this purpose. In case tapes lose their labels or when they're dubbed, or if you wonder just what microphone was used in a scene six months from now, the slate information will prove invaluable. While the slate is being recorded, you can read its information into a microphone. Once the slate is recorded and played back, you've performed a second check-out of the system. At this point, you will want to set your time code generator (if you have one) to encode the proper tape number and beginning frame.

Most field production is accomplished with one VCR and one camera; therefore, shots are not necessarily taped in order as written in the script. Rather, shots from each angle or location are recorded together (as you have seen in the previous chapter on pre-production planning). Editing together segments of footage shot from different angles gives the appearance of "switching" among different cameras. For instance, in a typical interview segment, the interview is conducted with the camera aimed at the *interviewee*, perhaps zooming in and out slightly for visual interest. After the questioning, the camera can be moved to get a long shot of the two people talking, close-up *reaction shots* of each person listening, and shots of the interviewer asking each question again. Always shoot close-ups and long shots in which the subject's lip movements can't be distinguished: these shots are then edited into the main body of the interview *over* the continuing audio track to provide visual variety and to "cover up" edits. Take the example where you conduct a 30-minute interview with a person and want to edit it down to 10 minutes. If you skip from a shot 2 minutes into the interview to one 10 minutes into the interview, the person most probably will have changed position slightly. Perhaps she had a pencil in her hand in the first shot, and somewhere between 2 and 10 minutes into the taping she put the pencil down. If you edit the second segment onto the first segment, it will appear as if somehow magically the pencil disappeared! This situation, called a *jump cut*, is avoided by inserting *cut-ins* or *cut-aways*. A cut-in is a tight shot of a particular aspect of the scene, such as a report on someone's desk. A cut-away is a shot away from the main scene, such as the outside of the building in which an interview is taking place.

Inserting a cut-in or cut-away shot distracts the viewers' focus, if only for a second or two, allowing them to imagine that something happened in the previous scene "while they weren't looking." Using our previous example, if between the first and second shots you inserted a reaction shot of the interviewer nodding and smiling, the viewers would imagine that while they were watching the interviewer, the interviewee put the pencil down. Cut-ins and cut-aways are also used to add visual variety, enliven the pace, and add focus to the sound track. For instance, if you tape the president of your company in his office delivering a message about a new product line, it would be appropriate to edit in shots of those new products as they are mentioned.

When you're shooting in the field with an expectation of editing later (as is most often the case), you'll want to shoot as many cut-ins and cut-aways as possible. While you may be able to use the same reaction shot twice, after one repeat of it, viewers will begin to recognize it, and the illusion of that reaction *really* happening while the other person was talking will be destroyed. Cut-ins and cut-aways are not always planned: in some cases you'll have no prior idea of how much a segment will need to be edited down. Sometimes inserts are necessary to cover up camera mistakes, such as accidental jiggling or getting out of focus, or to replace a section of video with technical problems, such as a dropout or roll. It's usually rather easy to shoot more video while on the scene—and you can never have too many cut-ins or cut-aways to choose from when you're editing.

Another technique necessary when shooting for editing is rolling adequate tape before and after each scene. Every time the videotape is stopped or paused, it needs a few seconds to get up to speed again to be able to record a stable signal. So the first few seconds of all recorded segments are generally unusable. People accustomed to studio-style production are in the habit of giving "tight" cues to the talent so that a program doesn't begin with five seconds or so of a narrator staring blankly at the camera. In field shooting, however, each segment is edited to the next, so awkward pauses before the talent begins are always cut out. In fact, as you will see later in the section on editing, it is necessary to have a few seconds of stable recording *before* the desired in-cue to each segment. The same holds true for ending a segment: too often the camera operator is "trigger happy" and stops the tape on the talent's last word. When played back, the last part of the segment will be unusable, since the tape was stopping on the last word. Always leave yourself at least five seconds of tape *before* and *after* your desired segment—and have the talent hold the position without talking so that you will have a little cushion around the needed shot. The in—and out-cues will be tightened during editing.

During recording, sound levels should be monitored through headphones and/or by watching audio-level meters on the VCR. Sometimes producers *double-mike* the talent, so if one microphone develops a problem, the other will have recorded properly. Usually each mike is plugged into a separate channel on a two-channel recorder. In between segments, a little of the last segment should be played back and checked to see if everything is still recording properly. If the camera loses power between recording shots, and unless it has "memory" to hold its color balance, you will need to white-and black-balance the camera each time.

Battery levels should also be checked periodically when using this form of power supply: there's nothing more frustrating than losing power at a crucial moment or finding later that part of the tape is unusable because the battery levels started to drop. Along that same line the amount of tape left should be monitored regularly—when it's getting down to its last few minutes, it's better to stop at a logical breaking point and change tapes than to wait until it just runs out. Generally, cameras will display small warning lights and may also send out beeps to the headphone when batteries and tapes are getting low.

If the segments being shot involve a number of actions that need to be edited together, the producer must be aware of *continuity*. This means making certain that elements in the scenes being edited together remain constant enough to give the illusion of continuous action. For instance, say you want a sequence of a physician seen from behind walking toward an operating room, putting his hand on the door to open it, cutting to a shot from inside the room showing the doctor, now head on, coming toward the camera. Of course, these two angles will have to be shot separately if you're using only one camera. You will need to be careful that everything about the doctor's appearance stays the same between the two shots: if the first shot is to end just as he reaches for the door, the second will have to begin with his hand in the same place. If he's wearing a mask over his face in the second shot, make sure it's there in the first as well. If he opens the door with his right hand in the first shot, make sure he doesn't use the left hand when you shoot it five minutes later from the reverse angle.

Sometimes a crew member is given the specific job of watching for continuity. This is especially crucial when there are significant gaps of time between the taping of shots meant to be edited together. It's particularly important when days go by between shooting to make sure that the talents' clothes, hair, and makeup remain constant as do little details in the background scene. It's amazing sometimes what happens to scenes when they're edited. I remember looking at a tape a client sent us for review, and in a split-screen shot depicting a phone conversation, the two men were wearing the identical loud tie. Obviously, the two were sharing a tie—and no one thought ahead to imagine what the shots would look like when placed side-by-side in post-production!

As each tape is used, remember to label the tape with the date, the subject matter, and the number of that tape in the sequence. If a crew member is free to do so, it's useful to take notes on the shots and then include this information inside the tape box itself. This greatly speeds up the process of reviewing the tapes and selecting portions for editing. Don't rely on your memory to identify tapes—too often precious tapes have been bulk-erased or taped over because their identity was mistaken. If your practice is to re-use tapes, keep track of how many "passes" it's had in recording and playback; after considerable use, tapes tend to wear out and cause dropouts in recording. Be sure to retire tapes from use periodically to maintain quality.

When shooting "hand-held," a number of additional considerations arise. The first should be: is it *really* necessary to discard the tripod? Holding even the smallest of cameras becomes tiring, and it's difficult to maintain smooth and steady shots. Of course, to some extent, hand-held camera moves add interest and a feeling of "really being there" for the audience. The camera can travel through crowds, move along a subject and examine it from different angles, and take the position of a person's eyes as a scene is depicted. Our first full-time videographer was quite an acrobat. One really memorable shot of his depicting the educational situations in low-income areas was produced by his lying on a rug in the back of a classroom and being pulled on it to the front of the room as he gradually rose to his feet and got a slanted shot of writing on the blackboard!

If you *must* shoot without a tripod, be sure you have a comfortable shoulder mount, balanced and fitted for the camera operator. Try to stay on wide shots, where camera movements and the breathing movements of the camera operator are not so noticeable. You may want to use a camera steadier—such as the *Steadicam*, a device rigging the camera so it maintains a perfectly smooth shot, no matter how or where it's held—even on horseback. Steadiers are, however, bulky and very expensive. Finally, use a person to guide the camera operator while moving; the operator's only vision will be through the camera lens, which usually prevents seeing objects from the periphery or on the ground. It's easy for a person to trip or walk into something unless guided gently by verbal cues or a hand on the shoulder.

After a recording session, carefully strike the equipment and return the site to its normal configuration. Hot lights shouldn't be jostled, since they're likely to burst or break a filament—they're also dangerous! This is a good time to play back segments of the tape to check them for quality and to give the talent some feedback. We always have clients on hand during tapings to review the footage for accuracy and appropriateness. Sometimes they'll notice some small policy or safety violation that would make the shot unusable later on—and the producers and talent would never be aware of this detail. The VCR and monitor can be left connected to do this while the other gear is being packed up. Remember, your equipment lists will aid you in remembering to pack everything up again; if there's one thing *worse* than leaving something behind at a shot, it's forgetting something on location—from whence it often can't be recovered.

BIBLIOGRAPHY

KENNEDY, T. (1988). *Directing the Video Program*. White Plains, NY: Knowledge Industry Publications.

LeTOURNEAU, T. (1987). *Lighting Techniques for Video Production*. White Plains, NY: Knowledge Industry Publications.

MATHIAS, H. AND R. PATTERSON (1985). *Electronic Cinematography*. Belmont, CA: Wadsworth, Inc.

UTZ, P. (1987). *Today's Video: Equipment, Set Up, and Production*. Englewood Cliffs, NJ: Prentice-Hall.

WIEGAND, I. (1985). *Professional Video Production*. White Plains, NY: Knowledge Industry Publications

8
EDITING AND MIXING

The technology that brought us portable video has also mandated a new production style—one in which raw footage is shot in the field and the program is *really* produced in the editing suite. From scissors and splicing tape to computer-controlled banks of video editors and special effects devices, editing encompasses not only technology, but also technique. While the hardware certainly must be mastered, the management and organization of the "rushes" and the art of combining them logically and appealingly are the real skills of editing pros.

Post-production has many functions: to cut out mistakes, to assemble scenes shot out of order, to add visuals to a sound track or a sound track to visuals, to incorporate special effects, to enhance the audio or video, to pace a program, or to make a scene shot with one camera look as if it were shot with several. Some programs may require all, some few, but almost *none* are accomplished without some work after the shooting.

PREPARING TO EDIT

Except for the patching up of occasional mistakes in a studio production, most editing is planned. When a script is being developed, the writer can usually estimate about how much will need to be shot in the field, how many different shots and camera set-ups will be required, and what sort of shooting ratio will be involved. For instance, it will be obvious that certain shots will need to be taken in different locations and, therefore, edited together. Documentary-style production also requires the taping of much more footage than ever makes it into the final production—and basically the final narration will be written *around* the shots you actually got or what was actually said in interviews.

As described earlier, scripts are broken down into *shooting scripts,* and shots in the same location or shots of similar scenes are produced together. This means that the *raw footage* or *rushes* or *masters* (unedited tapes) are likely to contain segments out of order with regard to the overall script. Furthermore, there may be quite a bit of tape that's unusable, either containing "bad takes," camera errors, or long-winded interviewees whose comments must be cut down considerably to avoid putting the viewers to sleep.

Just as production time is precious and expensive, so is editing time. Many producers need to rent outside facilities; these can cost from $100 to over $1,000 per hour, depending on the location and the sophistication of special-effects equipment. Even in an in-house studio, editing equipment is expensive, so there are usually just one or two systems to serve a number of producers. The bottom line is that editing systems must be used efficiently, and in order to do that, you must be prepared to edit. That means going into the post-production suite armed with an *editing script* or *edit decision list.*

The biggest mistake you can make is to wait until editing day to decide exactly which shots or "takes" you plan to use—and to find where in the stacks of raw tapes they happen to be. This sort of ill-preparedness not only costs extra money and ties up valuable editing machines for the mere viewing of shots, but it can drive an editing engineer to distraction. Before editing—in fact right after tapes are shot, if possible—the raw material must be *logged.* See Figures 8-1 and 8-2. Each tape has a *log* that describes each shot and its location according to minutes elapsed on the tape, or according to SMPTE *time cod*e recorded onto one of the tape's channels. SMPTE (for Society of Motion Picture and Television Engineers) time code is a standard reference for finding points on tapes; it is written on an audio channel, on a special time code channel, or in the picture's vertical blanking interval, and denotes hours, minutes, seconds, and frames by a special time-code reader plugged into a VCR during recording. It can be displayed on the screen by being played through a frame-code reader, though, of course, it does not appear in the final edit. For viewing purposes, often a 3/4-inch or 1/2-inch *window dub* of the master tapes is made with a window showing the time code numbers in a window. That way, clients and producers can look at the images and log tapes without fear of wearing out the masters, and without needing to tie up more expensive playback equipment if the tapes were shot on Betacam, M-II, or some other high-end format.

The more detail you can put into a tape log, the better, Often the segments are timed out, so you know just how long each scene takes. This is useful for timing out narration to fit over the video or for figuring out how many sequences can fit into a 20-minute program. Comments as to the acceptability of each segment are crucial as well. You may have nine or ten takes of a scene, each with certain mistakes or drawbacks, and you'll need to choose the right one come editing time. In complex projects, sometimes audiotapes are made so that typewritten transcripts like those shown in Figure 8-3 can be generated. In this way, there's a hard copy for clients or legal advisors to review details in wording without looking at the tapes themselves.

After logging each tape, you write up an *editing script.* This is just like your first complete script, except it includes addresses by tape counter number or SMPTE code for each segment (see Figure 8-4). Often the audio and video portions come from two different segments on the raw tapes—the voice track from an interview, for example, and video inserts from scenes shot in the field, stock footage, or graphics. At this stage, you'll write any final narration needed to tie in the footage. The key to this whole process of edit planning is to use the editing suite only for editing and to use simple playback machines for viewing the raw tapes and making decisions as to what will wind up in the final product.

Let me give you an example for a project we did for a special children's

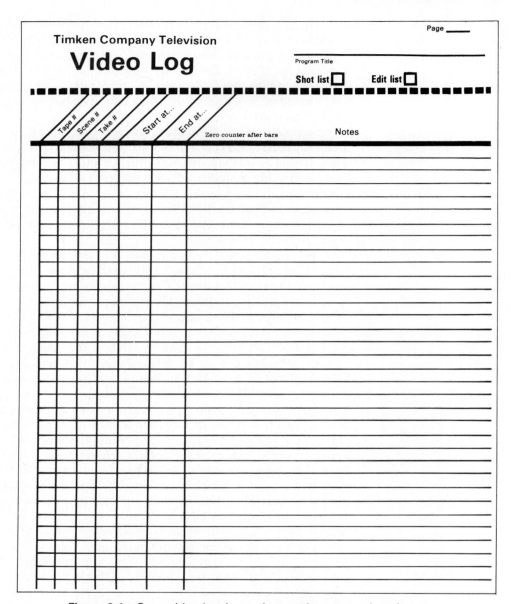

Figure 8-1 Once video has been shot, each tape needs to be logged so that you know where scenes are located (*courtesy, Timkin*).

center. The video was to demonstrate how the center was making use of a computer and software that had been donated to help children with various developmental disabilities and to encourage further similar support. We met with the center's administrators and got a general idea of what they were doing and wished to communicate. We spent a day shooting several teachers and therapists using the computer in classes and with individual clients and had them explain in their own words what they were doing. We shot a number of cut-aways of children and teachers at work, as well as general shots of the building. We logged all the tapes and found segments that were desirable to include. Then, we wrote a voice-over narration which served as an open, tied together various teachers' segments, and concluded the production. Finally, we selected music, edited a visually appealing "open," and edited together the opening narration, individual classroom segments,

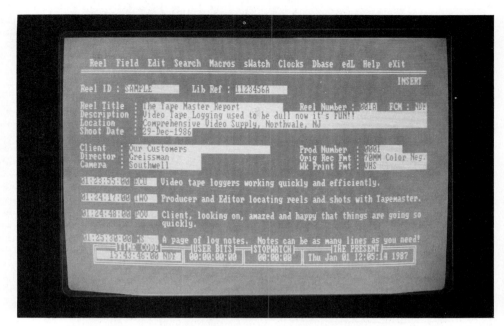

Figure 8-2 Computerized logging systems like this one make the job of identifying and finding scenes easier (*courtesy, Comprehensive Video*).

and the closing montage with music. You might say we violated the basic rule of never shooting without a script, but since we wanted a documentary-style production, we didn't want to "force" the scenes. We had an idea of the content and flow and wanted the teachers and children to speak for themselves—only using the narrator for the shortest time possible.

HOW EDITING WORKS

Videotape editing, unlike most other forms of media editing, is a process of duplication rather than cutting and splicing. All editing is electronic (performed by VCRs) rather than manually (using scissors and tape). In order to edit, you need to understand a bit about exactly what gets recorded onto videotape and why.

Before the days of electronic videotape editing, the cutting out or rearranging of program segments was done physically, much like audio tape or film. The tape was cut and spliced back together in the desired order. Often, however, this resulted in glitches or rolling pictures for a second or two around the edit point. Why?

We all know that videotape contains tracks for both audio (sound) and video (picture). What we can't perceive so readily is another track on most formats called the *control track* or *sync track*. Figure 8-5 illustrates how the tracks on 1-inch type C tape are laid out. This band of information along the tape has control pulses recorded on it, one for each video frame. There are 30 video frames per second— and 30 control pulses per second. These pulses can be thought of as "electronic sprocket holes." They keep the tape running at an even speed so that the VCR can "read" the signals correctly.

In order to perform a successful mechanical edit, you would have to cut the tape between control pulses and match up the tape segments so that the pulses were evenly spaced. This is just about impossible, since the control pulses are invisible, unless a special "developer" fluid is applied and the tape is examined under a

Begin tape 59

Diane: This is the first interview with Betty _____.

Kd directs.

Noise of a crowd.

#59

Diane: Betty, can you tell me a little bit about this gathering, who all is here today?

Betty: This is the _____ Cousins picnic and it consists of first cousins, the aunts and uncles, second, third cousins of a family of ten children of which seven aunts and uncles are still living and there are about 23 or 24 first cousins and their families. We have an annual picnic every year and we get together every two months, we have a family picnic, this is the third year in a row, but we have this family gathering to try to keep ourselves together because we're scattered all over the city and to different parts of the country. And that's basically what the picnic's all about, trying to keep our family together.

Diane: Why is it so important for all of you to keep your family together? What do you think you get out of this?

Betty: Well, I think the main thing is that we remember

Diane: Why is it so important for you to keep your family together? What do you feel you get out of this?

Betty: Well, I think we get this feeling of closeness which has disappeared from today's role because a lot of our young people have _____ and they don't
don't seem to get together and when we/live close to each other, so this is our way of getting together at least once a year where we see everybody and get to know a little bit about each other's families.

Diane: What does the Cousins Club do besides have this annual picnic?

Betty: We have a family dinner every year where we treat our aunts and uncles and we also gather every two months; we go to each other's houses and we just sit around and talk and reminisce about the old days and talk about the things we did when we were kids and the family traditions we try to keep up over the years and around the holidays you know we get together once in awhile and basically just try to remember what we did as we were kids and bring these things closer to us.

Diane: It seems really important for you to keep alive the kind of way that you were brought up when you were young; you seem to want to pass that on to your children. What was it about the way that you were brought up that you thought was so special that you want to pass on to your kids?

Betty: Well, the closeness of families. Years ago your grandparents lived around the corner, your aunts and uncles lived around the corner and our particular house, my mother being the oldest of ten,
our
KHK house was the expression there (Grand Central Station). They were in and out, there were parties all the time and with everybody being so far away from each other, there isn't that feeling today that there was years ago in the family neighborhood.

Diane: How do the young people here feel about it, a lot of young people are kind of getting away from families as you said today?

Betty: Well, this is sort of working together and they really like the idea and they like the idea of meeting cousins and they want to know who's who and how they're related and whether they're second, third or fourth cousins and when we do get together they all meet each other and at least if they see each other say in town or someplace KHK they can go up to each other and say, oh, hi, I met you at the picnic, or I met you at the square dance or I met you up at Fordham. The young kids really seem to be going back, getting back to th family which is really the main reason for these gatherings, to get the young people, let them have the feeling that we had when we were kids which you really don't get much of today because like I said we're all separated and we all live so far away from each other.

Diane: Do you think this kind of thing is a reaction to roots; a lot of young people now are interested

Betty: Very definitely, very definitely. A lot of your college students that I have met are working on these things, they're taking ethnic studies, people in the neighborhood are getting very interested in this; I'm personally involved in the KHKHKH Museum which has roots that go way back which were all brought over from Germany, from England and from all your foreign countries and really the young people are very definitely interested in this; they're really going back, they want to know who they are and what they are and where they came from.

Diane: Is that a factor in your family. Your family is mostly Italian with some Polish mixed in.

Betty: Yea, we have a few, we have a lot of Polish, we have Germans, Irish, we have quite a few that have married into, you know, Irish descent fellows and girls but the majority are Italian and I guess quite a few have married Polish.

Diane: Do you think the Italian back/ ground plays a large part in your kids background?

Betty: Very definitely. Very definitely. The food, the traditions, our Christmas Eve tradition, both on the Polish side and the Italian side.

Diane: Betty, what specific traditions are you trying to pass on to your kids, what kind of Italian traditions are you passing on?

Betty: Well, one main thing is the tradition of the respect for our elders that a lot of kids aren't with their grandparents, my children right now only have one grandparent. They were very young when their Italian grandparents died, they remember them, but not as well as I would like them to. They both died within the last ten or eleven years and they were a little too young to remember, like the Christmas eve dinners and the traditions that we had where we all sat down at the big table and we just ate and ate for hours everything from soup to nuts, the Italian soup, the lasagne, the ravioli. But in my cooking I try to, you know, I cook both in fact, both the Polish and the Italian but with their Polish grandmother we go there for breakfast on Easter and on Christmas and we have the traditional Polish breakfast and they look forward to that and during the year they'll say to me, gee Mom, how about if you cooked that, why wait till the holiday. So, that's one of the main things and the different, like Easter coats that my mother use to make and on New Year's there were specific things that she made but they don't remember, but I mean we try to you know cook them for the kids to let them get a taste and you know when kids are little they don't really want to taste, they have very funny taste but as they get older they try more and more different foods, they realize as they get older that as long as they taste it, they dont' know whether they like something until they taste it and they, that's one of the main reasons I like to keep up the different foods and the Easter tradition and the Christmas tradition are the two things, visiting relatives is one of the biggest things. Where families get together and vist each other, that was one of the really big things amongst the Italian people.

Diane: Now, your kids are half Polish and half Italian, a lot of people say now as the generations go on and on and everybody kind of melts in and is American; how do your kids feel, do they identify with the Polish or the Italian or neither one.

Betty: They really identify with both. I mean, they're teased on both sides with the Polish jokes and the Italian jokes but basically they're meshed on both sides because I keep up the Italian tradition and then with the Polish grandmom they, you know we keep up the Polish tradition too. So, they're really, they consider themselves both.

KHKHK

Tape 59 continued

Diane: Peachie, you're the founder of this Cousins Club, what gave you the idea to start it?

Pea chie: Well, the idea started when all you ever hear people say is, we only
each
see/other at wakes and weddings, why don't we get together, why don't we keep in touch more often. So, one day it just dawned on me that someone has to start this, so I figured let me try a trial run letter you know so I comprised this letter and sent it out to all the first cousins just for their reaction of the letter, not so much, are you ready to come to the event. So, I sent - recently an idea came to mind that I thought you might be interested in and I'm sure that you'll agree that it seems that the only time families see each other is at wakes and weddings. So, to avoid reunions at these rare and not too happy events, a sort of occasional get together might prove to be quite interesting. The Cousins Club would be an appropriate title for our group. The general idea is that we would get together as often as possible, approximately once a month, meeting in each other's homes. Also, a few times a year socially events can be planned such as dinner and a show, Palumbo's, weekend in New York or up the mo untains or any suggestions that might come to mind. And, its understandable that all of us could not possibly attend every event or gathering but I just wanted to share the idea with you and get your opinion. And, if you're interested please drop a note or call, whatever. And then about 26 reactions came in such as letters

Figure 8-3 Sometimes a complete transcript of videotapes is typed. Here, the underlined portions are the ones which will be included in the final production.

from one cousin who said, I hope the letter's not too late, the Cousins Club is really a great idea and you're right about the weddings and the funerals and one is too far, inbetween and too sad so this would be a great idea and another one came from South Carolina, what a great idea you came up with and Carol and I would be glad to make as many meetings as possible, we'll fly in on the week-ends and they all followed just the same.

Diane: What do you do with the Cousins Club? How often do you get together and what do the meetings consist of?

Peaches: Well, we usually meet about every two months and I thougt it was apropos that I start the first one so I made it a cocktail party with hors d'oeuvre and cocktails and we had a great turnout and then at the meetings we discussed like who will take the next meeting you know, so someone else will pick the home and they'll have whatever they want, they can do anything they want, dinner, hors d'oeuvres or pizza and beer, whatever and we discuss what we're going to do that coming year and to keep traditions together XXX and visit during holidays and outings and from this we came up with the family picnic which we're at now today and that's for first cousins, second cousins, children, aunts and uncles and also once a year we take the aunts and uncles out to dinner.

Diane: How many people are there in the Cousins Club and how far away do the peoplecome?

Peaches: Well, with husbands and wives, I would say about 49 or a little less maybe and once in awhile the couple from South Carolina, they'll fly up, one time the cousin from Chicago flew up and then we have an uncle in Pittsburgh and one in Wilmington. Basically they're in Philadelphia or Jersey and they do come, basically everyone comes about every two months and especially to the picnic which is in Lake once a year.

Diane: Why do you think its important that you keep your family together like this?

Peaches: Families nowadays they kind of dwindle away, and the only way you keep them together is a few strong people just about more or less forcing it to stay together, making it pleasant enough; let's go to that thing or let's go over here and she's right, let's keep everybody together to just spread the love and to keep all the family ties closer instead of farther apart.

Diane: How do the young people feel about it; why do young people kind of shun their families and go off with their friends; what's been the reaction to the younger people here?

Peaches: Well I think that's true about going off with their friends but once a year they kind of feel well this is once a year and once they get here they really say its not too bad at all being with everybody and they say who's that woman over there and realize its an aunt or you'll say, who's that little kid over there and its a cousin. This way the more you come to these picnics and meetings the more you realize that you know these people are your cousins and not a stranger any more, and they have the water and everything and everybody likes to eat so they really some of them are even thinking of starting their own, you know the second gener-ation cousins.

Diane: What kind of traditions are you trying to pass on to the younger generation here?

Peaches: Well, naturally it always starts with the food and the cooking, and you always want to instill in the children the importance of keeping close you know, staying together and keeping our love and respect, you know, and by coming to-gether that's what happens.

Diane: Ed, you've got to get that.

Diane: Are you taping it?

End tape 59

060

Diane: You said that you keep the Cousins Club together to kind of keep alive the traditions in your family. What kind of traditions are you trying to keep up?

Peaches: Well, basically it starts out with the food, different bakings, you know we make certain Easter cakes you know made with the ricotta cheese, and at Christmas time we have butter cookies and whatnots, you know. So, it starts with the food. But the other traditions is just the really closeness and we find out the talents in the family. The crocheting and then you find a little kid crocheting and wonder how they ever got started you know, so I guess each family has their own type of tradition and things that they do, you know and its nice to just pass it on to the children. You know, it makes the older relatives feel better and the children become more worldwide and they learn all the different things that have gone back in family times and to strangers it's a new thing, you know, its

a new activity or whatever, but to the family its been in there for ages.

Diane: How important is it to your family that their Italian, are you trying to keep up any thing specifically Italian about your heritage?

Peaches: Well, certain people have started to delve more into the Italian roots as they say, you know, the family tree and what not, you know, we came from there, or whatever and you pick up all the Italian customs, you know, again with the cooking you know, it starts there and you pass it on and improves it a little or whatever, I guess they'll do more research as time goes on; maybe it's the younger cousins might, you know know as far as the older ones, II just really grandparents and where they came from and their parents and so on and so forth, family tree type of thing.

Diane: Do you think your family was raised any different because you're an ethnic family, because you're an Italian family?

Peaches: Closeness, if anything. I feel that Italian people are very, very close and they make everyone else feel the same way. You just belong no matter who you are you know. You come into an Italian house, the food is there again, you know, and whoever you are, you know, you can have whatever. There's just no difference when it comes to, you know, for Italian people, all people are the same.

Diane: Are you guys recording? Tell me your name, address and telephone number.

Chris   , 137 S. California,   Pennsylvania

Diane: Chris, how do you like coming to these family get togethers?

Chris: I wouldn't miss them.

Diane: I understand that you're XXX thinking of starting a second cousins club for the younger generation. Why would you do something like that?

Chris: Well, ever since this one started we see a lot of each other, a lot more of each other.

Diane: Chris, how do you feel about coming to these family gatherings?

Chris: They're just great, I wouldn't miss them for anything.

Diane: I understand you're starting a second cousins club. What gave you the idea to do that?

Chris: Well, after this one started, you know, we see a lot of each other and I really like this side of my family and just to see them I guess and associate and have a good time. We really do get along very well.

Diane: Why do you think its important to keep the family together like this? What do you get out of it?

Chris: Just knowing how nice my family is, they're all very friendly, we get along with everybody. Everybody gets along really fine.

Diane: Do you think your family is any different than the family of some of your friends because you're raised as an Italian?

Chris: Without a doubt. Italians are close you know real close. Not all, you know, there are exceptions but, XXXXXXXXXXXXX I'd say our family is very knit.

Diane: You obviously didn't come over from Italy, you're probably third or fourth generation, how can you still identify as being Italian?

Chris: Well, I mean if everybody's going to cut you up about being Italian, you might as well stick to it, you know, stand up for yourself, why not.

Diane: What do you think is good about being Italian, what's important about your Italian heritage?

Chris: Well, I'm sure I'm no better than anybody else but, I like the food and the wine and the great times.

Diane: If you start a second cousins club, what will you do with it?

Chris: We'd have some wild parties. We would go out to eat; we have a place down on the shore now, me and my cousins got together and got a house for the summer. We got a job down there and we're going to have a really good time this summer. I think just every summer we're going to be getting a little closer all the time. And, by the time we're all these people age, all the other kids are going to start all over again, hopefully.

Diane: So, you think its going to keep up beyond your generation?

Chris: I hope so. I'd like to see, you know, my kids and   have a good time with each other.

Diane: Mr. Martelli, you came here all the way from Pittsburgh to New Jersey to attend this family reunion, what would make you drive so far to get together like this?

Mr. M: Well, this is a very closely knit family, and there's always some reason to get the family together. Now, we have a cousins club with all the nieces and

Figure 8-3 Continued

nephews who meet about every two months and once a year they invite the parents;
to entertain the parents and this is the result of the family reunion or family
picnic. This is all due to the cousins who pay all the expenses for everyone to
be here to entertain them.

Diane: How was the---------

Diane: Mr. Martelli, you came all the way from Pittsburgh to New Jersey to attend
this family picnic, what would you, make you make such a long trip to get together
with the family?

Mr. M: Well, this is an important affair that's held. Our nieces and nephews
have formed a Cousins Club and they invited the parents to attend a family reunion
picnic.

Diane: How did you raise your own family to keep the family so close; obviously
there must have been something instilled in you to keep the family ties so strong?

Mr. M: This has been a family tradition. My family was very closely knit. Our
family of actually 14 children, 10 of us lived and raised together and we were
very close and this is the way my parents had trained us from the time we were
children, that we are one family, we stay together and we live together and this
is what we have continued to do, we have raised our own families the same as we
were raised when we were children.

Diane: What kind of traditions did you pass on to your own sons, I know you have
one son here all the way from South Carolina; how in particular did you raise your
family to have such strong ties?

Mr. M: This is a followup of my training and my background. From the time my
children were infants we always stayed together and we always had our little
                                    like
conversations, llllll mornings preparing for school, we would have our breakfast
together and discuss our problems for the day, that we had the previous day and
what our plans were for that day. And, I train them the same as my parents
trained me. But, you know, we are one family and this is the way we are going
to stay, as one family.
                        were
Diane: You, yourself xxx raised in South Philadelphia and then you moved to
Pittsburgh, how did you maintain such close ties with the people back in South
Philadelphia?

Mr. M: Well, this again rates, reverts back to our training. We are close and
we like to stay close. I've made trips every two weeks for years, back and forth
before the turnpikes were built and our six dollar weekend excursions on the rail-
roads; I stay close to the family and I had my children do the same thing.

Diane: What about the experience of your parents. Now, they were Italian immigrants, do you think there's any special kind of ethnic or heritage that they

passed on to you as being an Italian? How important is it that this family's
Italian?

Mr. M: You'll find that most immigrants like to stay together and this was the
same with my parents and their families. As their brothers and sisters came to
this country they stayed together and that helped my parents to stay close to us.
Now we had a tradition, 6:00 or 5:00, between 5 and 6 was our dinner hour. And
that was a must. Ten children had to be at that table for dinner and you had to
have a darn good reason not to be there, you were still not excused and that was
our raising.

Diane: When you were growing up in South Philadelphia, how many people in the
neighborhood were actually part of your family?

Mr. M: Our family spread out in quite a hurry, as they started to marry off and
have

Diane: When you grew up in South Philadelphia, how many people in the neighborhood
were part of your family? How close did your family live to your actual house?

Mr. M: Well, we all lived within several blocks. As the family grew and married
off, they all lived within maybe three or four blocks of the parent house.

Diane: And as the upcoming generations kind of spread out, do you think they,
there was something about that living together that they missed that was kind
of the start of something like this Cousins Club?

Mr. M: The girls in South Phillie decided that something should be done to bring
the family closer together. We have spread out, I'd gone to Pittsburgh and my
brother has gone to Wilmington, Delaware and they started to move up to Germantown
and northeast and Chester and all over the surrounding areas and somebody had to
do something to get them together. However, in a family like we have, there's
always some reason someone will come up with a reason to have a party to get the
family together; a christening, a wedding, a birthday, be on the phone calling
everybody up, come on over. There's always a reason to get the family together.

Diane: Do you think that your family is different than the families of some of
the other, some of your other friends or some of the other people who might live
near you in Pittsburgh? Do you think that you're closer than the average American
family?

Mr. M: I don't know of another family that's closer than the Martelli family,
we are very, very close even though we're not living close together we're still
very close.

Diane: How important is your family to you?

Mr. M: I would say very important.

Figure 8-3 Continued

microscope. Therefore, most of these cut-and-splice edits result in picture break-up
and are used only in extreme emergencies for excising badly damaged sections from
a tape.

Electronic editing, on the other hand, leaves the master tapes untouched. The
portions of the raw footage desired in the final program are duplicated or *dubbed*
onto another *edited master* tape, segment by segment. In order to do this so that
there is no electronic disturbance, a special editing VCR is used to record the final
edited program. To cue up the playback or *master* machine and the editing or *slave*
machine perfectly so that you're recording exactly the segments you wish, an *editing
controller* or *edit interface* is used between the two VCRs (see Figure 8-6).

In order to edit, you lay down segment after segment from the master raw
tapes onto the master edited tape. But it's not as simple as just pressing record and
play. What would happen if you used one playback deck patched into a record
button to start each new edit? Well, there would be several seconds of disturbed
video right after each edit point. That's because tapes need to get up to speed
before they are able to record or play back properly. To allow them to get up to
speed, VCRs must be *prerolled* about five seconds before you actually want the edit
to take place—the editor plays back for five seconds while getting up to speed and
then goes into the "record" mode. This preroll of both master and slave decks is
also accomplished by means of the interface.

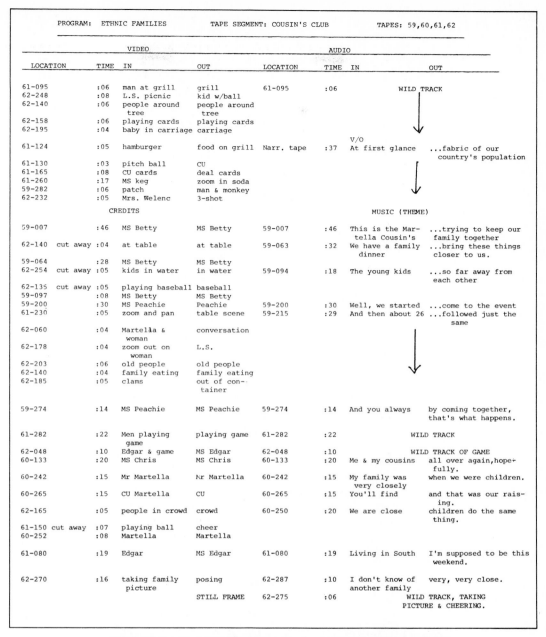

```
        PROGRAM:  ETHNIC FAMILIES        TAPE SEGMENT: COUSIN'S CLUB        TAPES: 59,60,61,62
```

LOCATION		TIME	VIDEO IN	OUT	LOCATION	TIME	AUDIO IN	OUT
61-095		:06	man at grill	grill	61-095	:06	WILD TRACK	
62-248		:08	L.S. picnic	kid w/ball				
62-140		:06	people around tree	people around tree				
62-158		:06	playing cards	playing cards				
62-195		:04	baby in carriage	carriage				
							V/O	
61-124		:05	hamburger	food on grill	Narr. tape	:37	At first glance	...fabric of our country's population
61-130		:03	pitch ball	CU				
61-165		:08	CU cards	deal cards				
61-260		:17	MS keg	zoom in soda				
59-282		:06	patch	man & monkey				
62-232		:05	Mrs. Welenc	3-shot				
			CREDITS				MUSIC (THEME)	
59-007		:46	MS Betty	MS Betty	59-007	:46	This is the Mar-tella Cousin's	...trying to keep our family together
62-140	cut away	:04	at table	at table	59-063	:32	We have a family dinner	...bring these things closer to us.
59-064		:28	MS Betty	MS Betty				
62-254	cut away	:05	kids in water	in water	59-094	:18	The young kids	...so far away from each other
62-135	cut away	:05	playing baseball	baseball				
59-097		:08	MS Betty	MS Betty				
59-200		:30	MS Peachie	Peachie	59-200	:30	Well, we started	...come to the event
61-230		:05	zoom and pan	table scene	59-215	:29	And then about 26	...followed just the same
62-060		:04	Martella & woman	conversation				
62-178		:04	zoom out on woman	L.S.				
62-203		:06	old people	old people				
62-140		:04	family eating	family eating				
62-185		:05	clams	out of con-tainer				
59-274		:14	MS Peachie	MS Peachie	59-274	:14	And you always	by coming together, that's what happens.
61-282		:22	Men playing game	playing game	61-282	:22	WILD TRACK	
62-048		:10	Edgar & game	MS Edgar	62-048	:10	WILD TRACK OF GAME	
60-133		:20	MS Chris	MS Chris	60-133	:20	Me & my cousins	all over again,hope-fully.
60-242		:15	Mr Martella	Mr Martella	60-242	:15	My family was very closely	when we were children.
60-265		:15	CU Martella	CU	60-265	:15	You'll find	and that was our rais-ing.
62-165		:05	people in crowd	crowd	60-250	:20	We are close	children do the same thing.
61-150	cut away	:07	playing ball	cheer				
60-252		:08	Martella	Martella				
61-080		:19	Edgar	MS Edgar	61-080	:19	Living in South	I'm supposed to be this weekend.
62-270		:16	taking family picture	posing	62-287	:10	I don't know of another family	very, very close.
				STILL FRAME	62-275	:06	WILD TRACK, TAKING PICTURE & CHEERING.	

Figure 8-4 Once all the tapes are logged, an editing script is developed. It contains all the in- and out-points for audio and video for the entire show. Notice how many different cuts are used to incorporate different interviews and cutaways over interview audio.

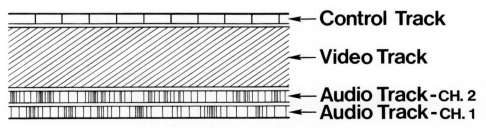

Figure 8-5 Tracks on Type-C tape.

To understand the need for preroll in a more concrete sense, take the example of relay racers. Before the baton is passed from racer 1 to racer 2, racer 2 starts to run alongside racer 1 to get up to speed. That's exactly what the VCRs do before each edit. You set your edit points and put each VCR in pause. Then when you press the "edit" button, the VCRs rewind about 5 seconds, playback those 5 seconds of preroll while getting up to speed, and then the units actually make the edit. While at first it may look disturbing when watching an editing session, you soon learn to ignore those five seconds of preroll. (Editing systems based on digital video or videodiscs don't need this kind of preroll, so although they're still rare, you should keep this distinction in mind.)

So, tapes must first be prerolled to get up to speed before each edit is made, but the preroll is also important for another reason. An editing VCR, or *editor* as they're usually called, must also perform a special function that differentiates it from a mere "recorder." In order to assemble edited segments into a program so that the edits are "clean" and have no disturbance, a perfect control track or sync track must be maintained on the final edited tape. In editing a *film,* you must be sure that all the sprocket holes are evenly spaced around the edit point so that the film doesn't jump through the projector at each edit. Likewise, when assembling an edited tape, the "electronic sprocket holes" or sync pulses on videotape must be evenly spaced. Here's how video tape editors make sure that a perfect sync track is maintained: during that preroll, when the tapes are getting up to speed in preparation for an edit, the editor "listens" to the sync coming in from the playback VCR and matches up its speed accordingly, using a capstan servo which can adjust the speed to the recorder's motor so that when an edit is made the sync pulses will line up perfectly with what is already on the tape. Regular nonediting VCRs can't do this, so they'll never produce reliable edits.

There are two types of edit modes, *assemble editing* and *insert editing.* They are used for different purposes and vary in the way that the signal is put down onto the edited tape. Refer to Figure 8-7. Assemble editing is used to join segments containing audio and video and the corresponding sync track together, one segment after another. Say, for instance, you interviewed a number of employees and asked their opinions of the new benefits package. If you wanted to string bits of each interview together to form a story, using both the audio and video of each interview, you'd use the assemble mode on your editor.

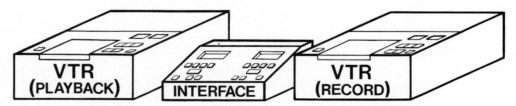

Figure 8-6 Simple editing is accomplished by a playback VCR and an editing VCR interfaced via a controller.

The insert mode, as its name implies, is used to insert material onto an existing recording. The material inserted can be audio only, video only, or both audio and video. But there must be an existing sync track laid down on your edited master to insert onto. For example, you decide to videotape the president of your organization delivering the annual report. To keep this 30-minute lecture from putting the viewers completely to sleep, you decide it would be a good idea to incorporate visuals supporting his statements—shots of the new products, graphics showing sales trends, scenes of the new manufacturing process, and so on. You first record his speech, edit it onto your edited master tape, and then going back and using the "video only" insert mode, replace some segments of his talking face with appropriate cut-aways, keeping his sound track intact. Similarly, by using "audio insert," you could insert only a sound track, say of narration or music, over previously recorded material, keeping the original video the same. On machines with more than one channel of audio, you can insert any one or any combination of audio tracks—adding narration, for example, over scenes with video and audio on the other track. You can also insert audio and video together: if you wanted to replace a segment of an existing tape with other scenes *exactly* the length of what you wanted to get rid of, you use an "audio and video insert."

In the insert mode, no sync is recorded: this means that you must insert over some existing video and control tracks. You never use the insert mode to "assemble" a new segment over blank tape, because you won't be recording a control track and therefore won't have the electronic control information needed to play back the

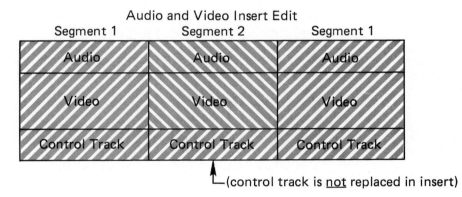

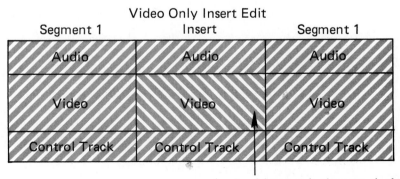

(control track is <u>not</u> replaced in insert)

(only video track changes during insert)

Figure 8-7 Assemble and insert edits. Notice which tracks are changed during each of the three different kinds of edits.

tape. It would be like trying to show a film that had no sprocket holes.

Since the insert mode doesn't disturb the underlying sync track, sometimes it's used exclusively when editing to ensure a perfect "glitch-free" edited master. To use it this way, you must first record a continuous video signal (color bars, black, or *anything* for that matter) the full length of the tape to be edited onto, then do all edits in the insert mode. You can't assemble *anything* using this process, since in that mode a new sync track is laid down, wiping out what was there before. So, assemble-edit over blank tape; insert-edit over previously "blacked" tape. To get the best edits, always black a tape first and make all insert edits.

TIME CODE AND CONTROL TRACK EDITING

Editing interface units are used for remote control of the VCRs during an editing session. Instead of operating the controls for rewind, pause, play, or edit on the actual machines, the interface unit duplicates these buttons so that the needed controls are all in one place. The interfaces also preroll each VCR and start them up at the same time so that edits take place exactly where they should. Finally, interface units are used to search for the desired in and out cues; interfaces allow you to search at various speeds—to whiz through portions of a tape or to creep along frame-by-frame while watching the picture to decide an exact edit point.

These interfaces need to keep track of where you are on the playback "master" and editing "slave" tapes. They do this by one of two methods: counting control pulses or monitoring SMPTE time code. The control-track interfaces are generally less expensive and do not rely on having SMPTE code laid down on the videotape. However, they're less accurate and do not provide for sophisticated automation of editing. Wherever control track is missing on the tape, such as between takes, or is disturbed for some reason, the interface will not register and will stop counting. Also when playing back very slowly or very quickly, a few control pulses usually get lost in the shuffle, making the interface's count a bit off.

SMPTE time-code interfaces are more expensive, but they're frame-accurate. This type of edit controller enables you to do computerized editing. Instead of performing edits one at a time, searching for your desired segments as you go, you can type in the entire SMPTE *edit decision list,* or in—and out-cues for each segment. Then the computer automatically cues up the tapes and performs the edits according to your list. This process allows you to make a new master edited tape right from the originals whenever you desire, without the need for an operator to sit down and do it in "real time." It also facilitates difficult editing, such as the rapid editing of extremely short segments. Of course, the interface can't change tapes in a VCR automatically, but many of them can control a number of different playback VCRs loaded with different tapes.

ON-LINE AND OFF-LINE EDITING

Simple editing, with one playback deck, one editing deck, and an interface, allows you to put together materials using straight *cuts* from one segment to the next. These video cuts look like "takes" between cameras going through a switcher. But let's say you want to add special effects, such as wiping from one segment to the next or squeezing one picture out of the screen while another replaces it. You *can* do this manually, with several VCRs, a switcher, and a conventional edit controller. But you'd better be pretty coordinated! And let's say you want to show your finished program to your client—and the client suggests that it looks great except for the one sentence a customer said right in the middle of the program. You simply can't cut out this segment physically, and unless you can find an acceptable substitute for it which is exactly the same length, you'll have to edit the whole program over again! Fortunately, computerized or *on-line* editing can rescue you.

Off-line editing refers to edits done with simple cuts-only systems (see Figure 8-8). Often a quick and dirty off-line edit is done to rough out a program and get client approval. Then the edit decision list created through this process is fed into a computerized editing interface in an *on-line* edit suite which may also contain higher quality VCRs as well as the gear needed for special effects.

Figure 8-8   An off-line editing system (*courtesy, Panasonic*).

Many organizational video departments have off-line edit suites for an initial edit but use rental post-production houses for final on-line editing and special effects. Post-production equipment is the most rapidly changing and expensive part of video gear, and often it's best to let specialists keep up with (and pay for) this exotica. However, many internal facilities do have extensive on-line systems like those shown in Figures 8-9 and 8-10.

But how do you prepare for on-line editing—especially when you want to add special effects transitions such as dissolves or wipes between segments? This is called A-B rolling because you're rolling two tapes (A and B) to combine their signals and record onto a third (C) editor. If, for instance, you want to dissolve from scene A to scene B, the scenes must first be placed on two separate tapes in two separate playback VCRs. The VCRs are cued up so that the shots to be dissolved into each other play back at the same time. The outputs of the VCRs are fed through a switcher, which is then fed into the editor and is used to perform the dissolve. A similar setup is used to superimpose character-generated titles over a video scene, except that instead of a "B" tape and recorder, the second source is the character generator. When more than one video source is used for playback, each playback VCR must be *time-base corrected* to match it to all the other sync sources.

So, there is a significant difference in price between a basic cuts-only off-line system and even a rather simple on-line system that can do dissolves or keying of graphics or titles over video during editing. The first system uses just one playback VCR, one edit controller, and one editing VCR. The second uses two playback VCRs, two time-base correctors, one character generator, a switcher, an editing interface that can read SMPTE time code and control multiple sources and finally, the edit VCR. High-end editing interfaces can "talk to" switchers and special digital

Figure 8-9 An on-line editing suite; note that a team is needed to enable sophisticated switching, audio mixing, and input of computer graphics along with the actual editing (*courtesy, Avid Communications*).

Figure 8-10 Another on-line suite; note the computer-like editing controller at the center of the photo.

effects devices so that you don't have to worry about when to execute your effects manually. Many programs require such elaborate edits, combining the inputs of multiple VCRs and audio sources and adding special effects, that you simply couldn't do it all yourself perfectly in "real time."

In order to produce a tape with dissolves or wipes, you must specially prepare your A and B tapes (see Figures 8-11 and 8-12). When the A tape is being recorded, there should be just black on the B tape. During the portion when you want to dissolve between A and B, there should be appropriate footage on both tapes. Once you've dissolved to B, there should be nothing but black on A. As you can see, it takes great planning—and basically two editing jobs—to assemble both your A and B tapes and then to edit those onto a final master. Also, as you can see, you lose an additional generation.

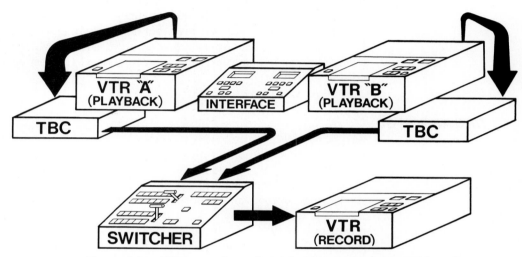

Figure 8-11 Effects such as dissolving between shots requires the use of A/B rolls. Two playback VCRs (both locked up by means of time-base correctors) and a switcher are interfaced to a recording VCR.

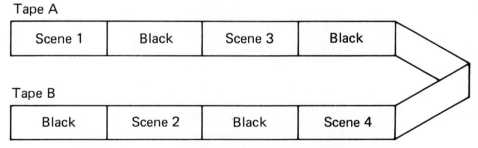

Figure 8-12 In order to A/B roll, two tapes must be prepared. When one tape is playing back a scene, the other tape has black.

The Next Generation of Editing Systems

In some ways, people are looking "back to the future" when envisioning new editing systems. While video can beat film in terms of immediacy of recording and playback, film was much easier to edit. You could physically add or subtract footage from the middle—without going back to re-edit everything else. You could hang up pieces of film and look at a number of them in your editing bay while deciding what to place where. With video you have the disadvantage of not being able simply to add or remove sequences from the master without redoing the whole thing. Also, it takes time to shuttle to segments on the tape, to cue up edit points, and to make edits.

New editing systems are becoming more like film in that a computer will be able to digitize segments you'd like to use, and play them back in any sequence. Once you've specified how you want the master to look, the computer will do the actual editing and lay the material down on tape. It's a bit like word-processing for video. Some high-end systems use videodiscs for editing, since they can find and cue up segments more quickly. Others digitize video and audio segments and save them on a computer medium such as a WORM; you can manipulate these segments to your heart's content, and the system will then create an edit decision list to take to a conventional on-line system. Digital video formats, such as D2, will allow you to go down multiple generations to make up complex special effects without degrading the signal. And multiple audio channels will make it easy to combine ambient sound, narration, music, and any other noises you'd like. Many new editing systems revolve around existing personal computers, such as Macintoshes, and will offer tremendous speed and flexibility for a fraction of the cost of today's conventional editing systems.

EDITING AS YOU GO

Post-production editing certainly involves a lot of time and expensive equipment. It also results in a loss of a generation, since the raw tapes are dubbed onto the edited master. There is one way to get around these drawbacks if you are producing a single program that can be shot in sequence.

Say, for instance, you want to produce a short demonstration tape on using a power saw to cut logs. The scenes are to be shot in sequence using a one-camera portable field unit. Many portable VCRs will automatically backspace the tape every time you pause between scenes; when you start up again, the VCR rolls and then makes an assemble edit to record the new material. You could use this function to record your program segment by segment, pressing the pause control between each shot as you re-position the camera, and cueing your talent each time you go back into "record." Of course, this can present some trouble if your talent "blows" a take; you have to go back and replay the last good scene, pausing just a moment before you make the edit into the bad take so that the unwanted segment will be completely erased. If you don't go back far enough, you'll have two "starts" to the new scene, with a few seconds of the bad take being left before the good take begins. Of course, if your talent continues to ruin takes, you'll gradually be chopping off more and more of the end of the last good scene—and may wind up having to do *it* over again, too. Many camcorders now have buttons to fade up and down automatically from black and can even superimpose simple characters over the video while recording.

EDITING TECHNIQUES

Knowing how to make technically good edits is only the beginning; the really interesting and creative decisions are when and where to edit and how to achieve the desired informational and aesthetic objectives. Good programs depend, of course, on having good raw material; you can't edit shots that don't exist nor magically change bad video quality. However, editing and special post-production effects *can* do a lot to pace a program, to enhance the video or audio, and to show off the better aspects of a sequence while wiping out or minimizing the negative.

The first rule of editing is *do it for a purpose.* The second is *don't let it call attention to itself.* It seems strange that the goal of all this technology and effort is to make itself invisible, but remember than instructional and informational programs are produced for a purpose—not as technical showpieces. When mistakes are made in post-production, the viewer becomes aware of the videotape itself and all its production mechanics—instead of paying attention to the content. Often when there's not much to say or the writer doesn't know how to explain something, the tendency is to pull out every special effect and editing technique in the book. But the final product rarely succeeds.

Editing together shots of a moving subject is one of the most common uses of editing. You might follow an inspector, for example, as he walks around a building. To string together smoothly shots taken in different locations, be sure to provide logical *transitions*. For instance, you can show the inspector walking out of the video frame at the end of one shot and walking into the frame in a new scene. You can shoot him walking away from the camera in one sequence and walking toward the camera in the next. Remember not to *reverse screen directions*. For example, if you are shooting someone walking out of the frame from right to left, don't have her walk into the next scene from the left to the right, lest it appear that she's suddenly walking back from whence she came. Never shift camera angles more than 180 degrees when following a moving subject. Another way to edit motion sequences is to *cut on action*: that is, to edit in the middle of some movement to another angle or perspective. If you are showing a technician using a group of tools, you might edit from a medium shot as he reaches for an instrument to a close-up of his hand and the item, making the edit with the hand in the exact same position in each shot.

Editing down a long interview is another common task. In documentary-style and news gathering shoots, interviewees are likely to say a lot more than you could ever use or are apt to make mistakes. In order to cut out unwanted portions without making the editing apparent, you'll need to eliminate jump cuts. To cover over these apparently sudden shifts in the subject's position, you can edit in video-only cut-aways of cut-ins. (For a more complete explanation of this technique, see the section on shooting in the field). Common video inserts are reaction shots of the interviewer nodding and listening, shots of subjects referred to in the interview, or extreme long-shots of the scene in which you can't lip-read what the interviewee is actually saying. These cut-aways need last only a second or two to "cover up" the edit. If you're editing together scenes in which there are two different angles of the subject, often no cut-away is needed—as long as the person didn't drastically shift positions. For instance, edits from an extreme close-up to a medium shot usually don't need a video insert to "cover" them; they look like they were merely shot "live" with two cameras.

Sometimes interviews are edited purposely to reveal jump cuts. This technique gives a "hard news" or "video verity" look to the program, emphasizing that certain segments *were*, in fact, cut out. The CBS program *Sixty Minutes* often uses this approach, as do many documentaries. Also, jump cuts are one of the major techniques in giving music videos their "look" that's often energetic and rather bizarre. This production style is not unlike that of architecture in which beams and pipes are left exposed. Whether or not you decide to use this approach, be sure to keep your style consistent so that the edits don't appear as mistakes or sloppiness.

Often interviewees will say in five minutes what could be summarized in 30 seconds. In order to save time and provide some audio contrast, you can utilize *voice-overs* to capsulize the person's comments, going back to the interview only for really crucial or memorable quotes. A narrator (or perhaps the person who was the interviewer) can introduce the speaker and the subject over a long shot of the interview or a shot depicting the topic. Throughout the segment, then, voice-overs can be used to provide summaries and transitions among topics.

If you want to show an interviewer in the scene, edit in a number of two-shots and close-ups of the interviewer asking questions. On the other hand, if the "reporter" is to stay in the background or be totally invisible, edit out his or her questions.

Compressing time can also be achieved through editing. In the old days, filmmakers showed the passage of time by a clock whizzing away the hours, newspapers piling up, or months being torn off calendars. Today's viewers are more visually literate, however, and can usually infer the passage of time without the use of any special techniques. The most common transition used to imply passage of time is the dissolve. Or you might want to show sequences such as the old trick of the cooking show, where the dish is shown in various stages of completion, down to the finished product coming out of the oven, having baked there for the previous four hours. Where you would not follow one subject through a process, you can use narration, keyed-in subtitles, or corner inserts of clocks to giver the viewer an accurate representation of elapsed time. Wipes and digital effects such as "flipping" the picture like a page in a book are also effective temporal transitions.

Creating montages to convey a certain mood or theme is common in motivational and informational programs. Often visuals are "cut to" music or sound effects. This can best be accomplished by selecting a sound track that fits the mood and pace of the sequence, estimating the length of the visuals, editing the audio and laying it down on tape, and finally editing the video *to* the audio, following its rhythm and themes. Generally, dissolves or "soft" wipes are used for slow pieces, but vibrant special effects are utilized for fast, energetic sequences. Look at the script excerpt in Figure 8-13 for examples of these concepts.

Editing together a series of interviews can be a challenging task. Say you interview six scholars on the subject of home health care for the aged. The show is primarily focused on these six individuals and their contrasting viewpoints: but how do you keep from producing a monotonous program of six five-minute interviews strung together? *Intercutting* is a very useful and effective technique: in it, you intercut or intersperse segments of different sequences. For instance, you'd present each expert's comments on one particular question together, editing short segments of each person as if they were reacting to the others' comments. This makes it much easier to compare and contrast viewpoints, and it breaks up the pace of the program. To distinguish each person further and to provide a more meaningful identity, the interviewee can be shown in this or his or her own environment. The changes in background scenery also help to relieve the monotony of talking heads. Of course, this requires a good deal more editing than merely performing five assemble edits to join up the six interviews, but it also lets you edit out material *within* an interview without falling back on more traditional and often forced-looking cut-aways. See Figure 8-14 for an example of intercutting.

Producing voice-overs is easy to do in post-production. The most common question is: do I edit the voice-over to the video, or the video to the voice? It all depends on which is the more crucial timewise. If, for instance, the most it's easiest to lay down the voice track first, then edit in video shots corresponding to the words spoken. If, however, you're showing processes where it's important to show a whole sequence from beginning to end, it's better to lay down the video first, then time narration to fit the video and dub the sound track in, following video cues. The narration can be a bit shorter than the video, of course; brief pauses between sentences or paragraphs give the viewer a "breather" from constant chatter and can be filled in with a music bed, if desired. The narration can be stretched out by editing in one or two sentences at a time, then leaving a short pause before starting the next.

Instead of editing so that the video changes with each sentence or exactly when the corresponding word is heard, you may wish to have the video lead the

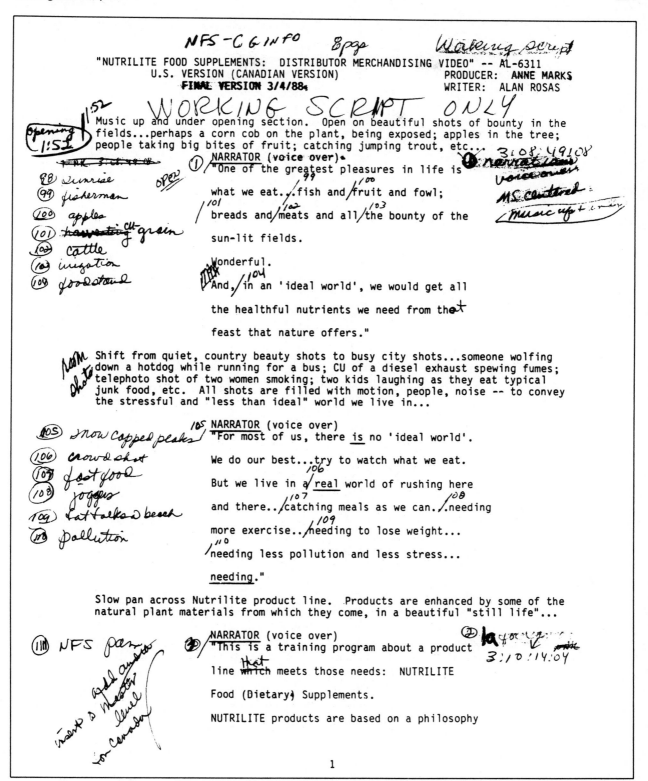

The script page reads:

NFS-CG INFO   8 pgs   Working script

"NUTRILITE FOOD SUPPLEMENTS: DISTRIBUTOR MERCHANDISING VIDEO" -- AL-6311
U.S. VERSION (CANADIAN VERSION)   PRODUCER: ANNE MARKS
FINAL VERSION 3/4/88   WRITER: ALAN ROSAS

WORKING SCRIPT ONLY

1:52
Opening 1:51

Music up and under opening section. Open on beautiful shots of bounty in the fields...perhaps a corn cob on the plant, being exposed; apples in the tree; people taking big bites of fruit; catching jumping trout, etc...   *3:08 49:08*

① NARRATOR (voice over).
"One of the greatest pleasures in life is

what we eat.../fish and /fruit and fowl;

breads and /meats and all /the bounty of the

sun-lit fields.

Wonderful.
And,/in an 'ideal world', we would get all

the healthful nutrients we need from the

feast that nature offers."

88 sunrise   *Open*
99 fisherman
100 apples
101 harvesting grain
102 cattle
103 irrigation
104 food stand

① *narration*
voice over
MS centered
music up + under

Shift from quiet, country beauty shots to busy city shots...someone wolfing down a hotdog while running for a bus; CU of a diesel exhaust spewing fumes; telephoto shot of two women smoking; two kids laughing as they eat typical junk food, etc. All shots are filled with motion, people, noise -- to convey the stressful and "less than ideal" world we live in...

105 snow capped peaks
106 crowd shot
107 fast food
108 joggers
109 fat folks @ beach
110 pollution

105 NARRATOR (voice over)
"For most of us, there <u>is</u> no 'ideal world'.

We do our best...try to watch what we eat.
But we live in a /<u>real</u> world of rushing here

and there../catching meals as we can./.needing

more exercise../needing to lose weight...

/needing less pollution and less stress...

<u>needing</u>."

Slow pan across Nutrilite product line. Products are enhanced by some of the natural plant materials from which they come, in a beautiful "still life"...

111 NFS pan
insert s master level for Canada

② NARRATOR (voice over)
"This is a training program about a product

line which meets those needs: NUTRILITE

Food (Dietary) Supplements.

NUTRILITE products are based on a philosophy

② *3:10 14:04*

1

Figure 8-13 This program uses a montage of scenes to create a mood; note the number of video shots required for this relatively short open (*courtesy, Ron Brown, Amway Corporation*).

```
PROGRAM: ETHNIC POLITICS
SEGMENT: MIKULSKI AND VENETOULIS ON DOMESTIC POLICY


Barbara in parade from front        V/O: Barbara Mikulski is the
                                    Democratic Congresswoman rep-
                                    resenting the 3rd district in
                                    Baltimore.
from back marching                  Born, raised, and educated in
                                    one of Baltimore's many
                                    ethnic neighborhoods,
waves to people                     she has emerged as a powerful
                                    force in national as well as
                                    local politics.
                                       MIKULSKI:
M.S. Mikulski                       It seems like ethnic politics...
                                    to make it one the national
                                    level.
cutaway interviewer                 Krupsak, Grasso,...

M.S. Mikulski                       it's a national phenomenon.

W.S. Venetoulis                     V/O: Ted Venetoulis is the
  (back time to incue, "we're       Baltimore County Executive &
  a colorful...)                    he ran for governor in MD.
                                    in 1978.  Like Barbara Mikul-
                                    ski, he believes that his
                                    ethnic heritage has given
                                    him special insights and stren-
                                    gths which have enabled him
                                    to better serve his constit-
                                    uency.
MS Venetoulis                       VENETOULIS: We're a colorful
                                    breed...children will have an
                                    opportunity to seek office
MS interviewer                      INTERVIEWER: How does being
                                    ethnic affect your political
                                    outlook?
MCU Venetoulis                      VENETOULIS: I'm the Executive
                                    of every...ethnic background.
MS Mikulski                         MIKULSKI: One of the things
                                    I fought in the Congress...
                                    when we deliver service.
LS Mikulski                         I have several constituents...
                                    we need to recognize.
```

Figure 8-14 This editing script intercuts inverviews and scenes from a variety of tapes to tell the story and add visual and auditory variety.

audio a bit or follow it by a beat or two. Showing a shot that will be explained in a second or two gives the viewer a chance to focus on the video for a while before having to attend to the narration. Conversely, you may wish to introduce a new visual scene over a graphic or a very neutral background so that the audio can receive the attention *it* deserves. Try to avoid a monotonous rhythm in editing so that the program doesn't resemble an amateur slide show, with the shots changing predictably at every new sentence. *Lead* the viewers from shot to shot, *arouse* their interest, and *direct* their attention to the most crucial elements in the program.

Video and audio enhancement can be achieved through post-production special effects. For instance, areas of the video frame can be emphasized by "spotlighting" portions, using an option available on most switchers. Superimposition of arrows, diagrams, or words can aid in focusing the viewer's attention. Split screens or inserts showing both long shots and close-ups or two different angles can aid in comprehension. Still frames can freeze action, and slow motion can let people see things not possible in "real time." Time lapse or *pixillation* speeds up action, so that you can see in a short time events taking place over a long period of time, such as a flower opening. And special effects such as dissolves, wipes, digital effects, and computer animation can all rouse interest and heighten a mood. Often, audio recorded in the field needs enhancement; it can be *equalized* or *filtered* to reduce hiss or background noise. It can also be mixed with music or narration, or in the case of voice-overs, the narration can be mixed with *ambient noise* of the sounds of the scene being shown. Video, too, can sometimes be electronically enhanced to produce more stable sync or more accurate colors through the use of time-based correctors or digital enhancers.

Figure 8-15   Audio is an important part of video; this is a typical audio sweetening and multi-track production suite (*courtesy, GTE California*).

Editing an interactive video program involves a totally new mind set. You're basically assembling segments onto a disc which may be randomly accessed by the viewer or a computer. In the end, the user does the "final edit." Since many interactive video programs use many still-frames, you may be editing many single frames—or at least just laying down 3 or more frames of a single image. Special still-store and digital devices are useful in storing hundreds of images, which can then be laid down, frame by frame, by computerized editing equipment. You can imagine what it would be like to edit 2,000 single frames—and a videodisc can hold up to 54,000 frames!

PACING A PROGRAM

Producers often wonder when to change shots, add special effects, or add music tracks. Sometimes these things are specified in a script, but there's a limit as to how completely a script *can* or *should* control exactly what's edited. In most of the programs we do, even if they're fully scripted, we select the exact music and video shots for the opening montage, and we decide how long cut-aways should be in between scene transitions. Unfortunately, there's no easy rule to help you decide how to make these final decisions, except to ask yourself "Why?" Today's post-production suites have made it easy and fun to edit, mix, and add a variety of dazzling computer graphics and special effects. However, many producers get carried away with these options, creating programs that may "wow" the viewer but leave little content behind. Of course, other productions fail because the audience falls asleep or turns the program off after the first three minutes.

Perhaps the best answers are found by analyzing the program's audience, topic, and purpose:

- Who is the audience? What is their age and attention span? What is their ability to process information quickly?

- How interesting is the topic to the audience? Is it an energetic encomium on the new time-saving hardware your company's just introduced or a thoughtful reflection on the beauty of a wildflower sanctuary in the spring?

- Is the program to be mostly instructional, informational, or entertaining? Teaching someone how to repair a new computer is different from introducing its features to potential customers or providing a motivational montage on its applications to kick off the annual sales meeting. Much more detail and time to process information must be provided in programs that are really designed to teach someone something.

- What is the nature of the shots? Sequences showing action—camera or subject movement—will hold viewers' attention much longer than static shots. How much information to process is in each shot? If you must include slides or stills, try zooming, panning, or digital effects for transitions.

- What is the "style" of the organization? Certainly flashy special effects, punk-rock music tracks, and tight editing may be fine for a young audience but are unsuited to a more conservative or serious group. Just as a company's letterhead and brochures convey a certain style, their productions *generally* should reflect that style—especially if it is made for management.

Be especially careful in the way you think out the pacing of a show. You may be so tired of the subject, once you get into the editing suite, that you race through the program at a pace that no novice could hope to follow. Conversely, you may be so taken with the footage you've shot or the personalities you've met who are now on tape that you're reluctant to cut out a single frame. Even though you may have been the perfect naive learner of the material when the client first contacted you, by the time editing rolls around, you may have difficulty in taking the learner's viewpoint. Question yourself if you find you're straying from the original pacing of the script—and when all else fails, get some advice from someone outside the program—or *even* from your client!

BIBLIOGRAPHY

ARWADY, J. AND D. GAYESKI (1989). *Using Video: Interactive and Linear Designs*. Englewood Cliffs, NJ: Educational Technology Publications.

ANDERSON, G. H. (1988). *Video Editing and Post-Production*. White Plains: Knowledge Industry Publications.

UTZ, P. (1987). *Today's Video: Equipment, Setup, and Production*. Englewood Cliffs, NJ: Prentice-Hall.

9

PROGRAM DISTRIBUTION

A lot of time and effort goes into program design and production. However, the real impact of a program begins once it leaves the media center and gets out to its intended audience. Often so much attention goes to the making of a production that relatively little is done about planning its dissemination.

New technologies have dramatically affected the dissemination of instructional and organizational video. Since one of the prime reasons for using video is its capability for rapid and efficient distribution, the distribution phase must receive due consideration. Whether an organization uses satellite teleconferences, microwave links, cable broadcasts, or learning stations in a media center to make programming accessible, the management and promotion of distribution is a vital link in the organizational communications system.

BROADCAST

The oldest and most pervasive means of video distribution, of course, is broadcast. Although most organizational communication has too narrow an audience for this technology to be appropriate, a wide range of educational and public information programs can be and are effectively distributed though this means.

Public television stations got their start as "educational television," emphasizing children's programming, in-school instructional TV, college-level telecourses, and cultural affairs. Even earlier, however, commercial television carried instructional programming; in fact, the early stations were often affiliated with universities. ITV soon took a back seat to entertainment and news on the commercial channels, but instructional and informational programs persisted, if only in the early morning. College-level telecourses such as "Sunrise Semester" and shows on agriculture, gardening, and child-rearing have continued to be run.

Because of its almost universal coverage, broadcast is a powerful means for the delivery of generalized programming. The impact of such programs as *Sesame Street*, documentaries by National Geographic, and network specials on current events is immeasurable—not only do they reach millions of viewers, but they set a standard in content and production style against which all other kinds of video are measured. Access is broadcasting's major strength—it cuts across boundaries of age, class, location, education, and culture.

Strangely enough, access is also perhaps broadcasting's biggest limitation, for every program must be justified on a mass-appeal basis. Special-interest groups are not a target. Another significant limitation of broadcasting is the fixed schedule for viewing; the audience must adopt its schedule to the broadcast, rather than the other way around. This problem has limited the curricular use of educational programs in the schools, since it is difficult to adjust classes to a station's timetable.

As more viewers have access to video recorders and gain rights to tape programs off-air, some of the constraints of broadcasting can be overcome. The distribution technology allows easy and widespread access to programming, which once on tape can be viewed at a time and in a style deemed appropriate for each user.

Broadcast has the potential to reach those who may most acutely need its message. For those who are homebound, geographically isolated, unlikely to actively seek training, or living and working out of the mainstream, it can provide information and skills. Britain has long benefited from its "Open University" program in which adults can earn college credit by participating in broadcast courses. The United States has started similar projects, on a smaller scale. Less industrialized nations use broadcast to disseminate programs on basic literacy, health and agriculture in areas where teachers are scarce and transportation is difficult.

Children's programming has met with great success—especially those shows with specific objectives and carefully researched techniques. Television serves as a "great equalizer," providing children from diverse backgrounds with a common set of skills and experiences. For this reason, substantial amounts of grant money have supported children's series on public broadcasting, and commercial networks have developed documentaries, arts programs, and news shows aimed at the younger set. Cable television began as an alternate means of distributing broadcast television; starting out as CATV (Community Antenna Television), operators constructed large antennas and fed the signals to homes otherwise unable to enjoy adequate reception. As the demand for this service grew and operators vied for franchises in individual communities, additional community programming was made mandatory. Today, the number of channels provided by cable has made feasible a greater variety in programming, in terms not only of entertainment but also of information and education.

Most cable outlets have facilities for local origination of programs and will train members of the community to produce simple shows. Head ends may also be located in local libraries, schools, or colleges, from which these institutions can deliver programs to the community. Because the signals do not have to be broadcast quality, cable shows can be produced with simple, inexpensive equipment, making this means of communication accessible to many groups. As many people find travel problematic owing to fuel costs or work schedules, cable can be an effective means of local information or political action. Community colleges are exploiting this medium to deliver course materials at a variety of times suitable for homemakers and workers. Local chapters of nonprofit associations, as well as businesses, can use this delivery system to provide increased outreach and inform the community about services and activities.

Cable provides an excellent means of community information exchange. Although used primarily by local governmental and nonprofit groups, the medium holds great potential for public relations and continuing education functions of businesses. Organizations can provide updates on their new policies, plans, and products, giving the local citizens a better idea of how they contribute to and affect the community. They can provide information about their services and tips to consumers on such matters as shopping and energy conservation; often this material is offered to the public in brochures or pamphlets that are not as effective or wide reaching. Education needed to upgrade skills or advance in careers can be transmitted during nonworking hours over a cable channel, allowing employees to continue their studies, if they choose, in their own homes.

Finally, as cable programming services increase in scope and number, a wide range of special-interest shows will be offered and in demand. This expanding distribution medium promises to be an effective outlet for producers of documentaries and art, educational, and cultural programs.

Many organizations use video to provide clips to broadcast news programs—much as they used to provide press releases. Often, these video news releases (sometimes called VNRs) make their way onto network or at least local news, providing good exposure. For example, when *Consumer Reports* magazine reported results of tests that showed the Suzuki Samurai four-wheel drive car was unsafe, Suzuki countered the very next day with a videotape featuring the general manager. That night, the same network news programs that had reported the *Consumer Reports* data the night before aired Suzuki's response. Many people credit video with saving the product and the company (Berger, 1989).

DISTRIBUTION OF TAPES

Ten years ago, many schools, universities, and training centers operated closed-circuit distribution systems or "dial access" systems where viewers could request or punch up a tape and watch it on a monitor in a carrel or classroom. The University of Maryland has used several such systems (Figure 9-1). Video equipment was too large, expensive, and finicky to roll around and have "mere users" operate the VCRs.

But as equipment has become less expensive and troublesome to operate, most organizations have decentralized equipment and playback control, while perhaps maintaining a central library of tapes. The advantages of having individual control over playback equipment outweigh the expense and effort. Moving one step further, more users are becoming owners of their own video playback units; learning centers may be able to lend out programs (or make copies of them on a viewer's own tape) to be viewed at home. Distribution systems are not obsolete, however; their application lies more in the area of simultaneous display of messages or programming throughout a building or area.

Distribution of tapes can occur over a broader geographic area than just a building or campus. For instance, we produced a program featuring the work of the Tompkins/Seneca County Healthy Heart Program which is distributed to local physicians, associations, and interested individuals.

PRIVATE VIDEO NETWORKS

Although the word "network" generally conjures up images of one of the commercial broadcasting giants, organizational nonbroadcast video has networks of its own. Corporations with branch offices in scattered locations set up playback facilities in those offices to which programs are mailed. These may include training or

a

b

c

Figure 9-1 A closed-circuit TV distribution system (*courtesy, Paul Malec, University of Maryland*).

product updates, corporate policies, or company news. According to a recent survey, the median number of viewing locations within organizations was 133, and more than half of the organizations had over 100 separate sites within their networks (Brush & Brush, 1988).

These networks are established in a variety of ways. Sometimes the equipment is provided free by corporate headquarters; sometimes the branch offices are required to buy it; and in other situations the equipment may be optional. If enough hardware is involved, the corporation may buy directly from a manufacturer and may itself become a "dealer" of sorts. The organization, in this case, may have to take responsibility for maintenance and repair of the hardware, since local dealers may not want to work on an item that they didn't sell.

Duplication of tape and purchase of raw stock are two problem areas with this distribution technology. Instead of sending out a copy to each location, some organizations "bicycle" tapes from one place to another. This, of course, delays the delivery of information, which may be time critical. Another approach is to recycle tapes by having the branches send back outdated programs, which get erased.

An even more crucial issue in this system is control. You, in the media production center at headquarters, may have no idea how the programs you send out are being used—or if they are. If a branch manager "doesn't believe in video," your efforts may be going to waste. The hardware may be set up in an inaccessible or unattractive environment; employees may not be told of programs' availability. Furthermore, the equipment may be in a state of disrepair and not work satisfactorily. In order to prevent these potential problems, a given person at each site should be made responsible for the playback system. Periodic checks, in person or through forms, are necessary to keep on top of the status of each location. Thorough orientation in the use and upkeep of the equipment should also be offered.

The advent of rapid duplication on tape has made this distribution technology feasible and effective. Videodisc has even more to offer in both ease and cost of mass duplication. Large organizations such as automobile manufacturers distribute marketing and training programs to their dealers using disc technology, which, of course, can also provide interactive capabilities. Since discs are relatively "user proof," they can be made accessible to the general public without requiring much, if any, training in operation of the hardware.

The ease and effectiveness of private video networks as a means of communication for large organizations has been a major factor in the growth of the field. Because video, which is a relatively expensive communications channel, can reach so many people, its relative cost per person is a bargain. As companies expand and diversify, their need to inform also grows. The availability of the technology to make feasible playback units in each branch office is in itself a major justification of video. However, the quality and quantity of use "out in the field" is of the greatest importance, and it is crucial to monitor and promote this utilization throughout the various locations to carry off a satisfactory video network. See Figure 9-2 for examples of good network management forms.

MICROWAVE AND ITFS

The need to transmit video over distances to a defined audience—to "narrowcast" rather than broadcast—has led to the development of microwave and ITFS (Instructional Television Fixed Service). Both are technologically similar to broadcast television but utilize higher frequencies. Signals on these frequencies travel shorter distances than those on broadcast channels, and they are generally used for point-to-point transmission of messages or programs. While microwave is used by commer-

MetroNet
Equipment Log

Office #_____

Page____of____

Updated   to:_____

Office Name:_____

Complete Office Address:_____

_____

☐ Branch
☐ District
☐ Regional
☐ Territory

Make	Model	Description	Serial Number	Date Received
Sony	KV-1923	TV Receiver		
Sony	SLO-323	VCR		
Sony	VCL-1206	Lens 12.5-75mm		
Sony	DFX-3	Viewfinder		
Sony	RM-300	R.A. Controller		
Sony	AVC-3260	Video Camera		
Sony	F-27	Microphone	N/A	
Bretford	VTRC-54E	Equipment Cart	N/A	
Lowell	1500	Softlight Kit		

Prepared by: (Please Print)_____

Date:_____

Office Use Only					
R	B	KI	B	VOL	REC

Figure 9-2 An important part of video network operations is managing and maintaining equipment (*courtesy, Metropolitan Life Insurance*).

cial broadcasters as well as industrial, educational, and governmental organizations, ITFS is strictly set aside for education.

These forms of distribution are used for signal transmission among fixed points, such as a group of hospitals in a region or schools within a district. Normally one or two locations are head ends or transmitters, while the others have receive-only dishes. Microwave is also commonly used to send a signal from a station's studio to its transmitter site or to relay live events from a field crew back to the studio. The "instant eye" live reports of important events on broadcast television

Metro**Net**
Office #_____
Page__of _____

Monthly Activity Record
For Month Ending:_____

Office Name_____ ☐ Branch ☐ Regional
☐ District ☐ Terrritory

Date	Activity	# of Hours	Remarks

Total Number of Hours:_____

Activity Code:
1 - Videotape Screening
2 - Role Play Session
3 - Other

Prepared by: (Please Print)_____

Return this form to:
MetroNet Administration
Corporate Audio Visual Services
New York Home Office - 22A

Figure 9-2 Continued

use microwave, since it eliminates the necessity of laying cable or renting special phone lines.

Both microwave and ITFS require a license, since they use part of the frequency spectrum. The number and location of these systems is limited by the amount of channel space available. Like broadcast, they can be affected by bad weather or geographic obstacles between the transmitter and the intended receiver.

A number of colleges and universities are using microwave to beam certain classes to regional "customers" in businesses. Participants in these courses can earn credit and gain in professional skills without having to leave the work site. Institu-

MetroNet

Supplies Request

Office #_____

Date:_____

Office Name:_____

☐ Branch ☐ Regional
☐ District ☐ Territory

Item	Quantity Needed
Gaffer Tape	
Test Tape	
Viewing Filter	
Video Cassette	
Lamp for Soft Light	
Air Bottle	
Lens Cleaner	
Lens Cleaning Tissue	
Cable (Describe)	

Prepared by: (Please Print)_____

Return this form to:
MetroNet Administration
Corporate Audio Visual Services
New York Home Office - Area 22A

Figure 9-2 Continued

tions offering the courses can thereby attract a whole new population of adult
learners. Several classrooms can be equipped with simple instructor-controlled
video equipment. Usually the instructor, perhaps with some help from a technician,
will be able to operate the equipment remotely, switching between shots of himself
or herself and close-ups of notes or diagrams. The lectures are done with a regular
"live" class and may include talk-back systems to allow the remote classes to ask
questions or engage in discussion.

Other uses of microwave links are at medical facilities for continuing education of personnel or for consultation among a group of professionals. A number of
hospitals, clinics, and medical schools can be tied together so that staff can partici-

pate in conferences, get a look at an unusual case or procedure, or get opinions from colleagues miles away.

The programs carried on these microwave systems obviously are not always fully scripted "shows"; often they're more like "picture-phone" conversations. For instance, corporations may utilize permanent microwave links between office buildings in a region to facilitate face-to-face conversations or meetings in which diagrams, sketches, or objects can be displayed, thus reducing local travel costs. This communications technology is usually put under the control of the video management and production department.

Narrowcasting may in some cases resemble a very specialized television station, with regularly scheduled programs and published program guides. Series of shows, either purchased externally or produced internally, may obtain the rights to send a series of elementary-level science programs to the buildings in its jurisdiction. Hospitals in private network can receive specialized educational programs for physicians and nurses as well as patient information programs that can be distributed in individual rooms.

SATELLITE TELECONFERENCING AND BUSINESS TV

Perhaps the distribution technology promising the greatest revolution in video communications is satellite. Signals can be fed to a satellite from an up-link, which can then be retransmitted to a large geographic area and received by a down-link or dish. Because all points within its broadcast pattern are considered equidistant, transmission of signals between widely separated cities is no problem. Companies that own the satellites lease or rent time on several satellite channels, either on a long-term basis or for periods as short as an hour or two.

Satellite transmission has six main instructional or informational uses:

- To transmit regular employee communications or new shows, as does Federal Express
- To broadcast generalized instructional fare to anyone with a down-link, as does the National Technical University
- To distribute televised college courses to corporations paying a flat "tuition fee" for their employees, as does Chico State University in California
- To transmit regularly scheduled professional training, as does the Hospital Satellite Network
- To enable small groups of two or three persons to hold ad hoc meetings or discussions over long distances, as does JC Penney (They allow store managers to choose merchandise in this way.)
- To conduct *ad hoc* teleconferences or conduct large multi-location conferences, as do some major corporations when they have a new product launch

Satellite communication is seen as a real solution to ever-increasing travel costs for formal instruction, continuing education, consultations, and business meetings. Because no cables or phone lines are needed to stretch over long distances, the systems are more reliable and maintenance free than some earlier distribution technologies. Costs for satellite telecasting are decreasing, and as it is applied more frequently, the arrangements for its use are becoming simplified. A number of companies can lease or sell the necessary hardware, and others are springing up that specialize just in the coordination of telemeetings and teleconferences. Time on either the Ku or C bands can be rented from corporations who own the satellites and can be had for as cheaply as $500 per hour. See Figures 9-3 and 9-4 for some sample rates.

Organizations regularly using teleconferencing or having their own networks include John Hancock Insurance, Texas Instruments, JC Penney, Federal Express, and Eastman Kodak. Big business is not the only user of satellite technology:

"Average" Cost for a 2-Hour KBTV Broadcast (Limited pre-production)

Pre-Production:
- o Graphics (4 hours) $140
- o Set-Up/Rehearsal (4 hours)   400
- o Scriptwriting (polish to drafts)   500
- o Broadcast coordination   250

Studio Package:
- o Complete broadcast facility (8 hours)   1,520

Satellite Time/Uplink Charges:
- o 2.5 x $850   2,125

Materials:
- o One videotape master and four VHS duplicate copies   500

Personnel:
- o Producer/Director, technical director, audio engineer,
     floor director, tape operator, camera operators, engineer-in-charge,
     electronic graphics operator, teleprompter operator, make-up
     artist/stylist, chief engineer   4,500

On-Camera Training:
- o Training for 1-4 people on presentation skills for live or
     pre-recorded videotaping.   800

Other:
- o Coffee carts, script typing, downlink contact, phone operators   250

TOTAL: $10,985

The costs shown above are for the broadcast and rehearsal of the broadcast. Added costs for a broadcast should include: pre-production of video segments, hand-out materials, additional instructional designer's time, sets, and/or professional talent costs.

This estimate is a "ballpark" figure to be used for budgeting purposes. Some broadcasts will cost more than this while others will cost less. We would be happy to meet with you to give you a more accurate estimate. Call 724-0079 for an appointment.

Figure 9-3 Estimates for Business TV programming (*courtesy, Holly Walkland, Eastman Kodak Company*).

MOBILE KU BAND UPLINK (personnel charges extra—see below)

1st day	$ 2,500 *(any part up to 24 hrs. = 1 Transmission Day)*
2nd day	2,250
3rd day	2,000
4th day	1,750
5th day	1,500
Per week (up to 7 days)	10,000

The above rates cover full use of all facilities, including:
- 26' BAF/WOLF Coach [IVECO chassis]
- 2.3 meter Andrew antenna
- Two LNR frequency synthesized exciters
- Two MCL 300-watt phase combined TWTA HPA's
- Two DX downlink receivers
- Standard and cellular phone
- Mobile/portable 450 MHz 2-way radio
- Onan 20Kw diesel generator with 70-hr. fuel cap.
- Test equipment (Tektronix vectorscope, waveform and spectrum monitors)
- Production equipment (Grass Valley 100 switcher, SONY BVW75 Betacam and BVU950 editors and MXP21 audio board, CHYRON VP-2 character generator)

Transponder Time is Additional. Please Inquire.

OPERATOR/ENGINEER (required)

Per day: *(up to 10 hours):* $250 each (1 full day minimum)
(after 10 hours in each 24 hour period): 40/hr. per person

OPERATOR EXPENSES

$35/day per person plus hotel

DRIVER (if more than one operator is required)

$75/day

MILEAGE

$1.00/mile (one-way only to site)

SET-UP/WAIT DAY

$750 (flat rate)

ADDITIONAL CHARGES

Current market rates *(where applicable, including site preparation, phone charges, camera crew and equipment, location/hook-up/parking fees, etc.)*

Media Services-ETV Center
NB13 MVR Hall
Cornell University
Ithaca, NY 14853

607/255-5431

Figure 9-4 Rate card for Cornell's satellite uplink truck (*courtesy, Cornell University ETV Center and Media Services*).

Cornell University recently outfitted a $500,000 satellite up-link truck so that it could put its professors on network TV programs if their expertise was desired—giving the University valuable coverage. They also cover their football games and rent out their truck to other users, including networks.

Other industry-specific providers of satellite training include HSN, the hospital satellite network, which charges its almost 1000 subscribers from $5,000 to

$30,000 per year and delivers a 24-hour stream of high-level medical training as well as entertainment and educational programs for hospital patients (Figure 9-5). Another service is the Automotive Satellite Television Network (ASTN), which beams generic automotive sales and product news to about 4,000 car dealerships (Levine, 1989).

WEEK-AT-A-GLANCE

Eastern Daylight Time	Saturday July 22	Sunday July 23	Monday July 24 Patient Education	Tuesday July 25 Nurse	Wednesday July 26 Manager	Thursday July 27 Physician	Friday July 28 Allied Health Professional
8:00am	CE MGR 6301 Hospitals Today: Crisis or Opportunity?	CNE 7733 Legal and Ethical Nursing Issues: Foundations	0595 The Postpartum Period Part II	CNE 7814 Implementing Universal Precautions: Managing AIDS in the OR	CE MGR 6829 A Question of Ethics: Physician/Nurse Relationships	A5210 Latissimus Dorsi Flap (35:00)	4809 Healthcare Today
8:30am	CE MGR 6302 History of Healthcare: From Privilege to Human Right		0549 Healthy Lifestyles	CNE 7615 Multilumen Central Venous Catheters	CE MGR 6823 Efficiency Is Not A Four-Letter Word		CE AHP 8616 Antibiotic Prophylaxis: Risks and Benefits
9:00am	CE MGR 6722 Developing Alternative Delivery Systems: PPOs and IPAs	CNE 7638 Basic Techniques For Transferring Patients Safely	9059 Diet and Cancer Prevention ★	CNE 7650 Nursing Management of Wounds ★	CE MGR 6737 Emergency Preparedness: The Joint Commission Approach ★	CME 5710 Valvular and Congenital Heart Disease ★	CE AHP 8530 Nutritional Parameters in the Trauma Patient ★
9:30am	CE MGR 6629 AWH Innovation and Enterprise Development	CNE 7640 Principles For Positioning Immobilized Patients		CNE 7711 A Child Dies ★	CE MGR 6539 Taking Control: Making Time Work For You ★		Video Bulletin Board ★
11:00am	CE MGR 6301 Hospitals Today: Crisis or Opportunity?	CNE 7733 Legal and Ethical Nursing Issues: Foundations	0595 The Postpartum Period Part II	CNE 7814 Implementing Universal Precautions: Managing AIDS in the OR	CE MGR 6829 A Question of Ethics: Physician/Nurse Relationships	A5210 Latissimus Dorsi Flap (35:00)	4809 Healthcare Today
11:30am	CE MGR 6302 History of Healthcare: From Privilege to Human Right		0549 Healthy Lifestyles	CNE 7615 Multilumen Central Venous Catheters	CE MGR 6823 Efficiency Is Not A Four-Letter Word		N2103 Healthwatch SPE
12:00pm	CE MGR 6722 Developing Alternative Delivery Systems: PPOs and IPAs	CNE 7638 Basic Techniques For Transferring Patients Safely	9059 Diet and Cancer Prevention ★	CNE 7650 Nursing Management of Wounds ★	CE MGR 6737 Emergency Preparedness: The Joint Commission Approach ★	United States Army Reserve (OSG) Medical Corps ★ SPE	CE AHP 8530 Nutritional Parameters in the Trauma Patient ★
12:30pm	CE MGR 6629 AWH Innovation and Enterprise Development	CNE 7640 Principles For Positioning Immobilized Patients		CLOSED CIRCUIT VIDEOCONFERENCE (3.5 hours)	CE MGR 6539 Taking Control: Making Time Work For You ★	CME 5614 Nutritional Assessment in Pediatrics ★	COUNTDOWN ★
1:00pm	8703 HSN SHOP TALK: Technology and Equipment (Rebroadcast) (1.5 hours)		9016 Aspects of Alcholism ★		CE MGR 6301 Hospitals Today: Crisis or Opportunity? ★	CME 5613 In vitro Fertilization and Tubal Surgery: The British Perspective ★	CE T8689 MIND & BODY: The Fine and Performing Arts: Stress & Health Issues LIVE (60 min.) ★
1:30pm					CE MGR 6302 History of Healthcare: From Privilege to Human Right ★	CME 5604 Pediatric Trauma: The Special Vulnerability of Children ★	
2:00-5:00pm							
early next day 5:00am			9016 Aspects of Alcholism ★		CE MGR 6301 Hospitals Today: Crisis or Opportunity? ★	CME 5613 In vitro Fertilization and Tubal Surgery: The British Perspective ★	CE T8689 MIND & BODY: The Fine and Performing Arts: Stress & Health Issues (Rebroadcast) (60 min.) ★
5:30am					CE MGR 6302 History of Healthcare: From Privilege to Human Right ★	CME 5604 Pediatric Trauma: The Special Vulnerability of Children ★	

Watch Video Bulletin Board for additional 10:00-11:00am and 2:00-5:00pm programming

Figure 9-5 Satellite educational programming schedule (*courtesy, Hospital Satellite Network*).

But many organizations produce only occasional teleconferences. Often the purpose of the teleconferences is the kickoff of a new sales campaign; other common themes are the CEO's delivery of the corporation's annual report and the sharing of research among members of a professional association. These video meetings may consist of one-way transmission of video and audio to a number of sites, or they may have audio or audio and video feedback capability from one or more remote sites. Of course, the number of up-links used affects the system's costs and complexity. Often prerecorded segments are interspersed with "live" communications, combining the styles of broadcast television and face-to-face meetings.

Texas Instruments produced an annual teleconference featuring leaders in the field of artificial intelligence. Part of the four-hour experience (which is free to

Figure 9-6 Cooordinators for KBTV can schedule downlinks across the nation (*courtesy, Holly Wlakland, Eastman Kodak Company*).

anyone interested in receiving it) contains prerecorded features, but part is a live round-table among experts who can then answer viewers' phoned-in questions "live." TI sends out packets of leaders' guides, posters, and the viewers' brochures, which not only detail the conference but also give information on how to obtain TI hardware and software.

Successful teleconferencing depends upon a great deal of planning. Meeting sites, origination facilities, satellite time, and feedback loops must be reserved far in advance. Potential viewers must be informed of the conference's times and locations as well as its objectives. Coordinators are needed at each site for both the technical aspects (such as setting up monitors or large-screen projectors and arranging microphones) and the people aspects (such as welcoming the group, managing their feedback to the conference, and explaining the setup). The structure of the event, such as speeches, question-and-answer periods, or prerecorded information, must be carefully laid out. Speakers, even those with plenty of traditional speaking experience, might well be coached for television performance. Finally, the hardware system must be checked out before use. The emergence of teleconferencing promises to reduce not only the monetary costs of large-scale travel by individuals and organizations, but also the personal costs of time away from home, lost work hours, and the fatigue inherent in travel. Many organizations find that electronic meetings save anywhere from 10 to 50 percent or more, compared to traditional means of conferring. The savings in nonrenewable energy are another important consideration from ecological and political perspectives.

As satellite technology advances and new regulations allow the expansion of the range and power of the "bird," down-links can become smaller and cheaper. Already many organizations are installing permanent teleconferencing facilities in their headquarters and branch offices. Hotel chains are establishing receiving equipment to attract conference business; an example is Holiday Inn's Hi-Net satellite. Holiday Inn can also use their physical plants to house regional sites for teleconferences, since they all have down-links. As more satellites are launched and the technology becomes more commonplace, the cost will decrease, and the quality will increase.

BIBLIOGRAPHY

BERGER, W. (1989, April). "When the walls come tumblin' down: Crisis video," *Corporate Video Decisions,* p. 40–45.

BRUSH, D. AND J. BRUSH (1988). *The Fourth Brush Report Update '88.* La Grangeville, NY: HI Press, Inc.

LEVINE, M. (1989, June). "Are generic business networks worth their costs?" *Corporate Video Decisions*, pp. 18–21.

MATHIAS, G. (1987) *How to Produce Your Own Teleconference.* White Plains, NY: Knowledge Industry Publications.

10

EVALUATION
OF PROGRAMS

Too many producers think their job is done when they've edited the last credit onto the end of a program. But how do they know if anyone really watched it? Would another format of program or medium have worked better? Most important, what will their answers be when their managers ask, "What have you really done for us lately?"

In video's infancy, it was considered adequate, even amazing, that a producer could actually make pictures appear on the TV screen. Today, however, managers are much more sophisticated, and merely running a TV camera is a pretty common skill—almost all managers have a camcorder at home and probably can even get decent pictures out of it. Programs must be shown to affect an organization's goals—to meet stated objectives and to do so efficiently. To accomplish this, video communications professionals must have a repertoire of evaluation methodologies through which to document the results of their work. While it's probably beyond the job description to become a statistician or expert researcher, a lot can be learned from reading reports or others' studies in professional journals.

The most important concept to keep in mind when assessing your work is to conduct a *bottom-line evaluation*. That is, don't just figure out whether people "liked" a program or talk about the technical perfection of your shots and editing. That information is nice—but it is superfluous to management. Your organization wants to see how video affects its bottom line—how has it saved money, made money, prevented accidents and down time, or spread its word to its shareholders and the public. Your job is to keep management aware of the impact you're making.

WE'ER MAKING A DIFFERENCE

Dear Diane,

    If everyone is as quick to respond to your request as I am, you may get your book finished sometime in the next century. Here are a couple of scripts and a treatment for a program we have not gotten to script yet. I hope they are of some help to you.

    I'd love to get back to Ithaca College some day and see what's happening. Amway A-V is very busy and is making a difference. Senior management gives some of the credit for a business turnaround to the use of video. Distributors in the field are so complimentary about the program that it is difficult to get the kind of information we need to make them even more useful. I've worked where we thought we were contributing, but never knew for sure. It's nice to be in a position to know that what you are doing is helping and making a difference.

Good luck with the book.

Sincerely,

Ron Brown, Audio-Visual Manager
Amway Corporation

EVALUATING OFF-THE-SHELF MATERIALS

Up to this point we've assumed that if a video program could solve an organization's problem, it should be produced. However, commercially produced materials are available on a wide range of subjects to provide a quicker and cheaper solution than custom-made productions. Many organizations resist buying "off-the-self" programs because they feel that they're "different" and that their needs are unique. Moreover, producers usually feel that, given a chance, they could do a better job than someone producing for a general audience.

In some ways, each business or school or hospital is unique, having special problems, ways of training, and products. Clearly, programs on assembling a specific product, on the history of the company, or on the layout of the plant need to be done on a custom basis. In fact, many such programs contain classified information and may not be released outside the organization. Some topics, however, can probably be covered fairly well by generic programs—such programs as phone manners, supervisory skills, or good health habits.

Because these programs are designed for the mass market, their producers can often afford to include features such as animation, interviews with high-powered experts, or shots from a number of geographical locations that add to the effectiveness of the program but might not be affordable by an in-house production group.

There are a number of ways to find out about commercially available programs. Professional journals, such as *Corporate Video, Training and Development Journal, Videography, Training, Biomedical Communications*, and *Tech Trends* carry announcements of new programs and advertisements by major distributors. These distributors also send out fliers and catalogs describing their offerings. A number of commercially available guides, such as *Educator's Guide to Free Audio and Video Material*, and the *NICEM* (National Information Center on Educational Media) *Index*, list materials by subject and/or format. Finally, professional organizations may also compile "mediagraphies" of programs available of interest to their constituencies, and magazines and journals for special-interest groups and professionals will also carry ads and reviews of commercially available programming.

But how do you evaluate these programs to determine their appropriateness for your own organization? First, attempt to get a complete description of the program—or several descriptions from different sources. What is the specific content? The media format? When was it produced and by whom? Do you feel that the producer or content expert would have a bias, making the program unsuitable for your organization? When was it produced; is the content or style out of date? How is the content presented? The more answers to these questions you can find by reading ads or reviews, the more effectively you can narrow down the list of potentially acceptable programs.

Of course, you must take the advertisers' "hype" associated with these commercial programs with a grain of salt. Often they use sweeping descriptions in order to make the program appealing to a wide range of potential users. Beware of such statements as "suitable for junior high to adult audiences." Some programs do have a wide appeal, but many wind up pleasing nobody by trying to please everybody. It's best to see if you can find a more unbiased review.

Most programs are offered for preview free or at a low cost from distributors. Unless the material is extremely inexpensive, this is a crucial step. Descriptions may tell you little or be quite misleading, and the only way to evaluate a program well is to see it. Just as you work closely with a client and content expert in producing a program, you should do the same in evaluating materials. Many organizations have standardized evaluation forms by which teachers, trainers, and media specialists can critique preview programs and make recommendations on their purchase or rental. See Figure 10-1 for one sample. These forms are kept on file so that others may refer to them when searching for the same sort of material. Important points to consider:

- Does the content fit in with our particular objectives?
- Is the style suitable for our audience?
- Does the scope of the program cover too much or too little information?
- Is the content accurate?
- Do the format and style provide the clearest possible explanation of the material?
- Is the presentation credible?
- Do the situations and talent adequately represent the cultures, ethnicity, sexual composition, and ages of our viewers?
- Is the content or style out of date?
- Is the pacing too slow or too fast?
- Does the program make the best use of the medium's available techniques?
- Is the length of the program appropriate?
- What do people have to know as a prerequisite for understanding the material?
- Does the program hold the audience's attention and encourage active participation?
- Does it come with a guide to assist teachers or trainers in its most effective use?

Sometimes you'll find that a program has many good points but some limitations. Perhaps one scene shows an outdated procedure; maybe the program is too

WHAT TO LOOK FOR IN A TRAINING PROGRAM DESIGN

1. **TRAINING OBJECTIVES**

   o Do they exist---in writing
   o Are they clear, understandable, & unambiguous
   o Are they attainable
   o Are they stated in 'Real World' terms

2. **TRAINING MATERIALS**

   o Instructions for 'How To Use'
      o How complete & understandable
   o Materials for Instructor use
      o Complete and in final form
      o Meet acceptable media materials design criteria
   o Materials for Learner Use
      o Complete and in final form
      o Clearly identified
   o Do materials assist Presenters/Learners move toward and/or to achieve stated objectives

3. **TRAINING DESIGN**

   o Does overall design include strategies for
      o Climate Setting & Motivation
      o Information & Content Delivery
      o Learner Acquisition of KS & A
      o Transfer & Application to Real World
   o What is Video's role in these strategies
   o Can/Does Video fulfill roles(s)
   o Is design of program
      o Single purpose (to be used one way only)
      o Versatile/multi-purpose

4. **PRODUCTION QUALITY**

   o Characters, Sets, Dialogue, Actions
      o Authentic - Realistic
         o Credibility Factors
         o Plausibility Factors
      o Up-to-date
         o Dress
         o Language
         o Settings
   o All production effects enhance, not detract, from message

5. **VALUE**

   o Is it worth the cost(s) as compared to other
      o Problem solution alternatives
      o Instructional design alternatives
   o Will it 'save'
      o Time
      o Money

(c)1987, Henry F Bohne, Parker, Colorado

Figure 10-1 Evaluation for training video programs (*courtesy, Henry Bohne*).

long, or it needs some way to keep the viewers more involved. Often you can use presentational techniques to overcome some of these deficiencies:

- There's no rule that a program must be watched in its entirety from count-down leader to closing credits. Unacceptable segments can be skipped over, with the instructor providing an alternate description of what was left out.
- You can show a program in sections, allowing time for discussion or exercises in between.
- An instructor can add "live voice-over" by merely turning down the audio and providing an alternate sound track with the visuals.
- Introductory or summary information can be provided "live" or through some mediated format. This can help relate the information to your specific audience and organization and provide local validity (applicability and credibility for the particular situation).
- You can show segments in a different order or replay parts for emphasis.
- With permission from the copyright holder, you can re-edit the program, taking out unwanted segments, adding in locally produced materials, or rearranging content.

FIELD TESTING YOUR PRODUCTIONS

One of the best measures of a program's success is the client's satisfaction. Being able to create a product that embodies your client's objectives, style, and taste is no mean feat. However, the program was designed for a target audience, and you can determine its real effectiveness only by seeing if it meets its goals out in the field.

Strategies for assessing a program's effectiveness range from informal conversations through questionnaires (like the one in Figure 10-2) to scientific experiments. Some projects are easier to evaluate than others, since they have more specific or short-term objectives. For instance, it's much easier to measure the results of a training tape for new workers on how to operate a cash register than a company news program designed for the broad purpose of enhancing employee morale. In general, instructional or informational material is easier to evaluate than motivational or purely artistic material. Not only is it difficult to change attitudes merely by presenting a video program, but it's doubly difficult to measure attitude change accurately.

There is no one correct methodology for evaluating programs, but there is one basic approach: evaluate a program on the basis of its objectives. In Chapter 2 we introduced the concept of instructional systems. If a project was developed using this model, you will have specified objectives and audiences. If this was not done, or was somehow not clearly communicated to the client, evaluation will probably be frustrating and meaningless. Just what was the purpose of the program? Specifically what should the viewers be able/motivated to do as a result? For whom was the program designed? Under what conditions is it to be used? The easiest approach to evaluation is to look at the behavioral objectives set out for a program and design a scheme to measure whether or not they've been met.

There are two categories of evaluation: formative and summative. Formative evaluation takes place during the production process and includes such measures as client evaluation of the script, previewing of rushers, and critiquing of rough-cut segments. Summative evaluation, done when the project is finished, seeks feedback on its final form.

A number of methodologies are available for evaluation, each with strengths and weaknesses and appropriate applications.

project _____

MEDIA SERVICES PROJECT EVALUATION FORM

Please take a few minutes to evaluate the project named above
that _____ of Media Services recently
produced for you. The form's first part addresses the final
product; the second, the producer's professionalism.

Answer questions with a number scale by circling the figure
closest to how you feel about it: 5 - strongly agree; 4 - agree;
3 - neutral; 2 - disagree; 1 - strongly disagree.

Honesty is important. Your feedback will be used in the
producer's performance appraisal. It will also help us
ultimately improve the quality of our work. Thank you.

<u>part one</u>
1. The project achieves its goals.

    1------------2------------3------------4------------5

2. The project's purpose is clear.

    1------------2------------3------------4------------5

3. The project's style is appropriated to the subject/audience.

    1------------2------------3------------4------------5

4. The project provides its audience with new information.

    1------------2------------3------------4------------5

5. The project's technical quality (lighting, sound,
    photography, layout) is acceptable.

    1------------2------------3------------4------------5

6. The project works.

    1------------2------------3------------4------------5

7. What do think is the project's main point?

    _____

    _____

8. Which, if any, aspects of the finished product do you
    especially like or dislike? _____

    _____

Figure 10-2 Having clients evaluate the programs you create will
help improve the quality of your services (*courtesy, Mark Weiss,
Georgia Power Company*).

9. Which, if any, aspects of the finished product would you
    change if given such an opportunity? _____

    _____

    _____

part two

10. The producer worked with me to define the results I
    anticipated.

        1------------2------------3-----------4-----------5

11. The producer knew why this project was important.

        1------------2------------3-----------4-----------5

12. The producer told me what my responsibilities would be at
    each of the project's stages.

        1------------2------------3-----------4-----------5

13. The producer accepted my suggestions or provided
    alternatives with explanation that were at least as good.

        1------------2------------3-----------4-----------5

14. The producer delivered the project by the negotiated
    deadline. (Explain negative answer at #20.)

        circle one: yes   no

15. The producer delivered the project within budget. (Explain
    negative answer at #20.)

        circle one: yes   no

16. The producer informed me of developments that could have
    affected the project's delivery date and/or costs.

        1------------2------------3-----------4-----------5

17. The producer knew hwat s/he was doing.

        1------------2------------3-----------4-----------5

18. I would enjoy working with this producer again.

        1------------2------------3-----------4-----------5

19. Which, if any, aspects of your working relationship with the
    producer would you change if given such an opportunity?

Figure 10-2 Continued

The structured interview consists of discussing the program with viewers, singly or in a group, following a set of planned questions or topics. The questions can cover specific information found in the program, as well as viewers' reactions to the content and style. Being able to follow up on a viewer's reactions often gives you insights into areas you would never have asked about. However, you may get inaccurate feedback because your subjects don't want to criticize a program—out of politeness or job politics. In a group interview, the tendency is for an opinion leader to take over, so you may not hear everyone's real feelings. This method is best for assessing opinions—it doesn't really measure what a viewer has learned or can now perform. Therefore, it's usually applied to the evaluation of motivational or "soft" informational programs, rather than specific training programs, or it's applied along with some other measure of content mastery to get feedback on production styles or formats.

Questionnaires are often used in place of interviews—again, usually to measure an audience's opinions about a program. They can contain open-ended questions that allow the viewer to write short "essays" on a topic or scales on which a viewer rates certain aspects of the program, say from "poor" to "excellent." Questionnaires provide "hard copy" of viewers' responses and can be administered by anyone. Further, they avoid the bias that may be injected when someone involved in the program summarizes or interprets structured interviews. Like the structured interview, however, a questionnaire may not reflect a person's true feelings. He or she may feel under pressure to respond in the "correct" fashion, knowing what the objectives of the program are. This tendency is strengthened if the questionnaire is not anonymous.

Posttests can be used to measure a person's comprehension of an instructional program. They can take the form of a traditional paper-and-pencil test, or they can be performance based, actually measuring a trainee's ability to perform some task. Of course, written tests are easy to score and can be administered in a group setting; this is not always the case in evaluating practical exercises. However, testing should reflect the objectives: just because a person can write about something doesn't necessarily mean he or she can perform a task; conversely, some people have trouble with written tests but not with hands-on skills. Posttests can be administered immediately after instruction or delayed for a period of time to measure retention. In the former case you're measuring immediate recall and may not be sure what occurred between the program viewing and the testing. Perhaps the trainees learned the procedure by some other means or received conflicting information.

One major problem with posttests is that you have no data about what the viewers knew before watching the program, so it's hard to pin down the real effectiveness of the instruction. Another problem particularly plaguing written tests is the difficulty of developing good questions that reliably and validly screen those who know the material from those who don't. We've all seen test questions to which a person could easily guess the correct answer without really knowing the content, as well as questions so poorly written or so "tricky" that they would foul up someone who really does know the information.

The pretest-posttest methodology attempts to zero in on what learning can be attributed directly to a given experience. Viewers are tested before and after a program, and the difference in scores is calculated. While this adds a level of information to the evaluation, it can create some problems. A pretest can "sensitize" viewers to the information to be covered on the posttest. If the same questions are used on both tests, the audience may simply have "learned the test." If different questions are used on each test, they must be shown to be equivalent in terms of content and difficulty—otherwise you're comparing "apples and oranges."

Experimental design, using "control groups" and "experimental groups," is another evaluation methodology. One group, the experimental, is exposed to a "treatment"—watching a program. The control group is exposed either to nothing or to some "placebo" condition. Then the groups are compared by some form of posttest. Of course, you must ensure that both groups are essentially similar in aspects that could affect test performance—sex, age, experience, education, intellectual ability, and so on. To even out these factors, you would normally assign individuals to each group randomly. This is often difficult to carry out ethically in a real world situation: if you have every reason to believe that a video program will teach them more effectively than some other means (or no instruction at all), you'll have a hard time denying it to one group for the sake of an experiment. Experimental methods are generally used to evaluate some new technique or medium rather than just to get feedback on a particular program.

Direct measures of performance are perhaps the most concrete way to measure the impact of a program, but they are difficult to pin down. For instance, if your training program is designed to reduce the number of mistakes made in filling out purchase orders, what is the actual rate of errors before and after the videotape? If your new program is supposed to encourage viewers to donate to the annual United Way drive, what is the actual amount of money donated by those persons who saw the tape? Of course, in many cases it's impossible to attribute such behaviors directly to a program. However, this measure is probably "closest to the heart" of most organizations and, added to other measures of evaluation, can make a strong case for the effectiveness of video.

Actual job performance may not be the only area to evaluate. Often training or communications programs have important side benefits. Perhaps employees now can perform a task efficiently or are informed about the organization's activities; these are obvious benefits. But has there been a decline in absenteeism and job turnover? Could this be because people feel more confident in their work, more valued by the organization, more like part of a team? Do students suddenly take more interest in a certain subject, enrolling in higher numbers or pursuing additional study? Certainly in the more global matters there can be no single cause; however, these matters are so crucial to the basic life of the organization that the mere demonstration that the video operation is a positive factor can be worth more than dozens of rigorous scientific studies.

A number of statistical techniques allow you to evaluate programs with more precision. Say, for instance, you had one group of ten students watch a videotape on interviewing techniques and another group of ten read about the same information in a pamphlet. When you give all of them a posttest, the "videotape group" scored an average of 95 percent and the "pamphlet group" an average of 90 percent. Therefore, you conclude that the videotape was a more effective way of teaching that subject matter. However, is that five-point difference enough to justify the costs of producing video rather than print? Is that difference subject to chance fluctuation? For instance, if you repeated the experiment, could the results favor the print format, or would the spread be even greater? Chances are, if you did repeat this little study, you'd come out with different figures. So how do you know when your difference is "real?"

Statistical formulas have been developed that allow you to tell if such a difference is significant (that it is probably not due to chance variation). While it is beyond the scope of this text to go into these procedures, some of the basic concepts are important to remember: What is the spread in the scores of the two groups? The larger the difference between the scores of the two groups, the more sure you can be that one is really superior. The variation in the individual scores between groups should be substantially greater than the spread of scores within each group.

After you've assessed a program, what do you do with the data? In some cases you'll find that certain parts of the program were not effective and should be changed before the program is used again. In other cases you may not have to redo the program but may gain some insights on what "works" with a particular audience. Your evaluations should be directed at several main groups: your client(s), the subject-matter expert, the instructors or managers who will use the program, and the target audience (see Figure 10-3). It's often difficult to satisfy all these constituencies—and it may take a while to get a good grasp on their tastes. Different methodologies will be appropriate for getting feedback from these different

ADVISORY COUNCIL QUESTIONNAIRE

NAME _____

ETHNIC OR INSTITUTIONAL AFFILIATION _____

DURING OUR MEETINGS AND THROUGH CORRESPONDANCE WITH PROJECT STAFF, SEVERAL GENERAL THEMES AND OBJECTIVES WERE IDENTIFIED AS ELEMENTS TO BE INCLUDED IN THE SERIES. PLEASE RATE THE PROGRAMS ON THE WAY THEY CARRIED THROUGH WITH THESE OBJECTIVES, USING THE FOLLOWING CRITERIA. PLEASE RATE THE FOLLOWING ITEMS ON A SCALE OF 0 THROUGH 4.

	0	1	2	3	4
	strongly disagree	disagree	neutral	agree	strongly agree

1. The videotape series covered the importance of ethnicity in modern society.

    0   1   2   3   4

2. The series covered adequately the relevance of ethnicity to young people.

    0   1   2   3   4

3. The series covered general topics on ethnicity rather than focusing on individual ethnic groups.

    0   1   2   3   4

4. The series presented ethnicity and ethnic traditions in a positive light.

    0   1   2   3   4

5. The series showed real people and real events rather than presenting abstract concepts.

    0   1   2   3   4

6. The series treated ethnicity as a dimension in the lives of many types of people living many different lifestyles.

    0   1   2   3   4

7. The series treated issues and people which counteracted stereotyped and negative images of ethnic Americans.

    0   1   2   3   4

a

Figure 10-3 Many grant projects use advisory councils; here is an instrument designed to collect their reactions to major program objectives.

8. The content was factually accurate.

           0   1   2   3   4

9. The technical quality of the videotapes was high.

           0   1   2   3   4

10. The style and content of the programs are appealing to a wide variety of audiences of different ages and lifestyles and backgrounds.

           0   1   2   3   4

11. In general, the series reflects the goals and suggestions developed by the Advisory Council.

           0   1   2   3   4

12. In general, the series served as a forum for ethnic Americans to tell their own story.

           0   1   2   3   4

GENERAL COMMENTS:

BEST ASPECTS OF THE SERIES:

WORST ASPECTS OF THE SERIES:

PLEASE COMMENT BRIEFLY ON HOW EFFECTIVE YOU PERCEIVED THE ADVISORY COUNCIL'S INPUT WAS IN THE DEVELOPMENT OF THE PROGRAMS.

IN GENERAL, DO YOU FEEL THAT THERE ARE ANY SIGNIFICANT DIFFERENCES IN TONE, QUALITY, OR EFFECTIVENESS AMONG THE FOUR VIDEOTAPE PROGRAMS? IF SO, WHAT ARE THE DIFFERENCES?

b

Figure 10-3 Continued

"audiences." Although the most important aspect is whether the material met its stated objectives, it's politically important to assess also the client's satisfaction with both the style and content of the program.

ASSESSING COST EFFECTIVENESS

As we've seen, organizational video differs from commercial video in that the programming is a means rather than an end. Corporations, schools, government agencies, and medical centers don't produce programs for their own sake, but rather to achieve certain organizational goals. At the root of those goals, more often than not, is money: either saving it or making more of it. Since, of course, video is not the only means of communication or training, a basic justification of it is cost effectiveness. The basic underlying question is: can we achieve the same results in a more efficient manner?

Cost-accounting measures are necessary for any production center that relies on the charge-back method of support. The manager must determine the true cost of each production—and of maintaining the facility between productions so that it can stay afloat. Television centers relying on annual budgets for support often neglect to calculate such figures, except perhaps for the usage of expendable materials. When budgets are in jeopardy, they find themselves without ammunition to defend their contribution to the organization's economic welfare.

The cost of each production—including labor, materials, travel, depreciation, and overhead—should be calculated and recorded. One way of then assessing cost-effectiveness is to divide the production cost by the number of viewers reached, thereby deriving a cost-per-viewer figure. Another very powerful technique is to assess the direct benefits of the program in terms of dollars and compare this figure to the production cost. For instance, if a safety program saved a company $3500 in one year in employee compensation and cost $5000 to produce, after a little over a year the program would be paid for and continuing to benefit the organization.

Quite often, video programs are compared to other media and delivery methods. A common comparison is made with "live" teachers in terms of cost per student. When trying to make these comparisons, however, it is first crucial to assess if the modes being compared are equally as effective and acceptable to managers, instructors, and students. Mediated methods, when used with a large audience over a period of time, will often be found to be more cost-effective than traditional face-to-face communication. Despite its high initial design and production costs, video can be used over and over and distributed to a wide variety of locations. Moving information rather than people is almost universally more economical.

A few basic questions can help determine the monetary benefits of a video program:

- How much did the program cost versus some other just as effective delivery format?
- How many people were reached via video versus those who could have been reached by some other means? For instance, a teacher may be able to teach four sections of 80 students in a class that is partially media-based but only two sections of 20 if using the lecture method only.
- Did video's ability to be used on an individual basis contribute to a wider outreach? For example, do more students sign up for a course that is partially taught via broadcast instructional programs than would enroll in a course at a fixed location? Can more employees get an opportunity to be exposed to company updates by viewing videotapes at a time convenient to them than could attend a given meeting?
- How many times can the same program be used? A consultant might be hired to deliver a short workshop on EEO guidelines; this might cost $2000 to be delivered to 30 employees at one site. A video program might cost $30,000 but could be used repeatedly and on demand in various locations.
- Does the nature of video actually motivate more people to pay attention to the material? While employees might deposit a memo in "the circular file," they might be tempted to see what's on the new tape just sent from headquarters.
- Does distribution of the video program eliminate the necessity of personal travel? Can students see some object or place under study on television rather

than in person? Can employees learn about management techniques without being sent to the company's training center or to a special workshop?

- Can video provide a simulation of something too expensive or risky to carry out in person? For instance, can a student nurse experiment with various treatments of cardiac arrest through interactive video rather than in real life? Can new recruits learn about operating a tank on video rather than using expensive and breakable equipment?
- Can information get out faster through video distribution than it would in individual meetings?
- Does video reduce the amount of training time? Can employees get back to the job faster and therefore be more productive?

These considerations should be kept in mind not only when evaluating programs, but also when doing a needs analysis for one. By keeping track of a number of budgetary figures for each situation, program costs as well as requests for additional equipment or personnel can easily be justified.

Sometimes traditional classroom training "looks" cheaper because people are not doing a total cost accounting of the entire process. Video may need to be paid for directly out of some budget, while trainers, classroom space, and trainees are just assumed to be "free." But, as the old saying goes, time is money. While trainers are planning and training and trainees are traveling or sitting in classrooms, they're being paid. Let's look at a simple example of how to do a cost accounting.

PROJECT: DEVELOP A HALF-DAY ORIENTATION SEMINAR FOR NEW EMPLOYEES (ESTIMATED 200 PER YEAR, AT 5 LOCATIONS)

Traditional classroom instruction cost **accounting**:

Development cost

Length of time to design 1/2 day course, **40 hours**

Hourly salary of course developer (including such items as benefits,) **$50**

Total design cost, **$2,000**

Total cost of traditional A/V support (such as slides and transparencies,) **$500**

Total development cost: **$2,500**

Delivery cost

Average number of trainees per class, **10**

Average student salary per hour, **$20**

Course length **4 hours**

Salaries of trainees while sitting in classes (200 students × $20/hour × 4 hours) = **$16,000**

Percentage of trainees who would have to travel to class **50%**

Average travel expenses for trainees who travel **$500**

Total travel expenses paid (100 trainees × $500 per trainee) **$50,000**

Instructor salary per hour **$30**

Total instructor salary for classes ($30/hour × 20 classes × 4 hours) = **$2,400**

Total delivery cost = **$68,400**

Total design and delivery cost for classroom training $70,900

Let's assume that you could develop a 2-hour video/workbook/computer-based training experience that employees could go through on their own when needed. (A general finding is that mediated instruction or information can greatly increase the speed at which information can be presented—with no loss of information. This is generally because people can go at their own pace and don't get bogged down by "nonessentials," such as side conversations, questions, and socializing.) This program would probably cost a lot more to design and produce up front but might be able to save money in the long run. I actually produced such a package for a client for a total of about $40,000 (excluding duplication), but it could have been done for quite a bit less if it had been done in-house. A workbook was used to provide a general introduction to the company. A computer-based "form-filler-outer" allowed employees to fill out their personal data on a computer, which then filled out necessary employment and tax forms for their signatures. A computer-based information program explained their flexible benefits package and adapted itself to part-time and full-time workers, giving people information only about those options available and appropriate for their situations. Finally, a 20-minute video presented an overview of the history and future of the company, showing various branches and "back-room" operations throughout its facilities.

DEVELOPMENT COST FOR VIDEO/WORKBOOK PACKAGE

Developer salary per hour, **$50**
Hours to develop workbook and script, **100**
Course developer total salary for project, **$5,000**
Production of 30-page workbook (desktop publishing), **$300**
Duplication of 100 workbooks, **$2,000**
Production of 20-minute videotape, **$20,000**
Creation of computer-based information program (200 hours at $50/hour, **$10,000**
Duplication of 10 VHS copies and 10 computer diskettes, **$100**
Total development cost, $37,400

DELIVERY COST FOR VIDEO/WORKBOOK/CBT PACKAGE

Average trainee salary per hour **$20**
Course length **2 hours**
*Total delivery cost (200 trainees × $20/hour × 2 hours) = **$8,000***

Total cost for Video/Workbook Package = $45,000

Total savings in using video (total classroom cost minus total video/workbook cost) = $25,900

As you can see from this example, the two major factors are the number of students and the need for some (moderate) travel. Play around with different examples—and see what you come up with. The $30,000 figure for the production of a videotape would be an approximate cost for a high-end production done in-house (using actors and perhaps custom special effects) or for a moderate production done out-of-house. Again, you can refer back to the chapter on budgeting and look at how to calculate in-house rates and look at the rate cards of production houses and see what it might take if it were done out-of-house. Of course, you'd also have to assess whether, in fact, your 2-hour workbook/video package communicated as much information *as well* as the "live" classes did—and what other benefits of getting a group of people together were given up by training people in isolation in their own offices.

Training is not the only category of video which can offer huge pay-backs. Employee information can help save companies money in insurance premiums and downtime, and information can alleviate employees' fears in tough times—making it easier for them to work productively. For example, GTE of Florida is producing a series on "Women's Wellness"—one program of which won a 1988 Golden Reel Award from the International Television Association. The company found that $3.9 million of the company's $17 million in insurance claims resulted from several female reproductive problems. Just one neonatal intensive care case could cost up to $200,000. Obviously, if the company could prevent just one case of caring for a premature baby, it could easily fund several video programs. Tapes in the series are costing them about $15,000 each (Kleyman, 1988).

Sometimes video programming can help a company *make* money. More and more firms are producing "video proposals" for jobs that are as diverse as building defense systems, designing large architectural projects, and providing communications systems. For example, US Sprint pulled out all the stops in its successful bid to win a large communications contract awarded by the government. A week-long presentation involved 15 videotapes, over 1,000 slides, live speakers, and a written proposal—and the video portion alone cost them over $1 million! Was it worth it? Well, they won a $10 *billion* contract (Luber, 1989).

FINDING INFORMATION: PROFESSIONAL LITERATURE AND ASSOCIATIONS

The organizational video producer often works in a professionally isolated atmosphere: there may be few or no other media people within the organization with whom to share ideas. For this reason, such producers are prone to "reinventing the wheel" when it comes to trying out production and evaluation strategies. Say, for instance, that you are interested in knowing whether different note-taking strategies affect student learning from video materials, or you want to know about the use of music, or superimposed key words, or the gender of the narrator? You may be inclined to rush out and conduct your own study. It is better to investigate first, however, whether anyone else had done some research on the topic.

A number of sources offer informative articles, research reports, or abstracts of studies. Depending upon your interests and needs, you can consult them for specific information or subscribe on a regular basis to keep up with a wide range of current issues in the field. There are three general categories of reference tools: books, periodicals, and data bases.

Books can provide general information on production techniques, educational technology, psychology, and management. Often it's helpful to get a thorough grounding in the theoretical aspects underlying your problem. For instance, if you're exploring the potential uses of interactive video in patient education, you may wish to examine books dealing with teaching methodologies, learning theory, new technology, and health care. Often these materials can provide background information on the principles underlying your topic and related research projects. If you're using a library card catalog, you might try the following headings: Selection of Nonbook Materials; Teaching Aids and Devices; Instructional Materials Centers; Media Programs; Educational Technology; or Instructional Materials Personnel.

Periodicals and scholarly journals offer more specific and current information, including articles on specific projects, approaches, or studies. Magazines aimed at the professional market, such as *Corporate Video Decisions, AV/Video*

Videography, Business Television, Training and Development Journal, Training, Educational Technology, Performance & Instruction, and *Tech Trends* mainly contain descriptive, "how-to," or opinion-based articles. Other journals, such as *Educational Communications and Technology Journal, Journal of Educational Technology Systems, Journal of Educational Psychology,* and the *Journal of Communications* publish articles of a more scholarly nature, generally summarizing original research on a very narrow topic. Magazines often contain more current but shallower articles than journals.

In finding articles, it's helpful to use indexes that survey a group of magazines and list articles by subject. Publications such as *Education Index, Business Index,* and *International Index to Multi-Media Information* may be of particular assistance. Often you'll find bibliographies at the end of articles that will lead you to further sources.

Finally, data bases list and abstract research materials on given topics; several of these are computer based, so that you can have computer-assisted as well as manual searches made. On-line information utilities such as *CompuServe, The Source, Knowledge Index,* and *Dialog* allow you to search through literature using key words or phrases, or authors' names. See Figure 10-4 which shows the output of a database search. A useful data base is *Dissertation Abstracts,* which summarizes doctoral dissertations by year and by topic. ERIC (for Education Research Information Clearinghouse) abstracts a wide variety of materials related to instruction. It is divided into two parts: *CIJE* (Current Index to Journals in Education), which abstracts published articles, and *RIE* (Research in Education), which abstracts unpublished monographs, reports, speeches, papers, and the like. *Psychological Abstracts,* another widely used data base, covers articles dealing with experimental methods, learning, perception, and human behavior.

By going through these indexes by hand or by having a computer search made, you can not only obtain titles but short summaries of the article or paper. Some on-line data bases can even print out an entire article for you. This saves you from hunting down an article with a promising title that turns out to be totally inapplicable to your needs. In order to use data bases, you need to come up with descriptors, words or phrases that describe the subject you're interested in. Each index has a thesaurus of descriptors that it uses to classify materials.

Through professional conferences and seminars, you may be able to gather additional research and meet the individual responsible for the study. Associations such as the Association for Educational Communications and Technology, American Society for Training and Development, National Society for Performance and Instruction, American Educational Research Association, and International Television Association have conventions during which members deliver presentations on specific topics. Other commercial entities such as publishing houses, production centers, or private consulting groups offer workshops and seminars as well. By attending these events, you can not only profit from formal presentations but can also build a network of colleagues upon whom you can call.

The area of interactive video has its own journals and associations. Magazines of interest include *Instruction Delivery Systems, Journal of Computer-based Instruction, Journal of Interactive Instruction Delivery,* and the newsletter *Videodisc Monitor.* Associations dealing with computer-based interactive media include the Society of Applied Learning Technology (SALT), the Association for the Development of Computer-based Instructional Systems (ADCIS), the Interactive Video Industry Association (IVIA), and the International Interactive Communications Society (IICS).

The information you can gather from all of these sources is especially useful when you're working with a new format, subject matter, or audience. Before investing in new programs or hardware, supervisors often want to know what research has

```
C:VIDPROD.REF                    November 4, 1989    8:08am    Page 1


  3/7/13
EJ320660    CE515820
  A Guide to Cost-Effective Video.
  Ingrisano, John R.
  Training, v22 n8 p41-44 Aug  1985
  Available from: UMI
  Language: English
  Document Type: JOURNAL ARTICLE (080); NON-CLASSROOM MATERIAL (055)
  Journal Announcement: CIJNOV85
  Planning   details   are   suggested  for producing a quality, cost-effective
training  video. Discusses choosing a video medium, writing the script, and
deciding  on production facilities. Tips to consider when hiring an outside
consultant are also given. (CT)


  5/7/14
ED289054    CE049279
  Originating   Conferences   and   Credit   Courses.   Using  WOI  Satellite
Transmission. A Basic Guide.
  Stinehart, Kathleen; And Others
  Iowa   State   Univ.  of Science and Technology, Ames. Office of Continuing
Education.
  1987
  15p.
  EDRS Price - MF01/PC01 Plus Postage.
  Language: English
  Document Type: NON-CLASSROOM MATERIAL (055)
  Geographic Source: U.S.; Iowa
  Journal Announcement: RIEMAY88
  Target Audience: Practitioners
  This  guide  was  developed to help administrators and educators plan and
implement  videoconferences  and  credit  courses  using  the  Iowa  State
University  studios (WOI). In a short narrative format, the guide leads the
reader  through  the  videoconference  or  course  process.  The  guide  is
organized  in three sections. The first section presents an overview of the
process,  including  information  on  what videoconferencing is, the signal
path,  the transponder, the studio, return audio, the "footprint"--the area
covered  by  a  satellite's  signal,  live  versus videotape programs, and
downlink  arrangements.  The  second  section  explains how to get started.
Topics  covered  are making the initial contact, scheduling, marketing your
event,  and  planning  the  budget.  The  final section covers planning for
effective  satellite-delivered  instruction.  The  guide  ends  with  a
"start-to-finish"  checklist  to  help  the  reader plan a teleconferencing
project. (KC)


  5/7/15
ED283514    IR012718
  A National Survey of Higher Education Media Services.
  McConeghy, Gary L.; McConeghy, Janet I.
  Apr 1987
  54p.;  Paper  presented at the Annual Meeting of the American Educational
Research Association (Washington, DC, April 20-24, 1987).
  EDRS Price - MF01/PC03 Plus Postage.
  Language: English
  Document  Type:  RESEARCH  REPORT  (143);  CONFERENCE  PAPER (150); TEST,
```

Figure 10-4 You can use on-line services to get abstracts of
articles and reports in your area of interest.

already been done and what documented "success stories" can be pointed to in support of your proposal. Having not only your own in-house evaluations but also having access to outside research can assist enormously in expanding the video operation.

CLOSING THE LOOP

Well, here we are at the end of the story. We started out talking about who does corporate video and why. Then we learned how to analyze problems, write scripts, negotiate contracts, plan and execute productions, and finally distribute programs—hopefully keeping the client and our audience happy the whole time. But communication is not one way—it's a continuous loop. Evaluation is that feedback you need to keep you in touch with your audience and to help you improve the ways in which you solve communication problems.

Corporate video's future is inextricably tied to evaluation. Whether the field or individual departments will continue to exist can't be left to chance, fad, or whim. As professionals in this field, we've got to continue to prove our worth and make a place in our organizations. Finally, we must continue to grow with the rapidly expanding technology and redefine exactly how we execute our work as communication professionals.

BIBLIOGRAPHY

BRANDT, R. (1987). *Videodisc Training: A Cost Analysis.* Arlington, VA: Future Systems, Inc.

KEARSLEY, G. (1982). *Costs, Benefits, and Productivity in Training Systems.* Reading, MA: Addison-Wesley Publishing Co.

KLEYMAN, P. (1988, November/December). "Women's wellness: GTE's bottom-line cure," *Corporate Television,* p 26.

LUBER, C. (1989, March/April). "US Sprint races for GSA contract," *Corporate Television,* pp. 24–25.

GLOSSARY

A and B rolling: the mixing of two sources from "A" and "B" tapes onto a master edited tape

Advance organizer: a preview of a program's content designed to ready the viewer for the information to follow.

AFTRA: the American Federation of TV and Radio Artists.

Ambient noise: background sound.

ASCAP: American Society of Composers, Authors, and Publishers.

Aspect ratio: the ratio of a picture height to width; in video, 3:4.

Assemble edit: to string together video segments recording each's audio, video, and control tracks.

Authoring language: a computer programming language designed for producing computer-assisted instruction.

Back light: the light used to illuminate the back of someone's head to separate the person from the background.

Bartering the swapping or exchange of goods or services "in kind" rather than for cash.

Behavioral objective: a statement of a desired goal in terms of someone's behavior.

Betamax: a half-inch cassette standard developed by the Sony Corporation.

BetaCam: a broadcast-quality half-inch video standard developed by the Sony Corporation.

Bicycle: to distribute by sending them to a succession of locations.

Bid: a price quoted for an object or service.

Blocking   the establishing of positions and movements for talent on the set.

BMI: Broadcast Music, Inc.

Branching   a program style in which viewers are presented with or "branched to" different segments of the program, depending upon their responses.

Bump-up: a dub onto a larger-format tape.

Business TV: the use of satellites or phone lines to distribute live video programs for information or education to a defined group of people

Capacitance: a format of videodisc.

Capital equipment: nonexpendible equipment with an expected life span of a few years.

CATV: community antenna television, an alternate name for cable distribution.

CCD: charge-coupled device, a method of electronically creating a video image within a camera; a newer technology than using tubes in cameras.

CCTV: closed-circuit TV, or video distribution through receiving sites physically wired to the source.

Character generator: a keyboard device used to create letters, numbers, and simple characters in a video form.

Charge-back: a funding scheme in which a department runs on fees charged for its services.

Chroma-keying: the replacement of part of a video picture with the corresponding part of another shot by punching a "hole" in a picture where a certain color appears. It is used to insert pictures on part of a set backdrop, as commonly seen in news programs, or to place a person in a setting in which he or she is not physically present.

Client: the person requesting a service; the customer.

Closed-circuit TV: a distribution system using receiving sites physically wired to the source.

Close-up: a shot filling the screen with a small detail or just a person's head and shoulders.

Color bars: a standard test signal used as a reference when setting up equipment.

Color temperature: the color of a light source, measured in degrees Kelvin.

Community constituency: the audience or community that is to be served.

Company news program: a program following the broadcast journalism format containing news of a particular organization produced by and for that organization.

Constructed answer: a "fill-in-the-blank" answer that must be remembered and spelled out rather than just selected from a list.

Consultant: a person who offers information and advice in a particular field.

Content expert: the subject-matter expert versed in the content of a program, also called subject-matter expert or SME.

Continuity: the illusion of continuous action, even when segments that were recorded at different times are edited together.

Control room: an area that contains audio and video controls, such as a mixer and a switcher for a TV studio.

Control track: a track on a tape of control pulses used to stabilize playback of the tape; sync track.

Copyright: a "patent" on an original creative work.

Cost-effectiveness: an assessment of the benefits versus the cost of something.

Counter numbers: a revolving number scale, indicating revolutions of a tape, used to roughly index sections of a tape on a playback unit.

Crawl: to move text lines from the right to the left, as commonly seen on lighted signs.

Criterion test: a test measuring specific criteria or objectives used to evaluate the success of a program.

Cut: to replace one picture immediately with another; a "take."

Cut-away: a shot showing something other than what is in the previous shot, usually to cover up edits.

Cut-in: a shot showing a tight close-up of something in the previous shot.

Cut on action: to change shots while an action is taking place.

Depreciation: the reduction in value of an item as it ages.

Descriptor: a word or phrase that describes a subject under which information can be found in an index.

DGA: Directors' Guild of America.

Dial-access: a receiving system in which a viewer dials up a requested program, which is automatically started up and fed to the viewer's location.

Digital video: analog video which has been digitized

Digital video effects device (DVE):   a special-effects device that can control the size and position of a shot.

Digital video interactive (DVI):   a standard for digitizing and compressing video which can then be manipulated by a computer program.

Direct annual budget: a funding system in which a department gets a lump sum to expend during the year.

Dish: an antenna designed to receive satellite transmission

Dissolve: to gradually fade out one shot while simultaneously fading in another.

Docu-drama: a program format in which actual events are re-created or dramatized.

Documentary: a program format documenting a real event rather than creating a scripted one.

Double-mike: the practice of using two microphones on a person as a precaution against failure.

Down-link: a receiving site for satellite transmissions.

Dropout: "glitches" or streaks in a picture caused by a breakdown in the tape coating.

Dub: to duplicate electronically.

Edit decision list: a printout of desired in-and-out cues of segments to be edited.

Edited master: the original copy of an edited program.

Editing controller: a device that controls VTR's during the editing process; editing interface.

Editing script: a script marked up with location numbers of each segment on the raw footage for expediency in assembling the final program.

Editor: a VTR that can perform clean edits.

EFP: electronic field production; shooting video generally with one camera out of the studio.

Electronic editing: rearranging and "cutting" segments by means of duplication.

ENG: electronic news gathering: a production style using small portable equipment for high mobility in the field, as pioneered by broadcast news.

Equalize: to filter an audio track to balance the reproduction of ranges of frequencies.

Essential area   the area in the center of a shot that will be reproduced in full by almost any TV monitor.

Exclusive rights   the right to use a given work and to prevent anyone else from using it.

Experimental design: a methodology in which groups given different treatments are compared with each other.

External sync: sync provided by a generator in common to all the cameras and VTR's in a system.

Extreme close-up: a very tight shot filling the screen with small detail.

Federal Communications Commission: the U.S. regulatory agency for communications technology using the public airwaves.

Field: any place not in the studio; also one half of a frame of video consisting of either the odd or the even scanning lines

Fill light: the light used to fill in shadows on the side opposite the key light.

Film chain: a video camera, slide projector, and film projector in a unit designed to transfer film images to video.

Film-style: shooting with one portable camera.

First generation: an original recording, not a copy.

Flowchart: a diagram of program segments and paths through those segments.

Font: a character set or alphabet style.

Formative evaluation: assessment that takes place during the development and production process, used for "midcourse" feedback and correction.

Frame: one scanned video picture, appearing at 1/30 of a second during normal playback of a video program.

F-stop: the aperture setting on a lens that controls the amount of light passing through it.

Gaffer tape: wide, heavy-duty, metalized cloth tape; duct tape.

Gen-lock: to be "driven by" or accept the sync of another piece of equipment.

Glitch: a picture problem.

Grant: an allocation of money awarded competitively for a particular project.

Hard copy: a printed document.

Hardware: machinery or devices.

Headend: a point of origin for cable distribution.

Helical scan: the way that most videotape is scanned by the heads.

Hi-8:   a video format for high-band 8 mm wide videotape

High angle: a shot taken from an elevation looking down on a subject.

Hue: the actual color of something.

IATSE: International Association of Theatrical and Stage Employees.

IBEW: International Brotherhood of Electrical Workers.

In-cue: the beginning of a given portion of tape.

Industrial quality: a grade of video equipment not necessarily meeting the specifications of broadcast gear, but better than consumer-type home units.

Industrial video: nonbroadcast video produced by an organization for instructional/informational use.

In-house: within the organization: owned by the parent company.

Insert edit: to drop in video and/or audio segments on a tape that already has a control track.

Insert stage: a small studio used for simple recording of voice or picture inserts.

Instructional design system: a process by which instructional programs are designed, produced, and evaluated in a methodological manner.

Instructor-control: program design that assumes an instructor will control the program's presentation.

Intelligent program: a program with imbedded logic in which segments displayed can vary, depending on responses of the viewer.

Interactive video: a program style in which the viewer must actively participate in the program and in which the presentation may vary depending upon the viewer's responses.

Intercutting: interspersing segments of several taped sequences to consolidate content and provide visual variety.

Interface card: a circuit board inserted in a computer so that it can interface with a videotape or disc player.

Internal sync: synchronizing pulses supplied by an individual piece of hardware.

Isolation: the technique of recording each camera on a separate VTR; the tapes are then edited together in postproduction. Also called iso.

ITFS: Instructional Television Fixed Service; a distribution technology using a special band of frequencies set aside for educational narrowcasting.

ITVA: International Television Association; the major professional association for corporate and educational video producers and users.

Jump-cut: a joining of two segments that creates visual discontinuity.

Key: to electronically cut one image into another.

Key light: the main light source.

Laser-optical: a videodisc format.

Licensing fees: money spent to obtain the rights to use something copyrighted by someone else.

Linear: a program style in which each viewer watches each segment of the program.

Local validity: credibility for the particular situation.

Log: a description of the contents of a tape, scene by scene.

Long shot: a shot showing the overall scene; also called a wide shot.

Low angle: a shot taken from a camera close to the ground aiming up at a subject.

Low-light-level gain: a boost of sensitivity for a camera when operating in dim surroundings.

M-II: a format for broadcast quality half-inch videotape developed by Panasonic

Magazine format: a program format consisting of a number of feature stories shot in different styles.

Master: the original tape and the VTR it is played back on when editing.

Matching funds: awarded on the basis of "matching" money obtained from other sources.

Mechanical editing: physical cutting of a tape.

Mediagraphy: a list of media materials available on a given subject.

Medium shot: a shot halfway between a close-up and a long shot; usually a person shot from the waist up.

Memory: the ability to retain a given setting.

Microwave: very short-wave frequencies used for point-to-point transmission; higher than those used by broadcast.

Model of Participatory Design: an instructional design system incorporating the participation of a program development team.

Model release: the form giving permission to photograph or record someone's voice or image.

Module: a lesson or unit of information.

Montage: a sequence of shots rapidly edited or mixed together to evoke a particular concept.

Multiple branching: a programmed instruction format in which different responses cause the viewer to be branched to different corresponding segments.

NABET: National Association for Broadcast Employees and Technicians.

Narrowcast: to distribute programming to a limited, well-defined audience.

Needle drop: a measure or unit of music determined by how many times a selection is played or the "needle dropped" on the record.

Nonbroadcast video: programming designed for limited access rather than broadcast distribution.

Nonexclusive rights: the right to use a work, but not prevent anyone else from those obtaining rights as well.

NTSC: the video standard used in the United States and several other countries.

Off-line editing: using inexpensive systems, allowing you to do "straight" editing only without special effects or without the control of a computer interface.

Off-the-self programs: commercially produced generic programs that can be rented or purchased.

One-inch: the width of videotape with which there are three formats: Type A, Type B, and Type C.

On-line editing: using VTR's with a computer interface, or with studio-type mixing and switching equipment.

On-the-air: a term used to mean that a particular device is "live" or its output is being recorded or broadcast. Also called on-line.

Open-ended question: a question that requires more than a short answer, giving the respondent an opportunity to express opinions.

Out-cue: the end of a given scene.

Overhead: the costs of running the physical facility.

Overt behavior: an action that can be seen.

Over-the-shoulder shot: a shot taken with the camera looking over someone's shoulder at another person.

Pacing: the timing and segmenting of a program to control the rate of presentation.

PAL: a video standard used in Great Britain and several other countries.

Pan: to turn or swivel the camera from side to side.

Peripheral: a "remote control" device sometimes used to accept viewer response.

Pin-registered camera: a very precise film camera that exposes images in exact registration from one frame to the next.

Pixillation: the cutting out of a certain percentage of frames in a sequence to produce a fast-motion, jumpy effect.

Point-of-purchase program: one designed to be viewed alongside a product it demonstrates in a store.

Positive feedback: information confirming that a response was correct.

Postproduction: the activities of finishing a program through editing, mixing, and duplicating after the original footage has been shot.

Posttest: an evaluation taking place after a subject has been exposed to some treatment or material.

Preproduction: the planning activities undertaken before a program is shot.

Preroll: the backing up of a tape before the desired in-cue so that the VTR can get up to speed.

Pretest: an assessment of students' entering abilities or opinions before they're exposed to some treatment or material.

Private video network: a video playback system set up by an organization to communicate to its various branch offices or affiliates.

Production house: a company that rents out video studio and/or portable production gear.

Program control: program design that assumes the program will be viewed straight through without intervention of an instructor or student.

Program development team: a group of people representing clients, content experts, media professionals, and representative audience members who together develop a program.

Program format: the style in which a subject is covered: documentary, interview, demonstration and so on.

Public domain: the status of not being copyrighted.

Quadruplex: a method of videotape scanning using four heads, found on two-inch machines.

Random assignment: a procedure for dividing people into groups by chance to eliminate biasing those groups, such as picking numbers out of a hat.

Rating scales: numerical standards by which evaluators can rate something-for example, on a "1–5 scale" with 1 being excellent and 5 being poor.

Raw footage: unedited tape footage.

Reaction shot: a shot of a person reacting while another speaks.

Reliable: consistent.

Remedial frame: a segment that provides further clarification of a concept not understood by a viewer.

Request for proposals (RFP):   an announcement of the availability of grant or contract money, soliciting proposals.

Requisition form: a form used by clients to request services.

Resolution: the picture sharpness; how much detail is produced.

Role-playing: an instructional exercise where students take assigned roles to practice skills.

Roll: to move text lines from the bottom to the top of the screen, as seen commonly in ending credits; also to start or "roll" tape

Rough-cut: an imprecise edit of a program without special effects.

Run-down sheet: a log of segments to be edited together and their locations.

Rushes: recently recorded raw footage.

SAG: the Screen Actors' Guild.

Saturation: the depth or richness of a color.

Scan converter: a device that converts one video standard to another.

Scanning area: the area of a shot actually scanned or reproduced by the camera.

Script: the audio and video plan or directions for a program word-for-word and shot-for-shot.

SECAM: a video standard used in France and several other countries.

Second generation: a copy of a first-generation original tape.

Shooting ratio: the ratio of total tape shot to that actually used in the final production.

Shooting script: the script broken down into locations and talent needed, so that similar scenes can conveniently be shot together.

Shot sheet: a rundown of shots in sequence for a given camera for a studio taping.

Signal-to-noise ratio: the ratio of a desired signal to an unwanted signal (static or noise).

Single branching: a programmed instruction format in which all wrong answers are treated in the same way—by branching to a single given segment.

Slate: a board or card on which program identification information is written.

Slave: the machine recording the output of a master machine.

Small-format video: smaller, less expensive video equipment generally used for nonbroadcast purposes.

SMPTE time code: an address in digital time readout used to identify exact places on a tape.

Soft money: grant or contract money that is not guaranteed from year to year.

Software: program material or computer programs.

Specs: specifications or technical descriptions of an item

Standards conversion: the duplication of a tape into another video standard-for instance, NTSC to PAL or PAL to SECAM.

Step: to go through a program frame by frame.

Still-frame: the capturing and playback of a single video frame to stop or "freeze" action.

Storyboard: a script complete with pictures representing each shot.

Summative evaluation: assessment of the final product.

Switcher: a device that takes in a variety of video inputs and selects or blends them, allowing you to cut, dissolve, superimpose, and so on.

Sync track: a track on a tape of control pulses used to stabilize playback of the tape; control track.

Take: a given recording of a scene.

Talent: those appearing or being heard in a program.

Talking heads: a rather disparaging term for a production consisting of static shots of people talking.

Teleconference: a meeting transmitted among a number of sites using satellite distribution.

Teleprompter: a device that displays the script to the talent as a prompt during taping.

Test recording: a brief recording made to test the correct operation of the equipment.

Third person: the style of writing that uses the third-person pronouns (he, she, they, it, and so on) rather than addressing the viewer directly (you, your, and yours).

Time-base corrector: a device that corrects minor electronic errors on a prerecorded tape.

Time-lapse: the presentation, compressed into a short segment, of events that took place over a long period of time.

Touch screen: a video screen that viewers can touch in various areas to register their responses.

Treatment: a narrative description of the way a subject will be treated and a program will look when completed; an experimental condition.

Truck: to move the whole camera right or left across an area.

Tweak up: to make fine adjustments.

Two-shot: a shot containing two people.

U-Matic: ¾- inch video cassette tape or the type of player that uses that format.

Up-link: a site sending signals up to a satellite.

Valid: authentic; something that measures what it's really supposed to.

VCR: video cassette recorder.

VHS: ½-inch cassette standard used by JVC, Panasonic, RCA, and some other manufacturers.

Vicarious travel: the simulation of a trip through interactive video.

Videodisc: a video recording pressed onto a laser optical disc format.

Video format: the size, housing, and recording configuration of video tape or disc and the type of playback hardware associated with it, such as ¾-inch or 1-inch Type C.

Video verite: a style of shooting in which the camera tries to capture real life without intrusion.

Viewer control: program design that assumes an individual viewer will control the program's presentation.

Viewfinder: the small monitor on a camera giving the cameraperson the image of what is being shot.

Visual literacy: the ability to express and interpret ideas visually rather than verbally.

Voice-over: narration dubbed or edited over video shots.

VTR: video tape recorder.

Walk-through: a rehearsal in which talent and cameras assume scripted positions, but sometimes abbreviating actual dialogue.

White-balance: to adjust a color camera so that it "sees" and reproduces white correctly, thus also reproducing all other colors correctly.

Zoom: to change the focal length of a lens, giving the appearance of moving closer to or further away from an object.

REFERENCES AND SOURCES

APPLICATIONS

ARWADY, J. and GAYESKI, D. *Using Video:Linear and Interactive Designs.* Englewood Cliffs, NJ: Educational Technology Press, 1989.

BRUSH, DOUGLAS O., and BRUSH, JUDITH M. *Private Television Communications: The New Directions.* Cold Spring, NY: HI Press of Cold Spring, Inc., 1986.

BUNYAN, J.A. *Why Video Works: New Applications for Management.* White Plains, NY: Knowledge Industry Publications, 1987.

IUPPA, N.V. and ANDERSON, K. *Advanced Interactive Video Design.* White Plains, NY: Knowledge Industry Publications, 1988.

KEARSLEY, G. *Costs, Benefits, and Productivity in Training Systems.* Reading, MA: Addison-Wesley Publishing Co, 1986.

MARLOW, E. *Managing Corporate Media.* White Plains, NY: Knowledge Industry Publications, 1990.

MATHIAS, G. *How to Produce Your Own Teleconference.* White Plains, NY: Knowledge Industry Publications, 1989.

MATRAZZO, D. *The Corporate Scriptwriting Book.* Portland, OR: Media Concepts Press, 1989.

MUNROE, M. *Inside Corporate AV.* Torrance, CA: Montage Publishing, 1986.

STOKES, J.T. *The Business of Nonbroadcast Television.* White Plains, NY: Knowledge Industry Publications, 1988.

UTZ, P. *Today's Video: Equipment, Setup, and Production.* Englewood Cliffs, NJ: Prentice-Hall, 1987.

PROFESSIONAL ASSOCIATIONS

American Society for Training and Development
1630 Duke Street
Alexandria, VA 22313

Association for Educational Communications and Technology
1025 Vermont Avenue, N.W.
Washington, D. C. 20005

Association of Media Producers
1101 Connecticut Avenue, N.W.
Washington, D. C. 20036

International Association of Business Communicators
870 Market Street
Suite 469
San Francisco, California 94102

International Television Association
6311 N. O'Connor Rd, LB-51
Irving, TX 75039

National Association of Broadcasters
1771 N Street, N.W.
Washington, D.C. 20036

Society of Motion Picture and Television Engineers
862 Scarsdale Avenue
Scardale, New York 10583

Women in Communications
8305-A Shoal Creek Blvd.
Austin, Texas 78758

PROFESSIONAL PERIODICALS

AVC: Presentation Technology & Applications
210 Crossways Park Dr.
Woodbury, NY 11797

AV/Video
Montage Publishing
25550 Hawthornd Blvd, Suite 314
Torrance, CA 90505

Business TV & Video Guide
TeleSpan Publishing Corp.
PO Box 6250
Altadena, CA 91001

Corporate Video Decisions
401 Park Ave. South
New York, NY 10016

Educational Technology
140 Sylvan Avenue
Englewood Cliffs, New Jersey 07632

Tech Trends
Association for Educational Communications and Technology
1025 Vermont Avenue, N.W.
Washington, D.C. 20005

Training
731 Hennepin Avenue
Minneapolis, Mimmesota 55403

Training and Development Journal
American Society for Training and Development
1630 Duke Street
Alexandria, VA 22313

Videodisc Monitor
PO Box 26
Falls Church, VA 22046

Videography
P.S.N. Publications
2 Park Avenue, Suite 1820
New York, NY 10016

APPENDIX A
SAMPLE SCRIPTS

SCRIPT APPROVED BY Approval Route

Memo To : Approval Route
          Ron Holwerda, Ron Brown,
          Ken McDonald, Nan Van Andel,
          Jim Stover, Greg Evans, Gerry Nehra
From   : Mahedi Lalani, A-V Dept.   Ex.6190
Date   : April 6, '88
Subject : "Car Care Products" video program

Attached copy of the script for your approval.

Objective: To present the Amway Car Care product line in an attention-getting but persuasive fashion. After seeing the program, viewers should

-- <u>believe</u> that Amway's Car Care products offer maximum performance at reasonable prices;

-- <u>feel</u> that when using these products, personal car maintenance is both economically advantageous and personally satisfying;

-- <u>want</u> to begin using one or more of the products as soon as the snow melts (or even before, weather permitting).

Audience: Customers

Program length: Approx. 7min

Release Format: VHS Video

Comments: Canadian version will not have Freedom Oil segment. The product is not available in the market.

Thank you. Let me know if you need more information.

AMWAY/Car Care Products Video

<u>MUSIC / SOUND DIRECTION</u>
Slam-bang music comes on strong.

1. Fast-paced montage of cars being forcefully bruised and battered --
on race tracks, in old movies, at demolition derbies, under the wheels
of monster trucks, at test sites with dummies behind the wheel, etc.

<u>MUSIC / SOUND DIRECTION</u>
Music down, under

vigorous male <u>VOICE-OVER</u>

How to destroy an automobile

... the <u>hard</u> way.

<u>MUSIC / SOUND DIRECTION</u>
Music up ... now quieter, more
relaxed.

2. CUT to montage of cars slowly decaying: from the merely scruffy ...
to rolling wrecks ... to those finally at rest in a junk yard or at
curb-side. FREEZE on one such car -- rusty, abandoned, worthless.

<u>MUSIC / SOUND DIRECTION</u>
Music down, under

<u>VOICE-OVER</u>

There is an easier way: it's

called doing nothing. Because

if your car isn't given

1

AMWAY/Car Care Products Video

regular maintenance and upkeep

... in time it will simply

self-destruct. And that's a

shame,

FADE out.

3. FADE in on late-20s man driving up to pleasant suburban home in brand-new economy car (sticker still in the window); as he honks the horn, his attractive wife emerges excitedly from the house, admires it with him. As they circle the car, he pointing out features, she peering in the window, etc., we hear

VOICE-OVER

because for most of us a car

is just about the most

expensive purchase we'll ever

make. And taking good care of

it can be almost as easy as

neglecting it to death.

4. CUT to MS of husband opening hood.

VOICE-OVER

Start with the heart of your

car -- its power plant --

2

AMWAY/Car Care Products Video

4-a. ZOOM in past him to CU of clean engine block ... FREEZE.

<u>VOICE-OVER</u>

by protecting it with a top

quality motor oil to reduce

metal-to-metal contact and

resulting engine wear.

5. F/X PAGE FLIP to Narr, dressed as Mr. Goodwrench-type auto mechanic;
he's standing in a service garage, next to a different open-hooded car.

<u>ON-CAMERA:</u>

Even under the best of conditions

motor oil takes a beating, as

engine temperatures rise, and

combustion gases, water vapor and other

contaminants can creep in. High

speeds, and cold-weather or

frequent stop-and-go driving

only make things worse. This

constant rubbing, scraping and

pounding can "shear" conventional

oils -- break them down,

physically and chemically.

3

6. F/X PAGE FLIP to Narr, now dressed as lab technician; he's in a lab, holding container of Freedom Motor Oil.

> ON-CAMERA:
>
> Amway's Freedom Motor Oil has
>
> been laboratory designed and
>
> tested to resist viscosity
>
> breakdown due to high-shear
>
> conditions better than
>
> conventional oils ... and better
>
> than the leading synthetic!

7. CUT to graphic bar chart (adapted from brochure) showing FMO's superior performance in terms of resistance to shear.

> VOICE-OVER
>
> Proof? Independent tests have
>
> shown that Freedom Motor Oil
>
> out-performs both leading
>
> conventional oils and the
>
> leading synthetic oil in its
>
> shear-resistance ability.
>
> Other tests proved that
>
> Freedom Motor Oil

8. DISSOLVE to similar bar graph showing FMO's acid-neutralizing

4

AMWAY/Car Care Products Video

capacity.

> VOICE-OVER
>
> also has greater
> acid-neutralizing capabilities
> than these competitors -- which
> means it provides greater
> resistance to the corrosion
> caused by combustion acids.
> And by controlling varnish and
> sludge build-up, it helps to
> keep your engine clean.

9. CUT back to CU Narr in lab.

> ON-CAMERA:
>
> That's superior performance. And
> it means freedom

CG GRAPHIC
Freedom From Excessive Engine Wear

> ON-CAMERA:
>
> -- freedom from excessive engine

wear ... and the costly repairs

it can lead to.

9-a.   CUT to MS and cutaways Hastings Police Chief - Testimonial

ON-CAMERA:

Happy with the car performance

Reduced costs, etc.

9-b. ZOOM OUT/PAN as Narr walks toward refrigerator, dons gloves,
removes labeled beakers of oil.

ON-CAMERA:

But that's not all. Many oils

can't handle extreme temperature

changes. They can become stiff

as molasses when very cold --

making it difficult to start the

engine on below-zero mornings.

We've chilled this conventional

oil to zero degrees fahrenheit ...

10.   CUT to CU of beaker as he tips it; oil does not readily pour.

AMWAY/Car Care Products Video

            VOICE-OVER

                              and you can see how thick and

                              flow-resistant it is. But

10-a. PAN to FMO beaker in his other hand.

                              VOICE-OVER

                              Amway's Freedom Motor Oil ...

                              at the same temperature ...

                              retains superior flow needed

                              to do the job.

9-b. CUT back to Narr as he puts beakers down.

            ON-CAMERA:

            So you can take winter in stride

                          CG GRAPHIC
            Freedom From Cold-Weather Starting Problems

            ON-CAMERA:

            ... and enjoy Freedom from

            cold-weather starting problems.

AMWAY/Car Care Products Video

11. F/X PAGE FLIP to Narr, business-suited, in new car showroom.

ON-CAMERA:

Fuel-efficient, and compatible

with conventional oils, Freedom

Motor Oil meets or exceeds all

vehicle manufacturers'

recommendations for premium motor

oils for all gasoline engines. It's

also ideal for the high temperature

demands of turbocharged engines. And

that's not all -- because while

you'd normally change your oil

every five thousand to

seventy-five hundred miles,

independent tests confirm

that Freedom Motor Oil can keep

going for as many as <u>twenty-five</u>

<u>thousand miles</u> ... or up to an

entire year ... between changes.

CG GRAPHIC
**The 25,000 miles/1 year change interval claim excludes Turbocharged
engines and severe service schedules. New car owners
should follow warranty instructions.**
Oil filters should be changed per vehicle manufacturer's
recommendations.

8

AMWAY/Car Care Products Video

ON-CAMERA:

That means freedom

CG GRAPHIC
Freedom From Frequent Oil Changes

ON-CAMERA:

... from frequent, costly, and
time-consuming oil changes.
Freedom Motor Oil.

12. DISSOLVE to CU product.

VOICE-OVER

For reduced engine wear. For
improved cold-weather
starting. And for less
frequent oil changes. If you
care about your car, care
for it -- with the motor
oil that provides true
freedom: peace of mind.

9

FADE OUT.

AMWAY/Car Care Products Video

13.   FADE IN the new car couple on a sunny Saturday morning in their
back yard. Both are dressed casually -- cut-off shorts, tee shirts,
bare feet. The car -- still new, but showing a bit of road dust, some
bugs on the hood, etc. -- is parked on the grass. Obviously enjoying
themselves, they are preparing to clean the car, bringing out buckets,
hose, sponges, etc.

VOICE-OVER (Narr)

Your car's exterior deserves

the same kind of care -- and

with Amway's Mint Condition

car care product, providing

it is not only a sound

investment ... it's easy

and satisfying.

14.   CUT to CU of man spraying BUG & Tar Remover on Grill.

VOICE-OVER

Begin with Mint Condition Gel

Bug & Tar Remover. Its

exclusive gel formula won't

run or drip ... but it does

penetrate through layers of

10

soil to get rid of baked-on

insects ... sticky road tar

... ground-in grime. You just
                        AMWAY/Car Care Product Video

spray it on, watch it work,

and wipe it away. Safe for

use on all exterior car

surfaces, and interior vinyl,

this super-penetrating cleaner

also beats the tar out of the

competition.

15. CUT to table-top demo, as described

                                    VOICE-OVER

                                    We're coating the insides of

                                    two identical jars with a

                                    heavy-duty anti-rust coating

                                    used by professionals.

                                    Designed to stick to metal

                                    surfaces through thick and

                                    thin, it's going to challenge

                                    our Bug & Tar Remover ...

                                    alongside another leading

                                    brand.

                                    Now we'll lightly spray the

                                    11

                                              interiors with the two

                                              products ... theirs ... and

                                                   AMWAY/Car Care Products Video

                                              ours ... and then fill each

                                              jar with plain water.

                                              Almost at once, the coating

                                              treated with Mint Condition Gel

                                              Bug and Tar Remover

                                              begins to loosen and float

                                              free ... and

15-a.   F/X CLOCK WIPE indicates time passing; continue real-time demo.

                                                   VOICE-OVER

                                              in just a few minutes -- with

                                              no rubbing or scrubbing -- the

                                              jar is almost completely

                                              clear. Contrast that with the

                                              competition.

15-b.   F/X SQUEEZE product shot out to dominate frame.

                                   CG GRAPHIC
                                   No-Drip Gel
                     Just Spray-On, Wipe-Off Application
                         Safe For All Exterior Car
                                   Surfaces

                                        12

                                        VOICE-OVER

                                        Mint Condition Gel Bug and Tar

                                        AMWAY/Car Care Products Videos

                                        Remover. The easiest way in

                                        the world to get tough with

                                        road grime.

16. CUT to user testimonial, if desired and available.

               MUSIC / SOUND DIRECTION
               Light, lively music up.

17. CUT to back yard. He admires gleaming grill, picks up container of
car wash as we ZOOM IN for product CU.

               MUSIC / SOUND DIRECTION
               Music down, under

                                        VOICE-OVER

                                        The concentrated cleaning

                                        power of Mint Condition Car

                                        Wash loosens surface dirt and

                                        grime without removing the

                                        shine.

17-a. CUT to man adding single teaspoon of Car Wash to empty bucket,
filling with water. Wife joins in sponging, rinsing, etc.

                                        13

                                        VOICE-OVER

                                        It's biodegradable, so it's

                                                AMWAY/Car Care Products Video

                                        environmentally safe ...
                                        and you can even use it with
                                        hard water. Best of all, it's
                                        economical: you'll get nearly
                                        two hundred safe, easy washes
                                        from a single quart.

18. CUT to new back yard shot; man in the background, drying car, while
wife shakes container of vinyl/leather cleaner; ZOOM to product CU.

                                        VOICE-OVER

                                        Caring for your car's leather
                                        and vinyl is easy
                                        with Mint Condition Vinyl and
                                        Leather Cleaner.

18-a. CUT to MS of her treating dash, arm rests, whatever.

                                        AMWAY/Car Care Products Video

                                        VOICE-OVER

                                        14

                                    It cleans all colors of vinyl
                                    and leather upholstery, as
                                    well as car and boat
                                    interiors, sporting goods,
                                    luggage -- even coats and
                                    jackets. Its special silicone
                                    formula removes soil and grime
                                    without harsh abrasive action
                                    -- leaving leather and vinyl
                                    surfaces with a beautiful
                                    protective gloss and a fresh,
                                    clean scent.

19. CUT to man picking up container of silicone glaze; ZOOM to product
CU.

                                    <u>VOICE-OVER</u>
                                    Protect your car's finish with
                                    durable, long-lasting <u>Mint</u>
                                    <u>Condition Silicone Glaze Auto</u>
                                    <u>Polish</u> --

19-a. CUT to MS as he applies glaze, buffs to a shine, etc.

                                    AMWAY/Car Care Products Video

                                    <u>VOICE-OVER</u>

                                    15

                                    a custom blend of cleaning and
                                    polishing agents that gently
                                    lift soil and old polish ...
                                    <u>without</u> harming the surface.
                                    Formulated with four silicones
                                    plus a wax, Mint Condition
                                    Silicone Glaze creates a
                                    show-room bright, detergent-
                                    resistant shine. Here's how
                                    good it really is:

20.   CUT to demo, as described

                                    <u>VOICE-OVER</u>

                                    We can demonstrate different
                                    levels of wear and tear on a car
                                    finish by using a polishing/rubbing
                                    compound, designed to remove heavy
                                    oxidation on painted surfaces, and a
                                    more abrasive competitor to
                                    Silicone Glaze.
                                    This black acrylic sheet serves as a
                                    scratch - sensitive surface similar
                                    in character to automotive paint.
                                    We have chosen number 7 White
                                    Polishing Compound as the
                                    polishing/rubbing compound and

                                    16

Simonize II liquid Auto Polish
as the competitive polish.
Apply the polish /rubbing compound
and the Simonize II to separate
areas of the acrylic sheet and
Silicone Glaze to the third area.
After each product dries, wipe off
the residue with a clean cloth,
using some water to ensure complete
removal.
As you can see, the Silicone Glaze
section is sparkling clear and un-
scarred ... just as you'd want your
car's finish to look. The areas
polished with the polishing/rubbing
compound and the Simonize II
show some scratching.
Now lets apply Silicone Glaze Auto
Polish to the two scratched and
dulled areas produced by the other
products. These scratched areas of
different severity represent two
levels of wear which car finishes
face in the environment. Notice
how Silicone Glaze has effectively
improved the appearance of both
scratche areas.

17

19-b. CUT to man finishing up with final spot buffing; ZOOM to CU of
product standing on car hood.

> VOICE-OVER
>
> Mint Condition Silicone Glaze
>
> Auto Polish.

CG GRAPHIC
Superior Polishing Action --
Without Damaging The Finish!

> VOICE-OVER
>
> For a beautiful shine ...
>
> durable, long-lasting
>
> > AMWAY/Car Care Products Video
>
> protection ... and no damage
>
> to your car's finish.

21. CUT to proud and happy couple admiring their sparkling car (now
parked in the driveway).

> VOICE-OVER
>
> Amway has everything you need
>
> to give your car total care
>
> ... inside, outside, under the
>
> hood. Freedom Motor Oil.
>
> Mint Condition Gel Bug and Tar

18

                                    Remover ... Car Wash ... Vinyl

                                    and Leather Cleaner ...

                                    Silicone Glaze Auto Polish.

                                    They help you do more than

                                    protect your transportation

                                    investment for years to come.

                                    They make it fun to do so.

21-a.   Couple embraces happily, disappears inside house leaving shining
car in the frame. FREEZE.

21-b.   KEY product stills as mentioned

                                    AMWAY/Car Care Products Video

                                    VOICE-OVER
                                    We've even thought of the
                                    finishing touches: See Spray
                                    Window Cleaner and Quiet
                                    Breezes Automotive Air Freshener
                                    to add sparkle and a refreshing
                                    scent.

22.   CUT to table-top set showing gas and oil additives, Wonder Mist
      Silicone Lubricant and Rust Inhibitor, Chrome and Glass Cleaner,
      Metal Cleaner, See Spray Concentrate and Aerosol, Quiet Breezes
      Automotive Air Freshner

19

> VOICE-OVER
>
> And ask your distributor about
> other Amway Products for your
> car to help protect and
> enhance your car's appearance
> and performance.

23.   Match DISSOLVE to end of shot 21-a, with car in driveway, as above, but now there's a new luxury car parked next to the equally shiny economy car. Hold the shot as husband appears, dressed for success, carrying briefcase; he's now ten years older.

> VOICE-OVER
>
> Remember: if you take good
> care of your car, it will take
> good care of you.
>
>   AMWAY/Car Care Products Video

He admires the big car, brushes off a spot of dust with pocket handkerchief, drives off. As he does so, wife (also 10 years older) emerges from house with two kids in tow; kids get in, wife brushes off spot of dust with her sleeve, drives off.

> VOICE-OVER
>
> ... for a long, long time.

<u>MUSIC / SOUND DIRECTION</u>
Music Up.

23-a. SCROLL product stills, graphic keys.

20

Figure A-1 Note the use of the on-camera narrator with extensive voice-overs in this script. Also look at the way the writer uses visual analogies to make the program's message clear and powerful (*courtesy, Ron Brown, Amway Corporation*).

TAKE CHARGE!

Final Draft

January 19, 1988

Client:

Joanne Hiss
Facilities Management

Prepared By:

Meta Ann Donohoe
Video Services

- 2 -

ESTABLISH SHOT AS CHILDREN WALK HOME FROM BUS STOP.	(MUSIC UP AND UNDER NAT. SOUND UP OF CHILDRENS' CONVERSATION)
C.U. FEET OF LITTLE GIRL, TILT UP TO ESTABLISH 9-YEAR OLD WALKING AWAY FROM FRIEND.	(CONVERSATION OF 2 LITTLE GIRLS AS THEY SAY THEIR GOODBYES; THEY CALL TO EACH OTHER LOUDER AS THE DISTANCE BETWEEN THEM GROWS GREATER)
9-YEAR OLD WALKS TOWARD HOME: ESTABLISH HOME	
CHILD'S P.O.V. AS SHE APPROACHES HOUSE; ESTABLISH HOUSE FROM CHILD'S P.O.V. C.U. WINDOWS, FRONT DOOR	APPROACHES HOUSE. SHE REACHES THE HOUSE AND OPENS DOOR WITH THE KEY SHE WEARS AROUND HER NECK.
INT. HOUSE, CHILD'S P.O.V.	SHE LOCKS DOOR BEHIND HER. CHILD
TRUCKING P.O.V. GLANCE INTO L.R.	FOLLOWS PROPER PROCEDURES AS SHE WALKS INTO KITCHEN.
EST. KITCHEN; CHILD'S P.O.V. AS SHE APPROACHES DRAWER AND PLACES KEY IN DRAWER. CALLS MOTHER. GETS A DRINK, PICKS UP BOOKS AND ENTERS DEN. TURNS ON TV.	(NATURAL SOUND ACCOMPANIES ACTION) (PHONE CONVERSATION IN B.G.) (TELEVISION UP)
PROMO FOR HORROR FLICK ON MONITOR.	
REACTION SHOT: CHILD (INDICATES SHE'S INTERESTED IN THE MOVIE, BUT ON EDGE. PICKS UP REMOTE CONTROL AND TURNS OFF TELEVISION.	

- 3 -

WIDE AS CAT APPROACHES CHILD AND KNOCKS OVER TRINKET	(CHILD GASPS)
	(KNOCK ON DOOR)
CHILD PUTS DOWN PENCIL; PICKS UP CAT AND HOLDS ON TO IT TIGHTLY AS SHE'S FORCED INTO MAKING A DECISION. Z.I. TO CHILD'S FACE AND FREEZE.	(KNOCK RECURRS)
KISS BLACK	(MUSICAL BRIDGE UP AND OUT)
EST. SHOT NARRATORS	<u>HOLTER ON CAMERA</u>

<u>HOLTER ON CAMERA</u>

What would you do in that
situation? Answer the door?
Hide? Or just ignore it?
The fact is, as many as 10
million kids between the ages
of 6 and 14 are home alone
everyday. That's a lot of us; so
chances are we all would react
a little differently.
Hi, I'm Holter Graham.

<u>DIEDRE ON CAMERA</u>

And I'm Dee Watkins.
There really is no 'correct'
answer to situations like the
one we just saw; because there
are so many things to consider.

- 4 -

B-ROLL TO SCENE #1

DIEDRE VOICE OVER

What we would be advised to do
is---if you're not expecting
anyone---check through a peep hole
or window to find out who's there.
Then, ask the visitor to come
back later, explaining that your
mother is busy. If you _were_

B-ROLL/DIFFERENT DAY

expecting someone, look out a
window or through the peep-
hole, accept the delivery,
remembering to lock the door
behind you.

NARRATORS ON CAMERA

HOLTER ON CAMERA

If you are one of the growing
number of kids who find themselves without a parent at some
point during the day, you've got
a lot of responsibility. Your
parents strongly believe in you
to follow their rules and to take
care of yourself---and if you're
old enough, your brothers and
sisters.

- 5 -

	It's a big job, and it's a group effort. You are all in it togeth-er--as a family--and as a family, you'll need to work through any obstacles.
ONE SHOT: DIEDRE	<u>DIEDRE ON CAMERA</u> Today we're going to take a look at this common situation.
	A situation so common that kids who are responsible for tak-ing care of themselves even have a name. We're called 'Latchkey Children'. This name comes from the familiar key, worn around our neck, that lets us into our house.
	<u>HOLTER ON CAMERA</u> So let's find out how we can Take Charge!
UP TITLE SLATE	(UP SFX, MUSIC)
EXT. MCU NARRATORS	<u>DIEDRE ON CAMERA</u> In fact, more and more kids are becoming responsible for tak-ing care of themselves. Why? We'll take a look at some of the reasons.

- 6 -

HOLTER ON CAMERA

And we'll meet people like me and you. We'll share experiences and discuss some guidelines and sug- gestions to help make our jobs easier.

DIEDRE ON CAMERA

We'll find out who we can turn to for help, if necessary. After all, we all need help sometimes. Even your parents. That's why they're relying on you to help them while they're at work!

MONTAGE DEPICTING AS MANY WOMEN AS MEN IN THE WORKPLACE. INCLUDE CITY SHOTS, LEAVING HOME FOR THE DAY, COLLEGE CAMPUS, HOSPITAL, FIREFIGHT- ERS, POLICE OFFICERS, UTILITY WORKERS

(NAT. SOUND OF CITY WITH UPBEAT MUSIC)

VOICE OVER: HOLTER

Look around...it's happening all over. The workforce continues to increase. Men and women--moms and dads--working...for a variety of reasons.

- 7 -

STILLS/PHOTOS OF TRADITIONAL FAMILY	Of course, it wasn't always this way. When your grandparents were young, their parents most likely led a more traditional lifestyle. By traditional I mean that your great grandmother proba- bly took care of the children and the household--a big job in itself --while your great grandfather supported the family financially. Their children, your grandparents, probably grew up in the same family structure...and some of your parents lived in a household where only one parent left the house every morning to go to work. (SFX: WAR SOUNDS AND UNDER)
FILM: WAR FOOTAGE	<u>VOICE OVER: DIEDRE</u> Something happened historically to change this once-common life- style. World War One and World War Two introduced the need for increased labor support. Many

- 8 -

FILM/STILLS: FACTORIES

men left the United States to
fight for our country, creating a
need for support materials, such
as food--we <u>all</u> have to eat--and
war supplies.

(UP MUSIC OF THE PERIOD)

FILM: WORKING WOMEN

For one of the first times in
history, women collectively joined
the labor force, manufacturing and
packaging weaponry and war support
items.

EMPTY FACTORIES

After the wars ended, many women
returned to their full-time jobs

STILLS OF WOMEN IN
1930'S AT WORK

at home. Yet this labor movement
proved significant, introducing
the concept--and acceptance--of
women in the workforce.

QUICK PACED MONTAGE OF
WOMEN WORKING FROM 1930'S
THRU 1980'S

The ice was broken. Some women
actually enjoyed work and it became common to see women working
for a variety of reasons...from
personal to financial.

EST. NARRATORS

<u>HOLTER ON CAMERA</u>:
So here we are today. Now you've

- 9 -

heard some of the reasons how and
why our lifestyle changed from the
traditional role of the father as
the sole provider to the mother
and father as providers. The
latchkey situation isn't new, but
rather exists today in greater
numbers and continues to increase.

<u>DIEDRE ON CAMERA</u>: (TO HOLTER)
In fact, Holter, it's very common
to find both parents working,
sometimes referred to as two-
income or dual families. It's
also more common to live with
only one parent; single parent
families are on the rise.
(TO AUDIENCE)
Do your parents work? Ask
them if both of <u>their</u> parents
worked when they were children.
Probably not.

EXT. NARRATOR: MCU HOLTER   <u>HOLTER ON CAMERA</u>
                                   Now let's take a look at five
                                   common situations that may happen,

- 10 -

TRANSITION: CUBE ROTATION: OPENING REPRISE	or may <u>have</u> happened, to you. <u>VOICE OVER HOLTER</u>: We'll review the opening scene to highlight the positive things that Allison did. (Up Telephone Conversation)
TRANSITION: CUBE ROTATION: FIRST AID KIT	<u>VOICE OVER DIEDRE</u>: Then we'll look at an emergency situation and discuss the proper procedures to help you stay calm and in control.
TRANSITION: CUBE ROTATION: LESLIE SEARCHING FOR KEY	<u>VOICE OVER HOLTER</u>: Oh boy! Forget the key today? It happens sometimes, and we'll review some pointers on how to remember <u>not</u> to forget, and what to do if you do forget. Most of our advice has to do with being prepared--planning ahead--as you'll soon see.
TRANSITION: CUBE ROTATION: LATCHKEYS PREPARING BREAKFAST	<u>VOICE OVER DIEDRE</u>: Some people associate latchkey children with afternoons. That's not always the case. Lots of kids

- 11 -

	send themselves, and if they're old enough, their brothers and sisters, off to school every morning without a hitch. We'll see how.
TRANSITION: CUBE ROTATION: LIGHTNING BOLTS, STORM FOOTAGE	(SFX: THUNDER) VOICE OVER HOLTER: Looks like it's going to rain, and rain hard! What should you do if the lights go out? HOLTER ON CAMERA:
NARRATORS	As you recall, Allison had a busy afternoon... DIEDRE ON CAMERA But the most important thing is that she handled each situation sensibly...
ANIMATED KEY 'OPENS' SCENE FULL SCREEN SCENE #1 REPRISE	(UP SFX) V.O. DIEDRE
REPRISE OF GROUP OF GIRLS ALLISON WALKS TOWARD HOME	Different parents have different rules. Maybe you don't agree with these rules, but they are important.

- 12 -

	They're designed to help <u>you</u>... in the long run.
REPRISE ALLISON WALKING HOME	Allison's parents have asked her to go directly home each day after school. This way, Allison's mom knows where she is.
SUBJECTIVE SHOT AS ALLISON APPROACHES HOUSE	Look your house over as you approach it. Quickly check to make sure everything's in its place: is the front door is pulled tight? Are there any strange cars or obstacles near the house?
ALLISON REACHES FOR KEY	Pull your key out only when you have reached your door. Never show it to strangers; this lets people know that you will be alone for a while. Your arrangement with your parents is a secret; keep it that way.
INT. AS ALLISON LOCKS DOOR BEHIND HER	Always lock the door behind you. Glance around as you walk through your house. We call this a home-coming check. Is everything in its place? Be aware of your sur-

- 13 -

ALLISON PLACES KEY IN DRAWER	roundings. Taking care of a key is a big responsibility in it- self. Allison and her parents have decided to keep the key in the kitchen drawer. This way, she'll know exactly where it is tomorrow when she leaves for school.
ALLISON CALLS PARENT	It's also a good idea to check in with a parent when you get home. Allison's mom expects a call from Allison between 2:30 and 3:00 on school days. Some parents can't receive calls at work, so your parent may want to call you. Either way, establish a routine and to stick to it!
ALLISON GETS DRINK, GOES INTO DEN	There are lots of things for Allison to do after school. To- gether with her parents, they've structured her after-school activities. It's up to Allison to decide how she wants to spend her free time, as long as she gets all her homework and chores done.

- 14 -

	Today she wanted to watch TV for a while, but then decided the
ALLISON TURNS	scary movie wasn't something to watch alone.
	(UP MUSIC AND OUT)
ALLISON AT DOOR	And Allison handled the visitor properly; her mother didn't tell her to expect a delivery man. So she asked him to come back another day when her mother 'wasn't busy.'
	(UP CONVERSATION)
ANIMATED KEY 'OPENS' NEXT SCENE	(UP MUSIC/SFX)
	<u>VOICE OVER HOLTER</u>:
INT. KITCHEN OR MUD ROOM; Z.O. FROM FIRST AID KIT ON WALL AS BOY OPENS IT	Even a small scrape or cut can be frightening if you don't have the proper supplies to help when you're hurt.
	Assemble an Emergency Kit. It's a great group project, and may someday be a life-saver. Be sure to include: a flashlight, a transistor radio, extra batteries, and a first aid kit.
C.U. FIRST AID KIT	A first aid kit is very important for obvious reasons.

- 15 -

FIRST AID KIT   Band-Aids, 1 and 2-inch gauze
                                 strips and some antiseptic are
                                 necessary for small emergencies.
                                 Check these kits every two months
                                 or so to make sure everything's
                                 there...just in case.

ALICE/CHILD WITH PLANS   No one likes to think about things
AT TABLE   like fires, but fire officials
                                 agree that the best way to handle
                                 a fire is to be prepared. That
                                 means developing a fire plan with
                                 your family, knowing how to handle
                                 fire, and knowing who to call for
                                 help.

C.U. INSTALLED SMOKE DETECTOR   Do you know what this is? You
                                 should. It's a smoke detector, a
                                 device designed to help you in
                                 case you're in danger. It's also
                                 required by law in many states,
                                 including Maryland. Do you
                                 know what it sounds like, and
                                 where it is in your house?
                                 Find out. It saves lives. Also
                                 remind your parents to check the
                                 batteries every month.

- 16 -

	(UP DETECTOR SOUND AND UNDER)
DRAMATIZATION	<u>V.O. NARRATOR</u>
	If the alarms sounds, and you see
	fire or smell fire, your next step
	is to get help.
CHILD TO NEIGHBOR'S HOUSE	Go to a neighbor's house and
	call 911. This is an emergency
	service with trained profes-
	sionals, who are there to help
	you. Stay calm and tell the
	operator your name first and
	then the nature of the emergency.
	The operator will ask you about
	the emergency. Give the operator
	your address. <u>Never</u> hang up
	before the operator; operators
	may want to ask you more
	questions, so don't cut them off.

When calling the Police or the Fire Department, remain as calm as possible. Also keep the phone numbers-if they're different than the 911 number-by the phone.

- 17 -

TRANSITION: ANIMATED KEY 'OPENS' SCENE	V.O. DIEDRE
CHILD APPROACHES HOUSE, REACHES FOR KEY, REALIZES IT'S NOT THERE.	It happens...to some more than others...but we all experience times when we've misplaced or lost our keys.
	So what should we do? First, don't panic. Again, if you plan for the possibility that you may forget your keys, you'll be prepared if and when it happens.
PARENTS/MARJA/NEIGHBOR DISCUSSING KEY	Keeping your house key with a trusted neighbor is probably the best way to avoid major inconveniences.
MARJA GOING TO NEIGHBOR'S HOUSE	Fortunately, Marja and her parents have decided that with the help of Mr. Gregory, their neighbor, Marja has an alternative. Mrs. Gregory is almost always home during the day, so he's a reliable friend who lives close by. Marja can rely on Mr. Gregory for a key.

```
                            - 18 -


LESLIE RETURNING KEY            And Marja never forgets to return

                                the key; this ensures that Mr.

                                Gregory will have it...for the

                                next time.

                                How do you remember not to forget

                                your key in the first place?

MARJA TAKING KEY IN             One way is to develop a routine or
KITCHEN DRAWER A.M.
                                schedule.  Keep your key in the

                                same place when it's not around

                                your neck...like in a kitchen

                                drawer.

C.U. KEY                        Take the key from the drawer at

                                the same time every morning, like

                                right before you leave for school.

MARJA RETURNING KEY IN          And return the key to the same
DRAWER P.M.
                                drawer when you get home in the

                                afternoon.  This is important, so

                                get into the routine.  Handling

                                your house key is a big

                                responsibility.  Take control.

TRANSITION:  ANIMATED KEY       (UP MUSIC)
             'OPENS' SCENE
INT. KITCHEN AS OLDER SISTER    (UP SFX)
PREPARES BREAKFAST.  SCENE
IS ESTABLISHED                  (DIALOGE FROM BREAKFAST SCENE UP)

CHILDREN IN KITCHEN             V. O. HOLTER:

                                Matthew and his older sister

                                Schylar work well together, after
```

- 19 -

all they've been responsible for
getting themselves ready for
school every morning for close to

a year now!! Their parents feel
comfortable with the arrangement
because Schylar is a very responsible and thinks quickly. Since
she's 13, Schylar is legally old
enough to take care of her younger
brother. You see, in many
states--including Maryland
--children under the age of eight
years old or older.

CHILDREN WITH MOTHER

Matthew and Schylar's parents have
developed a very organized system
to help the family every morning.
The night before, Matthew and
Schylar and their mother select
their clothes for the next day.
Schylar's mom also sets out the
breakfast food; so most of the
morning is planned the night
before.

V.O. HOLTER:

CHILDREN AT TABLE

The most important part of being
responsible is knowing how to take

- 20 -

	care of yourself in different situations. A phone call <u>seems</u> like a simple thing, but it's very important that you handle it properly.
C.U. PHONE SCHYLAR ANSWERS PHONE	(PHONE RINGS)
	<u>SCHYLAR</u> Hello...(PAUSE) Blum residence. My mother's busy right now and can't come to the phone (PAUSE)
REACHES FOR PEN	May I take a message? (SNEAK UNDER SCHYLAR'S AUDIO)
SCHYLAR ON TELEPHONE	Did you notice how Schylar answered the call? She didn't give the caller any details; only that her mother was busy. (UP PHONE CONVERSATION) "My mother is busy..." <u>V. O. NARRATOR</u> Do <u>not</u> under any circumstances tell a caller that you are home alone. This is a safety precaution and should become part of your telephone techniques. Offer to help by taking a message...

- 21 -

	that's why it's important to have
	a pen and paper near the phone.
	(UP MUSIC)
MCU MASTER PHONE LIST	Notice too that there are several
	phone numbers next to the phone.
HIGHLIGHT NUMBERS	This is called a Master Phone List
	and it's very important to keep
	this list updated. Include on it
	the numbers for the Police, Fire,
	Ambulance--if different than 911--
	at least one of your parent's work
	numbers, your grandparents, a
HIGHLIGHT SEPARATE NUMBERS	neighbor, your family Doctor,
	Dentist, the number of your
	school, Poison Control and the Gas
	and Electric Company. If you have
	a pet, you might want to include
	the number of your pet's
	veterinarian. Also include the
	number for one and the Kids' Line
	and Talk Line numbers--we'll talk
	about that in a minute.
HIGHLIGHT TOP OF BOARD	Another good suggestion is to
	write your name, address and
	telephone number at the top of the

— 22 —

<table>
<tr><td></td><td>Master Phone List because sometimes--during an emergency--remembering those things is difficult.</td></tr>
<tr><td>CHILDREN CLEANING/EXITING</td><td>Schylar and Matthew would be the first to tell us that another part of helping their parents is making sure the house is in order before they leave. They put away the perishable food--milk, butter, jelly--and places any dishes in the sink. Schylar makes sure all of the lights have been turned off in the house. And don't forget to lock the door behind you! Organizing your time means that you won't be late for school.</td></tr>
<tr><td>TRANSITION: ANIMATED KEY
'OPENS' SCENE</td><td>(SFX)
(NAT. SOUND OF RAIN, THUNDER.
MUSIC UP AND UNDER SCENE)</td></tr>
<tr><td>CHILD WATCHING TV; EST. RAIN OUTSIDE

LIGHTS GO OUT, CHILD RE-SPONDS WITH FLASHLIGHT, CALLS UTILITY</td><td>V. O. DIEDRE:

Fun times can turn into scary times if you lose electricity. Again, be prepared. Check to see if other houses on your street</td></tr>
</table>

- 23 -

    have lost their electricity.

    Then, get a flashlight. It's a

    good idea to keep one in the kit-

    chen and one in your bedroom.

    Never use candles; they're a fire

    hazard. If the street is dark,

    call your electric company to

    report the outage.

    Remember, the number is on your

    Master Phone List. Then call your

    parents for additional in-

    structions. If the phone doesn't

    work because of the storm, get

    your key from the drawer, and go

    to your neighbor's house. And

    don't forget to lock the door

    behind you!

    (SFX)

NARRATORS ON CAMERA   <u>HOLTER ON CAMERA</u>:

    We've just reviewed a number of

    different ways to help us make

    the most of our responsible time

    alone at home. Remember that there

    are lots of   resources

    available to help kids like us.

    Right Dee?

- 24 -

MCU DIEDRE

DIEDRE ON CAMERA:

Right! It's okay to be frightened
sometimes...everyone is. So, when
you do become frightened, use your
resources--call your parents, your
grandparents, a friend--and talk
to them a while. Holter, did you
know that there are even telephone
services for Latchkey Children
called Kid's Line, Talkline, Phone
Pal and Phone Friend? Calling
these services enables you to talk
to a group of trained professionals who are there for you, if
you're ever lonely, afraid, or
just feel like talking to someone.

HOLTER MCU

HOLTER ON CAMERA

And if your parents are interested
in other options rather than having you stay at home, there are
resources available to them.
Deciding what's best for your
family may be puzzling, but it's
a good idea to look into the
following.

- 25 -

GRAPHIC	Ask your parents to contact State Department of Social Services for a list of licensed family day care and in-home care options, relatives, center-based care, corporate child care and extended school programs.

Does your school have an extended school day? If not, why? Investigating other options helps your family solve the child care puzzle. Try to participate in after-school activities, like Cub Scouts, Girl Scouts, or sports. |
| C.U. DIEDRE | DIEDRE ON CAMERA:
We have also included phone numbers for various services at the end of the videotape that you and your parents should share.
So don't stop the tape too soon!
(MUSIC UP)
HOLTER ON CAMERA: |
| C.U. NARRATOR | You are one of a growing number of children who are very responsible and capable of helping your |

```
                                    - 26 -


                               parents in today's society.

                               Realize that in your parent's

                               absence--they believe in YOU to

                               TAKE CHARGE!

                               (MUSIC UP)


SLATE OF SERVICES              LATCHKEY RESOURCES

                               (LIST LOCAL RESOURCES)

                               CREDITS
```

Figure A-2 Not all programs produced by corporations are "industrial training." This program, produced by Baltimore Gas and Electric, is a public service message to educate children who are often at home alone. Note the use of the child's point of view (P.O.V.), demonstrations, and role-plays (*courtesy, Meta Ann Donohoe, Baltimore Gas & Electric*).

GTE CALIFORNIA   ZUM EXPANSION
88203

            "CUSTOMER CONTACT -- ZUM EXPANSION"

PRODUCED BY: *Patti Ryan* Information Communications Center

WRITTEN BY: David Alexander

DATE: October 30, 1988 (second draft)
              October 27, 1988 (first draft)

                              APPROVED FOR PRODUCTION

                              BY _____

                              DATE _____

```
Script - ZUM
88203 - Page One
10/30/88




        "CUSTOMER CONTACT -- ZUM EXPANSION"



FADE IN:

MUSIC UNDER.

MONTAGE

SHOTS of telephone poles and phone lines stretching across the
landscape (STOCK FOOTAGE, if available); STATE and COUNTY MAPS
(San Bernardino, Riverside and Ventura Counties, and San Fernando
Valley); GTE REPS in office settings; CUSTOMERS talking on the
telephone.

                        NARRATOR (V.O.)
                For years, GTE California has subscribed
                to a basic principle underlying the
                telecommunications industry: that no matter
                where a customer might live, he or she has
                the right to first-class telephone service
                at a fair price.

                Now, in an effort to standardize telephone
                rates throughout the state, the Public
                Utilities Commission has ordered three
                telephone companies -- GTE California,
                Pacific Bell and Continental Telephone --
                to take the first steps in expanding
                Zone Usage Measurement service.

LOWER THIRD TITLES FADE IN AND OUT:

"SAN BERNERDINO"
"RIVERSIDE"
"VENTURA"

"SAN FERNANDO VALLEY"

                        NARRATOR (V.O.) - cont.
                This new plan would realign rate centers
                and exchange boundaries in three counties
                -- San Bernardino, Riverside and Ventura --
                and in portions of the San Fernando Valley.

AURORA MOVE superimposing customers over maps.
```

```
Script - ZUM
88203 - Page Two
10/30/88



LOWER THIRD TITLES FADE IN AND OUT:

"BUSINESS AND RESIDENTIAL CUSTOMERS"
"LOCAL/ZUM/TOLL"
"FREQUENT CALLER PROGRAM"
"PRIVATE LINE"
"FOREIGN EXCHANGE"
"OFF PREMISES EXTENSIONS AND STATIONS"

                    NARRATOR (V.O.) - cont.
          These proposed changes will impact
          thousands of business and residential
          customers, and the way they are billed
          for local, ZUM and toll calls.  Also
          affected will be the Frequent Caller
          Program, Private Line and Foreign
          Exchange services, Off Premises Extensions
          and Stations, and a variety of other services.
          Customers will be notified of the proposed
          expansion beginning December first.

PAN of BSOC or CSOC office, with reps talking on their phones.

                    NARRATOR (V.O.) - cont.
          The purpose of this videotape is to
          examine the changes that will take
          place, and to review the best ways
          to handle communication with customers --
          how to address their concerns and offer
          viable alternatives to their current
          calling patterns.

MUSIC UP LOUDER.

PROGRAM TITLE FADES IN:

"CUSTOMER CONTACT -- ZUM EXPANSION"

TITLE AND MUSIC FADE OUT.


GRAPHIC EFFECTS

AURORA EFFECT of current ZUM MAPS (labeled "CURRENT").

                    NARRATOR (V.O.) - cont.
          Customers are familiar with their current
          calling patterns -- where they call, and
          how much those calls cost.
```

```
Script - ZUM
88203 - Page Three
10/30/88
```

AURORA EFFECT, as the boundaries on ZUM MAPS change to new
configurations (and become labeled "PROPOSED CHANGES").

                        NARRATOR (V.O.) - cont.
                  With the changes in exchange boundaries,
                  many customers will have to reexamine
                  those patterns, and look for new ways
                  to make their telephone use cost-effective.
                  At first, they may be confused, even
                  upset, about upcoming changes.

INT. BSOC/CSOC OFFICES - DAY

GTE representatives are talking on their phones (muted).

                        NARRATOR (V.O.) - cont.
                  Whether you work in a Business Service
                  Order Center, Customer Service Order Center,
                  Customer Billing Center, GTE-One Full
                  Service Business Center, or in Sales, it's
                  your job as a customer contact representative
                  to reassure callers -- and effectively
                  answer their questions. Let's take a look at
                  some situations that might take place after
                  customers receive notification.

DISSOLVE TO:

INT. BSOC OFFICE/CUSTOMER'S OFFICE - DAY

FREEZE FRAME of a REAL ESTATE AGENT (MR. KITCHNER) on the phone.

TITLES (WRITTEN IN SCRIPT) FADE IN AND OUT:

"WHAT DOES IT MEAN?"
"WHY ARE YOU TELLING ME NOW?"

INTERCUT between the FIRST GTE REP and the real estate agent.

                        REAL ESTATE AGENT
                     (holding GTE notice)
                  This came to me in the mail, but I don't
                  get it.

                        FIRST GTE REP
                  Mr. Kitchner, we're sending notices to
                  all of our customers who will be affected
                  by these proposed changes.

```
Script - ZUM
88203 - Page Four
10/30/88
```

                          REAL ESTATE AGENT
                 I run a small real estate office. What does
                 this mean to me? And why are you telling me
                 now? This says nothing's going to happen
                 for more than a year.

                          FIRST GTE REP
                 We want to tell you about these proposed
                 changes early, so you can review your
                 office's calling patterns, and look for
                 ways to keep costs down if the changes do
                 go into effect.

                          REAL ESTATE AGENT
                 I'm not up-to-date on all the terminology,
                 but I know I make a lot of calls outside
                 my local calling area. Is that what's going
                 to change?

       (*In all double-column dialogue, the Narrator's voice is dominant
                    over the muted conversation to the right.)

         NARRATOR (V.O.)   FIRST GTE REP
 In a situation like this, with   The Public Utilities
 a small business customer, you   Commission has asked GTE
 should explain the proposed   California, along with other
 changes in exchange boundaries,   telephone companies, to look
 and how rates may be affected by   into the possibility of
 calling routes. Always stress that   making changes in telephone
 the changes you mention are only   exchange boundaries.
 being proposed right now. No
 final decision will be made   REAL ESTATE AGENT
 until the Public Utilities   That would change my rates?
 Commission gives the matter a
 complete review.   FIRST GTE REP
                                         It would probably affect your
                                         rates on specific routes.

                        FIRST GTE REP - cont.
                 We're concerned about how the changes
                 might affect small business customers
                 like you, Mr. Kitchner. What we want to
                 do is, work with you to help you find
                 solutions...

 DISSOLVE TO:

```
Script - ZUM
88203 - Page Five
10/30/88



INT. CSOC OFFICE/WOMAN'S HOME - DAY

FREEZE FRAME of a WOMAN in her forties (MS. ROGERS) talking on the
telephone.

TITLES (WRITTEN IN SCRIPT) FADE IN AND OUT:

"IS THIS JUST ANOTHER WAY TO RAISE RATES?"
"WHAT'S THIS GOING TO COST?"

INTERCUT between the SECOND GTE REP and the woman.
```

NARRATOR (V.O.) In this case, a woman has called about her mother, who telephones her every day -- and who is concerned about being able to afford her phone bills in the future.	SECOND GTE REP Yes, Ms. Rogers. How may I help you? WOMAN I live in Agoura, she's in Camarillo, and even though we see each other often, she likes to stay in touch every day...

```
                    WOMAN - cont.
          Tell me the truth, is this just another
          way to raise our rates?

                    SECOND GTE REP
          Ms. Rogers, the reason for the proposed
          changes is not to increase your rates,
          but to provide uniform rates for calls of
          similar distances throughout the state.

                    WOMAN
          That may be, but my mother's on a fixed
          income.  What's it going to cost her to
          call me now?

                    SECOND GTE REP
                 (checking RATE SCHEDULE)
          Checking the proposed rate schedule...Oh!
          You'll be pleased to hear this.  Calls
          from the Camarillo exchange to your
          prefix in Agoura will be reduced from
          toll calls to ZUM calls, billed at a
          lower rate.

                    WOMAN
          She'll save money when she calls me?
```

```
Script - ZUM
88203 - Page Six
10/30/88



                      SECOND GTE REP
              Yes...

            NARRATOR (V.O.)                    SECOND GTE REP - cont.
This is the ideal way to handle     Agoura is currently a toll
a caller's concern: explain the     call, but it will become a
reasons for the proposed changes,   ZUM call, which is much
and help the customer understand    cheaper.
how he or she will be affected.
Looking further, this CSOC rep               WOMAN
discovers that Camarillo            Great...
may soon be included in the
Frequent Caller Program, thus              SECOND GTE REP
offering the customer another       Here's something else:  Under
cost-saving alternative.            the new plan, your mother
                                    would be eligible for our
                                    Frequent Caller Program,
                                    which could save her even
                                    more.

                      WOMAN
              That's good to hear.  I'm really
              glad I called...

DISSOLVE TO:


INT. CUSTOMER'S OFFICE - DAY

FREEZE FRAME of a CITY TELECOMMUNICATIONS MANAGER (SCOTT).

TITLE (WRITTEN IN SCRIPT) FADES IN AND OUT:

"WHEN WILL THIS CHANGE REALLY TAKE PLACE?"

A GTE NETWORK SALES ACCOUNT EXECUTIVE (FEMALE) is in the office with
the manager.

                    ACCOUNT EXECUTIVE
              ...sounds like quite a project, Scott.

                     CITY MANAGER
              It is.  Four square blocks on the
              East Side of town...a new City Hall,
              police, Municipal Courts building, other
              city services.

                    ACCOUNT EXECUTIVE
              Very ambitious.
```

```
Script - ZUM
88203 - Page Seven
10/30/88
```

                              CITY MANAGER
                Yes, but here's where I see a problem...

        NARRATOR (V.O.)   CITY MANAGER - cont.
A GTE network sales account   I can understand why the PUC
executive visits the   wants you to make these
telecommunications manager of   changes.
a local city government. The
manager is sophisticated about   ACCOUNT EXECUTIVE
phone service, and understands   With population centers
the need for the PUC's proposed   shifting so much, they want
changes. But his city is planning   everyone to have access to
to build a new government center.   low-cost ZUM rates.

                                            CITY MANAGER
                                     Right. But now you come to
                                     my situation...

                        CITY MANAGER - cont,
                ...and as far as I can tell, our new
                offices will be in a different exchange
                from the ones serving most of our
                residents.

                        ACCOUNT EXECUTIVE
                You're worried about being in a new
                rate center.

                        CITY MANAGER
                I've started making it known to our budget
                people that telephone service might need
                a greater allocation. It would be a big
                help if I knew what kind of time frame
                we're talking about here. When will this
                change really take place?

        NARRATOR (V.O.)   ACCOUNT EXECUTIVE
In a situation like this, let the   We've come up with what we
customer know our proposed   think is a pretty reasonable
implementation schedule.   schedule...

L/3 TITLES FADE IN AND OUT:

"JANUARY, 1989 -- FILE WITH PUC"
"THIRD QUARTER, 1989 --
 ANTICIPATED APPROVAL"
"1990/91 -- WITH FAVORABLE RULING,
 CHANGES BECOME EFFECTIVE"

```
Script - ZUM
88203 - Page Eight
10/30/88



          NARRATOR (V.O.) - cont.              ACCOUNT EXEC. - cont.
In January of 1989, we plan to       We'll file for ZUM expansion
file for ZUM expansion in the        in January of 1989.  We
areas previously mentioned.  We      anticipate the PUC will approve
anticipate the PUC will approve      our filing by the third
our filing by the third quarter      quarter, and we'll put the
of 1989.  The changes to ZUM and     changes into effect during 1990
our exchange boundaries would        and 1991.
then become effective during 1990
and 1991.                                      CITY MANAGER
                                     That sounds like a good,
Information like this is often       workable plan.  I think we
the most valuable commodity          can fit any changes into our
you can share with a customer.       budget.

                                               ACCOUNT EXECUTIVE
                                     Scott, we'll work with you to
                                     make your transition as easy
                                     as possible.


DISSOLVE TO:


INT. SECOND CUSTOMER'S OFFICE - DAY

FREEZE FRAME of an OFFICE MANAGER (LENORA).

TITLES (WRITTEN IN SCRIPT) FADE IN AND OUT:

"AM I AFFECTED?"
"WILL I HAVE TO CHANGE SOMETHING?"

The same network sales account executive is meeting with the office
manager.

          NARRATOR (V.O.) - cont.              OFFICE MANAGER
Here's another situation             I appreciate your coming by
involving a GTE account executive,   so quickly.
who's paying a call on the office
manager of a large Health                      ACCOUNT EXECUTIVE
Management Organization.             It's always a pleasure, Lenora.
                                     What can I do for you today?

                         OFFICE MANAGER
               As you know, we have private lines and
               FX.  Frankly, I'm concerned about your
               filing with the PUC.  Am I affected?
               Will I have to change something when
               you begin to implement your expansion?
```

```
Script - ZUM
88203 - Page Nine
10/30/88
```

                         ACCOUNT EXECUTIVE
                          (consulting folder)
            I've been looking at your account, Lenora,
            and I think I've got the answers you need.
            The charges for mileage will change for
            some private line circuits, because our
            mileage rates are higher for service between
            exchanges.

                          OFFICE MANAGER
            That includes us?

                         ACCOUNT EXECUTIVE
            Some of your lines, not all.

                          OFFICE MANAGER
            People have been saying we'll have
            to get rid of FX. I know it's being
            eliminated for certain residential lines.

                         ACCOUNT EXECUTIVE
            With FX, again, the charges for mileage
            will change. But business customers such
            as you will still have the option of keeping
            your FX service, even if our proposed
            boundary changes put you in a "noncontiguous"
            area. Why don't we take a more detailed
            look at your situation...

              NARRATOR (V.O.)   OFFICE MANAGER
    Many customers, residential and   (edging closer)
    business accounts, may be   All right.
    confused by the implications
    of our proposed changes. It's   ACCOUNT EXECUTIVE
    your job to help them understand   I can look at your calling
    exactly what ZUM expansion will   patterns during the last two
    mean to them, and their phone   years, break them down to
    service.   highlight both your private
                                        line service and ZUM...

    DISSOLVE TO:

    INT. BSOC OFFICE/CUSTOMER'S OFFICE - DAY

    FREEZE FRAME of a BUSINESS CUSTOMER (MR. PUTNAM) talking on the
    phone.

    TITLES (WRITTEN IN SCRIPT) FADE IN AND OUT:

    "WHY CAN'T YOU LEAVE THINGS ALONE?"
    "HOW CAN I MAKE MY OPINION HEARD?"

```
Script - ZUM
88203 - Page Ten
10/30/88


INTERCUT between the First GTE Rep and the Business Customer.

        NARRATOR (V.O.)                      BUSINESS CUSTOMER
Finally, we have a somewhat          I just got your notice about
irritated customer, calling to       the changes you're going to
complain about the notice he         make in my service, and I'm
recently received.  An open and      not happy about it!
helpful attitude is the best way
to defuse this situation.                    FIRST GTE REP
                                     Would you like me to explain
                                     what the changes mean,
                                     Mr. Putnam?

                    BUSINESS CUSTOMER
            I don't need you to explain anything.
            I run my own business, and I understand
            how the phones work.  What I want to know
            is, Why can't you leave things alone?

                    FIRST GTE REP
            Mr. Putnam, the proposed changes are only the
            latest step in a process to make telephone
            charges throughout the state as fair as
            possible.

                    BUSINESS CUSTOMER
            Uh-huh, well, maybe.  But as far as I'm
            concerned, they're already fair.  This
            isn't going to go through without some
            input from people like me, is it?  How
            can I make my opinion heard?

                    FIRST GTE REP
            As part of the filing process, we're
            soliciting, and appreciate, comments from
            our customers.

                    BUSINESS CUSTOMER
            Who do I write to?

                    FIRST GTE REP
            If you'd like to have your comments forwarded
            to the Public Utilities Commission, Mr. Putnam,
            write to...

LOWER THIRD TITLE FADES IN AND OUT:

"GTE CALIFORNIA
 JOHN MANN
 RC 3410B
 ONE GTE PLACE
 THOUSAND OAKS, CALIFORNIA 91362-3811"
```

```
Script - ZUM
88203 - Page Eleven
10/30/88
```

          NARRATOR (V.O.)   FIRST GTE REP - cont.
Give customers the opportunity   John Mann...GTE Calfornia...
to write to John Mann, rate   RC3410B...One GTE Place...
development administrator, at   Thousand Oaks, California...
this address. And let them know   91362-dash-3811. And Mr.
that when the PUC schedules public Putnam, we will let you know
hearings on this matter, we will   when the PUC schedules public
send all affected customers   hearings on this matter.
notices -- which will announce
the dates, times and locations
of all hearings.

                    BUSINESS CUSTOMER
              You can be sure I'll be there!

DISSOLVE TO:

GRAPHICS EFFECTS

AURORA EFFECTS HIGHLIGHTING SHOTS of customers in ISOLATED BOXES.

                    NARRATOR (V.O.)
          The customer is not a problem, but a
          person with a problem that can be solved
          by you. Let's review the key points we've
          learned in this program.

AURORA EFFECT of real estate agent.

LOWER THIRD TITLES FADE IN AND OUT:

"EXPLAIN CHANGES IN EXCHANGE BOUNDARIES"
"CHANGES ARE ONLY PROPOSED RIGHT NOW"

                    NARRATOR (V.O.) - cont.
          Explain the proposed changes in exchange
          boundaries, and how some calling rates may
          be affected. Always stress that the changes
          you mention are only being proposed for the
          time being -- with implementation anticipated
          for 1990 or 1991.

QUICK DISSOLVE TO:

AURORA EFFECT of woman caller.

LOWER THIRD TITLES FADE IN AND OUT:

"EXPLAIN REASONS FOR CHANGES"
"OFFER CUSTOMERS ALTERNATIVES"

```
Script - ZUM
88203 - Page Twelve
10/30/88
```

                              NARRATOR (V.O.) - cont.
          Explain the reasons for proposed changes,
          and help customers understand how they
          will be affected. Go one step further,
          and offer customers any available service
          alternatives.

QUICK DISSOLVE TO:

AURORA EFFECT of city manager.

LOWER THIRD TITLE FADES IN AND OUT:

"PROPOSED IMPLEMENTATION SCHEDULE"

                              NARRATOR (V.O.) - cont.
          Let customers know our proposed
          implementation schedule, and how this
          might affect their own future plans.

QUICK DISSOLVE TO:

AURORA EFFECT of office manager.

LOWER THIRD TITLE FADES IN AND OUT:

"EXPLAIN IMPACT ON SPECIAL SERVICES"

                              NARRATOR (V.O.) - cont.
          Many business customers, and a few
          residential customers as well, take
          advantage of services such as private
          lines, FX, and off-premises extensions
          and stations. They may require special
          attention from you in order to fully
          understand the impact our proposed changes
          will have on their sophisticated systems.

QUICK DISSOLVE TO:

AURORA EFFECT of business customer.

LOWER THIRD TITLE FADE IN AND OUT:

"ACCESS TO PUC"

```
Script - ZUM
88203 - Page Thirteen
10/30/88



                          NARRATOR (V.O.) - cont.
            And be sure to provide customers with a
            way to make their opinions known to the
            PUC, by writing to GTE California's
            John Mann.

DISSOLVE TO:


CLOSING MONTAGE

MUSIC UP.

MONTAGE of SHOTS already seen in this videotape.

                          NARRATOR (V.O.) - cont.
            We've covered a lot of ground in this
            videotape, but there's more for you to
            learn about our proposed ZUM expansion and
            exchange boundary changes.  For more
            information, review the printed materials
            that accompany this program, and talk with
            your supervisor.

            ZUM expansion is a positive step in the
            evolution of telephone service throughout
            the state of California, but it will raise
            many questions and concerns among our
            customers.  Always be thinking:  Is there
            another alternative that can meet the
            customer's calling needs?  By dealing with
            customers' questions courteously and efficiently,
            you will help us to smoothly implement these
            necessary changes -- now, and in the years
            to come.


FINAL CREDITS.


PICTURE AND MUSIC OUT.
```

Figure A-3 This script uses narration combined with dramatization to create role models. Note the use of the narration over the dramatization as the audio is muted (*courtesy, Patti Ryan, GTE of California*).

V-7056   PRODUCER:
                                              JOSE ALTONAGA

ACCIDENT INVESTIGATION:
GATHERING THE FACTS IN THE FIELD

by Ken Gullekson

~~GENERAL TELEPHONE~~
GTE CALIFORNIA

July 7, 1987

AUDIO FX UP: TELEPHONES RINGING, TYPEWRITERS, MUFFLED VOICES   1

FADE IN:

INT - LEGAL DEPARTMENT RECEPTION AREA - DAY

EXTREMELY CLOSE PROFILE OF CHRIS - USE LONG LENS - CHRIS is a cable maintainer
seriously out of his element in the offices of the legal department. Half
lost in his thoughts and more than a little anxious about what is in store for
him there, he bites his fingernail and glances about distractedly. Presently,
he glances in our direction.

REVERSE ANGLE - CLOSE FRONTAL SHOT OF BRIEFCASE AND UPPER LEGS OF A GTC
ATTORNEY - WE DOLLY BACK TO MAINTAIN FRAMING as the leather briefcase and
crisply creased suitpants walk directly toward us. The right hand reaches out
for us.

                         ATTORNEY (O.S.)
                    Chris...?

MEDIUM CLOSE SHOT OF CHRIS

                              CHRIS
                    Yeah.

CHRIS stands, but the CAMERA doesn't follow him up.   Instead, CHRIS's hand
meets the ATTORNEY'S hand MID-FRAME and they shake.

                         ATTORNEY (O.S.)
                    Don Baker, staff attorney.

                         CHRIS (O.S.)
                    How ya doin', Don?

                                                            CUT TO:

INT - CONFERENCE ROOM

MUSIC UP - SERIOUS BUT NOT HEAVY, PERHAPS CLASSICAL

CLOSE SHOT OF BARE TABLE TOP - Near TOP OF FRAME is the edge of the table with
the lower third of the conference room door in the BACKGROUND, OUT OF FOCUS.
Horizonal shadows cast by venetian blinds are seen on the table and wall.

SUPER TITLE: "ACCIDENT INVESTIGATION"

IN THE BACKGROUND WE SEE the conference room door open. WE SEE the feet of
the two men enter and approach the table.

ADD TITLE: "GATHERING THE FACTS IN THE FIELD"

The ATTORNEY's leather briefcase abruptly ENTERS FRAME. The ATTORNEY'S hands
snap open the latches of the briefcase, lift the lid, and reach in.

LOSE TITLE

WE HEAR THE ATTORNEY'S VOICE as he removes a file containing numerous letters, affidavits, photographs of a damaged SPORTS CAR, and other legal documents, spreading it all out on the table top.

MUSIC OUT

                              ATTORNEY (O.S.)
                    How's your memory, Chris?

CLOSE SHOT OF CHRIS

                                   CHRIS
                    Pretty good, I guess.

CHRIS is apprehensive as he listens and watches the ATTORNEY gather his notes.

                              ATTORNEY (O.S.)
                    Good...'cause you're gonna need it today.
                    Henderson Forbes has filed suit against
                    General Telephone regarding your collision
                    accident with him.

CHRIS furrows his brow, recalling with surprised alarm.

                                   CHRIS
                    Sports car...?

ALTERNATE SINGLES AND TWO-SHOTS AS APPROPRIATE

                                 ATTORNEY
                    Yeah....

                                   CHRIS
                              (a little stunned)
                    Geez...that was almost a year ago! I
                    figured that'd already been taken care of.

                                 ATTORNEY
                    Well the wheels turn slowly on these
                    things sometimes. I called you in to see
                    if we can put together some kind of
                    defense.

                                   CHRIS
                              (surprised)
                    Defense?! What do we need a defense for?
                    It wasn't my fault.

                                 ATTORNEY
                    They seem to think it was, and they've got
                    a pretty strong case....

                                   CHRIS
                    How much are they suing us for?

3

                              ATTORNEY
              A hundred and fifty thousand dollars....

                                CHRIS
              A hundred and fifty thousand dollars?!!!
              That's impossible! There was only a few
              hundred dollars worth of damage there at
              best!

                              ATTORNEY
              As it stands it's your word against his.
              And he's got <u>this</u> to back him up.

CLOSE SHOT OF OPEN FILE - The ATTORNEY's hand gestures toward the open file of
papers and photographs.

                                CHRIS
              What've <u>we</u> got?

                              ATTORNEY
                  (waving a single sheet of paper)
              Just your accident report...which, I'm
              sorry to say, isn't going to do us much
              good.

                                CHRIS
              Why, what's wrong with it?

                              ATTORNEY
              Well you left out the most important
              stuff.

CHRIS takes the accident report and looks it over, somewhat bewildered.

                          ATTORNEY (cont.)
              I called you in to see if you can put it
              all together.

                                CHRIS
              Well, I'll try....

CLOSE SHOT OF CHRIS AS HE RECALLS - PUSH IN SLOWLY

AUDIO FX UP - WE HEAR the final bars of some snappy western guitar-and-banjo
tune being played through a car radio speaker and SEE CHRIS'S mouth move as he
begins to relate the incident to the ATTORNEY.

                                                     SLOW DISSOLVE TO:

INT - SPORTS CAR - MOVING - DAY

WE ARE CRUISING down a city street in a zippy little SPORTS CAR. The street
ahead IS VISIBLE THROUGH THE WINDSHIELD OVER-THE-SHOULDER of the DRIVER. The
MUSIC ENDS and ANOTHER COUNTRY/WESTERN TUNE begins.

The DRIVER reaches to TURN UP THE RADIO as he proceeds toward an intersection controlled by a traffic signal. Far ahead, beyond the intersection, a GTC COMPANY VEHICLE, a cable maintainer's truck, can be seen coming toward us.

RADIO FX OUT

                                                                    CUT TO:

INT - COMPANY VEHICLE ON CITY STREET - MOVING

We are in the GTC COMPANY VEHICLE visible earlier from the SPORTS CAR, approaching the intersection from the opposite direction. OVER-THE-SHOULDER OF THE DRIVER, CHRIS, the SPORTS CAR can be seen in the distance zipping toward us. WE MOVE into the left lane, stop at the intersection, and wait for traffic to clear to make a left turn. Opposite us is a PASSENGER VAN, sitting in his own left lane, waiting to make a turn in the opposite direction.

Traffic seems to clear for us and WE PROCEED to make our turn. Suddenly, the SPORTS CAR appears in the lane we are crossing, darting from behind the PASSENGER VAN. CHRIS slams on the brakes as the SPORTS CAR DRIVER swerves. But the collision is inevitable.

MEDIUM CLOSE SHOT OF SPORTS CAR DRIVER FROM CAB OF COMPANY VEHICLE - Seeing the huge COMPANY VEHICLE crossing his path, the SPORTS CAR DRIVER grimaces in terror as he swerves, then slams on his brakes.

EXT - INTERSECTION

MEDIUM SHOT OF CHRIS FROM DIRECTLY IN FRONT OF COMPANY VEHICLE - WE SEE the sudden terror on CHRIS'S face as he stands on his brakes and braces for the impact.

AUDIO FX: TIRES SQUEALING, THEN METAL CRUNCHING

From our MEDIUM ANGLE ON CHRIS WE SEE the COMPANY VEHICLE lurch and shudder as though struck on the passenger side by the SPORTS CAR. (Budgetary Note: Since we are looking at CHRIS during impact, we do not need to see the actual collision of the vehicles. A subtle JOSTLING OF THE CAMERA can enhance the illusion of collision.)

WIDE ESTABLISHING SHOT OF INTERSECTION - The COMPANY VEHICLE and the SPORTS CAR are now at rest in the middle of the intersection, the front end of the SPORTS CAR apparently mashed into the passenger side of the COMPANY VEHICLE. For a few seconds there is the HUSH of stunned inactivity as our two DRIVERS, BYSTANDERS on the sidewalk, the DRIVER of the PASSENGER VAN, and the DRIVER of a PICKUP TRUCK situated on the cross street stare transfixed at the two vehicles now blocking the road.

Snapping to, CHRIS SWEARS UNDER HIS BREATH, anxiously jumps from the cab of his truck, and runs around the SPORTS CAR.

FULL SHOT OF CHRIS - CHRIS rounds the SPORTS CAR, surveying the damage to both vehicles as he approaches the SPORTS CAR DRIVER who is still seated in his vehicle somewhat stunned, not wearing his seatbelt. CHRIS goes up to the window of the SPORTS CAR.

CLOSE TWO-SHOT

                              CHRIS
                           (anxiously)
            Are you hurt?!!

                        SPORTS CAR DRIVER
                        (a little stunned)
            Nah, I don't think so....

                              CHRIS
            I'm really sorry, man, I didn't see ya....

The SPORTS CAR DRIVER eyes CHRIS with annoyance. CHRIS abruptly straightens up
and quickly surveys the scene, suddenly aware that they're blocking traffic -
although there is room for other vehicles to maneuver around them. He hastily
stoops again to the SPORTS CAR DRIVER.

                          CHRIS (cont.)
            We're blockin' traffic...we better get
            outta the intersection.

WIDE SHOT OF INTERSECTION - CHRIS runs back around and hops into the cab of
his truck. The PASSENGER VAN opposite the COMPANY VEHICLE waits to execute
his turn as the PICKUP TRUCK on the cross street waits for the intersection to
be cleared.

INT - COMPANY VEHICLE

OVER-THE-SHOULDER SHOT THROUGH COMPANY VEHICLE WINDSHIELD - CHRIS starts the
engine as the SPORTS CAR DRIVER backs off to allow us passage. CHRIS MUTTERS
to himself as he maneuvers to the far curb.

                              CHRIS
            Wouldn't you know it...! Wouldn't you
            just know it...!!! This is all I need....
            (etc.)

EXT - CURB WHERE COMPANY VEHICLE IS PARKING

As the COMPANY VEHICLE passes by us in the near FOREGROUND, WE SEE some damage
evident on the right fender. It CLEARS FRAME just in time for us to SEE, in
the BACKGROUND, the SPORTS CAR hobbling to the far curb, where three
BYSTANDERS stand watching the proceedings.

REVERSE ANGLE - CAMERA ON SIDEWALK NEAR SPORTS CAR - From this vantage point,
WE SEE CHRIS alight from his truck and start across the street against the red
light toward the waiting SPORTS CAR. The PICKUP is still sitting at the
crosswalk, hesitant to proceed into the intersection, even though he has a
green light. CHRIS impatiently waves him on, and the PICKUP MOVES OFF. As
CHRIS continues across the street, WE SEE the PASSENGER VAN in the BACKGROUND
finally execute his turn.

A little annoyed with the situation, the anxious CHRIS pushes past the
BYSTANDERS on the corner and moves directly to the SPORTS CAR DRIVER who is
now standing near his crumpled front end, inspecting the damage.

                            CHRIS
            I'm really sorry about this, man....

CLOSER ANGLES - Without looking up, the SPORTS CAR DRIVER continues to study
the damage to his vehicle.

                         CHRIS (cont.)
            I work for General Telephone and we're
            insured, so there shouldn't be any problem
            getting it taken care of....

                      SPORTS CAR DRIVER
                  (still not looking up)
            Yeah....

Now the SPORTS CAR DRIVER stands and moves to the sidewalk.

                   SPORTS CAR DRIVER (cont.)
            Well let's get this over with....

CHRIS follows him to the sidewalk where they pull out their wallets and
exchange drivers licenses.

REVERSE ANGLE

                            CHRIS
            That's my ID card, and there's the yard
            address.

The SPORTS CAR DRIVER nods. In the BACKGROUND, the BYSTANDERS become bored
with the incident. One of them MOVES OFF FRAME LEFT. The other two MOVE OFF
FRAME RIGHT. The DRIVERS fish for paper and pencils and start jotting down
contact information.

                      SPORTS CAR DRIVER
                  (pointing to address card)
            What're these numbers here...?

NEW ANGLE FAVORING CHRIS

                            CHRIS
                        (looking)
            That's my building number and mail
            code....

The SPORTS CAR DRIVER nods. As the two men jot down contact and insurance
information in the FOREGROUND, the two BYSTANDERS reach the far side of the
street in the BACKGROUND and continue on down the street.

NEW ANGLE FAVORING SPORTS CAR DRIVER - The SPORTS CAR DRIVER pulls out a
business card and extends it to CHRIS. As CHRIS studies the business card,
the single BYSTANDER enters his business in the BACKGROUND and is gone.

WIDE ANGLE - WE SEE the two DRIVERS recording each other's contact information
with the entire intersection visible in the BACKGROUND, completely devoid of
potential accident witnesses.

                                                          DISSOLVE TO:

INT - CONFERENCE ROOM - DAY

TWO-SHOT OF CHRIS AND ATTORNEY - CHRIS has just finished telling his story.
The ATTORNEY, listening with a hint of skeptical detactment, rests his cheek
on the butt of his pen. CHRIS turns his palms skyward.

> CHRIS
> That's about it.

MEDIUM SHOT OF ATTORNEY

> ATTORNEY
> You say _he_ hit _you_.

ALTERNATE SINGLES AND TWO SHOTS AS APPROPRIATE

> CHRIS
> Yeah.

> ATTORNEY
> (looking at accident report)
> Well your diagram doesn't show that
> clearly. In fact, before you described it
> to me, I didn't understand your diagram at
> all. But you're quite confident the other
> guy was at fault.

> CHRIS
> Oh, yeah!

> ATTORNEY
> (frowns and leans forward)
> Can you remember anything that would help
> us track down some witnesses to back that
> up...?

CHRIS looks off and furrows his brow. Failing to remember he just shakes his
head. During the ATTORNEY's following line, CHRIS just shakes his head in
response to each question.

> ATTORNEY (cont.)
> Residents or workers in the vicinity that
> might have seen the accident? License
> plates on the pickup truck and passenger
> van? Anything?

> CHRIS
> (shakes his head confirmationally)
> It's pretty hard to remember that kind of
> detail that long ago.

The ATTORNEY reluctantly accepts this and moves on.

> ATTORNEY
> You say he braked and skidded?

                              CHRIS
Yeah....

                            ATTORNEY
Did you happen to measure his skid marks
so we can determine if he was speeding?

                              CHRIS
No.

                            ATTORNEY
And you didn't get any photos of the
damage to his vehicle....

                              CHRIS
No.

                            ATTORNEY
And no police report?

                              CHRIS
Huh-uh.

                            ATTORNEY
                    (suppressing exasperation)
Look, Chris, let me tell you what we're up
against, here. They've built a very strong
case demonstrating that you made an improper
turn in front of their client. They've
documented everything in great detail and
it's gonna be tough convincing a judge or
jury you're not at fault. Listen to what
they're saying....

The ATTORNEY picks up the plaintiff's brief and scans it.

                         ATTORNEY (cont.)
...You turned in front of their client's
vehicle, which puts you at fault...you
apologized and stated you didn't see him,
thereby admitting fault...you told him the
phone company would take care of the
damage, confirming fault.

                              CHRIS
Geez...! I didn't even think he was
listening to half of what I said.

                            ATTORNEY
Well he was listening and he put it all
down in black and white for his insurance
company and his lawyer.

The ATTORNEY picks up several photos and hands then to CHRIS.

9

                                    ATTORNEY
                    They have numerous photos showing serious
                    damage to their client's vehicle....

                                     CHRIS
                             (viewing photos and interrupting)
                    Hey, I didn't do half of this damage...!!

                                    ATTORNEY
                    Well, without pictures there's no way to
                    distinguish the damage <u>you</u> did from the
                    damage that existed before the accident...
                    <u>or</u> damage that might have occured after
                    the accident.... They've got affidavits
                    from doctors confirming his injury,
                    hospital and therapy fees, loss of work...

                                     CHRIS
                              (interrupting again)
                    You gotta be kidding!! He told me he was
                    alright. He was walking around like
                    nothin' happened...!

                                    ATTORNEY
                    You don't say anything about that in your
                    accident report....

                                     CHRIS
                    You know this is a crock, Don! That
                    accident wasn't my fault. The lane was
                    clear when I started my turn and he zipped
                    into it and hit <u>me</u>!

                                    ATTORNEY
                                  (surprised)
                    He made a lane change?!

                                     CHRIS
                    Yeah! He was in the lane behind the
                    passenger van, so I started my turn. Then
                    he zipped into the next lane and plowed
                    into me.

The ATTORNEY quickly checks CHRIS's accident report, then the plaintiffs'
brief.

                                    ATTORNEY
                    You didn't mention that on your accident
                    report. And <u>they</u> certainly don't mention
                    it.

                                     CHRIS
                    I didn't think about it.

                              ATTORNEY
                    Well that could've been our defense - and
                    a very strong one at that - if you'd put
                    it in your report.

                               CHRIS
                    Well can we put it in now?

                              ATTORNEY
                    We can argue the point. But I think we're
                    gonna have a hard time convincing the
                    judge we're not just making it up in a
                    last ditch effort to win the case. The
                    problem is, Chris...your accident report
                    is just too sketchy.

CLOSE SHOT OF CHRIS

                          ATTORNEY (cont. O.S.)
                    In order to win a case like this you need
                    to have witnesses, photographs, detailed
                    diagrams, skid marks, a description of....

CHRIS plunges into thought as the ATTORNEY'S WORDS TRAIL OFF.

CROSS FADE TO CHRIS' VOICE-OVER THOUGHTS

                              CHRIS (V.O.)
                    No one had ever explained to me how to
                    fill out an accident report. I knew there
                    was a form in my glove compartment, but I
                    figured all I had to do was get the guy's
                    name, drivers license, and insurance
                    company and I'd be set. I never even
                    considered getting witnesses...much less
                    photos or measurements of skid marks....
                    Without a complete and accurate report, we
                    have no way of proving I was not at fault,
                    and the company is gonna have to pay. If
                    I could only go back...I know now what I'd
                    do differently.

                                                          DISSOLVE TO:

INT - SPORTS CAR - MOVING - DAY

WE ARE CRUISING down a city street in the zippy little SPORTS CAR. IN
ABBREVIATED FORM, THE ACCIDENT IS REPLAYED UP TO WHERE CHRIS FIRST HOPS FROM
THE CAB OF HIS TRUCK TO CHECK THE CONDITION OF THE SPORTS CAR DRIVER.

FULL SHOT OF CHRIS - CHRIS rounds the SPORTS CAR, surveying the damage to both
vehicles as he approaches the SPORTS CAR DRIVER who is still seated in his
vehicle somewhat stunned.

11

                              CHRIS (V.O.)
                    Naturally, I'd wanna find out if the other
                    guy was okay....

He goes up to the window of the SPORTS CAR.

CLOSE TWO-SHOT

                                CHRIS
                    Are you hurt?!!

                            SPORTS CAR DRIVER
                              (a little stunned)
                    Nah, I don't think so....

                                CHRIS
                    Good.

MEDIUM SHOT OF CHRIS - He straightens up, draws a deep breath, relaxes, and
glances at the damage to the vehicles.

                              CHRIS (V.O.)
                    I wouldn't apologize or say anything which
                    sounded like an admission of fault. If he
                    needed medical attention, I'd call an
                    ambulance before I did anything else. If
                    he's okay, I'd take a deep breath, relax,
                    and get a firm grip on myself....

WIDE SHOT OF INTERSECTION - Surveying the scene as he returns to his truck,
CHRIS observes that although traffic is partially blocked, there is enough
room for other vehicles to maneuver around. The PASSENGER VAN opposite the
COMPANY VEHICLE and the PICKUP TRUCK on the cross street remain in place.

                              CHRIS (V.O.)
                    Then I'd see if the vehicles were blocking
                    traffic. If there was enough room for
                    cars to get around, I'd let 'em sit till I
                    had a chance to make an accurate
                    diagram....

INT - COMPANY VEHICLE

CHRIS enters the cab and opens his glove compartment. He obtains an accident
report form, which he clips onto his clip board, and immediately makes a
notation on it.

                              CHRIS (V.O.)
                    As soon as possible, I'd get out the
                    accident report form and start making
                    notes...such as the condition of the other
                    driver....

                                                                      WIPE TO:

GRAPHIC OF ACCIDENT REPORT - The accident report form FILLS THE FRAME. The
section for victim's statements is HIGHLIGHTED, then ZOOMED OUT to FILL THE
FRAME. CHRIS's entry quickly appears as though hand-printed by an invisible
hand: "Asked driver: 'Are you hurt?' He answered: 'Nah, I don't think so.'"

                              CHRIS (V.O.)
                    I'd wanna get down exactly what he said in
                    the description section of the form....

                                                                    WIPE TO:

EXT - INTERSECTION

WIDE SHOT - CHRIS jumps from the cab of his truck with his clipboard in hand
and runs to the PICKUP TRUCK.

                              CHRIS (V.O.)
                    The very next thing would be to look for
                    witnesses before they disappeared. I'd
                    start with drivers in other vehicles....

CLOSE TWO-SHOT OF CHRIS AND THE PICKUP DRIVER

                           CHRIS (LIVE ACTION)
                    Would you mind sticking around a few
                    minutes and be a witness for me?

WE DON'T HEAR THE ANSWER, BUT WE SEE the DRIVER respond with a definite nod.

                              CHRIS (V.O.)
                    Some'll be eager to help....

ANGLE OVER CHRIS'S SHOULDER TO PASSENGER VAN IN BACKGROUND - CHRIS turns just
in time to see the PASSENGER VAN make his turn and drive off. He jots a note
on his report form during the following line.

                              CHRIS (V.O.)
                    Others'll drive away before I can talk to
                    them. I'd get their license plate and
                    vehicle description if I can....

FULL SHOT OF CHRIS - He moves to the corner where the three BYSTANDERS are.

                              CHRIS (V.O.)
                    People standing around who I thought of as
                    being "in my way" before, I would now
                    think of as "witnesses"....

WE SEE BUT DO NOT HEAR CHRIS ask the three BYSTANDERS if they will be
witnesses. Two of them nod affirmatively, while one shakes his head "no" and
walks up the walk toward his business, which is there on the corner. The
PICKUP DRIVER joins CHRIS and the other two BYSTANDERS on the corner.

                              CHRIS (V.O.)
                    Some'll cooperate and some won't....

CHRIS looks at the address of the uncoorperative BYSTANDER who is returning to his business, and jots it down on the accident report.

> **CHRIS (V.O.)**
> I'd get identifying information on those
> who don't cooperate...such as their
> physical description and the address of
> their residence or place of business.
> They may change their minds at a later
> date and can be subpoenaed if necessary.
> The name, address, and telephone number of
> each witness go on the accident report
> form in the block marked "witnesses"....

                                                                              WIPE TO:

GRAPHIC OF ACCIDENT REPORT - The accident report form FILLS THE FRAME. The section for witness information is HIGHLIGHTED, then ZOOMED OUT to FILL THE FRAME. The invisible hand prints the names, addresses, and phone numbers of the three willing witnesses, plus the address and physical description of the uncooperative BYSTANDER, in the boxes of the graphic accident report. In another box, the license plate and description of the PASSENGER VAN is already evident.

                                                                              WIPE TO:

INTERSECTION

WIDE SHOT - CHRIS surveys the position of the vehicles on the roadway, the positions of the vehicles relative to each other, and any skid marks, making notes on his clipboard.

> **CHRIS (V.O.)**
> Once I had a number of witnesses lined up,
> I'd sketch a diagram of the accident on
> the report form in the appropriate box,
> accurately showing the position of the
> vehicles on the roadway, the positions of
> the vehicles relative to each other, skid
> marks, and any other relevant details....

MEDIUM CLOSE SHOT OF CHRIS - He places his pen to his clipboard and starts to write as we:

                                                                              WIPE TO:

GRAPHIC OF ACCIDENT REPORT - The section for the diagram is HIGHLIGHTED, then ZOOMED OUT to FILL THE FRAME. The invisible hand quickly draws a clear and detailed sketch of the incident.

                                                                              WIPE TO:

INTERSECTION

WIDE SHOT - CHRIS hops into the cab of his truck, and the two vehicles clear the intersection as before, moving to the same positions shown in the previous accident portrayal.

> **CHRIS (V.O.)**
> Finally, I'd clear the intersection. If
> the vehicles were a major obstruction to
> the flow of traffic, I'd make an accurate
> mental note of their conditions and
> positions and clear the intersection
> immediately after rounding up my
> witnesses. Then I'd draw my diagram from
> my mental note....

INT - COMPANY VEHICLE

MEDIUM SHOT OF CHRIS - He picks up his radio microphone. WE SEE BUT DO NOT
HEAR HIM SPEAK into it.

> **CHRIS (V.O.)**
> Now I'd take this opportunity to radio my
> supervisor, let him know of the accident,
> and ask him to bring a camera out with
> him. If my truck didn't happen to be
> equiped with a radio, I'd find a phone to
> make the call....

ANGLE ON SPORTS CAR PARKING AT CURB - The SPORTS CAR DRIVER gets out as CHRIS
approaches with his clipboard. The two men exchange drivers licenses and
contact information.

> **CHRIS (V.O.)**
> In addition to getting all the information
> about the other driver called for on the
> accident report, I'd give him my name,
> drivers license number, company address,
> and company claim card. I would not give
> him an apology, admission of guilt, or the
> completed accident report, which I've
> heard of other people doing. The accident
> report goes to my supervisor....

                                                                          WIPE TO:

GRAPHIC OF ACCIDENT REPORT - The section for the other driver/vehicle "B" is
HIGHLIGHTED, then ZOOMED OUT to FILL THE FRAME. All the information called
for there quickly appears, printed by the invisible hand.

                                                                          WIPE TO:

CURB AT SPORTS CAR

FULL SHOT OF CHRIS - He is walking around the SPORTS CAR noting pre-existing
damage.

> **CHRIS (V.O.)**
> While I'm waiting for my supervisor to
> show up, I'd take a walk around the other
> vehicle and note on the accident report
> the damage done in the accident as well as
> any pre-existing damage....

                                                                          WIPE TO:

15

GRAPHIC OF ACCIDENT REPORT - The section for the damage to vehicle "B" is
HIGHLIGHTED, then ZOOMED OUT to FILL THE FRAME. The invisible hand prints a
description of the damage done by the COMPANY VEHICLE, plus various
pre-existing dents and scratches.

WIPE TO:

PHONE BOOTH

With the receiver to his ear, CHRIS drops dimes in the slot and dials.

                    CHRIS (V.O.)
          This would be a good time to report the
          accident to the police. The report they
          file can corroborate the report I turn
          in....

WIPE TO:

STREET

FULL SHOT OF CHRIS walking the street. He spots a pothole and notes it on his
clipboard.

                    CHRIS (V.O.)
          This would also be a good time to check
          the condition of the roadway for
          potholes, incorrect roadsigns, or
          conditions the state, county, or city are
          responsible for. If there's time, I'd
          write my description of the accident in
          the box marked "detailed account." If
          not, I'd write it as soon as possible that
          same day to keep from forgetting important
          details. This account would describe the
          accident in complete and accurate
          detail...including direction of travel and
          speed of both vehicles, as well as the
          fact that the other driver changed lanes
          at the last minute and was not wearing his
          seatbelt....

WIPE TO:

GRAPHIC OF ACCIDENT REPORT - The section marked "detailed account" is
HIGHLIGHTED, then ZOOMED OUT to FILL THE FRAME. The invisible hand prints a
complete description of the accident.

WIPE TO:

STREET

CHRIS'S SUPERVISOR pulls up and parks a COMPANY VEHICLE. He gets out with a
camera and moves to CHRIS and the SPORTS CAR DRIVER at the SPORTS CAR. CHRIS
points to the damage done in the accident, which the SUPERVISOR photographs,
then to some pre-existing damage, which the SUPERVISOR also shoots.

16

ANGLE ON the damaged panel of CHRIS's truck. PULL BACK as CHRIS and his
SUPERVISOR ENTER FRAME and take some shots.

ANGLE ON CHRIS and SUPERVISOR taking shots of the skid marks made by the
SPORTS CAR.

ANGLE ON CHRIS and SUPERVISOR taking a shot of the pot hole. To the back of
each shot CHRIS sticks a Picture Identification Label and fills in the blanks.

                          CHRIS (V.O.)
                I'd have my supervisor get photos of the
                damage done to the sports car in the
                accident...the pre-existing damage on the
                sports car...the damage done to the
                company truck...the skid marks left by the
                vehicles...and any street or traffic
                conditions the city is responsible for.
                Each shot needs to be identified and
                properly labeled....

ANGLE ON CHRIS and SUPERVISOR measuring the length of the SPORTS CAR's skid
marks. CHRIS notes it on the accident report.

                          CHRIS (V.O.)
                Finally, we'd measure the length of the
                skid marks....

Having finished their measurements WE SEE CHRIS thank his SUPERVISOR. The two
men move to their respective vehicles.

                          CHRIS (V.O.)
                If I'd given my original accident report
                careful thought and filled it out
                completely and accurately, I could've
                saved the company thousands of dollars....
                Naturally, I don't intend to have another
                accident. But accidents do happen....

INSERT SEGMENT FROM V4021: "HOW TO USE THE RAPID RESTORATION VAN" - The claw
of a ditch-digging machine scooping dirt from a ditch severs a water main. An
EMPLOYEE with a clipboard peers into the hole to assess the damage.

                          CHRIS (V.O.)
                The same care and attention to detail
                should be taken when investigating a
                property damage. A complete and accurate
                accident report needs to be filed in in
                these cases, too....

ANGLES ON CHRIS, his SUPERVISOR, and the SPORTS CAR DRIVER as they each drive
away from the scene.

17

CHRIS (V.O.)
Well, this was an expensive lesson in
filling out the accident report, but I'll
know next time how to do it right....

FADE OUT

FADE IN MUSIC AND CLOSING GTE LOGO

FADE OUT

Figure A-4 Look at the realistic dialogue in this dramatic script.
The re-creation of events is especially well visualized (*courtesy,
Patti Ryan, GTE of California*)

TV MONITOR	COMPUTER	SCRIPT

LIVE FOOTAGE

BLANK

DOCTOR: If you look, listen and feel, and there is no breathing, you must move rapidly to get air into the lungs, because you know now, that there is no oxygen getting to the body. To do that, you immediately blow air into the lungs with a technique we call rescue breathing.

(Video screen goes to illustration, computer screen goes to display reading "RESCUE BREATHING")

ILLUSTRATION

HAND ON FOREHEAD PINCHING NOSTRILS

RESCUE BREATHING

DOCTOR (SO) V/O: This is the way it's done...Once you've made sure the airway is open, move your hand forward on the victim's forehead so that you can pinch the nostrils tightly closed with the thumb and index finger while maintaining the headtilt/chinlift.

(Video screen goes to next illustration, computer screen holds display)

ILLUSTRATION

HAND HOLDING FOREHEAD/ PINCHING NOSTRILS MAKING AIRTIGHT SEAL

RESCUE BREATHING

DOCTOR (SO) V/O: Then you take a deep breath and make an airtight seal over the victim's mouth with your mouth, and you blow...

(Video screen changes to next illustration which is the same as the last with the addition of an arrow. Computer screen displays the word 'ventilation')

ILLUSTRATION

SAME DRAWING AS BEFORE ONLY ARROW TO INDICATE BLOWING

VENTILATION

DOCTOR (SO) V/O: We call this ventilation. When ventilation is successful, you will see the chest rise because it has filled with air.

(Video screen changes to next illustration – same as illustration in vocabulary bank under 'Exhaled Oxygen' only in color. Computer screen displays print-out reading "80% of the oxygen remains in an exhaled breath, more than enough for the victim")

ILLUSTRATION

80% OF THE OXYGEN REMAINS IN AN EXHALED...

DOCTOR (SO) V/O: Now, some people are concerned that the victim won't be getting enough oxygen when they blow their exhaled air into a victim's lungs, but don't worry, there's plenty of oxygen left in the air you exhale, and the victim sure can use it ...Now we'd like you to try a ventilation on the manikin -- Compy will guide you through it...Compy?

(Video screen goes to typed slide and computer screen goes blank)

TYPED SLIDE

VENTILATING THE VICTIM

BLANK

COMPY (SO) V/O: Okay, doctor, well here we go again ...You got pretty good at opening the airway a while ago...and you'll need to use that same technique in this segment too...

(Video screen goes to slide of hands cleaning manikin's mouth, computer screen goes to "Touch this spot...")

Figure A-5

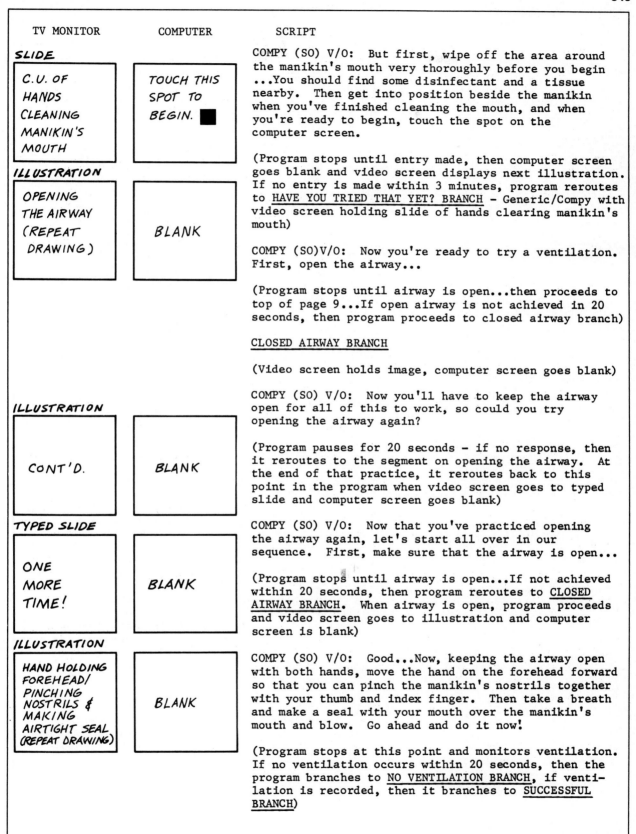

TV MONITOR	COMPUTER	SCRIPT

SLIDE

C.U. OF HANDS CLEANING MANIKIN'S MOUTH

TOUCH THIS SPOT TO BEGIN. ■

COMPY (SO) V/O: But first, wipe off the area around the manikin's mouth very thoroughly before you begin ...You should find some disinfectant and a tissue nearby. Then get into position beside the manikin when you've finished cleaning the mouth, and when you're ready to begin, touch the spot on the computer screen.

ILLUSTRATION

OPENING THE AIRWAY (REPEAT DRAWING)

BLANK

(Program stops until entry made, then computer screen goes blank and video screen displays next illustration. If no entry is made within 3 minutes, program reroutes to HAVE YOU TRIED THAT YET? BRANCH – Generic/Compy with video screen holding slide of hands clearing manikin's mouth)

COMPY (SO)V/O: Now you're ready to try a ventilation. First, open the airway...

(Program stops until airway is open...then proceeds to top of page 9...If open airway is not achieved in 20 seconds, then program proceeds to closed airway branch)

CLOSED AIRWAY BRANCH

(Video screen holds image, computer screen goes blank)

ILLUSTRATION

CONT'D.

BLANK

COMPY (SO) V/O: Now you'll have to keep the airway open for all of this to work, so could you try opening the airway again?

(Program pauses for 20 seconds – if no response, then it reroutes to the segment on opening the airway. At the end of that practice, it reroutes back to this point in the program when video screen goes to typed slide and computer screen goes blank)

TYPED SLIDE

ONE MORE TIME!

BLANK

COMPY (SO) V/O: Now that you've practiced opening the airway again, let's start all over in our sequence. First, make sure that the airway is open...

(Program stops until airway is open...If not achieved within 20 seconds, then program reroutes to CLOSED AIRWAY BRANCH. When airway is open, program proceeds and video screen goes to illustration and computer screen is blank)

ILLUSTRATION

HAND HOLDING FOREHEAD/ PINCHING NOSTRILS & MAKING AIRTIGHT SEAL (REPEAT DRAWING)

BLANK

COMPY (SO) V/O: Good...Now, keeping the airway open with both hands, move the hand on the forehead forward so that you can pinch the manikin's nostrils together with your thumb and index finger. Then take a breath and make a seal with your mouth over the manikin's mouth and blow. Go ahead and do it now!

(Program stops at this point and monitors ventilation. If no ventilation occurs within 20 seconds, then the program branches to NO VENTILATION BRANCH, if ventilation is recorded, then it branches to SUCCESSFUL BRANCH)

Figure A-5 This portion of an interactive script is for a CPR program which uses a mannekin as an input device. The trainee actually performs actions on the mannekin and gets feedback via audio and two video/computer monitors (*courtesy, American Heart Association*).

INDEX